JOSEPHUS IN GALILEE A

HIS VITA AND DEVELOPMENT AS A

BY

SHAYE J. D. COHEN

LEIDEN
E. J. BRILL
1979

Columbia Studies in the Classical Tradition *publishes monographs by members of the Columbia University faculty and by former Columbia students. Its subjects are the following: Greek and Latin literature, ancient philosophy, Greek and Roman history, classical archaeology, and the influence of the classical tradition on mediaeval, Renaissance and modern cultures.*

The publication of this work was aided by the Stanwood Cockey Lodge Foundation, the Jewish Theological Seminary of America, and the American Academy for Jewish Research

ISBN 90 04 05922 9

PRINTED IN THE NETHERLANDS

For Brenda
and My Parents

TABLE OF CONTENTS

PREFACE

This book is a revision of a doctoral dissertation submitted to the Faculties of Columbia University in October 1975. In revising the dissertation I have tried to make the work more accessible to the larger circle of non-specialists by removing much of the Greek from the text and by translating most of what Greek remained. Since chapters six and seven will, I hope, be of interest to all students of Jewish and classical antiquity, they contain practically no Greek at all and do not demand a detailed knowledge of Josephus. On the other hand, the first part of chapter one, and all of chapters two and three, in spite of my efforts, are very technical and assume familiarity with the Josephan corpus. Throughout the work, in order to save space, I have not given liberal and frequent citations from Josephus; I hope that the reader will have at his side a copy of the Josephan text. The translations throughout are my own, although I will not deny inspiration from the version of the Loeb Classical Library edition of Josephus. I have striven for comprehensibility in context, often best obtained by paraphrase rather than verbatim translation.

A few bibliographical notes: The Bible is cited according to the verse numeration of the Hebrew. The titles of Hebrew books and articles are transliterated except if an abstract or separate title page bears a western language title, in which case I cite the more widely comprehensible title and add "Heb." after the entry. Editions and translations of Josephus are regularly cited by the name of editor or translator alone. The bibliography should be consulted for the complete reference.

Schürer's *Geschichte des jüdischen Volkes* is cited as "Schürer" throughout. If no volume number precedes the page citation, volume I is intended. "Schürer-Vermes" is my designation of the new English edition of Schürer volume I by G. Vermes and F. Millar. To avoid confusion I write "Cambridge" as the place of publication for those books published in Cambridge, England, by the Cambridge University Press, but "Harvard" for those books published in Cambridge, Massachusetts, by Harvard University Press.

In the notes to the text, modern books which I found particularly helpful and which are frequently cited, receive a full citation in the first reference, an abbreviated citation (author's name alone or author's name and key word of title) after that. These works are listed in the bibliography. Books cited only infrequently are omitted from the bibliography and receive full citation every time they appear. In order to save space I have usually omitted the titles of articles in the notes; the more important articles receive full reference in the bibliography.

Without the aid of certain works, this book could not have been completed. I mention them here because the few times they are cited are not an adequate acknowledgement of their importance: M. Avi-Yonah, *Geographia Historit shel Erez Yisrael* [2] (Jerusalem 1951); L. H. Feldman's index to Josephus (at the end of volume nine of the Loeb Josephus); K. H. Rengstorf, *A Complete Concordance to Flavius Josephus* I and II (Leiden 1973ff); H. Schreckenberg, *Bibliographie zu Flavius Josephus* (Leiden 1968); idem, *Die Flavius-Josephus-Tradition in Antike und Mittelalter* (Leiden 1972); A. Schalit, *Namenwörterbuch zu Flavius Josephus* (Leiden 1968); the Loeb edition of Josephus.

My list of acknowledgements is long. First and foremost, I am grateful to Professor Morton Smith, my sponsor and dissertation supervisor, for his advice, criticism, questions, suggestions, and references. If I have achieved anything of value in this book, a good deal of the credit belongs to him. I am grateful also to the other members of my doctoral committee, Professors Roger S. Bagnall, Louis H. Feldman, William V. Harris, and John Schmidt, for their advice and criticism. Professor Elias Bickerman was kind enough not only to read and criticize an early version of chapter two, but also to discuss the entire work with me.

My friends Professors David Berger and Ivan Marcus have aided my discussion of the medieval Jewish traditions on the death of Agrippa II. Professors Eric Meyers and Lee Levine brought me up to date on the archaeological evidence. In addition Professor Levine carefully read the entire manuscript in its penultimate form, spotted several errors, pointed to a few matters which required further attention, and disagreed with several of my arguments. I am grateful to him for his comments. I received aid in numismatic matters from Dr. William E. Metcalf and Professor Peter R. Franke. Professor Saul Lieberman provided me with some references to Rabbinic texts; Professor Heinz Schreckenberg answered my questions about some Josephan textual problems.

Three friends have given me access to their scholarship before publication. Professor David Balch showed me his essay on Josephus and Menander the rhetorician; Professor Louis Feldman allowed me to study his critical bibliography on Josephus; Professor David Rhoads lent me an advance copy of his *Israel in Revolution*, a revision of his doctoral dissertation. I was able to obtain some rare or unpublished items through the courtesy of Professor Günther Wille, Professor Walther Ludwig, and the staffs of the Cambridge University Library and the library of the Jewish Theological Seminary.

I do not need to add that any errors which remain despite the aid of these individuals should be ascribed to me alone.

I am grateful to several institutions for their financial support: Columbia University, for the fellowships it provided me when I was a graduate student; the Abbell Publication Fund of the Jewish Theological Seminary of America, the American Academy for Jewish Research, and the Lodge Foundation, for generous grants towards the publication of this book.

15 April 77   S.J.D.C.

The publishers and the editor of this series have kindly allowed me to append a few addenda and corrigenda.

12 January 79   S.J.D.C.

ABBREVIATIONS

AJ	Josephus, *Antiquitates Judaicae*
AJP	*American Journal of Philology*
B	Babylonian Talmud (followed by the name of the tractate)
BASOR	*Bulletin of the American Schools of Oriental Research*
BIES	*Bulletin of the Israel Exploration Society*
BJ	Josephus, *Bellum Judaicum*
CA	Josephus, *Contra Apionem*
CP	*Classical Philology*
CQ	*Classical Quarterly*
CW	*Classical Weekly*
EI	*Eretz-Israel*
FGrH	F. Jacoby, *Die Fragmente der griechischen Historiker*
GRBS	*Greek, Roman, and Byzantine Studies*
HSCP	*Harvard Studies in Classical Philology*
HTR	*Harvard Theological Review*
HUCA	*Hebrew Union College Annual*
HZ	*Historische Zeitschrift*
IEJ	*Israel Exploration Journal*
IG	*Inscriptiones Graecae*
IGLS	*Inscriptions grecques et latines de la Syrie*
IGRR	*Inscriptiones Graecae ad Res Romanas pertinentes*
JAOS	*Journal of the American Oriental Society*
JBL	*Journal of Biblical Literature*
JJS	*Journal of Jewish Studies*
JQR	*Jewish Quarterly Review*
JRS	*Journal of Roman Studies*
JSS	*Journal of Semitic Studies*
JTS	*Journal of Theological Studies*
LSJ	Liddel-Scott-Jones, *Greek-English Lexicon*
LXX	Septuagint
M	Mishnah (followed by the name of the tractate)
MGWJ	*Monatschrift für die Geschichte und Wissenschaft des Judentums*
MH	*Museum Helveticum*
MT	Masoretic Text (the traditional text of the Hebrew Bible)
NC	*Numismatic Chronicle*
NT	*Novum Testamentum*
NWB	A. Schalit, *Namenwörterbuch zu Flavius Josephus*
OGIS	*Orientis Graeci Inscriptiones Selectae*, ed. W. Dittenberger
om.	omitted by
PAAJR	*Proceedings of the American Academy for Jewish Research*
PhW	*Philologische Wochenschrift*
PIR	*Prosopographia Imperii Romani*,[2] ed. Groag, Stein, et al.
PW	Pauly, Wissowa, Kroll, Ziegler, *Realencyclopädie*
RB	*Revue biblique*
RBPh	*Revue belge de philologie*
RhM	*Rheinisches Museum*
T	Tosefta (followed by the name of the tractate)
TAPA	*Transactions of the American Philological Association*

ThLZ   *Theologische Literaturzeitung*
V   Josephus, *Vita*
WS   *Wiener Studien*
Y   Palestinian (Yerushalmi) Talmud (followed by the name of the
            tractate)
ZDPV   *Zeitschrift des deutschen Palästina-Vereins*
ZNW   *Zeitschrift für die neutestamentliche Wissenschaft*
ZWT   *Zeitschrift für wissenschaftliche Theologie*
/ /   paralleled by

INTRODUCTION

In 66 CE a war was begun, in 70 a temple was destroyed, and
soon explanations were needed. Why did the Jews rebel? Why did
the Romans destroy the temple in Jerusalem? Who were these Jews,
the cause of so much trouble, and what was their history? Josephus,
a Palestinian Jew then residing in Rome, attempted to answer these
questions. First was his *Bellum Judaicum*, a detailed account of
the war preceded by a fairly long survey of the history of the
Jews in Palestine from the Maccabees until the outbreak of the
war. Less than twenty years later he completed his *Antiquitates
Judaicae*, a study of Jewish history from the creation to 66 CE.
These two works are now our most important sources for the
political history of the Jews in Greco-Roman antiquity.

Before arriving in Rome and embarking on this double career
as historian and apologist, Josephus had been a leader of the
rebels in Galilee during the war. How did Josephus in Rome
explain the actions of Josephus in Galilee? Why did he fight the
Romans? Was he any different from the nefarious tyrants who, in
his opinion, were responsible for causing the destruction of the
temple? Both of Josephus' large works deal with these issues.
In BJ Josephus' career is treated as a part—a large and significant
part, true, but only a part—of the war effort, while in the *Vita*, an
appendix to AJ, it is the dominant concern. Our main problem is
that the two accounts do not agree. Why did Josephus change his
story from the first version to the second? What is the relationship
of these accounts to each other? After we have studied these
questions and have analyzed the apologetic aims of each work,
we can attempt to reconstruct the history of Josephus' participation
in the war.

This problem has been discussed since the nineteenth century
but no consensus has yet been reached, in part because almost all
previous studies suffered from a lack of perspective. They treated
the V//BJ problem in isolation, as if it were not related to the

I

Josephan corpus as a whole. We shall see that V and the Galilean narrative of BJ can be understood only after we have investigated the motives and techniques of all of AJ and BJ. The study of V and BJ is the study of Josephus' development as historian, apologist, and Jew.

Our work is organized in the following manner. Chapter one delineates the specific contradictions between V and BJ and briefly surveys the scholarship on our topic. The first aspect of the problem which must be solved is the literary relationship of V to BJ. Chapter two investigates how Josephus treated his sources and examines the relationship of the first book and a half of BJ to books 13-20 of AJ. The results of this investigation are applied by chapter three to V//BJ.

Having clarified the literary relationship, we turn to the content of each work. BJ is analyzed in chapter four, V in chapter five. Thus the stage is set for a historical reconstruction which is attempted in chapter six. Chapter seven summarizes and concludes. Appendix one collects and analyzes all the external data relevant to the early history of the war. Appendix two is a synoptic survey of V and BJ.

CHAPTER ONE

VITA AND BELLUM JUDAICUM:
THE PROBLEM AND THE SOLUTIONS

The problem is clear. V and BJ disagree not only on the substance but also on the order of Josephus' activities in the Galilean war of 66-67 CE. How are the discrepancies to be explained? In this chapter we identify the disagreements and present a survey of the modern literature.

A. *The Problem*

Chronology is a crucial issue. Here in tabular form is the history of the first phase of the war as presented by BJ and V.[1]

V		BJ [2]	
		430-432	Rebels capture Antonia and attack royal palace (17 Loios)
20	Josephus takes refuge in temple after fall of Antonia		
		433-436	Menahem directs the siege
		437-440	Palace taken, Romans flee to towers (6 Gorpiaios) (= 556-558 below)
46-47	Philip flees to a village near Gamala five or more days after the fall of the palace (i.e. 11 Gorpiaios or later)		
		441-448	Menahem is murdered [2]
21-23	Josephus emerges from the temple after the murder of Menahem		
		449-457	Romans surrender and are massacred (17 Elul = Gorpiaios?); [3] "on the same

---

[1] The index in appendix II shows the literary structure of each work but neither V nor BJ adheres to a linear chronological scheme. Only rarely does Josephus synchronize various events. Wherever V's chronology is ambiguous I assume in the text that it agrees with that of BJ but I discuss the alternate possibilities in the notes. Many of these chronological problems will be discussed in chapter five.

[2] Menahem was executed a few days after 7 Gorpiaios (BJ 2.441) but it is impossible to determine whether before or after 11 Gorpiaios.

[3] Josephus provides no date but *Megillath Ta'anith* for 17 Elul (Gorpiaios)

			day and the same time of day" the Jews of Caesarea are massacred
42	Justus attacks villages of Gadara and Hippos [4]	458-460	Jewish attacks on gentile cities (including Gadara and Hippos)
25-26	Massacres of Jews in Syria and Scythopolis [5]	461-478	Massacres of Jews in Syria, Scythopolis, and coastal cities
		479-480	Antioch, Sidon, Apamaea, and Gerasa leave Jews unmolested
43-45	John defends Gischala against Tyrians and others [6]		

is usually invoked, "On the 17th of Elul the Romans departed (or, with another reading, were removed) from Jerusalem." The chronology supports the identification. See H. Lichtenstein, "Die Fastenrolle," *HUCA* 8-9 (1931-32) 304-305. The scroll does not mention the massacre of the Romans either (a) because Josephus is wrong and most of the Romans were not massacred (if this explanation is right, we may have to re-interpret a passage in Suetonius too—see appendix 1 note 24); or (b) because the author of the scroll does not want to remind the reader that the revolutionaries committed treachery. (b) seems more probable. The exegesis of B. Z. Lurie, *Megillath Ta'anith* (Jerusalem 1964) 142-143 (Heb.), is incorrect.

[4] These occurred before Josephus arrived in Galilee (cf. V 341) and the most likely context is the period before Cestius' expedition (although such fighting continued after Cestius' defeat as well; see V 81). BJ 2.458-460, a thematic list, gives the false impression of a single wave of Jewish attacks on the cities of Syria. Many of these conflicts were the result of local tensions —witness Justus and John as described by V—not of a centrally directed revolutionary movement. Chronological details are uncertain. Did the Ascalonites and Ptolemaeans massacre their Jews (477) before or after the Jewish attacks (459-460)? (πυρπολυθεῖσα is an obvious exaggeration). Did the Gerasenes preserve their Jews (480) after being attacked (458)? On the other hand there are some indications that Josephus is paying attention to the sequence of events. The Damascus incident (559-61) is not included here, presumably because it took place after the defeat of Cestius. The later campaign against Ascalon (BJ 3.9-28) is probably not here referred to. Accordingly we may suppose Josephus thought these disturbances, no matter what their relative chronology, mostly occurred before or during Cestius' campaign.

[5] V's chronology is ambiguous and hinges on the implication of προσγενομέ-νης of V 24. A pluperfect meaning seems intended. BJ's arrangement offers no legitimate ground for scepticism (V 27 calls BJ here ἀκριβέστερον) since no tendentiousness is evident. According to BJ only in Caesarea are the Jews passive victims. In Syria both Jews and Greeks share responsibility since each attacks the other. Contrast V 25-27 which suppresses any mention of Jewish attacks against the Greeks. The pagans are responsible, not the Jews (a further discussion of this point in chapter five).

[6] The exact sequence is uncertain. John's opponents are obscured by the faulty textual tradition. What brings the Gadarenes to attack Gischala

46-61	Massacre in Agrippa's kingdom; Philip flees to Gamala [7]	481-483	Massacre in Agrippa's kingdom
		484-486	Rebels take Cypros and Machaerus
		487-498	Riots in Alexandria
24, 30b, 31b	Expedition and defeat of Cestius	499-555	Expedition and defeat of Cestius (from the festival of Tabernacles to 8 Dios) [8]
	(= 46-47 above)	556-558	Philip and other distinguished Jews flee to Cestius [9]
27	Massacre of the Jews in Damascus [10]	559-561	Massacre of the Jews in Damascus
28-29	The foremost men of Jerusalem send Josephus and two other priests to Galilee	562-568	Those who defeated Cestius elect generals, among them Josephus for Galilee and Gamala
		3.9-28	Jewish attacks on Ascalon[11]

(V 44) ? They are likely opponents for Tiberias but not for a village of upper Galilee. See Christa Möller and Götz Schmitt, *Siedlungen Palästinas nach Flavius Josephus* (Wiesbaden 1976) 113. Γαβαρηνοί Σωγαναῖοι is an unfortunate conjecture (although adopted by Naber, Thackeray, and Pelletier) for the meaningless βαραγανεοι *vel similia* provided by the manuscripts. Gabara and Galilean Sogane were Jewish settlements, not Tyrian, and Gabara was later friendly to John. Sogane in Gaulan, like Gadara, is irrelevant for Gischala. For other conjectures see Haefeli ad loc. and S. Klein, *Galilee* (Jerusalem 1967) 42-43 (summarized in Schalit, *NWB* s.v. Καφαραγαναῖοι, and accepted by Möller and Schmitt 124-125).

[7] V 46-61 is composed of two strands: (a) the story of Noarus/Varus and (b) the story of Philip and Gamala (not in BJ). Both (b) in V and (a) in BJ agree that this episode took place before the invasion of Cestius. Modius, who replaced Noarus/Varus, was already at his post when Josephus came to Galilee (V 74).

[8] BJ 499-555 contains several dates: the feast of Tabernacles (515), the Sabbath especially honored by the Jews (517), 30 Hyperberetaios (= Tishri; 528), and 8 Dios (= Marḥeshvan; 555). The Sabbath especially honored by the Jews (517) is probably the festival of the eighth day (ʿAzereth) which may have coincided with a Sabbath. The Roman garrison capitulated on a Sabbath (456) and if that day was 17 Elul (see note 3 above), a thirty day Elul would make 22 Tishri (the date of ʿAzereth) a Sabbath. A discussion of the Josephan calendar would be out of place here. I agree with the view that in these sections Josephus employs the Jewish calendar but with Macedonian month names. See Schürer-Vermes 596-599.

[9] The account of Philip's movements here contradicts that in V 46-61, which suggests that Philip remained in Gamala and did not accompany Cestius to Jerusalem. See chapter five below, section C 2 e.

[10] V 27 includes this massacre with the others that preceded Cestius' expedition, but this chronology is probably the result of thematic association. See notes 4 and 5 above.

[11] These attacks took place shortly after the defeat of Cestius (3.9), and, presumably, after the selection of generals. The Ascalon expedition would then be contemporaneous with Josephus' early activities in Galilee.

30a, 31a	Josephus' arrival in Galilee and kindness to Sepphoris (= 79 below)	569	Josephus' arrival in Galilee and kindness to all
		570-571	Josephus establishes a supreme council
	(= 77a below)	572-575	Fortification of Galilean cities
	(= 186-189 below) (= 77b-78 below)	576-584	Josephus recruits and trains an army
62-69	Destruction of the palace in Tiberias		
70-76	Schemes of John of Gischala	585-592	Schemes of John of Gischala
77-78	Fortifications and military arrangements		(= 572-584 above)
79	Josephus establishes a supreme council		(= 570-571 above)
80-84	Josephus' integrity and popularity		
85-103	John at Tiberias		(= 614-623 below)
104-111	Josephus and Jesus at Sepphoris		
112-113	Refugees from Trachonitis		
179-186	Philip, Agrippa, Gamala [12]		
114	Agrippa attacks Gamala [13]		
115-121	Josephus skirmishes with Romans		
122-125	John tries to remove Josephus	593-594	John tries to remove Josephus
126-148	Dabaritta affair (= 85-103 above) (= 369-372 below)	595-613	Dabaritta affair
		614-623	John at Tiberias
		624-625	Dispersal of John's followers
	(= 190-335 below)	626-631	Delegation from Jerusalem
149-154	Refugees from Trachonitis		
155-173	Revolt of Tiberias		
174-178	Josephus and Justus	632-645	Revolt of Tiberias
187-189	Fortifications		
190-335	Delegation from Jerusalem		(= 573-575 above)
368-372	Dispersal of John's followers		(= 626-631 above) (= 622-625 above)
373-380	Revolt of Sepphoris	645-646	Revolt of Tiberias and Sepphoris
381-389	Revolt of Tiberias		

---

[12] V 179-186 forms a direct continuation to V 46-61 and needs but little transition to V 114. Josephus does not provide enough data for the determination of any precise chronology. See the discussion in chapter five below, section C 2 e.

[13] This siege was maintained for seven months but without success (BJ 4.10). Vespasian attacked Gamala in the fall of 67 (Gorpiaios and Hyperberetaios, BJ 4.83). The seven month siege had failed before Vespasian began his attempt. Therefore V 114 refers to an event of circa November 66 - January 67. See chapter five n. 194.

390-393 Flight of Justus
394-397 Revolt of Sepphoris
398-406 Fighting with Sulla

	647-651 Situation in Jerusalem
	652-654 Situation in Akrabatene and Idumaea [14]
	3.1-8 Appointment of Vespasian
407-411 Vespasian in Syria	3.29-34 Vespasian in Syria
	3.59-69, Galilean war [15]
	110ff

This index shows that V and BJ differ in the order of six episodes. The establishment of a supreme council and the fortification of the Galilean cities are juxtaposed and placed early in the narrative by BJ, but separated and postponed by V. The autobiography has the episode of John at Tiberias before the Dabaritta affair and the repulse of the delegation before the dispersal of John's followers, while BJ has the opposite sequence in both pairs.

V and BJ contradict each other in many other details, large and small. We find variations in proper names and numerals: *Noaros* has become *Varos* (BJ 481//V 50); [16] *Annaios* has produced *Dassion* and *Iannaios* (BJ 597//V 131); the names of the fortified cities are transmitted differently (BJ 573-574//V 187-88) as are the names of the members of the delegation from Jerusalem (BJ 628//V 197); either 500 (V 127) or 600 (BJ 595) gold pieces were taken at Dabaritta; Josephus' house was surrounded by 600 (V 145) or 2000 (BJ 610) soldiers; John received reinforcements from Jerusalem, either 1000 (V 200-201) or 2500 (BJ 628); the ultimatum to John's followers bore a time limit of five (BJ 624) or twenty (V 370) days; according to V 371-372, 4000 soldiers deserted John and only 1500 remained, but in BJ 625, 3000 deserted and only 2000 remained.[17] I omit from this list examples of mere variant

---

[14] BJ 647-654 describes events which are contemporary with Josephus' administration of Galilee but, again, Josephus does not provide enough data for a precise chronology.

[15] Josephus entered Jotapata on 21 Artemisios (BJ 3.142) or thereabout. His tenure had lasted about six months.

[16] Which name is correct is uncertain. For the name Νόαρος in Syria see IGLS 4052 and 4010 with the commentary on p. 36 top. Schürer 587 n. 6 = Schürer-Vermes 472 n. 7 identifies this Varus with the Varus of BJ 2.247.

[17] Σύρων in BJ is a mistake for Τυρίων as Reinach and Thackeray note. BJ 588 mentions the Tyrians but a total of only 400.

spellings (e.g. Σόεμος in V 52 versus Σόαιμος in BJ 481). Some of the cases listed here are certainly the result of manuscript corruption but other variations occur too. Was Soemus, the relative of Varus/ Noarus, a tetrarch of the Lebanon (V 52) or a king (BJ 481)? [18] How much profit did John make from his sale of Jewish oil (V 75//BJ 592)? Was the oil for the Jews of Syria or of Caesarea Philippi? Did the brigands of Dabaritta attack Ptolemy (BJ 595) or Ptolemy's wife (V 126)? In V 137 the sole bodyguard who remains with Josephus counsels him to commit suicide. In BJ 600-601, however, four bodyguards remain who counsel Josephus to flee. After the Dabaritta affair did Josephus whip many (BJ 612) or only one (V 147) of the ringleaders?

The most significant contradiction concerns the nature of the mission to Galillee. BJ portrays Josephus as a general selected by an assembly to carry on the war against Rome. He recruits a large army and prepares to meet the foe. He fights courageously and sincerely. But V claims that Josephus and two others were sent as emissaries of the Jerusalem aristocracy to maintain peace in Galilee. Instead of recruiting an army Josephus pays the brigands to refrain from any hostile activity. He desires a peaceful Galilee.

Aside from these and other contradictions, several important elements appear in only one work. V, but not BJ, contains extensive material on Philip ben Jacimus, Gamala, and Justus of Tiberias. Neither BJ nor V is friendly to John of Gischala but only BJ vilifies him.

B. *The Solutions*

The problems may seem obvious but for a long while they did not attract attention.[19] Pre-nineteenth century scholars noted that V and BJ were parallel, and that the two texts frequently disagreed, but they were unable to come to grips with the issue. The revision of J. Fabricius' *Bibliotheca Graeca*, published in 1796, described Josephus' life by summarizing V and ignoring BJ.[20]

---

[18] The identification of Soemus is uncertain. See Schürer 720-721 = Schürer-Vermes 569-570 as well as the pages cited in n. 16 above; Marcus on AJ 14.129.

[19] I do not mention here every work written on Josephus. I try instead to highlight the main contributions and to show the trends in the scholarship. Invaluable assistance is provided by H. Schreckenberg, *Bibliographie zu Flavius Josephus* (Leiden 1968).

[20] J. A. Fabricius, *Bibliotheca Graeca*, ed. G. C. Harles, vol. 5 (Hamburg

The Jewish historian I. M. Jost was the first [21] to appreciate the difficulties in reconstructing Josephus' career. His nine volume *Geschichte der Israeliten* (Berlin 1820-1828), the first extensive survey of Jewish history since the work of Basnage more than a century before, earned for him the title "father of modern study of Jewish history." [22] Jost assumed that BJ and V can be combined to produce a single reliable record. Josephus and the Jerusalem aristocracy, although sincere advocates of war (here Jost follows BJ), realized that Galilee must be kept peaceful as long as possible in order to allow time for the preparations for war. The Romans must not be aroused to a precipitous attack before the Jews were ready. Josephus' task was to unite the population of Galilee, to fortify the cities, raise an army, prepare for war, and simultaneously to disguise these militant activities and maintain peace. After the war Josephus was embarrassed by these contradictory policies and the seeming incoherence of his actions. BJ and V improve matters, BJ stressing militancy and V pacificity. Why does V differ so much from BJ even in incidental details? Because Josephus did not consult BJ when writing V and his memory had changed on many points. Jost theorized that V might be less or more accurate than BJ, less accurate when Josephus was responding to the accusations of Justus, and more accurate when Josephus had the benefit of extra information from Agrippa. Jost forgot to illustrate these excellent generalizations with specific examples. Finally, Jost was the first to note that neither V nor BJ establishes an organic connection between one event and the next. The story is narrated with little concern for cohesiveness or logical development, and, as a result, the reader often becomes confused.[23]

Jost had a firm grasp of the problem. If his account is somewhat obscure, it is because he could not work out all the details himself.

1796) 1-64 (by F. Oberthür). Cf. the original edition, vol. 4 (Hamburg 1708) 228-256. S. Havercamp, in his edition of Josephus (1726), summarizes the results of Josephan scholarship to his day.

[21] Frise's annotated German translation of V (Altona 1806) is capable of "cf. BJ" and nothing more. I have not been able to check J. F. Eckard's (Eckhard?) translation of V from 1782 but Oberthür (n. 20) 48 calls him a "passim negligentior interpres."

[22] For an appreciation of Jost's work see S. Baron, *History and Jewish Historians* (Philadelphia 1964) 240-262 and I. Schorsch, *Yearbook of the Leo Baeck Institute* 22 (1977) 109-128. We deal here with volume 2 (1821).

[23] See Jost 69-94 and the *Anhang* 88-90 (note 29), 93 (note 35), and 55-73 ("Ueber den Geschichtschreiber Joseph als solchen"), esp. 65-71.

He was a pioneer writing a history of three thousand years.[24] His notion that the Jews were trying to hide their revolt from the Romans (after the defeat of Cestius!) is implausible and contradicts even V. But his theory that V did not consult BJ and that shifts in memory are responsible for the disagreements between the two works, was a major contribution.

Twenty five years after Jost, Salvador independently assumed that V and BJ are contradictory because they reflect different facets of an inherently contradictory situation.[25] In this reconstruction too, Josephus was entrusted with a double mission but as to its nature Salvador preferred V. The aristocrats did not want war. They hoped only to control the situation and prevent the spread of "radicalism" until an arrangement could be worked out. In the interim they pretended to support the war. BJ emphasizes Josephus' official, public role; V, under the pressure of Justus and others, reveals the secret and authentic one. Salvador ignored the numerous disagreements in details and chronology.[26]

Jost and Salvador combined V and BJ by accepting V. Only the biography distinguishes between Josephus' covert and declared purposes, and thus reveals how complicated the situation was. BJ conceals these deceptions and presents only a single aspect of his activity, either the covert and real (Jost) or the public and pretended (Salvador). The historian's task was not to reject one account in favor of the other but to reconstruct a situation which could produce two accounts, conflicting and yet true. Jost's theory found few sympathizers and so it was Salvador's reconstruction which, usually unacknowledged, remained fundamental for the historians of the next generation (from 1847 to 1874, from Salvador to Schürer).[27] Apparently no one accepted his interpretation of BJ as representing the official version of the war but many agreed that V correctly characterizes Josephus and his associates as pro-Roman.

E. Reuss was the most sceptical of this group. He accepted the

---

[24] Jost later abandoned his reconstruction under the influence of Graetz; see note 29 below.

[25] J. Salvador, *Histoire de la Domination Romaine en Judée* (Paris 1847), 2.42-117, esp. 45-50.

[26] Salvador 46-47 adds that Josephus tried to make himself independent of the central command in Jerusalem so that he could negotiate with the Romans for himself on his own terms, but here Josephus failed.

[27] I have not been able to see Champagny, *Rome et la Judée au temps de la chute de Néron* (Paris 1865).

view that Josephus was a member of the "moderate" party (thus V) which was involuntarily drawn into the war. Josephus' election as general (thus BJ) by the revolutionary council may have been a victory either for the moderates who successfully advanced their candidate or for the extremists who were glad to remove any influential opponent from Jerusalem. Although Reuss tried to combine V and BJ he realized that they are fundamentally incompatible:

> In whose name, with what intention, for the defense of what interest did he go to Galilee? Was it to pacify the spirits and reconcile the parties, or was it to excite the passions and organize the resistance? Was he the agent of the moderates or the demagogues? What were all those interminable quarrels which absorbed him there, which he recounts with so much emphasis, but whose origin and resolution we do not understand? Why is his autobiography almost entirely devoted to these bloody intrigues which belonged to only one year, which exerted only a minor influence on the course of events, and why is he unable to give us distant and impartial spectators a clear and precise idea of these intrigues?

Neither Jost nor Salvador answered these questions. Reuss sensed that V is more an apology directed against Justus and less a biography but he neglected to ask whether V is therefore less reliable than BJ. Reuss' incisive formulation of the historical problem should have prevented the incautious acceptance of Salvador's position.[28]

But it did not. A year after Reuss, Graetz called Josephus a *Römling* and asked how such a man was chosen general of Galilee. Graetz' two answers are not as important as the question which shows that Salvador's was the accepted interpretation of Josephus' career.[29] Not only Graetz, but also Ewald,[30] Hausrath,[31] M. Baum-

---

[28] Ed. Reuss, *Nouvelle Revue de Theologie* 4 (1859) 253-319 (the quotation is from 260-261), an expanded French version of his German article in the *Allgemeine Encyclopädie der Wissenschaften und Künste*, ed. J. S. Ersch and J. G. Gruber, series 2, vol. 31 (Leipzig 1855) 104-116 s.v. Josephus (where the quotation is on page 107).

[29] H. Graetz, *Geschichte der Juden* III (Leipzig 1856) 391-419, esp. 401 (Salvador is invoked in n. 2). The text is almost identical in the fifth and last edition (1906) 476-503, esp. 484 (where Salvador is not mentioned), except for the addition of an important footnote; see below. Graetz' answers were that Josephus' friend Jesus ben Gamala (V 204) supported his election or that Josephus masqueraded so convincingly that he was accepted as a revolutionary. Graetz did notice that V's chronology contradicts BJ; see n. 46 below. Jost now abandoned his earlier scheme in favor of Graetz'.

garten,[32] von Gutschmid,[33] and Hitzig,[34] all were certain of Josephus' duplicity and concern to maintain peace. All ignored Reuss' questions.

During this period not all scholars preferred V to BJ. Lewitz [35] and Milman [36] accepted BJ's portrait of Josephus the revolutionary, but neglected to explain why V presented Josephus as a pacifist if BJ correctly pictured him as pro-war. This problem was faced by Raphall and Merivale.[37] They theorized that BJ presented Josephus as he would have liked to have been for the Jews—a militant patriot, while V presented Josephus as he would have liked to have been for the Romans—an inveterate pro-Roman. The impossibility of this theory was soon noted [38] but the important point was that the motives of each work had been questioned. Raphall and Merivale had at least asked not only which account is the more reliable but also why the two accounts disagree.

Now that this question had been raised, it led to new results. When the reaction against the Salvador-inspired preference for V

See his *Geschichte des Judenthums und seiner Secten* 1 (Leipzig 1857) 441-444.

[30] G. H. Ewald, *Geschichte des Volkes Israel* 6² (Göttingen 1858) and 6³ (Göttingen 1868) 700-713. Ewald based his account on V because he claimed (707 n. 2) that it is fuller and chronologically more exact than BJ. Ewald did not elaborate.

[31] A. Hausrath, *HZ* 12 (1864) 285-314, esp. 293-296. Hausrath thinks of Josephus as a noble and idealistic Pharisaic scholar who, upon arriving in Galilee, attempted to set up the ideal Pharisaic state with a council of seventy elders, courts of seven, etc. This view is repeated without change in his *Neutestamentliche Zeitgeschichte* ² (Heidelberg 1873-1877).

[32] M. Baumgarten, *Jahrbücher für Deutsche Theologie* 9 (1864) 616-648, accepts V and does not try to reconcile V with BJ.

[33] A. von Gutschmid, *Kleine Schriften*, ed. F. Rühl, vol. 4 (Leipzig 1893) 339-340. (This article was written in 1868 or 1869; see Rühl's footnote on page 336.)

[34] F. Hitzig, *Geschichte des Volkes Israel*² (Leipzig 1869) 603-604.

[35] F. Lewitz, *De Flavii Josephi Fide atque Auctoritate* (Königsberg 1857). Lewitz also emphasized (7) that Josephus himself was often confused because a firm policy had not been established by the Jerusalem government.

[36] H. Milman, *The History of the Jews from the Earliest Period down to Modern Times*, 3 vols. (London 1863, repr. N.Y. 1875) 2.228-243. Milman did make one great contribution but, because it was buried in a footnote, it went unnoticed; see chapter three below, n. 4.

[37] M. J. Raphall, *Post-Biblical History of the Jews* (Philadelphia 1855) 418, and C. Merivale, *History of the Romans under the Empire* 6 (N.Y. 1866) 431. Merivale followed BJ, Raphall was uncertain. Raphall 424 realized BJ's great exaggerations.

[38] K. Peter, *Flavius Josephus und der jüdische Krieg* (Perleberg 1871) 29-31. Peter himself accepted V but claimed that when Vespasian arrived in Galilee, even Josephus the half-hearted fought as best he could.

solidified in the 1870's, it was supported by the view that V cannot be trustworthy because it is polemical apology, not history. A small pamphlet published in Breslau in 1873 stated clearly that BJ is more trustworthy than V.[39] Schürer, in all the editions of his famous history, accepted BJ as the basis of his narrative.[40] A footnote now added to Graetz' history made another attempt to reconcile V with BJ but with the biography's share much reduced: Josephus began as a moderate, was caught by the passions of the moment, became a sincere zealot, gradually was disillusioned, and ended by joining the Romans in a secret compact.[41]

In the first dissertation devoted to our topic, A. Baerwald agreed that V falsely disassociates Josephus from the revolutionaries but claimed that the key to Josephus' activities in Galilee was a secret agreement between Josephus and Agrippa. Publicly the king was pro-Roman, but secretly he hoped for a Jewish victory and the restoration of his ancestral throne. Josephus supported Agrippa and, like him, played a double game. He therefore protected the king's property. With the arrival of Vespasian, Agrippa saw that the Jews had no hope of success and docilely returned to whole-hearted support of Rome. Josephus followed his lead and betrayed the cause. After the death of Agrippa Justus revealed this secret agreement and Josephus had to respond. Thus Baerwald, under the influence of Graetz.[42] This theory, which does not really come to grips with the V//BJ problem, is extraordinarily confused and has not won support.[43]

---

[39] I. Prager, *Ueber das Verhältniss des Flavius Josephus zur Zelotenpartei beim Ausbruch des jüdischen Krieges* (Breslau 1873).

[40] *Geschichte des jüdischen Volkes* I[3=4] (Leipzig 1901) 75, 86-87, and 607-609 = Schürer-Vermes 44, 53-54, and 489-491. The first edition appeared in 1874. Schürer accepts the chronology of BJ without comment. V is utilized only for biographical details and for the explanation that Josephus' heart was not in the struggle because he knew Rome too well to expect a Jewish victory.

[41] Graetz, *Geschichte der Juden* 3[3] (1878) 515 n. 2 = 3[5] (1906) 485 n. 1. I have been unable to see the second edition of 1863.

[42] A. Baerwald, *Flavius Josephus in Galiläa, sein Verhältnis zu den Parteien insbesondere zu Justus von Tiberias und König Agrippa II* (diss. Breslau 1877), esp. 13-16, 33-35, 59-63. Graetz taught at Breslau.

[43] See the review of Schürer, *ThLZ* (1878) 208-210, and the remarks of Luther (n. 45 below) 33-34. Baerwald never explains why V differs so much from BJ nor why Josephus had to respond as he did to the rival account of Justus. V should have emphasized according to Baerwald that Agrippa was militantly pro-Roman and that Josephus was militantly anti-Roman (i.e. not a traitor). But V does neither.

The next major step was taken by Niese in his outstanding survey article.[44] Graetz, Schürer, and Baerwald knew that V's motive was to show that Josephus went to Galilee for peace, not war. In his brief discussion of V, Niese isolated other tendentious elements: Josephus always protected Agrippa; Josephus attempted to prevent the defection of Sepphoris to the Romans; Josephus did not cause the revolt of Tiberias; Josephus was not friendly with John; Josephus was upright.

H. Luther continued Niese's work.[45] He demonstrated that V and BJ taken together show that Josephus was active in pursuing the enemy, establishing fortifications, and trying to maintain a united front against the Romans. Josephus was not the traitor pictured by Graetz and Baerwald, but a dedicated revolutionary. Therefore, concluded Luther, V's claim of pro-Romanism is false. Not that BJ was irreproachable—Luther tried to demonstrate that BJ contained at least two serious errors, one in chronology [46] and the other in the substance of an episode [47]—but Luther successfully showed that even V, with all its talk of pro-Romanism and duplicity, essentially agreed with BJ. Josephus fought Rome.

---

[44] B. Niese, "Der jüdische Historiker Josephus," *HZ* 76 (1896) 193-237. An English version of this article appeared in *Encyclopaedia of Religion and Ethics*, ed. J. Hastings, vol. 7 (Edinburgh 1914) 569-579; I cite from the German. See Niese 194 n. 4 and 228 with n. 2. A sign of the reaction in favor of BJ is provided by O. Holtzmann in B. Stade, *Geschichte des Volkes Israel* 2 (Berlin 1888) 645-654 who summarizes BJ, almost ignores V, and merely says (647) that BJ contains much *Unglaubliche*. Works of the post-Schürer era which still follow V are the history of E. Ledrain (Paris 1882) and A. Edersheim's article "Josephus" in Smith and Wace, *A Dictionary of Christian Biography* 3 (London 1882) 441-460.

[45] H. Luther, *Josephus und Justus von Tiberias: Ein Beitrag zur Geschichte des jüdischen Aufstandes* (diss. Halle 1910). Niese directed the dissertation.

[46] BJ, unlike V, places the Dabaritta affair before the Tiberias episode. Luther argues (26 n. 2) that this is incorrect because in the former Josephus and John are open enemies while in the latter Josephus does not suspect John. Note that Graetz 3¹ (1856) 405 n. 1 = 3⁵ (1906) 489 n. 1, accepted by Baerwald 45, argued just the reverse: V must be incorrect because it tries to blacken John. Since Josephus' suspicious conduct at Taricheae might have justified John's attack at Tiberias, V reversed the sequence in order to make John's attack unmotivated.

[47] BJ 606-609, in agreement with V 142-144, has Josephus promise fortifications to the Taricheaens first and the Tiberians second, but this, says Luther (28), is impossible because BJ 3.465 shows that Tiberias was fortified before Taricheae. This argument is not cogent because BJ 606-609 and V 142-144 relate only what Josephus said, not what he did. Luther should have cited V 156 which contradicts BJ 3.465.

Luther's other main contribution was a serious attempt to reconstruct Justus' account. It had long been obvious that Justus' work was an important factor in the interpretation of V, but Luther was the first to deduce from the variations between V and BJ the charges to which Josephus was responding. All the accusations thus revealed were attributed to Justus.[48] According to Luther, Justus attacked not only Josephus' personal conduct (Josephus was an ill-behaved revolutionary fanatic, cruel, rapacious, and greedy), but also his previous narrative (BJ was inaccurate and distorted). In response Josephus emphasized his probity, denied his revolutionary past, and corrected many of BJ's omissions and exaggerations which had been criticized by Justus.[49]

From his detailed synoptic study of BJ and V, Luther deduced some of the motives and gauged the relative historicity of the two works. Luther never stopped to consider, however, whether such a procedure was justified. Did V pay such close attention to BJ that every contradiction can be treated as significant? Many contradictions, notably those affecting chronology, were not explained;[50] many of these appear to be unmotivated (see above).

---

[48] See Luther 65-82.

[49] Here are some of Luther's more plausible arguments. V had to mention Josephus' two colleagues, the destruction of the palace in Tiberias, and the campaign into Syria (V 81), because Justus had criticized these omissions and had used the last two incidents as proofs of Josephus' revolutionary actions. Because Justus had accused him of being an associate of John of Gischala, Josephus responded that John was originally a member of the peace party (V 43) who obtained Josephus' reluctant approval for his schemes only through the intervention of Josephus' fellow emissaries (V 72-73). Justus harped on the exaggeration of BJ 591 and V 74 had to admit that John sold oil only to Caesarea Philippi, not all Syria. (But why is John's profit margin greater in V than BJ?) Luther should have noted that several other numerical discrepancies can be explained by the assumption that V is toning down the exaggerations of BJ. John received only 1000 reinforcements (V 200-201), not 2500 (BJ 628). Only 600 opponents were outsmarted by Josephus (V 145), not 2000 (BJ 610). The ultimatum to John's followers is less severe in V 370 (twenty days) than BJ 624 (five days). But this approach does not always work. V 137 knows only one bodyguard, BJ 601 four. The dispersal of John's forces is more effective in V 371-372 than BJ 625. Some of these examples had been noted by S. A. Naber, *Mnemosyne* n.s. 13 (1885) 269-270, but Naber nowhere ascribed the impetus for these changes to Justus.

[50] Regarding one chronological contradiction (see above) Luther tried to explain which account was right and which wrong, but he ignored the problem why the wrong account distorted the facts. Niese 228-229 thought these discrepancies were a sign of Josephus' conscientiousness—V corrects BJ even in incidental detail.

Furthermore, it is illegitimate to assume that all of the Josephan apologetic was directed solely against Justus. Josephus may also have wished to answer charges that circulated orally, and to introduce traits that would recommend him to persons of parties now become powerful, even though they were not attacking him. To determine his apologetic motives is, therefore, a complex problem requiring a complex solution. Luther himself sensed this when his assumption yielded a Justus simultaneously attacking Josephus as anti-Roman and insufficiently anti-Roman.[51]

The work of Richard Laqueur marked a major advance in Josephan studies.[52] In a reaction to contemporary source criticism (see chapter two below), Laqueur insisted that historiographic inquiry is more fruitful. Why does Josephus follow a particular source at a particular time? Why does he change his opinion from one work to the other? In short, why does Josephus say what he says? Here Laqueur was the heir of Niese and Luther but he progressed beyond them. His aim was to produce a biography of Josephus based on the works of Josephus himself. Therefore Laqueur was especially interested in contradictions and shifts in opinion, because these would reveal the development of Josephus' attitudes and, by extrapolation, the evolution of the circumstances in which he worked.[53] The numerous contradictions between V and BJ resulted when one work had a purpose or point of view different from the other's. When Laqueur thought he found such contradictions even within V and BJ, he concluded that Josephus revised his output several times, always interpolating his new material. In these cases the motives of the interpolated material differed from those of the original text. Laqueur thus distinguished between the motives of the early and late Josephus, between the motives of the

---

[51] V attempts to show that Josephus did his best to prevent Sepphoris from surrendering to the Romans. Luther 80 considers this motif a response to Justus even though it is hardly consistent with Justus' other accusations. See chapter five, section C 2 c. Niese had noticed this motif but prudently avoided involving Justus.

[52] R. Laqueur, *Der jüdische Historiker Flavius Josephus* (Giessen 1920, repr. Darmstadt 1967). L. H. Feldman, *Scholarship on Philo and Josephus 1937-1962* (N.Y. n.d.) 31b, calls Laqueur's book "the most important single work on Josephus."

[53] See especially chapter seven, "Eine methodische Grundfrage," 230-245, and chapter eight, "Der Werdegang des Josephus," 245-278. Laqueur regarded his work on Josephus as a vindication of his earlier book on Polybius (1912).

original texts and the interpolated passages. This analysis provided Laqueur with the framework he needed for his biography of Josephus and the history of his times. Although a vicious circle results—the analysis of the text provides information about the author which is used in the analysis of the text—this method can yield cogent results.[54] Laqueur's thesis consists of two parts and runs as follows.

1. Although V was published as an appendix to a second edition of AJ after 100 CE, it contains as its nucleus a work which was utilized by BJ twenty-five years before. This theory was supported by the argument that V is more 'original' and truthful than BJ and, therefore, is anterior to it. Laqueur attempted to show that BJ consistently revises this nucleus (as reconstructed from V) to make it accord with BJ's own motives and goals.

The autobiography was provoked by Justus who had written a history of the Jewish war in good Greek and thereby ruined the market for a revised edition of BJ on which Josephus had been working for some time. Josephus abandoned the project mid-way and wrote V in response to Justus. The BJ which has come down to us is not the text of the seventies but the partly revised text of the nineties. Thus, from V and BJ we can trace Josephus' development through five stages: (a) nucleus of V (before BJ), (b) the original BJ, (c) some revisions of V (i.e. the nucleus) made at the time BJ was written, (d) later revisions of BJ, and (e) the final revision of V. Laqueur claims that he can indicate precisely the boundaries of all five stages [55] and explain the motives of the changes. Moreover, he finds that, although V in its present form is an express retort to Justus, his name appears only in the interpolations of stage (e). Therefore V contains an earlier document, the nucleus (a).

2. This early work was an administrative report (*Rechenschafts-bericht*) which Josephus submitted to the authorities of Jerusalem in defense of his activities in Galilee. Since there had been complaints (V 190//BJ 2.626), the report is especially concerned to show that Josephus was the paragon of justice tempered with mercy and that

---

[54] For example, see the works on Josephus and the Pharisees listed in chapter five below, note 150.

[55] These five stages belong to four periods: 1. the writing of the original V (written in 67 before Vespasian's arrival in Galilee); 2. its revision and the writing of original BJ (c. 75); 3. the revision of BJ during the completion of the last books of AJ (c. 90); 4. the final revision of V (after 100). A good example of Laqueur's technique is his dissection of the two narratives of the Dabaritta affair; see Laqueur 57-79.

all his opponents were worthless scoundrels. The nucleus is embodied in V 28-406, i.e., from Josephus' appointment until just before the arrival of Vespasian. The administrative report went no further because it was sent to Jerusalem in spring 67 and so knew nothing of a war with Rome. When it was written, war did not yet seem inevitable.

Laqueur had no doubt that the nucleus of V, the administrative report, was the only reliable source for the history of Josephus in Galilee. BJ was a tendentious revision, useful only because it reveals Josephus' concerns of 75-79 CE and beyond.[56] The nucleus shows that Josephus was sent not as a general but as an emissary for peace. He established himself as the middleman between the Galileans and the brigands. From the one he exacted money, from the other he bought inactivity (V 77-78). This position proved so congenial that Josephus appointed himself *strategos* and became a tyrant. But to maintain his position he had to adjust himself to suit his supporters, the brigands, who were really revolutionaries. Thus Josephus was inextricably drawn into conflict with the Romans.

This brilliant book provoked a series of hostile reviews.[57] The more important criticisms are the following. The claim that because V is more truthful than BJ it must, therefore, precede BJ, is a *non sequitur*. Truth is no sign of priority. And vice versa: even if we grant the existence of an early nucleus, the historical problems are not solved. Every incident must be studied to determine which account is more reliable and why the other departs from the truth.

Laqueur's account oversimplifies the relationship between V and BJ. If Josephus was a skilled laborer trying to reconcile one work with the other, his procedure was strange. He changed nothing of his earlier text but was satisfied by interpolating his new material, oblivious to the fact that he thereby contradicted himself, destroyed the context of many passages, and all but ruined the integrity of his work. (Laqueur would respond that the procedure was fairly successful since for over eighteen hundred years no one suspected the existence of these interpolations.) Because the

---

[56] For the AJ//BJ parallels Laqueur proposed the same view but with the titles reversed: AJ is a tendentious revision of BJ. See next chapter.

[57] The hostile reviews were those of Helm, *PhW* 41 (1921) 481-493 (by far the most important review); Münzer, *OLZ* (1921) 213-216; and von Stern, *Literarisches Zentralblatt* (1921) 757-759 and 779-781. The numerous other reviews failed to come to grips with the book. For the criticisms of Drexler and Schalit, see below.

language of V differs markedly from that of BJ, either one work or both must have revised the text of the *Rechenschaftsbericht*. Did Josephus recast the language but reproduce the content without any change? If Josephus wanted to reconcile a *Rechenschaftsbericht* with another work, he would not have restricted his modifications almost exclusively to short intrusive paragraphs but would have rewritten the entire document to reconcile all details. But Josephus did not do this. Again, according to Laqueur V contains sections written more than thirty years apart (from 67 to 100 or after), but V maintains a uniformly mediocre style throughout and provides no sign of unevenness or stratification.[58] Thackeray observed that V's style is close to that of AJ 20, the latest stage of Josephan Greek.[59] If there is an early common source behind BJ and V, it has been rewritten so thoroughly that we cannot recover its exact wording and delineate the interpolations accurately, that is, we cannot do what Laqueur attempted to do. Furthermore, our next chapter will investigate Josephus' treatment of his sources and the problem of the relationship of BJ to AJ. We can state here that the procedure attributed to Josephus by Laqueur is non-Josephan.

Laqueur did not even attempt to explain many of the chronological and factual discrepancies noted above.[60] And if Josephus took such great pains with his work, why is V so sloppy? We can forgive Josephus if a long and involved work like AJ contains contradictions and unfulfilled cross references, but a short work like V should be coherent. Yet V 66 thinks that Jesus ben Sapphia had already been

---

[58] Pelletier has examined the grouping of verbs, the avoidance of hiatus, and the clausulae of the first 103 sections of V. According to Laqueur V 1-27 and 31 fin.-62 date from 100 CE, the remainder from 67 CE. But Pelletier's data reveal no unevenness in V's style. See *Flavius Josèphe adapteur de la lettre d'Aristée* (Paris 1962) 225-227, 242-244, and 245-249. The more extensive study by W. Hornbostel, *De Flavii Iosephi Studiis Rhetoricis Quaestiones Selectae* (diss. Halle 1912) 31-111, demonstrates a unity of style not only within V itself but also between V and CA (except that CA is more rhetorical).

[59] H. St. J. Thackeray, *Josephus the Man and the Historian* (1929, repr. N.Y. 1967) 18-19, 108, and 115. The details are listed in the introduction to the Loeb edition of V (1926) xv-xvi. A. Pelletier, *Flavius Josèphe: Autobiographie* (Paris 1959) xvi-xvii, gives a more complete list of the verbal parallels but he too omits μικρὰ καὶ ἡ τυχοῦσα αἰτία (AJ 20.215 and V 13) and ἔπεισί μοι θαυμάζειν (AJ 20.155 and V 357).

[60] For example, Laqueur himself (63-64) notes that Josephus' confrontation with the people during the Dabaritta affair took place in the stadium according to V, but in front of Josephus' house according to BJ—but he does not explain why BJ and V disagree.

introduced (presumably in V 35). V 89 thinks that Silas had been mentioned.[61] The genealogy of V 186 does not square with 177-178 although Josephus says "as we have already said above" (καθὼς ἤδη προείπομεν). The attack on Justus is confused (see chapter five below). Finally, many of Laqueur's deductions are exaggerated or incorrect.[62]

Even if it be granted that Laqueur's account of the literary relations of V and BJ is correct, it does not follow that his account of the source and purpose of the earliest element of V is correct. Why should Josephus have written an administrative report just before Vespasian's arrival? According to Laqueur's reconstruction, Josephus had already been confirmed at his post. We hear of no complaints to Jerusalem after the repulse of the delegation. The nucleus of V does know of the war with the Romans (e.g. V 149-150) which is not surprising, because after the defeat of Cestius everyone must have known that war was inevitable.

Laqueur's main contribution was the idea that Josephus' work can be interpreted best in the light of the history of Josephus' own time. We shall return to this point in later chapters. Laqueur also inaugurated a reaction against the BJ-centered historiography of the previous generation. But some scholars, not only the authors of the hostile reviews already mentioned, remained unconvinced. The search for Josephus' motives, in the manner of Niese and Luther, reappeared in the work of H. Drexler.[63] He emphasized that BJ, no less tendentious than V, tried to excuse Josephus and his class by claiming that the priesthood and aristocracy opposed the war. BJ itself shows that this construct is false.[64] Drexler generally followed Luther's analysis of V (the tendentious elements are a retort to Justus) but he never tried to glide over Josephus'

---

[61] The reference to BJ 2.616 supposed by Pelletier (following Thackeray) and Hans Drüner, *Untersuchungen über Josephus* (diss. Marburg 1896) 91, is dubious because when AJ refers to BJ the title of the earlier work is usually mentioned. See Drüner 54 n. 1 and the list on 85-91. This fact was noticed by J. von Destinon, *Die Quellen des Flavius Josephus* (Kiel 1882) 26. Apart from V 89 the only possible exceptions are AJ 7.393 and V 61, each of which has ὡς ἐν ἄλλοις ἐδηλώσαμεν. But Josephus is not known for rigorous terminological consistency.

[62] See Helm's review, and Motzo (n. 72 infra) 226-240.

[63] H. Drexler, "Untersuchungen zu Josephus und zur Geschichte des jüdischen Aufstandes," *Klio* 19 (1925) 277-312.

[64] See especially 277-289. See the fuller discussion of this point in chapters four and six below.

sloppiness and obfuscation. Laqueur's comparison of V and BJ was illegitimate, argued Drexler, because, as the variations in numbers and minor details show, V was written from memory without direct reliance on BJ. Back to Jost! Since both BJ and V are tendentious and sloppy, Drexler concluded that we know very little about the Jewish war of 66-70.

Schalit's retort to Laqueur was more direct.[65] The response to Justus is not interpolated into an earlier text, as Laqueur thought, but is an integral part of V. The autobiography throughout defends Josephus against charges of cruelty and harshness, charges raised by Justus. Stories which appear to be otiose (e.g. regarding Gamala) are not otiose at all but conceal polemic against Justus who had reported the facts differently. In effect, Schalit, like Drexler, used Luther to refute Laqueur. Since all of the major differences between V and BJ [66] can be explained by the attacks of Justus, V must be an organic whole conceived in response.

In spite of these criticisms, Laqueur's fundamental point—V contains an early nucleus written before and more reliable than BJ—gained widespread approval. Since most scholars could not endorse Laqueur's thesis in toto,[67] improvements were suggested.[68] Thackeray thought that the administrative report would have been written in Aramaic and that with this modification the theory was "unobjectionable and not improbable." [69] M. Gelzer agreed with

[65] A. Schalit, "Josephus und Justus: Studien zur Vita des Josephus," Klio 26 (1933) 67-95. I do not know whether this article contains the results of Schalit's 1925 dissertation, "Die Vita des Josephus," which he completed at the University of Vienna. The university no longer possesses a copy of the dissertation.

[66] Schalit 73 n. 1 and 81 n. 1 emphasized that V probably did not consult BJ and that only discrepancies in larger issues can be pressed.

[67] Laqueur's work was accepted by Haefeli and Stein in the introductions to their translations. The modifications suggested by R. Eisler, Jesous Basileus (Heidelberg 1929) 1.xxxviii and 261-292, are based on the Slavonic version. S. Zeitlin, JQR 56 (1969) 53 and 58 = Studies in the Early History of Judaism I (N.Y. 1973) 391 and 396, accepts Laqueur but also resurrects, without acknowledgement, the old view of Salvador, "War presents the official version; Life gives the true mission of Josephus" (39 = 377). Zeitlin, as usual, has repeated his opinions; see JQR 64 (1974) 192.

[68] W. Weber, Josephus und Vespasian (Stuttgart 1921) 98-99, also attempted to show that V conceals an early literary work, a Rechtfertigungs-schrift submitted by Josephus at the Roman court to win the support of Titus' Jewish courtiers. This Rechtfertigungsschrift was used in BJ 3 to supplement the "Flavian work." Weber ignored the autobiographical material of BJ 2 and his theory has won no adherents.

[69] See note 59 above. Thackeray did not realize that if the Rechenschafts-

Laqueur that V must be earlier than BJ because it appears to be more reliable—Laqueur's old argument with its *non sequitur* intact. This early work was not an administrative report, however, but an early draft of BJ, a *hypomnema*, which, in accordance with the laws of ancient historiography, Josephus had prepared before writing his final version. The central portion of V is a copy of this *hypomnema* in contrast to BJ which has changed many matters, both large and small, in order to achieve certain rhetorical effects and to portray Josephus as a great general.[70] We shall see in chapter three that this theory has much to recommend it although Gelzer neglected the best arguments in its behalf. Thus, aside from converting the *Rechenschaftsbericht* to a *hypomnema*, Gelzer did not much advance the study of our question. Neither did Y. Baer, who, in turn, converted Gelzer's *hypomnema* into notes jotted down during the war (CA 1.49).[71]

Even those who rejected Laqueur were influenced by him. In a return to the consensus of the mid-nineteenth century, V was again regarded as the more accurate work. Motzo, Schlatter, Dessau, Momigliano, A. H. M. Jones, Ricciotti, Shutt, M. Grant, Hengel, Schalit (yes, Schalit), Rhoads, Smallwood, and Brunt,[72] either

---

bericht had been written in Aramaic, Laqueur's case becomes more difficult, for how can we detect the additions to this nucleus if we do not have the original text before us in its original form? This was one of Münzer's points against Laqueur.

[70] M. Gelzer, "Die Vita des Josephus," *Hermes* 80 (1952) 67-90 = *Kleine Schriften* III (Wiesbaden 1964) 299-325.

[71] Y. Baer, *Zion* 36 (1971) 128-143 (Heb.). Baer seems to think that V is based on Josephus' contemporary notes but that BJ is not. P. Churgin, *Studies in the Times of the Second Temple* (N.Y. 1949) 353-356 (Heb.), suggests that the early work was a history of the Galilean war which Josephus wrote, while still a captive, to salve his vanity.

[72] B. Motzo, *Saggi di Storia e Letteratura Giudeo-Ellenistica* (Florence 1924) 214-240; A. Schlatter, *Geschichte Israels von Alexander dem Grossen bis Hadrian*³ (Stuttgart 1925) 328-329 and 336-337; H. Dessau, *Geschichte der römischen Kaiserzeit* II, 2 (Berlin 1930) 807-813; A. Momigliano in *Cambridge Ancient History* 10 (1934) 850-858 and 884-887 (who follows Motzo on two editions of V); A. H. M. Jones, *The Herods of Judaea* (Oxford 1938) 248-253; G. Ricciotti, *Flavio Giuseppe tradotto e commentato I*²: *Introduzione* (Torino 1949) 5-13; R. J. H. Shutt, *Studies in Josephus* (London 1961) 35-41; M. Grant, *The Ancient Historians* (N.Y. 1970) 243-268; M. Hengel, *Die Zeloten* (Leiden 1961) 376-381; A. Schalit in *Aufstieg und Niedergang der römischen Welt II*, 2, ed. H. Temporini (Berlin-N.Y. 1975) 276-278; D. Rhoads, *Israel in Revolution* (Philadelphia 1976); E. M. Smallwood, *The Jews under Roman Rule* (Leiden 1976) 303; P. A. Brunt, *Klio* 59 (1977) 149-153.

ignored Laqueur or criticized him, but used V as the basis for the early history of the Jewish war or for the characterization of Josephus' mission to Galilee.[73] Only patriotic Jewish historians still tried to deny that Josephus was a *Römling*.[74]

From this survey it is evident that the relative historical value of V and BJ can be determined only after we have solved two other problems. The first: what is the literary relationship of V to BJ? Most scholars, from Jost on, thought that V was written independently of BJ, but many, notably Niese and Luther, have assumed that V is a detailed revision of the earlier work, while others, notably Laqueur and those inspired by him, have thought BJ and V revisions of a lost early work. What is Josephus' standard procedure when narrating material in parallel texts? Are the discrepancies between V and BJ exceptional or typical? How does Josephus normally deal with his sources? Does he transcribe them and interpolate his additions and corrections? These topics will be treated in chapters two and three. The second problem—what are the tendentious elements of V and BJ?—can then be approached in chapters four and five with a bit more confidence.

---

[73] H. Lindner, *Die Geschichtsauffassung des Flavius Josephus im Bellum Judaicum* (Leiden 1972) 58 n. 1, has also remarked upon the dominance of Laqueur's position.

[74] A. Kaminka, *Kitbei Biqoret Historit* (N.Y. 1944) 57-79, esp. 66-75, and J. Klausner, *Historiah shel ha Bayyit ha Sheni V*[2] (Jerusalem 1951) 166-182. Against Kaminka see E. A. Auerbach, *Bitzaron* 7 (1942-43) 290-299 (Heb., with English summary on 311-312); on Klausner see N. Glatzer, *Bitzaron* 39 (1958-59) 101-105 (Heb.).

CHAPTER TWO

JOSEPHUS AND HIS SOURCES

In the first section of this chapter we investigate how Josephus used his sources. We are interested in the three aspects in which V differs strikingly from BJ: language, sequence, and content. The results of this discussion are applied in section two to the relationship of BJ to AJ. Only after we understand Josephus' methods can we turn to the literary relationship of BJ to V.

A. *Josephus and his Sources*

1. *Josephus' Statements and their Historiographic Background*

In several passages Josephus boasts of the method he allegedly used when transcribing the Bible. The most important is AJ 1.17:

> The narrative, as it progresses, will indicate in the proper place (κατὰ τὴν οἰκείαν τάξιν) the precise details of what is in the scriptures (ἐν ταῖς ἀναγραφαῖς). I have promised to follow this principle throughout this work, neither adding nor omitting anything (οὐδὲν προσθεὶς οὐδ' αὖ παραλιπών).

Although Josephus emphasizes his faithfulness in reproducing both the substance and sequence of the Biblical narrative, even an inattentive reader quickly realizes that AJ has added and omitted entire episodes, changed many details, and revised the order of the material. What, then, is the explanation of AJ 1.17? One avenue of escape is the contention that "scriptures" (ἀναγραφαί) includes Midrashic interpretations as well as the Biblical text with the implication that (all?) the material presented in AJ 1-11 stood before Josephus in written form.[1] But this path is blocked by CA 1.28-43, a description of the Jewish scriptures (ἀναγραφαί). These books have been under the care of priests (CA 1.29-36) and prophets (CA 1.29 and 37). The Jews possess a canon of only twenty two books [2] which agree with each other, unlike the thousands of books of the Greeks (CA 1.38-41). Josephus then returns (CA 1.42) to the

---

[1] L. H. Feldman, in *Religions in Antiquity: Essays ... E. R. Goodenough*, ed. J. Neusner (Leiden 1968) 336-339 with 336-337 n. 1. AJ 1.5 shows that 1.17 refers only to the first half of AJ, not the entire work.

[2] Which twenty-two books these were is not our concern.

Jew's reverence for his scriptures (γράμματα, cf. AJ 1.5). "No one has dared to add, omit, or change anything" (οὔτε προσθεῖναί τις οὐδὲν οὔτε ἀφελεῖν αὐτῶν οὔτε μεταθεῖναι τετόλμηκεν). Some Jews have even accepted martyrdom rather than profane the laws (τοὺς νόμους καὶ τὰς μετὰ τούτων ἀναγραφάς).[3] The context and content of this section, in language reminiscent of AJ 1.17, suggest that "the scriptures" (γράμματα and ἀναγραφαί) are the Biblical books, nothing else.

Collomp has sought an explanation by placing Josephus in a Hellenistic context.[4] AJ 1.17 is a retort to Dionysius of Halicarnassus, a champion of rhetorical history. Dionysius declared that history must be ornate. He chose Roman antiquity as his subject because it had previously been treated only by annalists (1.7.3) who had aimed at the accurate presentation of the traditions of the sacred writings ("Whatever writings they received, whether deposited in temples or in profane archives, these they brought to the common knowledge of all, neither adding nor omitting anything, εἴ τ' ἐν ἱεροῖς εἴ τ' ἐν βεβήλοις ἀποκείμεναι γραφαί, ταύτας εἰς τὴν κοινὴν ἁπάντων γνῶσιν ἐξενεγκεῖν, οἵας παρέλαβον, μήτε προστιθέντες αὐταῖς τι μήτε ἀφαιροῦντες, De Thucydide 5 p. 819 = FGrH I T 17a). AJ 1.17 proclaims a return to the style of these annalists, the faithful preservation of ancestral traditions without rhetorical pollution. Josephus' theory, of course, was better than his practice. Thus Collomp.

Collomp's fundamental error was his confusion of style and content. Dionysius says that he wrote his *Antiquitates* to refute the erroneous opinions current in the Greek world on the origins of Rome (1.5, esp. 1.5.4). The reference to some of the previous Greek accounts as mere outlines (κεφαλαιώδεις, 1.5.4-6.2) is a criticism not of their inelegance but their brevity. Dionysius emphasizes the accuracy, not the style, of his own work. He interviewed the most knowledgeable men in Rome and read the old Roman annalists (1.7.3). His history was not based on "chance reports", ἐπιτύχοντα

---

[3] Josephus is not necessarily implying a distinction between νόμοι and ἀναγραφαί since he regularly uses two words where one would have sufficed. See A. Wolff, *De Flavii Iosephi Belli Iudaici Scriptoris Studiis Rhetoricis* (diss. Halle 1908) 49-53 and Hornbostel 36-45. Or we could suggest that νόμοι are the legal portions of the Bible (or the Pentateuch) while ἀναγραφαί are the narrative portions (or the Prophets and the Writings). Cf. AJ 1.12.

[4] P. Collomp, in *Publications de la Faculté des Lettres de l'Université de Strasbourg 106: Études historiques* (Paris 1947) 81-92.

ἀκούσματα (1.1.4; 1.4.2; 1.6.1). All this sounds very much like the prefaces to BJ and AJ—and like those to other histories too.[5]

Similarly *De Thuc.* 5 p. 819 and AJ 1.17 refer not to style but to content. Josephus, Dionysius, and most Hellenistic writers agreed that truth and high style were the twin goals of the historian.[6] In AJ 14.2-3 Josephus realizes the necessity of "charm of exposition" and artistic narrative. The preface to BJ denounces previous attempts not because of their rhetoric but because of their mendacity. It is only in CA 1.24-27, a work ambivalent towards Greek culture, that Josephus criticizes rhetorical history, but here too he speaks more of content than of style: historians should not distort the truth for the sake of rhetoric.[7] AJ 1.2 implies the same thing. Thus in AJ 1.17 Josephus affirms accuracy and fidelity to his sources, but says nothing about style. Dionysius' old writers [8] were so faithful to their sources that they included myths, impossible tales [9] (*De Thuc.* 5 p. 819 and 7 p. 823), and also much reliable information (Dionysius *Antiquitates* 1.73.1). This interpretation of *De Thuc.* 5 p. 819 and

---

[5] G. Avenarius, *Lukians Schrift zur Geschichtsschreibung* (Meisenheim/Glan 1956) 71-80, esp. 76-77. On the similarity of the Josephan and Dionysian proems, see H. W. Attridge, *The Interpretation of Biblical History in the Antiquitates Judaicae of Flavius Josephus* (Missoula 1976) 43-60. A further mistake of Collomp is his description of Dionysius' attitude towards documentary history. Dionysius quotes documents verbatim (6.95; 10.32.2) and refers to documents to support his story (1.68; 4.26.5; 4.58.4). See H. Peter, *Die geschichtliche Literatur über die römische Kaiserzeit bis Theodosius I* (Leipzig 1879, repr. Hildesheim 1967) 1.251-252 or *Wahrheit und Kunst* (Leipzig 1911, repr. Hildesheim 1965) 338. On the relationship of Josephus to Dionysius, see Attridge 115, n. 2, 159-165, 172-176; I. Heinemann, *Zion* 5 (1940) 180-203, esp. 182 (Heb.); and Schalit, introduction xix-xxvi. R. J. H. Shutt, *Studies in Josephus* (London 1961), devotes a chapter to this problem but the whole matter needs further study.

[6] F. Wehrli in *Eumusia: Festgabe für E. Howald* (Zurich 1947) 54-71 = *Theoria und Humanitas: Gesammelte Schriften* (Zurich 1972) 132-144, and F. W. Walbank in *Bulletin of the Institute of Classical Studies* 2 (1955) 4-14. On truth and rhetoric in Dionysius, see F. Halbfas, *Theorie und Praxis in der Geschichtsschreibung bei Dionys von Halikarnass* (Münster 1910).

[7] Cf. the beginning of Plato's *Apology* where Socrates contends that he knows nothing about rhetoric but knows only how to tell the truth.

[8] *De Thuc.* 5 p. 819 refers to the Greek writers before Herodotus and Thucydides, notably Hecataeus of Miletus, Acusilaus of Argos, Charon of Lampsacus, Hellanicus of Lesbos, and Xanthus of Lydia (see the list on p. 818). Dionysius' introduction to the *Antiquitates* refers only to the old Roman annalists who are compared to χρονογραφίαι. Collomp 85 identifies the two groups on the basis of Cicero *De Oratore* 2.12 (52) but that passage too speaks of content, not style. See P. Scheller, *De Hellenistica Historiae Conscribendae Arte* (Leipzig 1911) 14-15.

AJ 1.17 is supported by the phrase "neither adding nor omitting anything" which refers to accuracy, not style (see below).

The preface to AJ can be understood in another context. Since the Greeks and Romans were always interested in the Wisdom of the Orient, many writers tried to satisfy this curiosity with *Ethnika*, books describing the history and customs of foreign nations. But how could the reader be certain that he had before him genuine traditions accurately transcribed and not an account debased with modern interpretations and interpolations? One intellectual, for example, expressed admiration for the original constitution of Moses but declared that following generations ruined it with their own legislation (FGrH 87 F 70 = Strabo 16.2.35-37). It was customary, therefore, for the writer to claim that his account was but a translation of the sacred texts. "Here is the Truth of the East!" Such statements are found in the works not only of Hellenized Orientals such as Berossus (FGrH 680 T 1 = F 1, though the text is somewhat uncertain), Manetho (FGrH 609 F 1 = CA 1.73), and Philo of Byblus (FGrH 790 F 1 = Eusebius *PE* 1.9.21 fin.; cf. section 20), but also of Greeks such as Ctesias (FGrH 688 F 5 = Diodorus Siculus 2.32.4) and Hecataeus of Abdera (FGrH 264 F 25 = Diodorus Siculus 1.69.7; cf. F 2).[10] Josephus too was a Hellenized Oriental writing the history of his people for the Greeks. He, like the other writers of this genre,[11] proclaimed his work a "translation" of the sacred texts (AJ 1.5).[12]

To this claim Josephus added another. He has not added or omitted anything (οὐδὲν προσθεὶς οὐδ' αὖ παραλιπών, AJ 1.17). This too was a traditional phrase which Josephus repeats in reference not only to his Biblical paraphrase (AJ 10.218, cf. 4.196 and 8.56) but also other matters (BJ 1.26 and 5.97).[13] Although the formula has

---

[9] Precisely what Josephus insists are *not* to be found in Moses' works (AJ 1.15).

[10] For other Hecataean references to ἀναγραφαί, see Jacoby's commentary to F 25, page 83. Josephus writes that Menander translated the Phoenician records into Greek and we may suppose that this was the claim of Menander himself. See FGrH 783 T 3 = AJ 8.144 and 9.283; CA 1.116. On the belief that oriental wisdom had been interpolated, see R. M. Grant, *The Letter and the Spirit* (London 1957) 21-30.

[11] The numerous parallels between Josephus and these writers have not yet received adequate treatment. Schalit, introduction xix-xx, asserts that Josephus has little in common with these writers but this is false.

[12] Cf. AJ 1.26; 2.347; 8.159; 10.218; CA 1.54.

[13] The normal formula has προστιθέναι and ἀφαιρεῖν. Josephus varies the

several meanings, it regularly describes an author's fidelity to his sources or a historian's care with his facts.[14] Dionysius used this phrase to affirm the accuracy of the logographers (see above) and Thucydides (*De Thuc.* 8 p. 824). Lucian declares that the historian must follow those sources "which he should suppose were least likely to omit or add anything out of favor or malice" (*Quomodo Historia Conscribenda Sit* 47). The closest parallel to AJ's preface is the pseudepigraphic letter of Cornelius Nepos to Sallust which introduces the work of Dares Phrygius:

> When I was busying myself with many things at Athens, I discovered the history of Dares Phrygius written in his own hand. I loved it greatly and translated it line for line. I thought that nothing should be added or omitted lest the history be changed and appear to be my own (*cui nihil adiciendum vel diminuendum rei reformandae causa putavi, alioquin mea posset videri*).

Here too we have the formula with the claim of translation.[15]

Since AJ 1.17 consists of historiographical commonplaces—as do practically all of Josephus' pronouncements on the duties and methods of the historian [16]—we may suppose these pronouncements

---

second element (παραλείπειν, ἀποκρύπτεσθαι, ὑφαιρεῖν) but this is not significant. AJ 10.218, which has ἀφαιρεῖν, explicitly refers to AJ 1.17 (ἐν ἀρχῇ τῆς ἱστορίας) which has παραλείπειν.

[14] See especially W. C. van Unnik, *Vigiliae Christianae* 3 (1949) 1-36 and C. Schäublin, *MH* 31 (1974) 144-149. See too Avenarius 44-45 (why he cites Diod. Sic. 21.17.2 in this connection is unclear); W. Speyer, *Die literarische Fälschung im heidnischen und christlichen Altertum* (Munich 1971) index s.v. Hinzufügen; H. Cancik, *Mythische und historische Wahrheit* (Stuttgart 1970) 24-27 and 99-103. Van Unnik and Schäublin discuss the history of the formula. On its Egyptian origin see J. Leipoldt and S. Morenz, *Heilige Schriften* (Leipzig 1953) 56-62.

[15] The text of Dares' last sentence is not certain and so the phrase ambiguously describes either the quality of the source (cf. CA 1.42) or the task of the historian (or "translator," cf. AJ 1.17). Van Unnik's article focuses on the former usage. In any event, Josephus and ps.-Nepos were surely not the first to combine the formula with the claim of translation.

[16] Avenarius shows that Lucian's *Quomodo Historia Conscribenda Sit* is a collection of historiographical commonplaces, many of which originated in Isocratean rhetoric. To illustrate the first part of this thesis, Avenarius collected parallels to Lucian from many historians, including Josephus, thereby showing that all these historians were merely repeating historiographical commonplaces. Just as Lucian's *How to Write History* provides the key for understanding Josephus' historiographical statements and methods, Menander's *How One Praises Cities* provides the key for understanding the structure and content of the latter half of CA 2. (My friend David L. Balch has a fine paper on Josephus and Menander which should be published soon.) Josephus contributed nothing new to Greek historiography. Collomp 92 recognized

are not to be taken very seriously. Probably none of the writers quoted above fulfilled his promise to present a translation only and not to add or omit anything.[17]

Not only Josephus' formulae but Josephus' methods too are those of the Greeks. Rhetoricians long before the first century had considered the relationship of an author to his source and had decided that the historian was expected to improve upon, or at least vary, the diction of his source. What was important was not novelty of content but of form. "Do not shun those subjects about which others have already spoken, but attempt to speak better than they did", says Isocrates 4.8. "Better" means "with better style" or "with finer eloquence". The new account will, on the whole, be faithful to its source but factual discrepancies are bound to appear from the nature of the paraphrasing process.[18] Several examples will suffice to illustrate this principle.

Aeschines 2.172-176 is an adaptation which preserves the structure and content (an incredible account of the *pentekontetia*) of the source, Andocides 3.3-12, but varies the language so conscientiously that only a few phrases are retained verbatim. Livy (7.9.6-10.14) models his account of the exploits of one of the heroes of ancient Rome on that of Claudius Quadrigarius (fragment 10B Peter). Here too a few verbal reminiscences remain (*scuto scutum*; Claudius' *scuto pedestri et gladio Hispanico cinctus* becomes *pedestre scutum capit, Hispano cingitur gladio*) and though the general impression of each is the same, Livy has added, omitted, and changed many details for reasons of his own.[19] An even better

---

that AJ 1.17 might be a commonplace. I have emphasized the Greco-Roman background of AJ 1.17 and CA 1.42 and see no reason to connect these passages to *Deuteronomy* 4.2 and 13.1. Perhaps the similarity of Greek pretension to Biblical precept was noticed by Josephus but the Biblical precept, too, failed to secure observance. See Van Unnik 18-19 and 34-35.

[17] Although it is possible that Philo of Byblus and Berossus did use ancient sources, as they claimed, it is certain that they also added and omitted a great deal. See Albert I. Baumgarten, "The *Phoenician History* of Philo of Byblos," (PhD thesis, Columbia University, 1972); E. G. Kraeling, *JAOS* 67 (1947) 178-179 and G. Komoróczy, *Acta Antiqua Academiae Scientiarum Hungaricae* 21 (1973) 125-152 (on Berossus).

[18] The classic studies are H. Nissen, *Kritische Untersuchungen über die Quellen der vierten und fünften Dekade des Livius* (Berlin 1863) 76-83; Peter, *Wahrheit* 416-455, esp. 431-452; idem, *Geschichtliche Literatur* 2.260-264. Note the good summary by H. J. Cadbury, *The Making of Luke-Acts* (N.Y. 1927) chapter twelve, "The Treatment of Predecessors," 155-168. I am deliberately avoiding the New Testament problems.

[19] M. von Albrecht, *Meister römischer Prosa von Cato bis Apuleius* (Heidel-

illustration of Livy's technique is his "translation" of Polybius. Occasionally he remains close to the original but he can, as with Quadrigarius, add, omit, change, shorten, or expand. Livy is inconsistent in the application of these methods and here too we see a parallel to Josephus.[20]

Diodorus of Sicily rewrites so extensively that he produces a uniform Diodorean paste in which the literary characteristics of his sources are indistinguishable. A detailed investigation of his relationship to Agatharchides shows well how Diodorus 'normalizes' a colorful, variegated, rhetorical style. The vocabulary becomes more pedestrian, grammatical oddities vanish, striking metaphors are toned down. And yet, even when we add the fact that he may vary the language of Agatharcides for no particular reason at all, he still manages to retain quite a bit of the diction of the original.[21]

A particularly interesting case is Plutarch's *Coriolanus* which is based on the history of Dionysius of Halicarnassus.[22] Plutarch has let hardly a phrase of the original remain intact and, moreover, has modified the material to his own taste. The account abounds in invented detail. Coriolanus is endowed with an education and a youthful history suitable for his role as a foil to Alcibiades. Im-

---

berg 1971) 110-126 and W. Schibel, *Sprachbehandlung und Darstellungsweise in römischer Prosa: Claudius Quadrigarius, Livius, Aulus Gellius* (Amsterdam 1971). Quadrigarius is extant only in the transcription of Aulus Gellius.

[20] See Nissen 18-36. The statement on p. 33 could as easily apply to Josephus as to Livy:

> Es lässt sich ferner kein bestimmtes Prinzip bezeichnen, dass [sic] mit strengen Consequenz in seiner Bearbeitung durchgeführt ist. Er schwankt in seinen rhetorischen wie seinen römischen [for Josephus read apologetischen, polemischen, etc.] Neigungen und nur in Allgemeinen dürfen die aufgestellten Geschichtspunkte gelten.

For a convenient survey of Livy's methods, see P. G. Walsh, *Livy: His Historical Aims and Methods* (Cambridge 1961) 138-172. A somewhat different picture is drawn by H. Tränkle, *Livius und Polybios* (Basel/Stuttgart 1977), who emphasizes Livy's essential fidelity to Polybius and minimizes the intrusion of Livy's own interpretations and prejudices into the narrative. See Tränkle's summary 243-245. Whether Livy is thus an exception to the classical norm requires confirmation.

[21] J. Palm, *Ueber Sprache und Stil des Diodorus von Sizilien* (Lund 1955) 27-55, especially the summaries on 47-48 and 55. Diodorus follows the same technique with Thucydides (Palm 60-62).

[22] I see no reason to assume that Plutarch used a second source. See D. A. Russell, "Plutarch's Life of Coriolanus," *JRS* 53 (1963) 21-28. For another good example of a biography based on a history, see F. Kolb, *Literarische Beziehungen zwischen Cassius Dio, Herodian, und der Historia Augusta* (Bonn 1972) 8-24.

portant episodes are expanded and dramatized [23] while material which is of little interest is condensed ruthlessly.

Enough has been cited for our purposes. An author was expected to take some liberties with his source. He could freely invent details to increase the color and dramatic interest of the account. He was expected to recast the narrative, to place his own stamp upon it, to use the material for his own purposes, to create something new. But on the whole he was faithful to the content and sequence of the original. Minor variations were bound to appear but, if noticed at all, they were readily forgiven. The details of this procedure could vary greatly from one author to the next and there was no law requiring consistency. A tight paraphrase of one source could be followed by the free rendition of another.[24] But the ground rules were accepted: too close adherence to the source raised the specter of plagiarism or, at least, of unprofessionalism.[25] All this is dramatically different from the procedure of the Chronicler in his parallels to *Samuel* and *Kings*. He rewrites history to suit his own purposes, as his Greek counterparts do, but does not hestitate to quote extensive sections verbatim.[26] Greek rhetorical theory was of no concern to him and Hebrew, if any, is unknown to us.

Josephus stands squarely in the Greek tradition.[27] The excerpts from Dius, Menander, and Berossus which appear in CA and AJ in substantially the same language show that Josephus can quote verbatim if he wishes,[28] but citation and utilization are two different

---

[23] For two good examples, compare the descriptions by Dionysius 8.1.4 and Plutarch 23.1-3 of Coriolanus' appearance before Tullus and the description by Dionysius 6.93.1 and Plutarch 9.5 of the announcement of victory. Plutarch 15.1 conjectured that Coriolanus' military career lasted seventeen years, a figure without any support from Dionysius.

[24] See the sage remarks of Peter, *Geschichtliche Literatur* 2.262-264 and 266-269.

[25] Eusebius *PE* 10.3 quotes a long extract from Porphyry to prove that the Greeks were plagiarists (κλέπται). The major complaint is the transcription of a source verbatim (αὐταῖς λέξεσιν, section 3). But it is apparent that many of the criticized writers did make an effort to vary the language of the source (e.g. section 9-11). The problem of plagiarism in antiquity is too complicated to be discussed here; the standard work is E. Stemplinger, *Das Plagiat in der griechischen Literatur* (Leipzig 1912).

[26] A glance at any Biblical synopsis makes this evident.

[27] This is well known. See e.g. H. St. J. Thackeray, *Josephus the Man and the Historian* (1929, repr. N.Y. 1967) 107, and S. Jellicoe, *The Septuagint and Modern Study* (Oxford 1968) 288-289.

[28] Dius: CA 1.113-115//AJ 8.147-149 (CA 113 adds ἐν νήσῳ; CA 113 ναῶν// AJ 147 ἱερῶν); Menander: CA 1.117-120//AJ 8.144-146 (CA 118 adds κέδρινα

matters. Normally Josephus paraphrases the language of his source but preserves its content, although even that can be sacrificed if necessary. The ancient readers of AJ would have understood this procedure and would not have been troubled by the declaration in AJ 1.17. After all, Josephus was reasonably faithful to the essence of the Biblical story and that was all that was required of him.

AJ 1.17 also promised that everything would be narrated in its proper order (οἰκεία τάξις). Josephus' rearrangement of the Bible does not contradict this principle since at least twice he explains what he means by "proper order." When about to begin his summary of the laws of the Pentateuch, Josephus insists again on his fidelity to the text (AJ 4.196) but admits to one innovation: the arrangement by subject (νενεωτέρισται δ' ἡμῖν τὸ κατὰ γένος ἕκαστα τάξαι). "Moses' writings were left behind in a scattered state just as he learned everything from God" and therefore require rearrangement (AJ 4.197). Josephus adds that he expects objections to this procedure from his fellow Jews, but had he wished, he could have appealed to the precedent set by Philo and, perhaps, others as well.[29] Narrative material too is reorganized (AJ 8.224):

> I shall describe first the actions of Jeroboam the king of Israel and then, following these, the actions of Roboamos the king of the two tribes. In this manner the proper order (τὸ εὔτακτον) can be maintained throughout the entire history.

This is a declaration against the arrangement of *Kings* in favor of another, putatively superior.[30] The point of both AJ 4.196 and AJ 8.224 is clear. Items which belong together should be juxtaposed, no matter the chronology or the disposition of the source.

We find this principle illustrated throughout the Josephan corpus

---

ξύλα); Berossus: CA 1.135-141//AJ 10.220-226 (the largest variation occurs in CA 140 μακρὸν ἴσως ἔσται ἐάν τις ἐξηγῆται//AJ 225 περισσὸν ἴσως ἂν εἴη λέγειν; CA 141 ὀρείας//AJ 226 οἰκείας are scribal variants). Cf. the references to Megasthenes in CA 1.144//AJ 10.227 which are not direct quotations and therefore show more variation than do the preceding parallels. It is uncertain whether CA is based on AJ in these examples or whether both works quote the original source directly. This is not the place to discuss the use of quotations in ancient historiography.

[29] It is possible that the Pharisees and other sects had already begun to codify their oral law.

[30] Schalit, introduction liv-lvii, has tables showing the relationship of AJ to *Kings* and *Chronicles*.

(see below).[31] BJ too explicitly refers to it at least twice. BJ 4.491-495 is a short digression on Roman history which concludes with the excuse (BJ 4.496) that the author need not dwell upon well known facts. He has summarized them briefly in one passage "for the sake of the connection of the events and in order not to interrupt the narrative." Josephus admits that he is concerned more about the coherence of his narrative than about the accuracy of his relative chronology. The second example is BJ 7.43-53 which describes the history of the Jews of Antioch from Seleucid times until 67 CE. The account is placed in BJ 7 in order to make the story "easy to follow" (εὐπαρακολούθητον, BJ 7.42), i.e., Josephus explains why he has ignored the chronological order in favor of a thematic one.

Here too there was ample Greek precedent. In contrast to Thucydides, who had adhered to a strict chronological scheme, Ephorus preferred a thematic arrangement (κατὰ γένος, FGrH 70 T 11 = Diod. Sic. 5.1.4). Later writers, arguing that the narrative units of a history had to be clear (σαφής) and readily understandable, determined that this goal was attained best through thematic organization. Precise chronology should be sacrificed for the sake of clarity.[32] Polybius agreed that a history had to be clear but claimed that his own chronological method was as clear as, and more accurate than, the accepted thematic method.[33] Livy and Tacitus struggled, not always with success, to reconcile the Roman annalistic tradition with the demands of Greek historiography.[34] With his reference to "proper order" in AJ 1.17 and his use of the thematic method, Josephus follows the mainstream of ancient historical writing.

2. The Problem of Numbers and Names

Numbers and names pose special problems which we shall not consider here. The transmission of numerals in our manuscripts of

---

[31] Schalit, introduction lvii, cites a suggestion of B. Z. Dinburg that AJ has focused its attention on certain figures and has used them to organize the narrative. This is one aspect of the thematic method and is found in Livy too; see Burck, *Wege* (n. 34 infra) 342-347.

[32] For numerous testimonia see Scheller 23 and 43-46; P. S. Everts, *De Tacitea Historiae Conscribendae Ratione* (diss. Utrecht 1926) 13 n. 2; Avenarius 119-127.

[33] See especially Polybius 38.5-6 with Avenarius' remarks 125-127. See too Walbank's commentary on Polybius 5.31.6.

[34] On Tacitus see Everts; on Livy see E. Burck, *Die Erzählungskunst des T. Livius* (Berlin 1934, repr. 1964) and *Wege zu Livius*, ed. E. Burck (Darmstadt 1967; *Wege der Forschung* 132) 331-351.

all classical literature is notoriously unreliable. Similarly, Josephus' manuscripts and testimonia rarely accord unanimous support to the reading of any slightly unusual name, whether Semitic, Greek, or Roman.[35] As often as not, the numbers and names of the first half of AJ do not correspond to any of the forms preserved in any of the versions of the Bible.[36] In these cases we do not know whether our manuscripts of Josephus are corrupt, whether our manuscripts of Josephus' source are corrupt, or both. Perhaps Josephus intentionally modified the text of his source to produce a desired literary effect. (I do not speak here of the understandable tendency to Hellenize Semitic names.) Prudence dictates that we refrain from any conclusions based on these variations.

3. Josephus and Aristeas

The paraphrase of the Letter of *Aristeas* is the least questionable demonstration of how Josephus worked. It is the least questionable because Josephus used a text of *Aristeas* very similar to that extant and used no other source. The relationship of these two works, examined recently in a full length study,[37] resembles that of Diodorus to Agatharchides. While adhering scrupulously to the sequence of the original, Josephus freely recasts its language. The result is Josephan Greek. The rich vocabulary of *Aristeas* has been denatured, the syntax has been simplified, the bold colors have been dimmed.[38] Although the urge to rewrite is so strong that even phrases of unobjectionable style and acceptable content are thoroughly revised,[39] Josephus has retained some of *Aristeas'* language.[40] Three documents in particular are paraphrased closely.[41]

---

[35] The foundations for work on this problem are A. Schlatter, *Die hebräischen Namen bei Josephus* (Gütersloh 1913) and Schalit, NWB.

[36] Cf. the citation of Herodotus 2.99.2 and 100.1 in AJ 8.157-158 (Μιναίας, Νικαύλη) which does not agree with our texts (Μίν, Νίτωκρις). The reference is otherwise inaccurate too because Herodotus says clearly that the queen was included among the 330 rulers and nowhere says that she was the last. The spelling of names in Plutarch's *Coriolanus* often disagrees with that of Dionysius, his source, and that problem too defies solution. See Russell 22.

[37] A. Pelletier, *Flavius Josèphe adapteur de la lettre d'Aristée: une réaction atticisante contre la Koinè* (Paris 1962), who prints a serviceable synopsis of the two texts (307-327).

[38] Pelletier, *Aristée* 207-260.

[39] Pelletier, *Aristée* 260-261; Palm 47-48.

[40] E.g. *Aristeas* 183-184//AJ 12.96-97; *Aristeas* 301//AJ 12.103; et alibi.

[41] *Aristeas* 22-25//AJ 12.28-31; *Aristeas* 29-32//AJ 12.36-39; *Aristeas* 41-46 //AJ 12.51-56. Livy too closely paraphrased the documents of Polybius.

In matters of content Josephus is very faithful.[42] His omissions of extraneous matter (e.g. the symposium), his additions of explicative detail, his small, insignificant modifications, are expected.[43] One set of changes, however, deserves mention as an illustration of Josephus' inconsistent technique. In *Aristeas* 56 Philadelphus directs the workmen to fashion the table carefully in accordance with the Biblical prescriptions. AJ 12.63 has the king himself show the technicians what to do. AJ 12.58 and 12.84, in contrast to *Aristeas* 51 and 81, emphasize Philadelphus' personal supervision and concern.[44] But note that when the king is first presented with the Torah, *Aristeas* 177 reports that he stood for a long time, did obeisance some seven times, and then praised God. Not only does Josephus not expand here, he (AJ 12.90) omits the seven-fold obeisance. What a magnificent opportunity missed for underscoring the king's respect for the Law! But AJ 12.114 retains the obeisance mentioned by *Aristeas* 317. Josephus was either unwilling or unable to carry through his tendentious revision consistently.

4. *Josephus and the Bible*

The sources of better than half of AJ are extant. But whereas Josephus' use of *Aristeas* is fairly clear, his relationship to the Bible and 1 *Macc.* is uncertain. We do not know to what extent he used a Hebrew text, if at all; we do not know if he used an Aramaic Targum. He seems to have used the LXX, but in what form? Research in this field has been sloppy [45] and we cannot here attempt to settle

Josephus' inconsistency is evident because his procedure with the documents of 1 *Macc.* is quite different; see below. Philadelphus' letter (*Aristeas* 35-40//AJ 12.45-50) is not paraphrased so closely.

[42] We find discrepancies in numbers: *Aristeas* 19//AJ 12.24 (100,000 vs. 110,000), perhaps a transcriptional error; Aristeas 20, 22, 27//AJ 12.25, 28, 33 (the ransom for the Jewish slaves which Josephus seems to have increased without changing the total sum; see Schreckenberg, *Gnomon* 36 [1964] 570); *Aristeas* 275//AJ 12.99 (length of the banquet). AJ twice (57 and 86) speaks of 70 elders instead of 72. Some proper names too are different: *Aristeas* 184 ('Ελεάζαρον—there is no reason to change the text)//AJ 12.97 ('Ελισσαῖον) and, of course, 'Αριστέας//'Αρισταῖος (although CA 2.46 has 'Αριστέας).

[43] Pelletier, *Aristée* 268-271, lists the additions, omissions, and discrepancies, and provides some rather forced explanations.

[44] Pelletier, *Aristée* 134, 162, 270.

[45] A recent comprehensive discussion is Schalit, introduction xxvii-xxxv. Although some of his proofs for Josephus' use of the Hebrew text are sound, not one of the ten proofs for the use of a Targum is decisive. If Josephan exegesis shows similarity to an extant Aramaic Targum, can we assume that Josephus is dependent on it? The Aramaic transliterations show that

these questions. But we may suppose that any Hebrew text or version Josephus might have used would generally, at least in the Pentateuch and the historical books, have agreed very closely with the substantial content and sequence of the masoretic text (MT). Accordingly, our investigation will focus on content and sequence, deal only briefly with language, and ignore numerals and the spelling of proper names.

Josephus' paraphrase of the Bible bears little linguistic resemblance to the LXX and two explanations readily suggest themselves. When Josephus is working directly from a Hebrew or Aramaic text, his paraphrase is independent of the Greek version. Even when the LXX was the source, its 'semitic' character precluded any extensive verbal borrowings.[46] For example, Josephus' version of the Hebrew *Esther* contains no significant parallels to the LXX, but his paraphrase of the Greek additions is often very close.[47] (The fact that some of these additions masqueraded as royal documents was an added inducement to remain close to the original; cf. the procedure with *Aristeas* above).

Since a full discussion of Josephan technique in the presentation of the Bible would be out of place here,[48] a few notes illustrated by

---

Josephus spoke Aramaic, not that he used a Targum. (The same critique applies to S. Rappaport, *Agada und Exegese bei Flavius Josephus* [Vienna 1930] xx-xxiv.) See Attridge 31-32. Only four of Schalit's twenty proofs for the use of the LXX are more than conjecture. Should we not at least entertain the notion that Josephus used a Hebrew text which occasionally was closer to the LXX *Vorlage* than to the MT? Josephus' dependence on the LXX can be demonstrated only by showing that his source was a Greek text and that this text was the LXX. We have some indications of this sort: extensive or striking parallels in language (as in Schalit's proofs nrs. 1 and 15, from AJ 6.187 and 7.343); Josephus' reconciliation of LXX and MT (Schalit nr. 17 = AJ 8.189); Josephus' explanation of LXX (e.g. Schalit nr. 20 = AJ 8.85); the echoes of LXX howlers (e.g. the famous cynicism of Nabal, AJ 6.296). It is unfortunate that in trying to determine Josephus' Bible, scholars have most often appealed to numbers and the spelling of proper names—the two elements most unreliably transmitted in our texts of both Josephus and the LXX. On the corruption of proper names in the LXX, see Origen *In Johannem* 6.41 (or 6.212-215 in the recent edition by C. Blanc) on *John* 1.28.

[46] Schalit, introduction lx. Hölscher, *PW* 9,2 (1916) 1953-1954, collects the verbal coincidences of AJ 1 and the LXX. Their paucity and general insignificance are striking.

[47] Noted by Marcus on AJ 11.215 and 272. On the Greek origin of the additions closely paraphrased by Josephus, see the classic article of E. Bickerman, *PAAJR* 20 (1951) 101-133, and, more recently, C. A. Moore, *JBL* 92 (1973) 382-393.

[48] See the fine article of Heinemann cited in note 5 above and Schalit's

select examples will suffice. As with *Aristeas*, Josephus freely omits whatever he does not need: long lists of Semitic names,[49] incidents embarrassing (Reuben and Bilhah; Judah and Tamar; the golden calf; the complaint of Aaron and Miriam against Moses' wife) or difficult (the mention of Goliath in 2 *Samuel* 21.19), a few miracles which he thought a bit too much (the pillars of cloud and fire of *Exodus* 13; Elijah's translation to heaven). Some passages he just forgot (the pestilence of the Ten Plagues; the reign of Tola). He condenses technical material (the laws and rituals of the Pentateuch) and uninteresting details (the complications of the apportionment of Canaan among the tribes).[50] But we should note that Josephus is not consistent. He sometimes includes lists of Semitic names (e.g. AJ 1.79 and 83-88; 2.4-6; 8.35-37), embarrassing incidents (e.g. kidnaping of Joseph; revolt of Korah), fantastic miracles (Balaam's ass; Jonah and the fish), and technical matters (details of the Tabernacle, the Temple, and the priestly vestments[51]).

In spite of its omissions, AJ is characterized by additions to the Biblical narrative. Aside from the testimonies of Greek authors adduced to support the veracity of the Bible, the additions are mostly for explication and dramatization. Why did Terah leave Chaldea, and why did the later patriarchs not live so long as those before the flood (1.152)? Why did Korah revolt (4.11ff)? Why did the Israelites need a miracle to cross the Jordan (5.16)? How did Harbonah know that Haman erected gallows for Mordechai (11.261 and 266)? [52] Dramatizations too abound, e.g. Abraham's sacrifice of Isaac (1.222-236), the entire Joseph saga,[53] the affair of the

---

introduction lviii-lxxxii; Schalit's debt to Heinemann is inadequately acknowledged. L. H. Feldman has embarked recently on a series of articles on "Hellenizations" in AJ. See the article cited in note 1 above; *TAPA* 99 (1968) 143-156; *TAPA* 101 (1970) 143-170; *Aspects of Religious Propaganda in Judaism and Early Christianity*, ed. E. S. Fiorenza (Notre Dame 1976) 69-98. Attridge has a somewhat different approach.

[49] See AJ 1.129 with Thackeray's note. An author had to preserve the integrity (τὸ καθαρόν) of the narrative; see Avenarius 60.

[50] See Thackeray's note to AJ 5.79.

[51] Cf. *Aristeas'* lengthy description of Philadelphus' table. Josephus and *Aristeas* follow the Greek tradition of describing ancient or non-existent works of art at great length.

[52] Thus Feldman, *TAPA* 101 (1970) 167 against 158 (added for drama).

[53] See M. Braun, *Griechischer Roman und hellenistische Geschichtsschreibung* (Frankfurt 1934); H. Sprödowsky, *Die Hellenisierung der Geschichte von Joseph in Aegypten bei Flavius Josephus* (Greifswald 1937); M. Braun, *History and Romance in Greco-oriental Literature* (Oxford 1938); H. R. Moeh-

Israelites and the daughters of Moab (4.126-155), and Manoah's beautiful wife (5.276). The rhetorical and dramatic speeches need not be illustrated.

Rewriting history often meant defining the indefinite. Josephus is particularly fond of inventing figures to fill gaps in the narrative and, as often as not, the figures are impossible exaggerations. The Egyptians attacking the Jews at the Red Sea numbered 50,000 horse and 200,000 infantry (AJ 2.324). Joshua was faced by over 300,000 Canaanites (AJ 5.64). Saul slew 60,000 of the enemy (AJ 6.129).[54] Josephus may also have invented names occasionally although no certain instance can be cited.[55] The technique of defining the indefinite was not created by Josephus but was commonly applied in Rabbinic and non-Rabbinic Aggadah,[56] and by Greek mythographers, genealogists,[57] and historians.[58] His penchant for exaggerated numbers has many parallels too.[59]

Some of Josephus' modifications of the Bible were the result not of the literary factors just discussed but of a concern to resolve theological difficulties posed by the text. We see again, however, that Josephus is either unwilling or unable to adhere to this apologetic consistently. A frequent theme in AJ (e.g. AJ 8.116-117) is the refutation of the charges of exclusiveness and hatred of foreign-

---

ring, "Novelistic Elements in the Writings of Flavius Josephus" (diss. Chicago 1957).

[54] These examples were collected by Drüner 36-39 with 38 n. 2.

[55] The most likely example is Demoteles the letter carrier in AJ 12.227 and 13.167. Drüner 43-44 with 44 n. 2 proposes several others, all from AJ: Druma, 5.233; Sebee, 5.270; Ourios, 8.76; Iadon, 8.231; Amanos, 8.414. But see Thackeray/Marcus and Schalit ad loc. and Heinemann, *Zion* 5 (1940) 180.

[56] B. Heller, "Die Scheu vor Unbekanntem, Unbenanntem in Agada und Apokryphen," *MGWJ* 83 (1939) 170-184; L. Baeck, *The Pharisees and Other Essays* (N.Y. 1947, repr. 1966) 53-67 ("Tradition in Judaism") = *Judaism and Christianity: Essays by Leo Baeck*, ed. W. Kaufmann (1958, repr. N.Y. 1970) 45-62; I. Heinemann, *Darkhe ha Aggadah* (Jerusalem 1954, repr. 1970) 21-34.

[57] E. J. Forsdyke, *Greece before Homer* (London 1956); F. Jacoby, *Atthis: The Local Chronicles of Ancient Athens* (Oxford 1949).

[58] Theopompus invented a name for a previously anonymous figure (FGrH 115 F 70 from Porphyry in Eusebius *PE* 10.3.6-9). The process of rewriting a source would inevitably lead to an increase in detail.

[59] Naber, *Mnemosyne* n.s. 13 (1885) 267-268; Niese, *HZ* 76 (1896) 207; Peter, *Geschichtliche Literatur* 1.399. Lucian reports that one historian wrote that at the battle of Europus the Parthian casualties amounted to 70,236 dead, the Roman to two dead and nine wounded (*Quomodo Historia Conscribenda Sit* 20). Aggadic literature frequently invokes fantastic figures.

ers, often made against the Jews, but at least twice Josephus confirms these charges by additions of his own (circumcision was
introduced to keep the Jews separate from other peoples, 1.192; [60]
Jacob hates the Canaanites and refuses to lodge with them, 1.278).
His inconsistent attitude towards miracles has been noted already:
he can omit, transcribe without comment, transcribe with the
apology that every reader should decide for himself on the veracity,[61]
or rationalize (e.g. 3.8).[62] Josephus often (e.g. 7.72 and 294), but
not always (e.g. 1.257),[63] interjects an intermediary between God
and man where the Bible has simply "And God said." Josephus
does not even refrain from rewriting the Biblical text. Jacob
immediately believed his sons when told that Joseph was still
alive (2.169). Not Moses but some anonymous fellow doubted
God's omnipotence (3.298). Jehoash King of Ephraim, who con-
versed with Elisha and defeated Aram, must have been a good
king (9.178).[64] In short: Josephus' paraphrase of the Bible, in spite
of his protestations of unsurpassable fidelity, is freer than his
version of *Aristeas*.[65]

We turn now to sequence. In spite of all his other modifications,

---

[60] βουλόμενος τὸ ἀπ' αὐτοῦ γένος μένειν τοῖς ἄλλοις οὐ συμφυρόμενον. Cf.
Tacitus *Historiae* 5.5.2, *circumcidere genitalia instituerunt ut diversitate
noscantur* and the statement of Haman, the arch antisemite, in *Targum
Sheni* on *Esther* 3.9, ed. M. David (Berlin 1898) 23, "On the eighth day they
(the Jews) cut off the foreskin of their sons ... and say, 'Let us be different
from (the other) nations'."

[61] This apology is at least as old as Herodotus 2.123 (cf. 5.45) and Thucydides 6.2.1 and became a commonplace in Hellenistic-Roman historiography.
See Lucian *Quomodo Historia Conscribenda Sit* 60. Avenarius 163-164 notes
that this casts doubt on Thackeray's assertion (*Josephus* 57-58) of Dionysian
origin. It is important to realize that Josephus does not restrict these phrases
to mythology. Cf. AJ 4.158 (Thackeray's comment is incorrect), 8.262,
19.108; BJ 5.257; V 430.

[62] Josephus' treatment of Biblical miracles has been discussed at length.
See I. Heinemann in *Jubilee Volume in Honour of B. Heller*, ed. A. Scheiber
(Budapest 1941) 189; G. Delling, *NT* 2 (1958) 291-309; G. W. MacRae in
Miracles: Cambridge Studies, ed. C. F. D. Moule (London 1965) 127-147;
H. R. Moehring in *Studia Evangelica* VI, ed. E. A. Livingstone (Berlin 1973;
Texte und Untersuchungen 112) 376-383; O. Betz in *Josephus-Studien:
Untersuchungen ... O. Michel ... gewidmet* (Göttingen 1974) 23-44.

[63] Rabbinic exegesis did introduce an intermediary here; see Genesis
Rabbah 45.10 p. 457 ed. Theodor-Albeck with parallels. The Targumim
and the LXX are similarly inconsistent.

[64] Against 2 *Kings* 13.11. Or has Josephus confused him with Jehoash
king of Judah?

[65] N. G. Cohen, *JQR* 54 (1963-64) 311-332, observes that AJ 6-11, on the
whole, is more faithful to the Bible than is AJ 1-5.

Josephus normally follows the order of the Bible, except when he strives to produce a coherent, thematic narrative. This principle has been discussed above; here are the examples of AJ 1-10:

1.140-142 connects the story of Noah, Ham and Canaan (*Genesis* 9.20-27) to the genealogical list of Ham's descendants (AJ 1.130-139) and therefore inserts it in the middle of *Genesis* 10.

1.212 unites the story of Abimelekh by juxtaposing *Genesis* 20.15 to 21.31-32.

1.220 unites the story of Ishmael by juxtaposing *Genesis* 21.21 to 25.12.

3.224-286 is a collection of laws on sacrifices and rituals and has many subsections easily segregated by theme (e.g. 224-257 on sacrifices). A similar melange is presented in 4.199-301 where too subsections can be discerned (e.g. 244-259 on marriage and divorce; 277-288 on damage and torts).[66] Cf. too 4.67-75, a collection of the laws on the gifts to Levites and priests, and 4.172-173 on the cities of refuge.

8.50-140 presents the following order: Solomon builds the temple; dedication ceremonies and prayers; Solomon's dream; Solomon builds the palace and its furnishings. Both MT and LXX place the building of the palace before the dedication ceremonies, but MT places it before (1 *Kings* 7.1-12), LXX after (7.38-50), the construction of the temple equipment. Since the dedication ceremonies referred only to the temple and not the palace, Josephus has rearranged accordingly. Similarly, he appends to the construction of the palace (AJ 8.133-139) a description of Solomon's throne (AJ 8.140) although *Kings* 10.18-20 separated them.

8.175 finishes the story of the Queen of Sheba before embarking on a description of Solomon's wealth. *Kings* 10.11-12 rudely interrupts the Queen, as Marcus notes.

The reorganization of the material on the *diadochi* of Solomon has been mentioned above with reference to AJ 8.224.

Sometimes material is postponed only to be included later in the narrative at a convenient place. Note the following:

1.309 omits the story of Laban's sheep (*Genesis* 30.27-42) but Jacob's later reference to it in *Genesis* 31.41 (= AJ 1.320-321) is expanded.

---

[66] See the outlines in Schalit, introduction l-li. I do not fully understand the order in which these sections have been arranged.

2.2-3 introduces Esau's loss of the birthright and the aetiological explanation of the name "Edom" (*Genesis* 25.29-34) in reference to *Genesis* 36.8 "Esau who is Edom."

7.113 mentions Mephibosheth's lameness (2 *Samuel* 4.4) only in conjunction with David's kindness (2 *Samuel* 9.3ff).

Josephus will change the sequence for other reasons too.[67] His tendency towards compression often produces rearrangement.[68] He may wish a better literary effect than the original provides. For example, *Esther* 4.11, the prohibition of approaching the throne uninvited, is advanced in the narrative (AJ 11.205-206). It is not a newly-introduced difficulty which confronts the heroine later in the story but one for which the reader was long prepared. Josephus has improved the Biblical description of the construction of the desert Tabernacle (*Exodus* 25-27 and 36-38) and the priestly vestments (*Exodus* 28 and 39) by imposing a logical order. The Tabernacle is described from the outside in, from the outer court (AJ 3.108-113) and the laver (3.114) to the Tabernacle itself (3.115-150). The dress of the common priest is described first, from the floor up (3.151-158), and then the additional garments of the high priest are mentioned (3.159-178).[69]

A difficulty in the Bible is also cause for rearrangement.

1.113-120 places the story of the Tower of Babel (*Genesis* 11. 1-9) before 1.122-147, the genealogy of the descendants of Noah (*Genesis* 10), to answer the obvious problem: how can *Genesis* 10 say that the earth was populated by different tribes dwelling in different places, when *Genesis* 11 assumes that all the earth was monoglottal and dwelling together? Josephus avoids the difficulty by reversing the order.

---

[67] The variations in the order of minor details within a given narrative are of no concern here, since such variations usually arise in retelling a story. Our focus is on the change in order of entire pericopae, on details severed from their original context, and on variations which affect the meaning. Similarly, the preference for the order of the LXX over that of the MT is another matter.

[68] See AJ 2.315-319; 3.9-12 and 95ff with Thackeray's note on 99 (unless these two should be considered examples of thematic arrangement: 3.9-12 combines three separate attacks on Moses, 3.95ff combines Moses' two ascents to Sinai); 4.302-314; 5.68-75 (the narrative of the conquest of Canaan is much condensed).

[69] The LXX in these chapters differs radically from the MT (see D. W. Gooding, *The Account of the Tabernacle: Translation and Textual Problems of the Greek Exodus* [Cambridge 1959]), but there is no sign that Josephus used the Greek version.

4.159-164 juxtaposes *Numbers* 31, the Midianite war, to AJ 4.156-158 = *Numbers* 25.16-18, the exhortation to destroy the Midianites. This rearrangement is another example of thematic construction but it also obviates a clear difficulty. *Numbers* 27.15-23 = AJ 4.165 describes the appointment of Joshua as Moses' successor But shortly thereafter, during the Midianite war, the second in command is nowhere to be found. Josephus solves the problem.

5. *Josephus and Esdras*

For the Persian period Josephus' main source was the Greek book of *Esdras*, as is shown by the large number of verbal reminiscences.[70] There are other indications as well: the constant repetition of "Syria and Phoenicia"; [71] the separation of Ezra from Nehemiah and the placement of *Nehemiah* 8 at the end of the Ezra story (AJ 11.154ff); the inclusion of the story of the three guardsmen; the acceptance of the reading of *Esdras* where it disagrees with LXX and MT.[72] Nevertheless Josephus seems to be aware of the textual tradition represented by MT as well, whether through the LXX, the Hebrew original, or some other source, and this fact complicates the situation.[73]

As a whole the paraphrase is faithful to the source. The problem of names and numbers continues here [74] but the most striking

---

[70] Some of these are collected by H. Bloch, *Die Quellen des Flavius Josephus in seiner Archäologie* (Leipzig 1879) 69-77. A. Büchler, *MGWJ* 41 (1897) 57-66, argues, on the basis of the minor and infrequent variations in details, that AJ and *Esdras* are independent revisions of the same story, but Büchler is not aware of normal Josephan procedure.

[71] Συρία καὶ Φοινίκη is the Ptolemaic designation of Palestine (V. A. Tcherikover, *Corpus Papyrorum Judaicarum* I [Harvard 1957] 5 with n. 13), which appears in *Esdras* but not in MT or LXX.

[72] E.g. AJ 11.26 = *Esdras* 2.19 vs. MT 4.17; AJ 11.108 = *Esdras* 7.9 vs. MT 6.18.

[73] After citing Cyrus' letter (a fabrication by Josephus himself) in its chronological position, which corresponds to *Esdras* 2 = MT 1, AJ 11.18ff proceeds to *Esdras* 5.41 = MT 2.64, then to *Esdras* 5.63 = MT 4.1, only to revert in AJ 11.21 to *Esdras* 2.13 = MT 4.7f. Only consultation with MT or cognate traditions explains why *Esdras* 5.41 and 63 are presented before *Esdras* 2.13. Note that this material is repeated later in the positions which correspond to their place in *Esdras*: AJ 11.69 repeats *Esdras* 5.41 and AJ 11.84ff repeats *Esdras* 5.63 (where it is clear that Josephus is using *Esdras* because he, with *Esdras* but against LXX and MT 4.1, takes וַיָּשִׂמְעוּ with the תְּרוּעָה גְדוֹלָה of the preceding verse).

[74] Proper names are an endemic problem; for numerical discrepancies see AJ 11.61 (fifty talents) vs. *Esdras* 4.51 (twenty) and AJ 11.107 (ninth year) vs. *Esdras* 7.5 = MT 6.15 (sixth).

changes are those introduced to correct the chronology. As is well known, the Bible (both MT and *Esdras*) is confused and seems to be ignorant of the correct sequence of the Persian kings. Embarrassed by this, Josephus rewrote extensively, identifying uncertain royal names with whatever kings seemed appropriate. He smoothed over other difficulties too,[75] and his imagination is at work even when there are no problems. The "in the first year" of AJ 11.33 is an invention, as is the figure of 40,742 women and children returning from Babylonia (AJ 11.69). Cyrus reads the prophecies of Isaiah (AJ 11.5-6), the first Passover after the return is lavishly celebrated (AJ 11.109-111). These and similar other details enliven the narrative.[76]

The story often is compressed in the normal fashion. A good illustration is AJ 11.121-138, an intelligent condensation of the account of Ezra's journey to Palestine. First Josephus records the letter of Artaxerxes (*Esdras* 8.9-24 = MT 7.12-26), then the notice of *Esdras* 8.5 = MT 7.7 on the priests and Levites, and finally, the rest of the return story (*Esdras* 8.41ff = MT 8.15ff). AJ 11.135 juxtaposes the chronological data of *Esdras* 8.5 = MT 7.8 to *Esdras* 8.60 = MT 8.31. The valuables brought by Ezra to Palestine are mentioned twice in *Esdras* (8.56 and 61 = MT 8.26-27 and 33) but only once in AJ 11.136. Where the Bible narrates retrospectively or indirectly, Josephus simplifies by narrating chronologically or directly. Thus Cyrus' letter appears in its chronological position at AJ 11.12-17 although it was not mentioned by *Esdras* until chapter 6 (= AJ 11.92-93). The Persian delegation to Jerusalem is described by *Esdras* 6 only as part of a retrospective report but is narrated directly by AJ 11.90-94.

---

[75] AJ 11.32 takes Zerubabel back to Persia in time for his appearance before the king as a sage and guardsman. *Esdras* did not. AJ 11.154 places the assembly of the seventh month on σκηνοπηγία although *Esdras* 9.37 and 40 = MT 8.2 date it to the first of the month. Perhaps Josephus wanted to make Ezra conform to *Deuteronomy* 31.10-12 = AJ 4.209-211. The chronological modifications are carried through consistently; see Marcus' notes on AJ 11.21, 78, 86, 106, and 120.

[76] Perhaps to increase the drama AJ 11.96 mentions the activity of Haggai and Zechariah (*Esdras* 6.1 = MT 5.1) after *Esdras* 6.21 = MT 5.17. In AJ 11.35-37 Darius assigns each guardsman the topic on which he should expatiate but *Esdras* 3.4-16 has the guards themselves invent the contest. Here Josephus was trying to inject the literary motif of a king posing questions (or riddles) to a group of sages. Cf. Plutarch *Alexander* 64; FGrH 153 F 9; L. Wallach, *PAAJR* 11 (1941) 47-83. Josephus was familiar with this motif from *Aristeas*.

6. *Josephus and 1 Maccabees* [77]

Although we are fairly certain that for the history of the Maccabean period Josephus used the Greek version of 1 *Maccabees* as the basis of his account, our analysis of his modifications is complicated by the fact that he has supplemented and corrected 1 *Macc.* with a lost Hellenistic source. In AJ 12 and 13 excerpts from this

---

[77] Of the enormous bibliography on this problem I cite only a selection: the commentary of C. L. W. Grimm to 1 *Maccabees* in *Kurzgefasstes exegetisches Handbuch zu den Apokryphen des AT* III (Leipzig 1853) xxvii-xxx and passim; Bloch 80-90; Justus von Destinon, *Die Quellen des Flavius Josephus I* (Kiel 1882) 60-80; Drüner 35-50; H. W. Ettelson, *The Integrity of I Maccabees* (New Haven 1925) 255-280 and 335-341; Cadbury 169-179; A. Momigliano, *Prime linee di storia della tradizione maccabaica* (Torino 1931, repr. Amsterdam 1968) 18-48; F. M. Abel, *Les livres des Maccabees* (Paris 1949) xi-xv and lviii; E. Z. Melamed, *EI* I (1951) 122-130 (Heb.). Here as elsewhere G. Hölscher, *Die Quellen des Flavius Josephus für die Zeit vom Exil bis zum jüdischen Krieg* (Leipzig 1904) 52, argues that Josephus was too stupid to have used 1 *Macc.* directly. The most recent discussion of this issue is by Jonathan Goldstein, *I Maccabees* (N.Y. 1976) esp. 55-61 and 558-574. Goldstein's views are radically new but this is not the proper place to discuss them. I must indicate, however, why I believe his methods and conclusions are incorrect. His basic flaw is that he does not understand normal Josephan procedure. "... Josephus was emending the text of First Maccabees and departing from its narrative as he would never have done with sacred scripture" (26) is plainly wrong. Goldstein does not realize that Josephus can freely revise his source, even when he does not have another source to support his revision and even when he is not confronted by a difficulty in the text. Josephus' fondness for thematic organization is not appreciated (Goldstein 382-383). I agree with Goldstein that we cannot force Josephus to abide by the "one-source theory" (see my discussion in part B below), but when Goldstein argues that Josephus studied *Daniel*, the Hebrew original of 1 *Macc.* (now lost; see Goldstein 14), the Greek version of 1 *Macc.*, the work of Jason of Cyrene (now lost), 2 *Macc.* (see Goldstein 56 n. 10), the *Testament of Moses* (Goldstein 559 and 568), and a propagandistic history by Onias IV (Goldstein 57-59; the existence of this work was not suspected until Goldstein discovered it); compared these accounts one with another, analyzed their motives, and assessed their veracity; carefully transposed columns of text in order to solve various difficulties (Goldstein 382-383 and 562-566); and made certain that his final account would not contradict the consensus of Greco-Roman historians (Goldstein 56 and 424) —all this is unbelievable. Goldstein uses source criticism with a confidence worthy of Bismarckian Germany. He knows all the sources, whether extant or not, of Josephus, 1 *Macc.* and 2 *Macc.* The position we have adopted is that of Drüner, anticipated by Schürer, *ThLZ* (1882) 390: Josephus' treatment of 1 *Macc.* differs hardly at all, in principle, from his treatment of the Bible.

The source of BJ 1.31-49 is not known; Goldstein's (60-61) is not the only possible explanation.

source which supplement 1 *Macc.* are often framed by the enigmatic
"as we have explained elsewhere." [78] As examples of corrections
based on this source, I note: AJ 12.242-250 knows of two expeditions
of Antiochus (albeit in confused detail), 1 *Macc.* 1.16-24 knows of
only one; Philometor invaded Coele-Syria to aid his son-in-law
and only later shifted his loyalty (AJ 13.103f with Diodorus
Siculus 32.9 against 1 *Macc.* 11.1f); the capture of Demetrius II by
the Parthians is placed earlier (AJ 13.184-186) than in 1 *Macc.*
(14.1-3). [79]

In spite of this source we can examine some aspects of Josephus'
work. Although he revises thoroughly the barbarous Greek of 1
Macc., he retains in the normal manner some of the original's
language. These reminiscences show that Josephus' basic source was
the Greek version, not the Hebrew. [80]

---

[78] The theory that Josephus mindlessly cribbed this phrase from his
source some dozen times, is improbable. Niese's solution is still the best:
the phrase is a convenient and meaningless way to cut short a discussion
and punctuate the narrative. See *HZ* 76 (1896) 235.

[79] The document of 1 *Macc.* 13.36-40 is omitted because of this rearrangement. See Marcus' note on AJ 13.187. Josephus departs more and more
from 1 *Macc.* as his account proceeds so that it is not much of a surprise
when 1 *Macc.* is dropped completely at about 1 *Macc.* 13.42 = AJ 13.214.
The document in 1 *Macc.* 15.16-21 seems to reappear in AJ 14.145-148 in
different form. Whence Josephus derived his version is obscure; see Abel's
commentary 275-276. Discrepancies in small details need not always be
assigned to extraneous sources. I note *exempli gratia*: Judas' offering of
ὁλοκαυτώματα upon his return to Jerusalem (1 *Macc.* 5.54) becomes χαριστη-
ρίους θυσίας (AJ 12.349; is Josephus rewriting to make Judas conform to
Halachah? See B. Berakhoth 54b which requires a *todah* from those who
escape danger). AJ 12.379-380 assigns to Eupator a more active role than
1 *Macc.* 6.55-60. 1 *Macc.* 7.43 emphasizes that Nicanor was the first to fall
in battle, AJ 12.409 that he was the last. Modein is a *polis* in 1 *Macc.* 2.15
but a *kome* in AJ 12.265 (and BJ 1.36). Josephus may be correcting 1 *Macc.*
but he himself is notoriously inaccurate on this very matter (e.g. V 115—
Gaba is not a *polis*).

[80] Bloch gives a list of some of the verbal parallels but others too can be
noted: 1 *Macc.* 4.15//AJ 12.308 (mainly a list of place names); 1 *Macc.*
10.29-30//AJ 13.49; 1 *Macc.* 10.89//AJ 13.102. Cadbury discusses the stylistic
modifications. As in his treatment of *Aristeas*, Josephus sometimes makes
an effort to paraphrase documents closely; cf. 1 *Macc.* 11.30-37//AJ 13.126-
128 (here the original was rather like a Greek document). Elsewhere Josephus
exercises great freedom (AJ 13.48-57 is almost a new 'improved' version of
1 *Macc.* 10.25-45; AJ 12.417-419 and 13.166-170 rewrite the documents of
1 *Macc.* 8.23-32 and 12.6-18 to make them conform more closely to Greek
style) as well as carelessness (a parenthetical remark of 1 *Macc.* 10.20 becomes an integral part of the document in AJ 13.45).

The effects of Josephus' own hand are sometimes evident. The dramatic scene of the death of Antiochus IV (the king stricken with remorse for molesting the Jews) is perhaps Josephan (AJ 12.356-357). Simon's speech (1 *Macc.* 13.3-6) is beautifully embellished (AJ 13.198-200). Josephus explains how Judas surprised Gorgias (AJ 12.306) and why Simon decided to redeem Jonathan (AJ 13.206). Geographical and topographical data are frequently added to help the reader. The elaborate preparations for battle (1 *Macc.* 3.42-57) are condensed to one dramatic scene (AJ 12.300-301). Note too the thematic re-arrangement in AJ 13.11 and 18-21. Josephus, unlike 1 *Macc.* 9.37-42, does not want to interrupt the narrative with the story of Jonathan's and Simon's attack on the marriage party of Iambri. The letter of Areius to Onias (1 *Macc.* 12.20-23) is placed where Josephus thinks it belongs (AJ 12.225-228).

Certain tendentious elements seem to be Josephus' own. 1 *Macc.* admires both Mattathias and Judah but AJ admires them even more. Mattathias is elected leader (AJ 12.275 and cf. BJ 1.37) and does not usurp the position for himself (1 *Macc.* 2.39). Mattathias (AJ 12.276),[81] not some anonymous collective (1 *Macc.* 2.40f), decides to fight on the Sabbath. The rewriting in the case of Judah is even clearer. Forceful Judas does not need the advice of a great assembly (AJ 12.332; cf. 1 *Macc.* 5.16). After his defeat at Beth Zechariah, according to 1 *Macc.* 6.47, Judas retires to some destination unknown (BJ 1.45: to Gophnah) not to reappear until the invasion of Bacchides under Demetrius I (1 *Macc.* 7). For admirers of the hero this is quite unsatisfactory. Josephus therefore places Judas in Jerusalem and makes him a signator of the peace with Eupator (AJ 12.375-382). He even bestows the high priesthood on Judas (AJ 12.414)—the first and greatest of the Hasmoneans must surely have attained that honor. Therefore Alcimus has to be removed from this world before his time (AJ 12.413; cf. 1 *Macc.* 9.18f, 54-57) and a treaty is explicitly dated, "when Judas was high priest" (AJ 12.419, om. 1 *Macc.* 8).[82] But even with this admiration Josephus does not transcribe 1 *Macc.* 5.62 (Joseph and Azariah were defeated because they were not of the seed to which the salvation of Israel

---

[81] Marcus' note on AJ 12.277 misses the point.
[82] For a good discussion of Josephus' departures from the chronology of 1 *Macc.*, see Goldstein 569-574 (although I do not agree with all his conclusions).

was entrusted) but replaces it with the much less significant praise of Judas' foresight (AJ 12.352). Josephus' inconsistency is again evident.[83]

7. *Summary*

On the whole Josephus was faithful to his sources: he neither invented new episodes nor disorted the essential content of those previously narrated. However, he did not confuse fidelity with slavish imitation. Like all ancient historians, he molded his material to suit his own tendentious and literary aims. He inserted dramatic and explicative details; he condensed, expanded, and omitted. The original sequence could be sacrificed in order to resolve a difficulty or to produce a shorter, more coherent narrative, often through thematic composition.[84] All of these modifications were combined with the original material to form a new organic whole. Although the language of the source was not reproduced but was entirely recast, the Josephan version still retained significant echoes of the original, especially of documentary material. In the final analysis these verbal reminiscences are our only sure way to identify Josephus' sources. They show that Josephus used *Esdras, Aristeas,* and 1 *Maccabees* and that he used them directly.

In all these procedures we must allow some inconsistency. Careful and tendentious revision often coexists with the transcription of embarrassing details. A source could be paraphrased closely or rewritten freely, expanded or condensed, with no reason apparent to explain the shift in procedure. Even if we ignore the variations in minor details and the ostensibly arbitrary reproduction of names and numerals, we may conclude that Josephus was not a meticulous and attentive craftsman.

---

[83] Goldstein 56 n. 9, 73-75, and 304, explains that Josephus, aware of the abuses and failings of the later Maccabees, did not want to claim that Judas and his brothers belonged to a family to which the salvation of Israel was entrusted. This explanation is plausible, but the other two examples of this tendency which Goldstein cites are unconvincing. Even if the explanation is correct for AJ 12.352, Josephus is still inconsistent, because he revises for this reason only inconsistently; see Goldstein 56. In any event, AJ 12.352 omits Judas' brothers because they had not figured in the original instructions to Joseph and Azariah (1 *Macc.* 5.18-19).

[84] Variations in sequence not explicable by this rule appear only in the Biblical paraphrase. I note AJ 1.238-255 which reverses *Genesis* 24 and 25; AJ 2.284-287 which confuses *Exodus* 5.1-4 and *Exodus* 7.8-13; AJ 4.76-81 which rearranges the stories of Israel and Edom, the death of Miriam, and the law of the red heifer; AJ 5.136-178 which reverses *Judges* 18 and 19-21 (see Attridge 133-139).

B. *BJ and AJ*

1. *Introduction*

The second half of AJ is parallel to the first book and a half of BJ. What is the relationship of these two works? Here Josephus provides no explicit statements to explain his procedure. Does the later work use the earlier? Do they derive independently from the same source(s)? With what presumptions can we turn to the BJ//V parallels? [85] Our primary interest is not *Quellenkritik*, the reconstruction and identification of lost sources, but the analysis of a literary relationship.

2. *Previous Research*

In 1863, H. Nissen published his *Kritische Untersuchungen über die Quellen der IV und V Dekade des Livius*. This work proved that for extensive portions of his narrative Livy generally followed Polybius. From this fact Nissen and later scholars developed the "one-source theory" which stated that ancient historians used only one source at a time. The ancients' claims of diligent research were false since each had derived all his data from some earlier work. The theory was applied to many different writers, including Tacitus, Plutarch, and the Historia Augusta. Dissent was not silent, but source criticism of this sort dominated the field.[86]

---

[85] There was no uniform theory of self-repetition in antiquity. Much of Xenophon's *Agesilaus* is verbally identical with the *Hellenica*. F. Blass, however, in the preface to his *editio major* of Demosthenes (Leipzig 1903) xxiv-xxvi, assumes that Demosthenes would not repeat himself verbatim and regards the repetitive speeches as spurious. Plutarch generally revises his diction when telling the same story twice in his *Vitae*. Cf. *Marius* 10.2-6 with *Sulla* 3.2-4. *Themistocles* 20.1-2 is exceptionally close to *Aristides* 22.2. Tertullian provides two famous examples of self-repetition in which nearly identical sections appear in two different works. On the relationship of the *Apologeticum* to the *Ad Nationes*, see C. Becker, *Tertullians Apologeticum: Werden und Leistung* (Munich 1954); on the relationship of the *Adversus Judaeos* to the *Adversus Marcionem*, see H. Tränkle, *Q.S.F. Tertulliani Adversus Judaeos* (Wiesbaden 1964), Einleitung. Eusebius repeats his own work with only minor stylistic modifications; see the introduction by I. Heikel to his edition of the *Vita Constantini* (Leipzig 1902), "Die Selbst-citate des Eusebius," xxviii-xxxviii. I know of no general study of this problem. Re-edition is another matter and is discussed below in chapter four, note 13, and chapter five, notes 235 and 236.

[86] See Nissen 76-83. For a reaction to this theory, see the sensible remarks of Peter, *Geschichtliche Literatur* 2.264-275. Because ancient books were papyrus scrolls, it was very difficult in antiquity to inspect several works at once. Therefore the "one-source theory" is intrinsically plausible; nevertheless the theory was applied much too rigorously.

In 1882 J. von Destinon conjectured that AJ 12-13 was a paraphrase not of two or more sources (including 1 *Maccabees*) but of a single anonymous work which had used 1 *Macc.* The source for AJ 14-17, Destinon said, was Nicolaus of Damascus. In this form the theory did not sufficiently account for the discrepancies between BJ and AJ and so later versions became more elaborate. Layers of intervening sources were introduced. Destinon and his followers were agreed on one principle: the first one and one half books of BJ and the parallel sections in AJ were not the original work of Josephus but were cribbed from some lost historian or historians. Josephus may have spruced things up a bit with an added quotation here, an embellishment there, but the basis was non-Josephan. This school supposed AJ and BJ to be independent versions of lost works. Niese and his school (notably Drüner) rejected this approach and theorized that BJ was the product of Josephus' own research while AJ was a reworking of BJ with the addition of new material. Between these two positions arose compromises of all sorts.[87]

The difficulties of the investigation were increased by the expectation of rigorous consistency. If AJ 14 was shown to be a revision of BJ, then, it was argued, all AJ 14-20 must be a revision of BJ. If a scholar demonstrated that AJ 13 was based on a single anonymous, he argued that all AJ 13-17 (or 13-20) must be based on a single anonymous. Why not grant Josephus a little freedom? We have already seen that we cannot expect consistency from our author.[88] Perhaps the relationship of BJ to AJ will be uniform throughout, the same for AJ 14 as for AJ 20, but this cannot be assumed; it must be proven. Similarly, we cannot assume that Josephus has always used only one source. Some of the anonymists, puzzled by AJ 15's alternating pro- and anti- Herodian bias, theorized that Josephus contaminated two contradictory sources. Thus even some advocates of the "one-source theory" could not maintain loyalty to their principle. Josephus, surely, could not either.

The second part of AJ is clearly divided in two with the break somewhere in AJ 17 (for simplicity I shall include all of AJ 17 in

---

[87] See the short but useful historiographical survey by Lindner 3-8.

[88] In one respect Josephus is consistent; he rarely copies a source verbatim. Those who conjecture lost sources must remember that Josephus' text would not preserve them intact. Some anonymists erred here too, notably W. Otto, *Herodes* (Stuttgart 1913) 12-14, esp. 14.

the first block). AJ 18-20, the history of the post-Herodian era, is quite different from the previous books. The two sections will be treated separately here.

3. *BJ 1-2 and AJ 13-17*

a. BJ and AJ 13-14

From about BJ 1.51//AJ 13.225 to BJ 1.357//AJ 14 fin. the two accounts are especially close. AJ follows BJ's sequence (with the exception of a few details rearranged for literary reasons) and has, especially from 14.268 to the end of the book, many verbal reminiscences of BJ.[89] AJ 14.479-486//BJ 1.351-356 is the extreme case of almost verbatim parallelism which is most easily explained on the theory that AJ is based on BJ. Ancient authors did occasionally plagiarize their own work.[90]

It is clear, however, that AJ is the result also of original research. Some of the new material in AJ 13-14 is perhaps from extraneous sources (e.g. the famous series of documents in AJ 14) but some seems to derive from the sources used by BJ and to be an integral part of the text. The Josephan penchant for dramatic invention will not explain the following: AJ 13.237-248, an extensive description of Antiochus VII Sidetes before Jerusalem; 277-280, Cyzicenus' use of Egyptian troops against Hyrcanus; 321-322, Hyrcanus' dislike of Jannaeus; 324-355, the wars of Jannaeus, Lathyrus, and

---

[89] See for example BJ 1.52-53//AJ 13.226-227; BJ 1.68-69//AJ 13.299-300; BJ 1.86-87//AJ 13.356-357; BJ 1.133-134//AJ 14.48-49; BJ 1.201-207//AJ 14.156-162; BJ 1.290ff//AJ 14.394ff. For the rearrangement of details, see BJ 1.154//AJ 14.71; BJ 1.320-327//AJ 14.438-450.

[90] See note 85. Even where there are no significant verbal reminiscences the account of AJ 14 is close to BJ. Cf. BJ 1.141-144//AJ 14.57-60 and BJ 1.210-211//AJ 14.169-170. Niese, *HZ* 76 (1896) 219 n. 1, remarks that the verbal repetition is very hard to explain on the theory that AJ and BJ are independent reworkings of the same source(s). It would be an amazing coincidence that only here did both BJ and AJ copy the source exactly. Josephus, especially in the second half of AJ 14, was obviously ready to stay very close to the language of BJ and a short section with verbatim transcription was a natural result. Thackeray, *Josephus* 106-109, theorizes that Josephus "wearied" near the end of AJ 14, and, instead of working from his source (Nicolaus of Damascus), he turned to his own earlier work and copied it. But if Josephus was so tired, why not copy Nicolaus directly? Why bother with BJ at all? After his stint with BJ he somehow managed, even according to Thackeray, to return to Nicolaus before closing the book (14.487-491). The cross references which appear in both works (cf. BJ 1.179//AJ 14.119; BJ 1.182//AJ 14.122; BJ 1.344//AJ 14.467) are no proof for the common source theory since those in AJ are modeled directly on those in BJ.

Cleopatra (BJ 1.86 seems to be a compressed excerpt); [91] 14.83, the presence of Romans in Jerusalem; 14.100, Alexander's siege of Gerizim; 14.378, Herod's aid in the restoration of Rhodes.

The natural conclusion is that Josephus based AJ 13-14 primarily on BJ, but also on his original source(s) and, perhaps, on new sources too.[92] Who or what these sources were is not our concern. These books of AJ occasionally supplement or disagree with BJ, either because of the additional information which Josephus extracted from his source(s), or because of the literary activity of Josephus himself, whether his sloppiness, tendentiousness, or inventiveness.[93] For example, two dramatic passages appear only in AJ (14.168 and 354-358) but we cannot know whether they were invented for the occasion by Josephus or whether he found them in his source. One of them, at least, is a historiographical common-place.[94] What is clear, as always, is Josephus' inconsistency. BJ 1.328, a dramatic scene, is toned down by AJ 14.451.[95]

---

[91] The battle of Lathyrus and Jannaeus at Asochis is only one incident in a long struggle (AJ 13.324-355). BJ 1.86 mentions only the battle of Asochis and states that Lathyrus was victorious but suffered heavy losses. AJ 13.337 agrees that Lathyrus was the victor but mentions nothing about losses. That detail comes from 338 which describes his losses at Sepphoris. BJ has excerpted one incident (Asochis) and, by condensation, added an extra detail. Similarly, the capture of Gaza mentioned in BJ 1.87 is paralleled in AJ 13.358-364 by an extensive description.

[92] Schürer's compromise (83 n. 16, omitted in Schürer-Vermes) is different. I do not know why Lindner 8 assigns this view (AJ used BJ plus the original source) to Schürer and Thackeray. B. Z. Wacholder, *Nicolaus of Damascus* (Berkeley 1962) 58-64, successfully avoids any definite statement on this issue. On Nicolaus as a source of Josephus, see M. Stern in *Studies ... Dedicated to ... J. Liver*, ed. B. Uffenheimer (Tel Aviv 1971) 381-389 (Heb.).

[93] On the whole AJ 14 is quite close to BJ with only few variations. Some numbers are transmitted differently (AJ 14.30, 71, 135, 340) and a few inexplicable contradictions appear (14.351, 427, 436, 487, on all of which see Marcus' notes [for 487 see note d on 479]). AJ 13-14 sometimes seems to be a correction of BJ. BJ 1.99 describes Antiochus XII Dionysius as the last of the Seleucids, a mistake omitted by AJ 13.387. In BJ 1.65 the Samaritans invoke the aid of Antiochus Aspendius = Grypus, in AJ 13.276 and 282, Cyzicenus. This contradiction is perhaps a sign not of different sources, but of Josephus' (or the source's) confusion when dealing with a confusing period.

[94] Women departing with their sobbing infants (AJ 14.354) is a standard scene in tragic history; see FGrH 81 F 53 (= Polyb. 2.56.7) and Tacitus *Annales* 1.40.4-1.41.1.

[95] See Marcus' notes d on 451 and b on 458.

b. BJ and AJ 15-16

The close correspondence between AJ 13-14 and BJ presents ample opportunity for the study of Josephus' motives. Since AJ used BJ we may seek an explanation for almost every variation. But with AJ 15 the situation changes.[96] Extensive verbal reminicences disappear, not to return again in AJ, and only isolated paragraphs recall to mind the earlier work. Our natural assumption that AJ 15-17 continued the practice of AJ 13-14 and utilized BJ, is weakened. On the whole AJ 15-17 agrees with BJ but there are more variations in small and insignificant matters between AJ 15-17 and BJ than between AJ 13-14 and BJ.[97] Another indicator is the amount of detail. In the parallel to AJ 13-14, BJ rarely gives more details than AJ; in the parallel to AJ 15-16, it often does. Finally, the order of AJ 15.5 to 16.159 is different from that of BJ 1.358-466. In contrast to AJ which is arranged chronologically, BJ has a thematic order: after a chronological section (1.358-400), it describes Herod's building program and munificence (400-428), his physical prowess and success in war (429-430), and his family disasters (431ff).

If AJ 15-16 is not a direct paraphrase of BJ, what is the relationship between these two accounts? Sequence is here the crucial criterion and all possible theories have been defended:

---

[96] Thackeray 107 well says, "For some time the two narratives have been running so closely parallel as to make the minor changes significant and purposeful; and it is not accidental that Laqueur selects just this fourteenth book for a detailed analysis and comparison of the different points of view presented. He could not have done the same for Book XV." Laqueur claimed the validity of his method for all of AJ (and V), but he restricted his investigation (so he said) because of lack of space (Laqueur 134 n. 1).

[97] AJ 15 is still rather close to BJ. I have noted only three discrepancies: AJ 15.332//BJ 1.410 (AJ's phrase κατὰ τὸν Περαῖα is ambiguous), AJ 15.334 //BJ 1.411 and AJ 15.380//BJ 1.401 (both cases of numerals). But in AJ 16 the situation is different. See AJ 16.90-91//BJ 1.452; AJ 16.193//BJ 1.477; AJ 16.201-204//BJ 1.478-479 (see Otto, Herodes 133 note, line 39ff); AJ 16.270//BJ 1.510; AJ 16.314-316//BJ 1.527-528. AJ 17 is even further from BJ, even if we disregard the discrepancies in numbers (AJ 17.199//BJ 1.673; AJ 17.264//BJ 2.50; AJ 17.320//BJ 2.97; AJ 17.323//BJ 2.100; Wikgren's interpretation of BJ 1.673 in his note to AJ 17.199 is baseless conjecture). See AJ 17.10//BJ 1.566; AJ 17.34//BJ 1.568 (see Marcus' note on AJ 17.34); AJ 17.106//BJ 1.636; AJ 17.134//BJ 1.641; AJ 17.194//BJ 1.667; AJ 17.295// BJ 2.76. Since the common source of BJ 1//AJ 15-17, Nicolaus of Damascus, was utilized until about AJ 17.323//BJ 2.100 (see Jacoby, FGrH 2 C p. 232-233), the discrepancies after AJ 17.323 must be treated separately.

(1) BJ represents the order of the original source,
    AJ the Josephan revision,
(2) AJ represents the order of the original source,
    BJ the Josephan version;
(3) BJ and AJ are based on different sources;
(4) both BJ and AJ are 'Josephan'.[98]

I think (2) is correct. We have already seen Josephus' fondness for thematic construction. Therefore, it is probable that the thematic structure of BJ represents his rearrangement of the material he had and that he would not have departed from this rearrangement in AJ unless he had been following a source arranged chronologically. His reason for following it may have been a combination of laziness and a desire to include the additional material it contained, which he had formerly omitted because it would not easily fit the thematic pattern of BJ. BJ, after all, promised to provide only a "brief summary" (BJ 1.18) of these events and thus could neglect many details and depart from strict chronology.[99]

This analysis of BJ//AJ 15-16 is confirmed by the following observations. BJ's thematic structure is punctuated by transitional phrases which connect one section to the next. With one exception the items within each section are narrated in the same order in which they appear in AJ, i.e. in the putative chronological order. These transitional phrases are Josephan, with no parallel in AJ (again there is one exception), and merely allow the historian to begin a new series of items under a new rubric. Josephus has imposed a thematic order on a chronological frame. A schematic presentation will illustrate the relationship. (Note that T = transitional phrase).

---

[98] For these opinions see: Destinon 101; Paul Otto, "Strabonis ΙΣΤΟΡΙ-ΚΩΝ ΥΠΟΜΝΗΜΑΤΩΝ Fragmenta," *Leipziger Studien zur classischen Philologie* 11 (1889) Supplementheft 234-236; C. Wachsmuth, *Einleitung in das Studium der alten Geschichte* (Leipzig 1895) 445; B. Niese, *HZ* 76 (1896) 209-210; Drüner 57-64; Hölscher, *Die Quellen* 26; W. Otto, *Herodes* 9 and 11; Hölscher, *PW* 9,2 (1916) 1948, cf. 1977; R. Laqueur, *PW* 17 (1936) 374, gives a hint. The opinion endorsed here is that of Schürer, *ThLZ* (1882) 393, followed by Stern (n. 92) 382.
[99] BJ and AJ belong to different genres, AJ being primarily a history of the past, BJ a history of contemporary events. On the ancient terminology for these two genres, see Scheller 11-14, a discussion of Gellius *Noctes Atticae* 5.18.1, and Weber 7-10 (followed by Schalit, introduction xiii-xv), a discussion of Cicero *Ad Familiares* 5.12. Many histories of contemporary events would include an extensive introduction to orient the reader; cf. Polybius, Ammianus Marcellinus, Zosimus, etc. Josephus had so much material on the Herodian period that he had to abbreviate it in BJ.

BJ 1			AJ 15
400	T:	Herod's prosperity turns him to works of piety	——
401		Herod builds temple and Antonia [100]	380-409
402		Herod builds royal palace	318
403	T:	Herod immortalizes the name of his patrons not only in palaces but even in whole cities	——
		builds Sebaste [101]	292 and 296-298
404-406		builds Paneion	363-364
407a		builds Jericho	——
407b	T:	After filling up his entire country with monuments and temples, Herod turns to his eparchy and cities [102]	——
408-414		builds Caesarea [103]	331-341 (cf. 293)
415		establishes games at Caesarea	16.136-138 (with 139-141)
416		builds Anthedon	——
417a	T:	Herod loved his father	——
417b-418		builds Antipatris, Cypros, Phaselis	16.142-145
419a	T:	Herod also perpetuated his own name	——
419b-421		builds Herodium [104]	323-325
422a	T:	Herod generous too to cities outside his kingdom	16.146

[100] BJ 401 πεντεκαιδεκάτῳ ἔτει, AJ 380 ὀκτωδεκάτου ἐνιαυτοῦ, i.e. a confusion of IE and IH. On the order here (temple before the royal palace) see below.

[101] BJ has many details not in AJ (6000 inhabitants; temple dedicated to Caesar; εὐνομία). The account in AJ seems to be a confused conflation of two or more sources. See Drüner 65-69; W. Otto 79-80n.; Schürer 366-367 n. 8 = Schürer-Vermes 290-291 n. 9.

[102] I am not sure what Josephus means by *eparchia*. Why are Caesarea and Anthedon in the eparchy in contrast to Sebaste, Paneas, Jericho? If Josephus means to distinguish the area given by the senate, presumably the Maccabean ethnarchy as organized by Gabinius, from the later extensions of territory by Augustus ("the eparchy"), he errs by including Sebaste in the former. AJ 15.328-329 says that Herod did not construct temples ἐν τῇ τῶν Ἰουδαίων. Since our BJ statement is a worthless rhetorical exaggeration, the apparent contradiction is not significant. Contra Drüner 58 n. 3 and L. Levine, *Caesarea under Roman Rule* (Leiden 1975) 152 n. 71. It is very possible that AJ 15.326-330 is from a different source than 323-325 and 331-341. Its tone is quite hostile to Herod in contrast to the other two sections although all three speak on the same theme. It is, perhaps, a critique by Josephus himself.

[103] BJ 411-413 has some substantial verbal agreement with AJ 334-338. I am not sure whether they are significant enough to indicate that AJ has utilized BJ *here*. The technical language in the description of the harbor may have been paraphrased closely from the source by both AJ and BJ. Josephus' description of the table manufactured by Philadelphus is very close to that of *Aristeas*.

[104] Note the parallel τὸν δὲ μαστοειδῆ κολωνὸν ὄντα χειροποίητον, BJ//ἔστι ... κολωνός, εἰς ὕψος ἀνιὼν χειροποίητον, ὡς εἶναι μαστοειδῆ τὴν περιφοράν, AJ. But the simile is striking enough.

422-425		list of cities aided by Herod	16.146-148
426	T:	Herod aids whole *oikoumene*	——
427		aids Olympic games	16.149
428	T:	Herod alleviates debts of many cities	——
		helps Phaselis, Balanaea, Cilicia	——
429	T:	Herod's body like his soul	——
429-430		Herod's physical prowess and good	(contrast AJ
		fortune [105]	16.150-159)
431	T:	Nemesis	——
432-444		execution of Mariamme [106]	202-242
445f		Herod and his sons	16.66f

The transitional phrases do not always cover the entire section which they head. The first transition refers to piety which cannot explain the construction of the royal palace. (Because of this transition, the construction of the temple and Antonia has been placed before the royal palace. The temple should come first in any event because of its importance.[107] It is the only exception to the rule of order.) The fourth transition refers to Herod only as *philopator* although BJ 417-418 speaks of his familial devotion in general. BJ insists on headings even where none are needed. The Olympic games, Phaselis, et al., formed part of the original list of foreign cities aided by Herod, and although BJ mentions them in their proper place, it adds two transitional phrases.

For almost all the items on this list AJ provides a chronological framework ("at about this time", or "after this", etc.).[108] Although the BJ list has a close affinity to AJ 16.136-149 and repeats the

---

[105] BJ 429-430 corresponds by position to AJ 16.150-159 but the contrast is evident. It is probable that BJ repeats the apologetic of the source since elsewhere too Herod's military defeats are ascribed to his troops' recklessness and treachery; see BJ 369//AJ om. and BJ 375//AJ 15.139-140. AJ 16.150-159 is probably by Josephus himself.

[106] BJ contaminates the details of two analogous stories, AJ 15.62-87 (Mariamme is almost executed) and 202-242. See Schürer 385 n. 51 = Schürer-Vermes 302 n. 49; E. Täubler, *Hermes* 51 (1916) 229-232; A. Schalit, *König Herodes* (Berlin 1969) 114-119. Moehring (n. 53) 92-117 does not even discuss this possibility. For the combination of doublets into a single story cf. AJ 3.9-12 and 95ff (see n. 68 above) and chapter three below.

[107] Thus Drüner 58 n. 2. Drüner's analysis of "Die Ueberlieferung über die Bauten des Herodes" (57-69) has many fine observations although I disagree with his conclusions.

[108] Otto often declares that these chronological links are by Josephus himself and historically worthless. See *Herodes* 72n., 79n., 81, 81n., 96n., 131, 180n., and 186. I do not doubt that this is sometimes the case (see chapter three below) but the indisputable examples Otto cites in 180n. are the result of the contamination of sources. They are irrelevant for Josephan procedure in a homogeneous narrative. See below note 131.

same material in the same order, the AJ section contains chronological information ("at about this time" with a date, 16.136, and "after this festival", 16.142) omitted in BJ. Only one thematic transition occurs in both works (cf. AJ 16.146, "it is impossible to mention all the other benefactions which he bestowed on the cities of both Syria and Greece", with BJ 1.422, "he demonstrated his generosity to very many cities outside Judaea") but the reason for this exception is clear. Since Herod's aid to foreign cities extended over his entire reign, it was only natural for a historian, even for one writing a chronological account, to lump all the names together under a rubric such as appears in BJ and AJ.[109] Was anyone interested in the precise dates of these royal grants? Nicolaus of Damascus, rhetorician, court historian, and putative source of AJ 15-17, would certainly not have been. Although both AJ and BJ have thematic lists, it is plain that the list in AJ is a drastic abbreviation of the original—the few items it has all appear in BJ's list and come in the same order.[110] In his earlier work, written under the aegis of Herod Agrippa II and the Romans (V 361-366), Josephus was willing to transcribe the whole of the list compiled by his source as well as other passages in praise of Herod. In fact, because of the thematic condensation and the transitional phrases, BJ's account is almost an encomium (or a biography) rather than a history.[111] By the time he wrote AJ, both he and the

---

[109] Josephus bothers with chronological data only when Herod, on his visits to Asia Minor and Greece, personally took part in the construction. Cf. AJ 14.378 (Rhodes, which appears again in the list here) and 16.18-19 and 26 (Chios and Ilium, omitted here). This one thematic section is no proof that the rest of the original source was arranged thematically; contra Drüner 60 and Otto 11. The thematic passage in AJ 15.326-330 is of a different type; it cites no examples and names no names, and probably comes from Josephus himself (see note 102 above). AJ 16.141 contains the same information as BJ 1.395, a Josephan transition, but it does not serve as a transition. BJ 1.395-396 is parallel to AJ 15.200-201 and 217.

[110] Instead of cataloguing ten Syrian cities (BJ 1.422), AJ 16.146 writes "Syria." BJ 1.423-425 lists nine cities of Greece and Asia Minor while AJ 16.146-147 mentions only two cities by name (Rhodes and Nicopolis). Antioch and Elis appear in both works (BJ 1.425-426//AJ 16.148-149). Finally, BJ mentions Phaselis, Balanaea, and Cilicia (BJ 1.428) which AJ omits. The tone of AJ is favorable to Herod but BJ is even more favorable.

[111] Cf. Xenophon's *Agesilaus*, an encomium which, after a historical introduction (c. 1-2), arranges the virtues of the hero by topic (c. 3-10). See F. Leo, *Die griechisch-römische Biographie nach ihrer litterarischen Form* (Leipzig 1901) 90-91 and A. Momigliano, *The Development of Greek Biography* (Harvard 1971) 50-51. Many later biographers (notably Suetonius) adhered

times had changed. The Jews most influential with the Romans now had no great love for Herod's memory and so, although Josephus copied his source more fully, he was able to express his own ambivalence. He omitted many of Herod's benefactions and inserted criticisms of Herod's actions.[112]

Thematic arrangement in BJ is clear elsewhere, as well as in 1.400-466. BJ 1.467-482 describes the discord in Herod's household caused by Antipater and the women of the court (Glaphyra and Salome). AJ 16.188-205 presents the same story but with the unkind interruption of Herod and Pheroras (194-200). BJ allows Aristobulus and the women to quarrel in peace by introducing Pheroras only in 483-484, which begins with a typical Josephan transitional phrase—a free rhetorical construct unparalleled in AJ and historically worthless.[113] Now that Pheroras was properly introduced, he could become an active figure in the rest of the story (BJ 1.485ff//AJ 16.206ff). Another result of this thematic rearrangement was that Pheroras' tetrarchy and 100 talent income were sundered from their chronological context (AJ 15.362) and transferred here (BJ 1.483).

We conclude that AJ 15-16 revises not BJ but a common source and preserves the chronological notations and structure of the original. Of course, we must allow some inconsistency. If AJ 14 is essentially a revision of BJ with occasional borrowings from the original source(s), AJ 15-16 may be a revision of the original source with occasional borrowings from BJ.[114] But even if we allow

---

to this form. See chapter five below, part A. BJ 1.431, the transition from Herod the virtuous to Herod the monster, has the same function as many Suetonian transitions and could easily be replaced by Suetonius *Caligula* 22.1 or *Nero* 19 fin. or (here the parallel is especially close) *Augustus* 61.1:

> Quoniam qualis in imperis ac magistratibus regendaque per terrarum orbem pace belloque re publica fuerit, exposui, referam nunc interiorem ac familiarem eius vitam quibusque moribus atque fortuna domi et inter suos egerit a iuventa usque ad supremum vitae diem.

[112] For criticism of Herod see AJ 15.267, 274-276, 326-330; 16.1, 5, 150-159, 395-404; 17.180-181. None of these appear in BJ. As always Josephus is inconsistent. AJ includes some pro-Herod material which does not appear even in BJ (e.g. AJ 15.299-316). On the differences between AJ and BJ see chapter five below, sections C 2 b and d.

[113] The fact that BJ condenses drastically and paraphrases 196 while ignoring the rest of the story is not our concern. I cannot explain the relationship of BJ 1.485-486 to AJ 16.206-219.

[114] See notes 103 and 104. The historical implication of this discussion is that AJ's chronology is that of the source and not a Josephan invention. This is no guarantee that the chronology is correct. The literary implication

for this inconsistency, the relationship of BJ to AJ 13-14 is fundamentally different from that of BJ to AJ 15-16. Why this is so,
I do not know.

c. BJ and AJ 17

Although AJ 17 provides much less material for analysis, the
cupboard is not bare. The level of verbal reminiscence is much
lower, the frequency of minor variation is much higher, than
in AJ 14. It therefore seems unlikely that AJ 17 is a direct paraphrase of BJ; indeed, we have at least one good indication that
AJ 17 and BJ are reworkings of a common source. AJ 16.299 and
335-355 describe at length the mission of Nicolaus of Damascus to
Rome on behalf of Herod while BJ omits the entire affair. But in
BJ 1.574//AJ 17.54 an oblique reference to Nicolaus' journey appears, utterly incomprehensible to the reader of BJ.[115] The simplest
explanation is that the source spoke of Nicolaus' activities (to no
one's surprise, since the source was the work of Nicolaus himself).
BJ focused on Herod's domestic tragedies and omitted all references
to Nicolaus' mission—except for one aside which remained unnoticed. AJ presents the material in depth. In spite of this, certain
stretches of AJ seem to be rather close paraphrases of BJ, e.g.
AJ 17.182-208//BJ 1.661-673 and 2.1-8, and AJ 17.286-299//
BJ 2.66-79. Thus AJ 17 may be the product both of the revision
of BJ and of consultation of the original source. When AJ 17.19-22
places a disquisition on the Herodian family at the end of a section,
an improvement on the arrangement of BJ 1.562-563, we cannot
be sure whether AJ is rewriting BJ or the source.

4. BJ and AJ 18-20

With AJ 18-20 the situation changes again. BJ 2.117-118 and
167-279 covers sixty years of Judaean history (6-66 CE) in only
one hundred and fifteen sections. Contrast the lengthy and detailed
account of the reign of Herod! The explanation no doubt is to be
sought in the fact that for the post-Herodian period Josephus had
no source comparable to Nicolaus' history of Herod. It is also
likely that Josephus did not wish to record a good deal of what he
did know about the period leading up to the revolt. It might have

---

is that AJ and BJ derive from a single extensive account of the Herodian
period, i.e. Nicolaus.

[115] Thackeray ad loc. notes the facts but neglects the conclusion.

incriminated the wrong people, i.e., those whom Josephus wished to exculpate. AJ provides additional data but our author is able to fill up the three books necessary to obtain the Dionysian twenty only by including much extraneous material, notably the long descriptions of the activities of the Parthians, Romans, and the Jews of Rome, Alexandria, Adiabene, and Babylonia. None of this appears in BJ. Only a German source critic could claim that AJ 18-20 is a paraphrase of a single source—anonymous, of course.[116]

What concerns us is the relationship of BJ to AJ. All of the usual options are available with the added complication that a sizable amount of the paralleled material could derive from Josephus' own experience, and much of the rest from stories he had heard from father, grandfather,[117] and friends (including Agrippa II). We shall apply our three tests of language, content, and sequence.

The extraordinarily small number of verbal reminiscences of BJ indicates that AJ is not a simple paraphrase of the earlier work. Only two parallels of note can be cited; "shall you go to war, then, against Caesar?" (πολεμήσετε ἄρα Καίσαρι, BJ 2.197//AJ 18.271) and "the festival became a day of mourning for the entire people; there was lamentation in every household" (γενέσθαι δὲ τὴν ἑορτὴν πένθος μὲν ὅλῳ τῷ ἔθνει, θρῆνον δὲ καθ' ἑκάστην οἰκίαν, BJ 2.227)// "instead of the festival, there was mourning; all turned to lamentation and wailing" (πένθος δ' ἦν . . . ἀντὶ τῆς ἑορτῆς καὶ πάντες . . . ἐπὶ θρήνους καὶ κλαυθμοὺς ἐτράποντο, AJ 20.112). But Josephus may have remembered these even without direct consultation of BJ. The first is a dramatic question in a dramatic story while the second is a highly rhetorical phrase which may have appealed to Josephus for its Biblical affinities.[118] In any event nothing can be deduced

---

[116] F. Schemann, *Die Quellen des Flavius Josephus in der jüdischen Archaeologie Buch XVIII-XX = Polemos II cap. vii-xiv, 3* (diss. Marburg 1887), theorized that most of AJ 18-20//BJ 2 is a reworking of a very detailed universal history traces of which can be found in BJ too. Only a few sections (e.g. the description of the sects) escape Schemann's net. Schemann relies on the unfulfilled cross references in AJ 19-20 which, he says, must have come from the source Josephus was cribbing, as if Josephus were infallible when referring to his own work or could not plan to write a work and later change his mind or not live long enough to complete it. Cf. Petersen, *AJP* 79 (1958) 273-274, with Feldman's note on AJ 20.96. Hölscher, *Quellen*, 59-80 and *PW* 9,2 (1916) 1983-1993, accepts Schemann's approach with modifications of his own which do not simplify the picture.

[117] For the dates of Josephus' father and grandfather, see V 5. Bloch 151-156 assigns as much as possible to these oral sources.

[118] See *Amos* 8.10 (LXX καὶ μεταστρέψω τὰς ἑορτὰς ὑμῶν εἰς πένθος καὶ πάσας τὰς ᾠδὰς ὑμῶν εἰς θρῆνον) and *Lamentations* 5.15.

from these solitary cases [119] and in only one passage is the use of BJ
clear and unequivocal.[120] After the section on Albinus (AJ 20.215),
to be discussed below, Josephus describes some doings of Agrippa II
(20.216-223) and proceeds to a brief history of the high-priesthood
(20.224-251). The short account of the reign of Florus (20.252-257)
which ends the book (20.258-268 are the closing remarks) is taken
directly from BJ 2.277-279. The best evidence for this is the large
number of verbal parallels.[121] Furthermore, the picture of Albinus
in AJ 253 does not match the preceding description in AJ. In
contrast to AJ 20.215 which said nothing of misdeeds by Albinus
before the last stage of his career, AJ 20.253-254 implies a long
record of malfeasance, in accord only with BJ 2.272-276. We may
conjecture that when Josephus neared the end of AJ 20, he unrolled
BJ in search for an appropriate place to end the narrative. He
chose the administration of Florus and paraphrased, in his normal
manner, what he had previously written. The discrepancy between
the two descriptions in AJ was probably not noticed since, super-
ficially at least, they were compatible.

But even if this one passage of AJ is based on BJ, it seems
likely, as we have indicated, that AJ 18-20 on the whole is not a
direct paraphrase of BJ. This conclusion is confirmed by the fact
that the variations in minor details are more frequent in AJ 18-20//
BJ than in AJ 13-14//BJ. The most striking contradiction concerns
the tenure of Albinus.[122] This man, the penultimate procurator
before the war, is thoroughly vilified by BJ 2.272-276. He was a
villain who gave free hand to the brigands. Bribed to release the
prisoners, he filled the country with revolutionaries. In short,
"from that time the seeds of the future capture of the city were
sown" (BJ 2.276). AJ, even more than BJ, tends to increase the
guilt of the Roman governors (see chapter five below, section C 2 d).
How, then, can we explain its picture of Albinus? The Roman at
first takes a tough stand against the *Sicarii* (AJ 20.204). Political

---

[119] Schemann and Hölscher use these and other (all insignificant) verbal
reminiscences to show that AJ and BJ are using a common source.

[120] Niese, *HZ* 76 (1896) 220, claims, and O. Henning, "Römische Stücke
aus Josephus" (diss. Tübingen 1922) 1-8, assumes, the use of BJ by AJ
18-19.

[121] Schemann 8 noted the parallels but claimed them for his common
source.

[122] The disagreements caused by the different motives of each work are
another matter entirely and will be discussed in chapter five below.

terrorism—not bribery—forces him to release some revolutionaries from detention (20.209). The lawless mobs assembled by some Jewish aristocrats have no connection with Albinus in AJ 20.213-214 although the governor is an accomplice in their crimes according to BJ 2.274-275. The war-guilt which Albinus shares in BJ 2.276 belongs to the aristocrats alone in AJ 20.214 ("from that time, above all, it happened that our city became diseased, everything proceeding from bad to worse").

Thus far in AJ Albinus has done no wrong. The problems begin with AJ 20.215:

> When Albinus heard that Gessius Florus was coming as his successor, he wished to become famous by providing (or: he wished to seem to have provided, βουλόμενος δοκεῖν τι ... παρεσχῆσθαι) something for the Jerusalemites. He led forth the captives and ordered the destruction of all those who clearly deserved to die, while those who had been placed in detention on account of a minor and trifling charge (ἐκ μικρᾶς καὶ τῆς τυχούσης αἰτίας), these he released after accepting money. Thus the prison was cleansed of its captives, while the countryside was filled with brigands (or: revolutionaries, λῃστῶν).

The first half of this passage fits well with everything AJ had already said about Albinus. The governor executed those prisoners who deserved execution. The only ambiguity here is the word δοκεῖν, which might mean "to gain a reputation, to become famous" (thus Feldman) or "to pretend, to seem". The second half, however, is decidedly negative and has Albinus receive bribes and release brigands into the countryside. The problem here is the phrase "on account of a minor and trifling charge". V 13 shows that this was a phrase Josephus would use to cover revolutionary activities. Priests were not sent to Rome to make their defense before the emperor for petty peculations nor, if they had been, would a young man soon to be in command of the revolutionary forces in Galilee have gone after them to help them. In the first part of the autobiography Josephus pretends that he was pro-Roman and therefore claims that the priests were *not* revolutionaries. They were in trouble because of a "minor and trifling charge" (μικρὰ καὶ ἡ τυχοῦσα αἰτία). In AJ 20.215 too the phrase seems to be apologetic. Albinus released not revolutionaries worthy of death but men imprisoned [123] because of a "minor and trifling charge". If so,

---

[123] They were being held in pre-trial custody or were being punished by a term in jail. Imprisonment was not, in principle, a legal penalty but the

how can we explain the last clause, "the land was filled with *lestai*"? Even if *lestai* refers not to "revolutionaries" but to "brigands", the clause comes as a surprise after the explanation that the men who were released had been jailed only for minor reasons. And why the sudden reference to Albinus' acceptance of bribes? Thus the tone of AJ 20.215 is peculiarly ambiguous and/or self-contradictory.[124]

If we suppose that both AJ and BJ followed a written account favorable to Albinus and rather like the initial description of AJ, the situation becomes clearer. BJ and AJ will then be independent attempts to blacken Albinus. In BJ, when the need of an apology for the revolt was still pressing, Josephus could not admit that Albinus had waged a vigorous campaign against the revolutionaries through most of his stay and had, at the end of his term, executed the guilty. Instead BJ concentrates on the fact(?) that the governor released brigands in return for bribes and represents this as his policy throughout. He was an associate of corrupt Jewish aristocrats. AJ, written twenty years after the war, could more readily admit the truth about Albinus' administration. Throughout his tenure the Roman proceeded vigorously against the revolutionaries. The Jewish aristocrats embarked on their criminal behavior without consulting Albinus. Only when reporting the end of his career did Josephus remember to attack Albinus. AJ 20.215, like BJ, accuses Albinus of accepting bribes and filling the country with brigands but the source was not revised thoroughly enough to disguise a more favorable account. It is only in AJ 20.253-254, copied directly from BJ, that AJ assumes Albinus' guilt throughout his term.

If this conjecture is correct, it follows that BJ and AJ 18-20 had a common source. Although the overall sequence of the two works is identical,[125] one exception may provide additional support for this conjecture. BJ 2.221-223 has the sequence: death and family of Herod of Chalcis; Chalcis given to Agrippa II; the replacement of Tiberius Alexander by Cumanus; the disturbances under Cumanus (224f). AJ 20.103-104, however, presents the removal of a high priest by Herod of Chalcis (not in BJ), the arrival of

---

principle was often disregarded. See *Digesta* 48.19 section 8.9 and section 35, translated by J. Crook, *Law and Life of Rome* (Ithaca 1967) 274.

[124] Cf. Smallwood, *Jews* 282 n. 88.

[125] AJ transposed BJ 2.284 to a position shortly after 271 (//AJ 20.182-184) in order to let AJ finish the story.

Cumanus, the death and family of Herod of Chalcis (less detailed than BJ), and the disturbances (105ff). If AJ is rewriting on the basis of BJ, why has the arrival of Cumanus been advanced to an intrusive position in the middle of a piece on Herod of Chalcis? But if AJ here preserves the arrangement of a common source which attempts to be chronologically exact, the order of BJ is readily understandable. In accordance with his principle of thematic composition, Josephus first presents all the material on Herod of Chalcis and then all the material on Cumanus.[126] Therefore, it may be that a common written source lies behind parts of BJ and AJ 18-20.[127]

The second example of divergent sequence is much more complicated and provides no support for our conjecture.

BJ 2		AJ 18	
167a	Antipas and Philip	27a	Antipas and Philip
167b	Death of Salome		(= 31b below)
168a	Death of Augustus accession of Tiberius		(= 32b-33a below)
	(= 168c below)	27b	Antipas builds Sepphoris and Julias in Peraea

[126] The alternate explanation is that AJ, longer and chronologically more exact than BJ, corrected BJ's account on the basis of extra information and that there is no common source at all. This explanation is possible but unlikely because AJ does not repeat all of BJ's data here.

[127] We cannot hope to restore the exact words of the source because of Josephus' habit of rewriting the language of his sources. It is possible that the common source of BJ//AJ 18-20 was a Josephan *hypomnema* in which the bare facts alone were narrated in chronological order. This theory seems especially plausible according to those who interpret AJ 20.259 to mean that Josephus began work on AJ before BJ. I mention this option only to indicate that the existence of a written source need not necessarily imply that Josephus used another historian's work for the events of his own lifetime. Gelzer has proposed a similar explanation for the V//BJ problem (see chapter one) and he may be right (see chapter three). E. Norden, *Neue Jahrbücher für das klassische Altertum* 31 (1913) 639-645 = *Kleine Schriften*, ed. B. Kytzler (Berlin 1966) 244-250, tried to demonstrate that the common source was a Roman chronicle of the procurators of Judaea. This conjecture is compatible with our analysis of AJ 20.213-215 because such a source, presumably, would have been favorable to Albinus. In the text I have phrased my conclusion in cautious terms because I realize that the evidence for a common written source is insufficient. While it is clear, I think, that AJ 20 was confronted by a source favorable to Albinus with which it could not totally agree, BJ's use of this source is nothing more than conjecture. The major strength of the conjecture is that it explains, in a neat and economical way, why Josephus contradicted himself in describing the tenure of Albinus.

168b	Philip builds Caesarea-Philippi and Julias in Gaulan	28	Philip builds Caesarea-Philippi and Julias in Gaulan
168c	Antipas builds Tiberias and Julias in Peraea		(= 36-38 below)
			(= 27b above)
		29-30	Samaritans pollute Temple
		31a	Ambivulus succeeds Coponius
	(= 167b above)	31b	Death of Salome
		32a	Rufus succeeds Ambivulus
	(= 168a above)	32b-33a	Death of Augustus, accession of Tiberius
		33b-35a	Gratus succeeds Ambivulus
169a	Arrival of Pilate	35b	Pilate succeeds Gratus
	(= 168c above)	36-38	Antipas builds Tiberias

The differences in order are three. The death of Salome and the death of Augustus appear in BJ before, in AJ after, the section on the construction of cities. The building of Tiberias in AJ is no longer connected with its thematic context but is postponed until after the arrival of Pilate, although both BJ and AJ place it after the death or Augustus.

AJ, except for one item, is chronologically accurate. Although the date for Sepphoris is uncertain, Caesarea-Philippi, Julias-Bethsaida, and Julias-Betharamphtha (Livias) were all built before the death of Augustus.[128] Since Tiberias was built in 19 CE,[129] Josephus has done well in AJ by interposing the death of Augustus in the proper place. That Josephus knows the correct date of the foundation of Tiberias is clear from the following sections, a survey of Parthian affairs from 3-19 CE (AJ 18.39-52) and a note on Germanicus in the East (AJ 18.53-54). The material is placed here because Orodes (AJ 18.52) occupied the Armenian throne from about 15 to 18 CE and was replaced by an appointee of Germanicus in 18 or 19 CE.[130] It is the reign of Orodes which Josephus thought

---

[128] Schürer 2.205-206, 208, 210, 214-215; H. W. Hoehner, *Herod Antipas* (Cambridge 1972) 84-91.

[129] This vexing problem has been solved by numismatic evidence. Antipas issued coins with his regnal year 24 = 19/20 CE on the obverse and TIBE-RIAC on the reverse. This was a special issue because Antipas did not begin a consecutive series until regnal year 33. See Ya'akov Meshorer, *Jewish Coins of the Second Temple Period*, trans. I. H. Levine (Tel-Aviv 1967) 74-75 and catalogue numbers 63, 64, and 65. Before the discovery of the numismatic evidence M. Avi-Yonah, *IEJ* 1 (1950/51) 160-169, had decided on 18 CE. Since Hoehner was unaware of the coins (93-95), his errors can remain unrefuted.

[130] See Feldman's note to AJ 18.52.

approximately contemporaneous ("at about this time", AJ 18.39) with the foundation of Tiberias (although his syntax obscures the relationship). Unfortunately, Josephus has confused later historians by narrating (AJ 18.35) the arrival of Pilate (26 CE) before (AJ 18.36-38) the construction of Tiberias (18/19 CE). Sympathetic critics may dignify the confusion with the title chronological anticipation [131] but on this point AJ is incorrect. Perhaps Josephus had reliable information to justify the third change, the post-ponement of the death of Salome.

The BJ account is obviously thematic. After an introductory note on Antipas and Philip which resumes the narrative after the description of the three sects (BJ 2.167a), Josephus reports the deaths of two important individuals (167b-168a) and lists the cities founded by two potentates (168b-c). Why the deaths are placed before the cities, against AJ, and why the cities of Philip precede those of Antipas, against AJ, is unclear. Thus BJ here is not explicable as a thematic revision of a source whose order was similar to AJ's. It is more likely that AJ is correcting BJ on the basis of additional information but all is uncertain.

5. *Summary*

We have seen that the Josephan technique of self-paraphrase is identical with the Josephan technique of paraphrasing other sources. AJ 13-14 revises BJ much as AJ 12 revises *Aristeas* (the major difference being that AJ 12 had no extra sources in its paraphrase).

However, the relationship between the two works soon changes. AJ 15-17 is for the most part an independent reworking of the source of BJ although occasional reminiscences of BJ seem to occur. AJ 18-20 is a melange of different sources and there are indications that one of these sources was used by BJ too. But at least one passage was borrowed directly from BJ and another seems to correct some errors of the earlier account. In sum, the natural assumption of continual and detailed consultation of BJ by AJ is unjustified.

---

[131] S. Giet, *Revue des études augustiniennes* 2 (1956) 243-249. This anti-cipation occurs frequently in AJ 8 and AJ 9 where Josephus paraphrases *Kings* and *Chronicles* (*Kings* itself anticipates very often) and in AJ 18-20 where Josephus is using many different sources. He finds it necessary to mention Tiberius' death three times in AJ 18 (18.89, 124, and 224). Otto, *Herodes* 180n., is an unsympathetic critic. The misdating of Pilate's arrival is not, I think, the result of contamination.

Josephus' inconsistency is demonstrated again. I do not know why the relationship of BJ to AJ varies so markedly. What is important for us is the realization that we cannot approach the V//BJ problem with any preconceived notion regarding the literary relationship of the two works. V may be a close paraphrase of BJ, a revision of a common source, an independent work, or a combination of these possibilities.

CHAPTER THREE

VITA AND BELLUM JUDAICUM:
THE LITERARY RELATIONSHIP

The previous chapter has analyzed Josephus' treatment of his sources and the different types of relationship which exist between BJ and AJ. Which of these types provides the closest analogy to the V//BJ parallel? We have three possibilities: (a) V is a revision of BJ much as AJ 13-14 is a revision of BJ; (b) V and BJ derive from a common source, much as AJ 15-17 and BJ derive from Nicolaus; (c) V is based primarily on Josephus' memory and was written with relatively little or no consultation of BJ. The three are not mutually exclusive. V may be a revision of BJ with occasional (or frequent) glances at a common source. V may be a revision of a common source with occasional (or frequent) glances at BJ. Shifts in Josephus' memory will be a factor according to whatever theory we adopt. But (a), (b), and (c) as stated above are the fundamental possibilities from which we shall have to choose. We apply here the same criteria which were utilized in the previous chapter: language, substance, and sequence.

As we have seen, linguistic comparison is the surest way to determine Josephus' sources. Parallels of content are not as decisive as parallels of language. And it is precisely by this criterion that V and BJ show their mutual independence. Three episodes appear in both works in great detail: John at Tiberias (V 85-103//BJ 614-623), the Dabaritta affair (V 126-148//BJ 595-613), and the first revolt of Tiberias (or the "sham fleet" episode, V 155-173//BJ 632-645). The verbal parallels are isolated and insignificant, the result of the repetition of essentially the same story. The greatest parallel, χρήσασθαι τοῖς ἐν Τιβεριάδι θερμοῖς ὕδασιν (V 85//BJ 614), is normal Greek for "to bathe in the hot baths of Tiberias" and does not indicate very much.[1] We cannot explain why Josephus' procedure here should have been so different from his procedure in AJ 14 by appealing merely to his inconsistency because, as far as can be determined, Josephus was never inconsistent in this respect.

---

[1] The verbal reminiscences are most frequent in two short sections: V 85-87a//BJ 614-615 and V 168b-173//BJ 641-644.

Unless some other explanation for the verbal difference of BJ from
V can be found, the conclusion will be that the relationship of V
to BJ (and BJ to V) is not that of a Josephan text to its source.
Only two of our possibilities remain.

The paraphrases of *Esdras, Aristeas,* 1 *Maccabees,* and of BJ 1
by AJ 14, are rather close to the content of their originals with
few inexplicable variations.[2] Even AJ 15-17, which is not based
directly on BJ, agrees on the whole with the earlier work.[3]
V frequently differs from BJ in minor details but we do not yet
know whether these contradictions are an intentional response to
Justus or a further sign of V's independence or both.

The criterion of sequence provides much more material for
analysis. The divergent chronologies of Josephus' activities in
Galilee are set forth in chapter one above; in this chapter we
deal with literary sequence. Here in tabular form is the narrative
of BJ with cross references to V. The reader should compare the
table in appendix II below which follows V and gives the cross
references to BJ. Note that T = transitional phrase.

V			BJ
30a		Josephus' arrival in Galilee	569a
——	T:	Josephus seeks goodwill of the populace	569b
79		Josephus establishes a supreme council	570-571
——	T:	Josephus protects cities against external threats	572
77a and 186b-89		Fortification of cities	573-575
77b		Recruitment of an army and procurement of weapons	576
——		Josephus trains his army in Roman fashion	577-580
77c-78		Josephus cautions his army to refrain from plunder and arranges their salary	581-584
——	T:	While Josephus was administering in this manner	585a
70		John and his character	585b-589
——	T:	John needs money to support his plan	590a
71-76		Schemes of John	590b-592a
——	T:	John uses his money against Josephus	592b
122-125		John tries to remove Josephus	593-594
——	T:	At this time	595a
126-148		Dabaritta affair	595-613
cf. 85a	T:	John is jealous and	614a
——		prepares a second plot against Josephus	614b

[2] See chapter two notes 42 and 43 (for *Aristeas*), 74-76 (for *Esdras*), 79
(for *Maccabees*) and 93 (for AJ 14).

[3] See chapter two note 97. We do not speak here of motivated corrections.

85b-101		John at Tiberias	614c-621
102-103 and		Josephus restrains a Galilean attack against	622-623
368-369a		John	
369b-372		Dispersal of John's followers	624-625a
———	T:	John again turns to secret plots	625b
190-335		Delegation from Jerusalem	626-631
372b		John is restricted to Gischala	632a
———	T:	After a few days	632b
155-173		Revolt of Tiberias	632c-645a
cf. 373	T:	After a few days	645b
373-389		Revolt of Tiberias and Sepphoris	645c-646

Since historical considerations do not suffice to determine which sequence is primary (see below), we must turn to literary criteria. The relationship of V to BJ seems similar to that of AJ 15-16 to BJ 1. The events of Herod's reign were narrated by AJ 15-16 in great detail and in chronological order, by BJ 1 in much less detail and in thematic order. We argued in the previous chapter that BJ 1 was Josephus' rearrangement of a source whose chronological order was preserved by AJ 15-16. We shall now try to show that BJ 2 is arranged thematically, V chronologically,[4] and that BJ's sequence is explicable as a revision of V's. We shall argue that the same literary principles are responsible for the Herodian narrative of BJ 1 and the Galilean narrative of BJ 2. Both narratives focused on certain themes and arranged them to produce a definite effect. Both narratives used rhetorical phrases to manage the transitions from one thematic unit to the next. Within each thematic unit, however, both narratives maintained the original chronological order.

BJ 2 contains two major themes, each composed of smaller thematic units. The first is Josephus the great leader who concerns himself not only about his army and fortifications (572-584) but also about the goodwill of the populace (569b-571). The second theme is Josephus the dominant leader who emerges victorious

---

[4] Over a century ago H. Milman theorized that BJ was thematically arranged; see his *History* (see chapter one above n. 36) 2.243 n. 2:

> In the 'Jewish War' it is not difficult to trace a certain order of these events, if not strictly chronological, yet of historical arrangement. Josephus first relates his reception in Galilee and the measures which he took for the organization of the province, the levying and disciplining of his army, the defensive fortification of the chief cities. He then passes to his strife with John of Gischala, and the long and obstinate struggle in Galilee and in Jerusalem with this noted rival. This may account for some transposition of events, and some discrepancy with the Life.

from his disputes with John (585-632) and the rebellious cities (632b-646). BJ 647, the rhetorical transition which changes the scene from Galilee to Jerusalem, ends the Galilean narrative of BJ 2 by referring to these two themes, "the disturbances and civil strife" (τὰ κινήματα καὶ οἱ ἐμφύλιοι θόρυβοι), and "the preparations against the Romans" (αἱ πρὸς Ῥωμαίους παρασκευαί). We shall see in the next chapter that BJ 2 and 3 portray Josephus as the ideal general and that both of these themes are part of the larger picture. In contrast to all this, no thematic order of any kind can be detected in V. Its content cannot be so readily catalogued.

The first theme consists of descriptions (569b-584) of protracted processes rather than single isolated events. The selection of seven judges for every *polis* (Galilee had 204 *poleis* and *komai*, V 235) [5] would have been a time consuming affair. The list of fortified cities is an obvious result of thematic compression (see the discussion below). The army training program would have demanded months. Since Josephus is interested in portraying himself as a great general we understand why he has advanced this material which is not chronologically defined. He could have placed it anywhere in his account, but he placed it here, at the beginning of the description of his administration, in order to indicate that he embarked on these admirable projects immediately upon arrival in Galilee. Josephus did what a leader was supposed to do and he did it from the very beginning of his tenure. Perhaps BJ wanted to give prominence to his desire for "good will", εὔνοια, (a word which frames the Galilean narrative at the beginning and end, 569 and 646), and so placed the formation of the council first.

Now BJ turns to the *stasis* theme (585-646) and introduces John, whose devious character (585b-589) contrasts with Josephan nobility ("while Josephus was administering in this manner", διοικοῦντι οὕτως τῷ Ἰωσήπῳ, 585a). BJ, in agreement with V, proceeds immediately to John's two schemes (590b-592a), but interprets them, in a transitional phrase which does not appear in V, as the result of John's lack of money (590a). John's profitable schemes induce him (592b, another transitional phrase) to formulate

---

[5] As we have seen already (chapter two note 79 fin.) Josephus uses *polis* and *kome* almost indiscriminately. *Polis* indicates any large settlement no matter what its juridical status. See A. N. Sherwin-White, *Roman Society and Roman Law in the New Testament* (Oxford 1963, repr. 1969) 130. Josephus is very sloppy with all his political and legal terminology. See V. A. Tcherikover, *IEJ* 14 (1964) 61-78.

a double-edged plan which was to result in the defamation or death of his rival. The plan, of course, fails to achieve its goal (593-594). Next comes the Dabaritta affair which, although chronologically anchored both fore and aft (BJ 595 and 614) in the middle of the anti-John section, originally had nothing to do with John. A Josephan 'gloss' in BJ 599 (absent from V), παρώξυνεν δὲ τοὺς πολλοὺς ὁ Ἰωάννης ("John aroused the multitude"), introduces John into the story but his appearance is sudden and inexplicable, his departure unnoticed and unmotivated.[6] BJ 594 ends with "John busied himself with many such actions in order to destroy Josephus." This is the sort of rhetorical generalization which often serves as a transitional phrase although it does not do so here. By his "gloss" in 599, Josephus gives a specific example in support of this generalization. Just as John followed a double-edged plan to destroy Josephus either by slander or by murder (593-594), so too the mob in Taricheae, encouraged by John (599), denounced Josephus as a traitor and intended to kill him. It is clear that Josephus has tried to make the Dabaritta affair support his anti-John polemic. We understand that he could not omit the story which he saw as a wonderful example of his craftiness and dexterity, but why did he narrate it in the anti-John section where it really does not belong? [7] And why did he place it, against V, before the Tiberias episode? The most likely explanation is that even in the original chronology (i.e. V's chronology), John's attempts to supplant Josephus (BJ 593-594//V 122-125) were linked to the Dabaritta affair.[8]

---

[6] Note that if V were not extant we would think that the appearance of Jesus too is a gloss since he enters and departs with John. But V shows that Jesus did take part in the events. Absolutely sure ground is a rarity in Josephan studies.

[7] He could have juxtaposed it to the revolts of Tiberias and Sepphoris, as a further example of civil strife.

[8] BJ's (595) connective (καθ'ὃν καιρόν) is simply chronological, V's (125) is somewhat ambiguous (καὶ δὴ ἀφικόμην εἰς κίνδυνον τὸν μέγιστον διὰ τοιαύτην αἰτίαν). τοιαύτη αἰτία is prospective, "the following reason," which is normal Josephan style (V 24, 31, 46, 179, 272, 381; BJ 7.219, 422; AJ 20.17; etc.; see G. C. Richards, CQ 33 [1939] 38 and the concordance s.v. αἰτία). The editors have posited a break after αἰτίαν because the following sentence begins the body of the exposition and is asyndetic. The problem is καὶ δὴ which may be connective or non-connective in both Josephan and classical Greek (H. St. J. Thackeray and R. Marcus, A Lexicon to Josephus 2 [Paris 1934] 132 s.v. δή (1) (d) and (e); J. D. Denniston, The Greek Particles² [Oxford 1954, repr. 1970] 248-253). Since καὶ δὴ in AJ 20 and V, with but two exceptions (AJ 20.150 and V 275), always introduces a statement which

When BJ 593-594 was advanced to serve the anti-John polemic, the Dabaritta affair was advanced too, and then "glossed." Thus BJ correctly coordinated the Dabaritta affair with the events of BJ 593-594 but misplaced it in the chronological sequence as a whole.

After the interruption of the Dabaritta affair BJ returns to the original order with the story of John at Tiberias (BJ 614-621// V 85-101). The transitional sentence in 614a explains that John was motivated by jealousy of Josephus' success in the Dabaritta affair (πρὸς ταῦτα) and formulated a further [9] plot (ἐπιβουλή) against him. V too uses John's jealousy as a transition (85a) [10] but, unlike BJ, does not use it to connect two episodes. Instead it appears at the end of a thematic section on Josephus' widespread popularity and general success (80-84). Therefore V 85a parallels the content, but not the function, of BJ 614a (see below). The Tiberias episode ends with a Galilean request, countered by Josephus (BJ 622-23//V 102-103), to destroy Gischala and kill John. A similar scene occurs in V 368 after the repulse of the delegation when a Galilean council asks Josephus to punish John. He rejects the suggestion (V 369a) but engineers the defection of John's adherents (V 369b-372). In order to avoid this doublet BJ identified the two scenes and so linked the dispersal of John's forces to the story of John at Tiberias (BJ 624-625). BJ 1 similarly compressed the two stories on the trial and execution of Mariamme.[11] In the original chronology the dispersal of John's forces meant the end of John's independent action (V 372b). Since BJ still had to narrate the delegation story, it replaced V 372b by a transitional phrase

---

is a continuation, or describes the result, of the preceding statement (AJ 20.2, 16, 35, 55, 77, 163, 257; V 53, 105, 196, 247, 258, 414) it seems reasonable to assume that καὶ δή is used here in a consecutive sense ("whereby", Thackeray). Even if the phrase here is non-connective, a chronological sequence is, at least, implied.

[9] If Josephus meant δευτέραν as "second," he should have said τρίτην (the first two being the plots of BJ 593-594 and the Dabaritta affair). However it is more likely to understand δευτέραν as merely "another," "a further," "a subsequent," a sense it often has in classical and Josephan Greek. See Thackeray's *Lexicon* s.v. δεύτερος (1) (b). The phrase δευτέραν ἐπιβουλήν may have been suggested by V 148 (= the *hypomnema*) δευτέραν ἐπιβουλήν, but that refers to the second stage of the Dabaritta affair itself (cf. BJ 611, ἀπάτη δευτέρα), whereas BJ 614 refers to what followed it.

[10] Cf. V 122. Josephus' opponents often are jealous: BJ 620, 627, and V 80, 204, 423. See below.

[11] See chapter two note 106 and, for a similar rearrangement in AJ, note 68. On doublets, see further below.

(BJ 625b) which reminded the reader of John's plots (ἐπιβουλαί). 372b was put aside to be used after the repulse of the delegation (BJ 626-631) when BJ could finally stow John away in Gischala (632a//V 372b). The anti-John section is now complete.

The revolts of Sepphoris and Tiberias, BJ's final subject (632b-646), are introduced not by a real transitional phrase but by a chronological indication ("and after a few days", καὶ μετ᾽ ὀλίγας ἡμέρας), perhaps because Josephus wanted to make sure to distinguish these revolts from those described by BJ 629-630 (including "without weapons", a precursor of 632-645a). BJ therefore emphasizes "again", πάλιν (632b and 645a). The last revolt too (645b) is introduced by "after a few days", μετὰ δ᾽ ἡμέρας ὀλίγας, which contradicts V 373 ("at about this time", κατὰ τοῦτον δὲ τὸν καιρόν) since the two works refer to different antecedents. But in spite of its chronological transitions BJ conflates the details of different episodes. The datum that Josephus returned the booty (BJ 646) is derived from the story told in V 328-335.

Most of these explanations are nothing but conjecture. They do show, however, that the structure of BJ can be more or less understood if we assume that V's sequence is primary and that BJ 2 has employed the same literary methods used in the BJ 1 parallel to AJ 15-16.[12]

Before we can accept this view, we must consider the objections and the alternatives. Thematic structure does not necessarily imply violation of chronology. We could argue that BJ selected its material in accordance with certain themes but adhered to the original chronological sequence. The crucial difference between BJ 2//V and BJ 1//AJ 15-16 is that BJ 1 nowhere pretends to be chronological. There the transitional phrases are rhetorical generalizations and the thematic structure is clear. But BJ 2 occasionally has definite chronological transitions and even appears to have more chronological data than V. Thus BJ places the episode of John at Tiberias in a definite chronological context (614a) while V links it to a thematic report which interrupts the narrative (see above). Similarly, BJ 592-593 places the antecedent to the Dabaritta

---

[12] BJ's concern for literary criteria may be further indicated by the use of certain key words. The use of *eunoia* has been noted above. The section on Josephus as a general is framed by the word *asphaleia* (572 and 584), the section on John (after the introduction) by *teichos* (590 and 632a). But this is, of course, no argument against BJ's sequence.

affair in a definite chronological context whereas V 122 links it to another rhetorical generalization about Josephus' popularity. V provides no parallel to BJ's "after a few days" which introduces the revolt of Tiberias (632). BJ's anti-John "gloss" in the Dabaritta affair is not necessarily an indication that the story is out of sequence. On the contrary, we could explain that BJ wanted to abandon neither the chronological order nor the anti-John polemic and therefore retained the story in proper sequence but glossed it so it would fit its literary context. V omits some detailed chronological information provided by BJ ("by night," BJ 483: "by night" and "towards dawn," 598; "after two days," 615) and employs retroactive summaries (V 31-61, 179-187). V thus evinces little interest in detailed chronology.[13]

But these objections pose no real problem because it cannot be assumed that the presence or the lack of explicit chronological indications proves that material is or is not chronologically arranged. The lack may indicate mere negligence, the presence, invention. It seems more prudent, therefore, to judge not by such unreliable details but by the question, whether or not the sections, by their main content, show thematic arrangement. On the basis of this criterion, it seems that V's arrangement, which makes no sense on any grounds (see below), is, perhaps, mainly chronological, whereas BJ's is probably thematic. If so, BJ, just as AJ did occasionally,[14] may have invented some chronological data for use as literary transitions.

The list of fortified cities (V 186-189//BJ 573-575) is a more significant case. After allowing for the numerous textual corruptions (see Niese's apparatus), we note that the lists contain the same names (although Seph is omitted by V) but in different orders. BJ lists the cities of lower Galilee, of upper Galilee, of the Gaulan, and appends a note on Sepphoris and Gischala. V has Gaulan (which connects the list to the narrative), upper Galilee, lower Galilee (which now includes Sepphoris) and finally returns to Gischala. Neither BJ nor V wins praise for its knowledge of geography.[15]

---

[13] V does provide chronological data (usually rather vague) when it supplies extra material not in BJ. See V 112, 390, 407, and the whole delegation story.

[14] See chapter two notes 108 and 131.

[15] For the identification of these places and an analysis of the topography see M. Avi-Yonah, *IEJ* 3 (1953) 94-98; M. Har-El, *IEJ* 22 (1972) 123-130;

The position of the list in V is important. After the revolt of Tiberias, according to V 174-178, Josephus and Justus had a discussion in which reference was made to Philip and certain relatives of Justus. V 179-186a is a digression explaining that reference. V 186b mentions Josephus' assistance to the rebels in Gamala for the fortification of the city walls which leads to the thematic list of fortified cities (V 187-188//BJ 573-574). The last item on BJ's list was the fortification of Gischala by John (BJ 575). The corresponding passage in V 189 not only closes the list but also introduces the pericope on the delegation from Jerusalem. The position of that very long account (V 190-335), therefore, seems to depend on a reference in a list which was appended to a digression which, in turn, explained an obscurity in the main narrative. If this appearance is not deceptive, we should suppose that V, at least here, is not arranged chronologically.

But appearances can be deceptive. If we return to our hypothesis that V is arranged chronologically, the problem can be resolved differently. We may conjecture that originally the delegation story was juxtaposed directly to Josephus' suppression of Tiberias. The intervening sections are all accretions to this structure. The discussion with Justus, part of V's apology and polemic, led Josephus to include what seems to be an excerpt from an independent written work on Gamala and Agrippa (see chapter five below, section C 2 e). This excerpt ended with a mention of Josephus' assistance in the building of the walls of Gamala. In order to return to the narrative, Josephus took the fortification list from

---

B. Bar-Kochva, *IEJ* 24 (1974) 108-116. See the maps in Avi-Yonah 96, Har-El 125, and Bar-Kochva 109. The only city whose identification is doubtful is Καφαραθκωμος = Καφαρεκχω. If we accept Avi-Yonah's identification, a counter-clockwise list beginning with Tiberias would be Tiberias, Arbel, Taricheae, Beer-Sheva, Selame, Sogane, Jotapata, Aphrata (the mystery name), Sepphoris, Japhia, and Itabyrion. V remotely approximates this list. BJ begins its circuit in the middle with Jotapata and is even more aribtrary. I have been unable to find a parallel to the relationship of these two lists. BJ 1.156//AJ 14.75-76 preserves a list of 13 cities (14 in AJ) arranged by region but without geographical order within each region. AJ follows BJ closely with one addition (Dium) and one insignificant change in order. BJ 1.166 presents a similar list arranged by region but without geographical order within each region. But AJ 14.88 not only condenses the text but completely destroys the order. AJ 14.18 repeats six names of the list of AJ 13.397, and five of them in the same sequence, but the texts are so corrupt and the identifications of the sites are so uncertain that any deductions are illegitimate.

BJ (see below) and used it as a transition. In fact, the transition in V 189 (᾽Ιωάννῃ δὲ τῷ τοῦ Ληουει τὸ κατ᾽ ἐμοῦ μῖσος προσηύξετο βαρέως φέροντι τὴν ἐμὴν εὐπραγίαν) recalls two other non-chronological transitions, V 122 (ὁ δὲ τοῦ Λευὶ παῖς ᾽Ιωάννης . . . κατάλυσιν δ᾽ αὐτῷ τὴν ἐμὴν εὐπραγίαν φέρειν νομίζων εἰς φθόνον ἐξώκειλεν οὔτι μέτριον) and V 85a.[16]

The main argument in favor of the theory that V reflects a chronology of which BJ is a thematic revision, is that V's sequence otherwise is incomprehensible. There is no way to derive V's sequence from BJ's nor can a *tertium quid* be reconstructed from which the divergent sequences of V and BJ could have been reasonably produced. Thematic organization will not explain V. Polemical reasons for V's rearrangement of BJ are unlikely because nowhere do V's polemics depend on the chronological points in which it disagrees with BJ.[17] Whether John's followers were dispersed before or after the repulse of the delegation seems irrelevant to any apologetic concern. There was no reason for V to "improve" BJ's sequence and, in fact we cannot now determine, whether V's is more reliable than BJ's.[18] A plausible history of the activities in Galilee could be written to accord with the order of either V or BJ; if only one of these works were extant, its sequence would have been readily accepted. Why then does V differ from

---

[16] For εὐπραγία leading to φθόνος, cf. BJ 1.67//AJ 13.288 and BJ 1.208 (cf. AJ 14.163). The transitions in both V 189 and 85a come after intrusive material directed against Justus (on V 85a, see chapter five below, section C 1). The rhetorical transition in V 122 returns the reader to John after a brief hiatus but the intervening material has no apparent connection with Justus.

[17] Graetz 489 n. 1, echoed by Baerwald 45, argued that V falsely advanced the Tiberias story because Josephus' suspicious conduct during the Dabaritta affair might have justified John's attack at Tiberias and V wanted to blacken John. Graetz neglected to point out that BJ was even more anti-John than V and that both BJ and V had already described an unmotivated attack by John (BJ 593-594//V 122-125). Thackeray's note on BJ 2.614 misses the difficulty altogether. True, a context in V helps to explain the Tiberias episode, but how can it be shown that the context was not invented to do so?

[18] Theodore Reinach, in his note on BJ 2.625, argued that the dispersal of John's forces must have taken place after the arrival of the delegation (as in V) because before John was reinforced by the delegation it is hard to see how he could have commanded 5000 or 5500 troops (V 371-372//BJ 625). Ricciotti (note on BJ 2.625) added that only after the repulse of the delegation would Josephus have been strong enough to neutralize John. These arguments are indecisive. I do not understand Luther's argument (74) against V's placement of the sham-fleet story.

BJ? The only solution aside from that suggested would be to suppose one (or both!) of the works incorrect by mere accident. Since V is more remote than BJ from the events, we should probably assume that V would be the less accurate [19] and this assumption could be supported by appeal to V's misstatements, occasional contradictions, and general confusion.

We therefore have a choice between a theory which interprets both V and BJ as rational and, to some extent, artistic productions (V a chronological account, BJ a thematic revision) and a theory which would make V the result of indifference, sloppiness, and faulty memory (BJ is chronological and correct, V is incorrect). Analogy with the relationship of BJ 1 to AJ 15-16 makes the former theory attractive. V and BJ are, for the most part, independent [20] revisions of a "common source" (see below), BJ giving a literary sequence, V a chronological sequence. We cannot determine whether V is correct but its sequence more closely resembles the original sequence of events than does BJ's.

Not only V's sequence but some of its content too seems more "original" than BJ's, i.e., we understand how BJ might be derived from V but not the reverse. V 77-78 discusses Josephus' dealings with the brigands (λῃσταί) and mentions the tribute (μισθοφορά or μισθός) exacted from the populace. Although the parallel passage [21] in BJ pretends that Josephus commanded an army numbering in the myriads (BJ 576 and 583) and trained in proper Roman fashion (BJ 577-580), nevertheless, it too refers to the accustomed brigandage (λῃστεία) of the troops (BJ 581) and calls some of them mercenaries (μισθοφόροι, BJ 583-584). V's scheme for extortion and bribery seems to have been transmuted in BJ to the claim that one-half of the "army" supported the other. Another example: both

---

[19] Niese, *HZ* 76 (1896) 228-229, noticed the variations in chronology but interpreted them as V's corrections of BJ and as proof of Josephus' conscientiousness! Niese forgot to explain why BJ erred in the first place. Reinach's note on BJ 2.646 summarizes the situation very well. "Ces divergences chronologiques entre la *Vita* et la *Guerre* sont troublantes. La *Guerre*, rédigée plus près des événements, semble en général mériter la préférence; mais on ne comprend pas que Josèphe, ayant sous les yeux son premier ouvrage, ne s'y soit pas conformé dans la *Vita* ou n'ait pas signalé les 'corrections' qu'il y apportait." A similar statement appears in Smallwood, *Jews* 302 n. 30.

[20] I.e., when writing V, Josephus either did not remember what he had written in BJ or remembered but did not care.

[21] Noted by Drexler 301.

BJ and V describe John's plots before the Dabaritta affair, but only BJ talks of John's intention to slander or murder Josephus (BJ 593-594). The autobiography, which is generally much less hostile than BJ towards John, narrates instead that John wrote to three cities but gained the (covert) support of only one.[22] BJ presumably changed this account in order to give a darker picture of John, to show the dangers that beset Josephus whatever course he followed, and to discredit, as John's slander, the story that he had been negotiating with the Romans. BJ therefore invented a scene which would fit its black portrait of John and which could be regarded as the result (BJ 592b, a transitional phrase) of his profitable speculations. BJ similarly invented John's participation in the Dabaritta affair (BJ 599). Tendentious revision explains how these sections of BJ were produced from V but not how V might have been produced from BJ. V would not have converted Josephus' mighty army to a band of brigands nor would it have gone out of its way to tone down BJ's polemic against John.

Thus in both sequence and (at least to some degree) content V has a more pristine form of the material than BJ. But, as we remarked in chapter one above in our criticism of Laqueur, that which is more pristine is not necessarily that which is earlier. Therefore a more significant example of V's primacy is the parallel V 86//BJ 615, from the episode of John at Tiberias. "He (Josephus) did not yet suspect the plotter (John)," οὔπω γὰρ ὑπώπτευεν τὸν ἐπίβουλον (BJ 615), makes little sense in BJ, after John's murderous plots of BJ 593-594 and the "Josephan gloss" of 599, and seems to be a careless paraphrase of V's "I did not suspect that he would do anything wicked," κἀγὼ μηδὲν ὑποπτεύσας πράξειν αὐτὸν πονηρόν. In V the words make sense because John's machinations, as described by V 70-76, were not such as to arouse suspicion. Here then is a good indication of the literary priority of V.[23]

By priority we mean that V, although written after BJ, contains as its nucleus a document which was written much earlier and

---

[22] Especially if we accept Naber's οὐδέ for the καὶ [om. R] αὐτοῦ δέ of the manuscripts at V 124. But even according to the *textus receptus* Tiberias gave John only lukewarm support.

[23] That BJ derived this *phrase* from the memory of the actual *event*, is much less plausible. Luther 26 n. 2, echoed by Ricciotti on BJ 2.614, noticed BJ's anomaly and deduced that V's sequence was more reliable than BJ's. They, and even Laqueur 79-90, overlooked this as evidence of V's literary priority.

was utilized by BJ. The existence of this document is supported by more than just the parallel V 86//BJ 615. The relationship of BJ 2 to V is similar to the relationship of BJ 1 to AJ 15-16 (see above) and this analogy suggests that the "common source" behind BJ 2 and V was not just Josephus' memory but a written document. The "original sequence", preserved by V and thematically revised by BJ, is the sequence of this work. This theory also explains the literary peculiarities of V. If V were a mere sloppy retelling of the story of Josephus' career in Galilee, written all at one time some thirty years after the events in order to refute Justus and based primarily on Josephus' memory (perhaps refreshed by a quick perusal of BJ), we could not explain why the clear organization of BJ was not followed more closely, why Justus' role is so spotty and peripheral, and why his name often appears in sentences which have no connection with their context and no consequence for the action (see chapter five below, section C 1). This argument in favor of the common source theory was emphasized (actually over-emphasized) by Laqueur. The only other systematic way to explain Justus' marginal role is to suppose that Josephus had written an autobiography, attached it to AJ, but later, after Justus' attack, converted it to serve his need for a self-defense. But if this auto-biography is our V minus the glosses, it is amazing that even before the attack of Justus Josephus prepared a long apologetic account which included precisely those elements he would later need in his self-defense. Therefore it has been suggested that the original autobiography was a short work consisting mostly of information on Josephus' background and family. The frame of our V is a remnant of this alleged edition (V 1-27 and 414-430). A few years later, in order to respond to Justus, Josephus expanded his earlier work in order to produce an apologetic and polemic.[24] But this suggestion does not solve our problem (why is the polemic against Justus so easily separable from the text?),[25] and is intrinsically implausible (why did Josephus not write a separate retort to Justus

---

[24] G. Hölscher, *PW* 9,2 (1916) 1941n., and B. Motzo, *Saggi di Storia e Letteratura Giudeo-Ellenistica* (Florence 1924) 214-226.

[25] Motzo also suggested that our V is an excerpt from the new history which Josephus was preparing (AJ 20.267) but never published. Thus Motzo explained why Justus appears only in glosses. But V is much too long to have been part of a history which Josephus could describe as κατὰ περιδρομὴν (or, with Laqueur 32 n. 1, παραδρομὴν) ὑπομνήσω.

if his autobiography were already complete?) [26] as well as chronologically difficult (Agrippa probably died before 93/4 and so there is
no reason to postulate two different editions of V).[27]

What is the nature of this hypothetical common source? The
least uncertain thing about it is that it was arranged chronologically much like V. If it was a literary work, a polished account
like, say, that of Nicolaus of Damascus, we must explain why there
are so many discrepancies between V and BJ, many more than
between AJ 15-16 and BJ 1. Some of these, no doubt, are Josephus'
responses to Justus (see chapter five below) but many are too
picayune to be of any significance. It is apparent that Josephus'
memory, in addition to this written source, must have played a
large part in both V and BJ. Thus we need a document fixed enough
to have a definite order but free enough to allow remarkable
divergences caused by shifts in memory. The most likely candidate
is a *hypomnema*, a dry sketch or outline of the events in Galilee,
which Josephus prepared before writing BJ. CA 1.50, "when my
entire narrative was prepared", (πάσης μοι τῆς πραγματείας ἐν
παρασκευῇ γεγενημένης) may well refer to this sketch. Ancient
historians were expected to prepare such *hypomnemata* before
proceeding to their literary works.[28] BJ, a rhetorical history,
drastically shortened, thematically rearranged, and freely modified
the *hypomnema*.[29] V, a hasty polemic and apologetic, retained the
scope, structure, and, in general, the dryness of the original but
added anti-Justus material (including the "glosses") and extensive
self-defense.[30] A similar theory has been advanced to account for the
differences between the *Vita Constantini* and the sections parallel

---

[26] F. Rühl, *RhM* 71 (1916) 297, and T. Rajak, *CQ* 23 (1973) 361 n. 4. If
the frame of our V derives from a short autobiography, why does it twice
narrate the birth of Josephus' children? In a long autobiography, which V
is now, the reason is clear: V 5 is a thematic context, V 426-427 chronological.

[27] See the last part of chapter five below for a full discussion of this
problem.

[28] On the use of *hypomnemata* see Lucian *Quomodo Historia Conscribenda
Sit* 48 with the rich documentation assembled by Avenarius 85-104. Avenarius
88 suggests that CA 1.50 refers to Josephus' *hypomnema*.

[29] Lucian (c. 48) explicitly says that the artistic arrangement (τάξις) of
the material belongs to the literary work, not the *hypomnema*: πρῶτα μὲν
ὑπόμνημά τι συνυφαινέτω ... καὶ σῶμα ποιείτω ἀκαλλὲς ἔτι καὶ ἀδιάρθρωτον
(i.e. ἄτακτον) εἶτα ἐπιθεὶς τὴν τάξιν ἐπαγέτω τὸ κάλλος.

[30] Gelzer was the first to suggest that V reflects an early *hypomnema*;
see chapter one note 70. Gelzer conjectured further that the *hypomnema*
was written before 70 but for this he has no evidence.

to it in the *Historia Ecclesiastica* of Eusebius. The one, a biography, and the other, a history, describe events of Eusebius' own lifetime but disagree on many details and on the order of events. Perhaps these two works derive from a Eusebian *hypomnema*.[31]

We cannot now determine the exact content and form of this work. Josephus has rewritten everything not only because this was his normal procedure (see chapter two), but also because the *hypomnema* was meant to be rewritten. Therefore it is no surprise that V's style resembles that of AJ 20 and that V contains several dramatic passages.[32] Our uncertainty can be seen clearly in the matter of doublets. When confronted with two similar narratives, Josephus will often compress them into one. We have adduced above several conjectural examples of this process from BJ 2. But Josephus also has the habit of describing similar incidents in similar language and so the reader cannot be sure whether he is reading about two discrete incidents or about one incident artificially duplicated.[33] We shall note in chapter five below many extensive repetitions of formulae and themes in V and we cite here two additional examples. The Sepphorites invoke a Roman garrison in both 373 ("They send to Cestius Gallus beseeching him either to come quickly himself to take their city or to send men to guard it", πέμπουσι δὴ πρὸς Κέστιον Γάλλον . . . παρακαλοῦντες ἢ αὐτὸν ἥκειν θᾶττον παραληψόμενον αὐτῶν τὴν πόλιν ἢ πέμψαι τοὺς φρουρήσοντας) and 394 ("They sent to Cestius Gallus beseeching him to come to them quickly to take the city or to send an army", πρὸς Κέστιον Γάλλον ἔπεμψαν ἥκειν παρακαλοῦντες ὡς αὐτοὺς παραληψόμενον τὴν πόλιν ἢ πέμπειν δύναμιν . . .).[34] The structure of the entire narrative of V 84-103 is similar to that of V 271-308. In both a revolt is begun against Josephus in Tiberias, Josephus is warned by Silas, addresses the people, flees from John by boat to Taricheae, dissuades the

---

[31] See I. Heikel's introduction to his edition of the *Vita Constantini* (Leipzig 1902) xxxi-xxxii. Heikel supports his theory by appealing to some stylistic matters, not the historical contradictions. In this Eusebian example, it is the biography which has rhetorically rearranged the material; see Heikel lix (note on 34,11). In chapter two above we conjectured that AJ 18-20//BJ 2 may derive from a *hypomnema*; see chapter two note 127.

[32] On the resemblance of the style of V to that of AJ 20, see chapter one n. 59; on V's dramatic passages, which have no place in a *hypomnema*, see chapter four below, section B. Gelzer assumes that V is a verbatim copy of the *hypomnema*, but this is most unlikely.

[33] For a good example see B. Justus, *Theokratia* 2 (1970-72) 107-136.

[34] Noted by Hornbostel 78.

Galileans from attacking John, and John retires to Gischala.[35] There is some verbal repetition too.[36] In all of these cases it is nearly impossible to determine the content of the original *hypomnema*. Perhaps even in the *hypomnema* Josephus described similar scenes with similar language. Perhaps it was only when writing V that Josephus reiterated certain themes and situations for apologetic reasons (e.g. his restraint of the Galileans). Certainty is unattainable.

Similarly, we cannot know what degree of detail the *hypomnema* provided. For example, the fortification list which appears in both BJ and V may not have been in the *hypomnema* at all. BJ might have produced it by thematic compression from the sketch's scattered references to Josephus' fortifications,[37] and V took the list from BJ. Alternatively, even the *hypomnema* had such a thematic list [38]—in what context we do not know—which BJ and V "independently" adopted and inserted.

We must remember that this hypothesis does not solve any of our historical problems. Even if we could assume that the *hypomnema* was essentially truthful—a near incredible assumption—we have no way to reconstruct it. Perhaps V reflects the scope and structure of the *hypomnema* more accurately than BJ but it is not a verbatim transcript. Josephus has added drama and pathos, remembered

---

[35] I need not mention that V 271-308 differs in many respects from V 84-103, notably that V 276-293, the maneuvers and counter-maneuvers of Josephus and the delegation, depicts events of several days while V 84-103 depicts the events of only one day. Neither story is wholly implausible.

[36] V 89 (ἧκεν γὰρ ἄγγελός μοι παρὰ Σίλα, ὃν ἐγὼ καθεστάκειν τῆς Τιβεριάδος στρατηγόν, ὡς προεῖπον, τὴν τῶν Τιβεριέων γνώμην ἀπαγγέλλων κἀμὲ σπεύδειν παρακαλῶν)//V 272 (ἀπαγγέλλει δέ μοι ταῦτα Σίλας διὰ γραμμάτων, ὃν ἔφην τῆς Τιβεριάδος ἐπιμελητὴν καταλελοιπέναι, καὶ σπεύδειν ἠξίου) and V 96 (ὁδηγηθεὶς ... ἐπὶ τὴν λίμνην καὶ πλοίου λαβόμενος καὶ ἐπιβάς, παρὰ δόξαν τοὺς ἐχθροὺς διαφυγὼν εἰς Ταριχέας ἀφικόμην)//V 304 (ἐπὶ τὴν λίμνην σωθεὶς καὶ πλοίου λαβόμενος, ἐμβὰς εἰς τὰς Ταριχαίας διεπεραιώθην ἀπροσδοκήτως τὸν κίνδυνον διαφυγών). Note too V 86 (κἀγὼ μηδὲν ὑποπτεύσας)//V 276 (κἀγὼ μηδὲν ὑπονοήσας—where Josephus is playing innocent; or is κἀγὼ ὡς μηδὲν ὑπονοήσας to be read, as Morton Smith suggests? Hiatus is not rare in V.) and the appearance of Justus in V 88 and 279.

[37] These references appear not only in V (45, 71, 156, 347) but also BJ (2.590, 638; 3.61, 159, 464-65; 4.9, 56). I do not claim that these passages are taken from the *hypomnema* (V 347 obviously is not) but they represent the type of material from which BJ's list may have been constructed (with the aid of Josephus' memory and imagination).

[38] Nicolaus of Damascus wrote a history which was arranged chronologically but nevertheless contained a thematic list of city donations; see chapter two above p. 56.

(invented?) new details and episodes, committed new mistakes. Therefore in matters of chronology V deserves preference but otherwise we cannot assume that V is more reliable than BJ. Every episode must be investigated separately.

To summarize: the near lack of verbal parallels between V and BJ proves that one text is not the direct source of the other. We have attempted to show that BJ thematically arranges the chronological sequence found in V. Thus the relationship of V to BJ is similar to the relationship of AJ 15-16 to BJ and this similarity, in addition to some literary peculiarities of the autobiography, suggests that V and BJ are reworkings of a common written source. We have conjectured that this written source was a *hypomnema*, a brief sketch which historians normally prepared before proceeding to their final draft. BJ thoroughly rewrote and rearranged the document, V rewrote less drastically and retained the original chronological order. Since in both works Josephus supplemented the *hypomnema* with his fresh recollection of the events, numerous discrepancies were the result. Which discrepancies were the result of the anti-Justus polemic and apologetic, will be investigated in chapter five.

CHAPTER FOUR

BELLUM JUDAICUM: AIMS AND METHODS

We turn now to the second aspect of our study. Since the literary relationship of BJ to V is not entirely clear, and since we depend almost exclusively on BJ and V for our knowledge of the early stages of the war, the only way we shall be able to separate historical fact from Josephan fiction is by historiographic inquiry. What are the aims and methods of both works? In this chapter we restrict our discussion to the relevant features of BJ.[1]

A. *Date*

Since we are interested in the variations between BJ and V, we need to know the date of each work. For BJ two views are encountered. The *communis opinio* places BJ between 75 and 79 CE.[2] Evidence: BJ 7.158-161 mentions the dedication of the *Templum Pacis* which took place in 75 (Dio Cassius 66.15.1). Vespasian himself, who died 23 June 79, received copies of BJ from the obsequious author (V 361 and CA 1.50-51). Hence book seven, at least, is later than 75 and no part of BJ is later than mid-79. Laqueur and Eisler introduce a new factor, re-edition, which allows them, in spite of this evidence, to propose a broader time span. Eisler determines that the first Greek version of BJ was finished in 71 but the work gradually expanded until, by 79, it reached its present dimensions,[3] although Eisler agrees with Laqueur that even after 79 BJ was frequently revised.[4] Let us examine the evidence for these views.

Was Vespasian presented with the entire BJ? At first sight V 361 and CA 1.51 suggest he was, but "the books" (τὰ βίβλια) does not necessarily refer to all seven books of BJ. Agrippa's

---

[1] Therefore I do not discuss such topics as the title of BJ, the Aramaic edition (Hatta, *JQR* 66 [1975-76] 89-108), Flavian political propaganda (Yavetz, *GRBS* 16 [1975] 411-432), BJ and Flavian foreign policy. In general I can be brief in this chapter since BJ's motives have been investigated many times.

[2] Established by von Gutschmid 344-345.

[3] Eisler 1.233, 250-260, and passim.

[4] See the summary of Laqueur's position in chapter one above.

letter (V 365) shows that Josephus circulated books (or sections) of BJ separately (probably one book per roll) and that Agrippa had to request future installments (πέμπε δέ μοι καὶ τὰς λοιπάς). Only in V 367 does Josephus clearly refer to a completed product ("when my history was polished off", ἀπαρτισθείσης τῆς ἱστορίας), but there he does not mention presentation or dedication. Our *terminus ante quem* is not so unambiguous after all. Furthermore, a date of publication under Titus seems rather attractive. Only Titus gave BJ the royal *imprimatur* (V 363) and only he appears in the proem to BJ. It was Titus who rescued Josephus at Jotapata (BJ 3.396-397). Vespasian is certainly not treated badly by BJ but Titus fares much better.[5] The son's speeches are more numerous and more magnificent. Josephus never tires of lauding this *amor ac deliciae generis humani*, a great warrior (BJ 5.88-97, 287-288, 340-341, 486-488) who does not delight in slaughter but pities the surviving populace of Jerusalem (3.501; 4.92, 117-119; 5.450-456, 519, 522; 6.324, 383). He wants to save the city (5.332-334) and does not boast of its capture (7.112-113). He is not responsible for the barbarities committed by the Jews (6.215-219) and he condemns those committed by the Romans (5.553-560). He has no desire to destroy the temple (6.127-128, 236-243) and even tries to save it (6.254-266). Vespasian receives this treatment only occasionally (3.127, he allows the Jews of Galilee to repent; 4.412, he pities the misfortunes of Jerusalem). His treachery towards the Jews (3.537-542), based on the advice of his friends, "there is nothing impious when fighting against the Jews" (3.536), receives no apology. Titus would never have pursued such a policy. The contrast is best explained by the view that BJ was completed under Titus.

Another observation confirms. Aulus Caecina Alienus was an enthusiastic Vitellian in the troubles of 69 until he deserted to the Flavians before the battle of Cremona (see PIR[2] C 99). Tacitus analyzes Caecina's motives:

> The historians, who, after the Flavian house rose to power, have narrated the memorable features of this war, have reported that Caecina and Bassus were motivated by concern for peace and love of the state (*cura pacis et amor rei publicae*), but the desire for adulation has corrupted their report; it seems to me that Caecina and Bassus destroyed Vitellius through their innate fickleness and

---

[5] Noted by Weber 57 and 135. I do not present here a complete list of passages. On the apologetic for Titus, see Yavetz, *GRBS* 16 (1975) 411-432.

because, after Galba had been betrayed, loyalty soon lost its value through the competition and jealousy among Vitellius' followers to be the first to cross over to Vespasian.

(an elucidatory paraphrase of *Historiae* 2.101.1)

If any historian was a Flavian lackey, it was Josephus. And yet, BJ's account of Caecina's activities (4.634ff) stresses his treachery. Nowhere do we encounter *cura pacis et amor rei publicae*. Caecina plotted treason (4.635), deserted to Antonius (4.639), and, viewed as a traitor, was bound by the soldiers (4.641). Even Vespasian's gifts barely covered the disgrace of his treason (644). Josephus' hostility to Caecina is surely explained by the events of 79 when, just before the death of Vespasian, Caecina was executed by Titus for an alleged plot against the emperor (Dio 66.16.3; Suetonius *Titus* 6). Titus' favorite explained in his history that Caecina had always been treacherous and unfaithful. The earlier Flavian propaganda, castigated by the Roman consular, had to yield to the political exigencies of a later period.[6] Thus BJ 4.634ff clearly obtained its present form no earlier than mid-79. We have no reason to regard it as an insertion into an earlier text, since the narrative, coherent, direct, and concise, is the last of a series of passages in BJ 4 about the dynastic wars of 69 (BJ 4.491-496, 545-49, 585-587, 630-655). A post-Vespasianic date for BJ 4 seems assured.[7]

---

[6] A full discussion of Caecina is in A. Briessman, *Tacitus und das Flavische Geschichtsbild* (Wiesbaden 1955) 28-45, esp. 29-36. See too M. Durry in *Fondation Hardt: Entretiens sur l'antiquité classique IV: Histoire et historiens* (Vandoeuvres-Geneva 1956) 226-230.

[7] M. Grant, *The Ancient Historians* (N.Y. 1970) 447 n. 20, draws this conclusion from Briessman's work although Briessman himself was non-committal on this point (see Briessman 34). G. E. F. Chilver, *JRS* 46 (1956) 204, remarks that "It may be that his [Josephus'] process of 'publication' was more elaborate than is generally understood." Briessman's thesis has been attacked by G. B. Townend, *AJP* 85 (1964) 338-342, who agrees that our passage is not an addition to the text but claims that Josephus could have denounced Caecina even before 79. Perhaps he *could* have, but why *would* he? Josephus was not a man to take unnecessary risks or to stand on principle. Townend conjectures that the *Historiae* of Pliny had anti-Flavian sentiments, including criticism of Caecina, which caused the author to suppress publication. Did Josephus have more spine than Pliny? The historian (BJ 4.642) and the encyclopedist (Tacitus *Hist.* 3.28) could blame Antonius Primus (PIR² A 866) for the sack of Cremona because Primus was deposed from eminence and power even in 70 (*Hist.* 4.80). As a result, he was allowed to finish his life in secure obscurity. Caecina moved in high circles under Vespasian and was important enough to be executed by Titus. On the political situation in 79 see J. A. Crook, *AJP* 72 (1951) 168-169. Townend writes that a pre-79 date for BJ "is as clear as anything can be from Josephus' own words" (339).

If BJ 1-6 was completed under Titus, BJ 7 is Domitianic. Its style, markedly inferior, is rather close to AJ and V. The literary assistants have not been at work here.[8] A telling indication of date is the attitude towards Domitian. The first six books mention Domitian only three times and only in the continuation of the passage of Flavian propaganda discussed above (on Caecina). The references (BJ 4.646, 649, 654) are bald statements with only moderate adulation ("the greatest portion of the hopes for victory" rested upon Domitian, 646). Perhaps Josephus is hiding Domitian's cowardice and incompetence, gleefully recounted by Tacitus, but BJ 1-6 knows no royal heroics or royal victories. Contrast BJ 7.85-88 which extols Domitian's prowess. The Germans are terrified merely by the rumor of his approach. Domitian single-handedly subdues rebellious Gaul. The Domitian of book seven is much more forceful than the Domitian of book four. Nor does Josephus neglect to mention that Domitian, who took no part in the destruction of Jerusalem, rode in the triumphal procession, magnificently attired and astride a great horse (7.152). Comparable details are lacking for Vespasian and Titus. Since BJ 6 forms an admirable close for the entire work, BJ 7 is presumably a Domitianic addition.[9]

This view is supported by the characterization of John in BJ 7.264. BJ 4-6 frequently accuses the revolutionaries of lawless

---

[8] Thackeray, *Josephus* 35 and 105; S. Michaelson and A. Q. Morton, *Revue* of the *Organisation internationale pour l'étude des langues anciennes par ordinateur* (known as the *R.E.L.O. Revue*), 1973 number 3, pp. 33-56, esp. 41-42 and 52 (on elision).

[9] Weber 55 makes similar observations but avoids the conclusion. Eisler too said that most of BJ 7 was added later to the main text. BJ 7 cannot be a part of the projected history from the war until 93/4 (AJ 20.267) because it does not fit κατὰ παραδρομήν (Laqueur's correction [32 n. 1] for the vulgate κατὰ περιδρομήν). The fact that BJ 7.97 knows that Arkea belongs to Agrippa's kingdom while BJ 3.56-57 does not, is no indication of the chronology of the two books. Perhaps Agrippa did receive Arkea from Vespasian after the war (cf. Photius cod. 33 = FGrH 734 T 2 section 3) but BJ 3.56-57 does not purport to give a complete description of Agrippa's kingdom. Nowhere does the geographical excursus (3.35-58) mention that Tiberias, Taricheae, and Julias-Betharamphtha belong to Agrippa (AJ 20.159). Schürer 594-595 = Schürer-Vermes 477-478 explains that Arkea is omitted because BJ 3.56-57 describes only those areas heavily populated by Jews. This explanation would do if we could be sure that first century Arkea was nearly *Judenrein*. See Michel-Bauernfeind's note 51 to BJ 7.97; Smallwood, *Jews* 339 n. 35. Weber considers book seven up to 158-162, the dedication of the *Templum Pacis*, an integral part of his Flavian work. I am uncertain whether a stylistic examination will justify the bisection.

behavior (παρανομία) and impiety (ἀσέβεια).[10] Which particular crimes are intended by theses words? Some of the accusations are general condemnations, but some have contexts specific enough to show that the crimes are of two sorts: capital crimes, notably murder (BJ 4.144, 182-184, 258, 348, 351; 5.402), and interference with the temple cult (BJ 6.95, 99-102; cf. 4.157). The laws which the brigands violate and the Romans defend are the universal norms of society and cult. No reference here to Jewish Halachah, e.g. the laws of purity, food taboos, festivals, prayer, etc. The two crimes are combined when Josephus charges the revolutionaries with polluting (usually μιαίνειν) the temple (BJ 4.150, 201, 242; 5.380, 402; 6.122, 124-127; cf. 2.424). The temple is defiled not by a violation of Halachah (ritual impurity) but by a violation of universally held principles (the crimes of murder, etc.). Only once (BJ 5.100) does Josephus state that the temple was invaded by impure men (ἄναγνοι) but there—even if the word is used in its literal cultic sense—he forgets to mention that the temple was polluted by the ritual impurity. John is guilty of impiety (ἀσέβεια) for using the sacred timber (BJ 5.36-39), of sacrilege (ἱεροσυλία) for using the sacred wine and oil (BJ 5.562-566), but not of a violation of the laws of purity. Contrast BJ 7.264 which defines John's impiety as the violation of the traditional laws of purity (τὴν νενομισμένην καὶ πάτριον ἁγνείαν). He is accused too of serving improper food (τράπεζαν ἄθεσμον). This Halachic formulation of the crimes of the revolutionaries is not found in BJ 4-6 but typifies the attitude of AJ.[11] Food taboos and laws of purity were prominent

---

[10] See the passages collected by Hengel 188-190 and Michel-Bauernfeind in excursus four on BJ 4.154.

[11] Michel-Bauernfeind, note 141 on BJ 7.264, suggest that τράπεζα ἄθεσμος refers partly to BJ 5.562-566 (John's use of the sacred wine and oil). This may be right but what is important is that BJ 5 expresses shock at the ἱεροσυλία, BJ 7 at the ἀθεσμία. BJ 4.402 describes an attack by some revolutionaries on Passover but Josephus does not refer to their παρανομία or even imply condemnation. BJ 4.98-106 does not say that John actually desecrated the Sabbath (John fled after nightfall, 106). It does say that John cared more for his own safety than for the Sabbath (103) but this is not a charge of παρανομία. The religious innovations of which the revolutionaries are guilty in BJ 2.414 consist of interference with the temple cult. BJ 2.456 and 517 point out that the revolutionaries fought on Sabbath but these passages are best explained by BJ 2.391-394: by fighting on the Sabbath the Jews lost God's aid. Pagan authors attributed Jewish defeats to the Jews' abstinence from fighting on the Sabbath (e.g. see CA 1.209-211); Josephus retorts that the Jews were defeated *because* they fought on the Sabbath. These passages are not part of the larger *paranomia* theme. In any event,

subjects in the Rabbinic discussions at Yavneh (and, indeed, in all
varieties of sectarian Judaism). BJ 7.264 tells the Rabbis that
John, a long time friend of Simon ben Gamaliel (V 192), was
really a wicked Jew who violated the most important canons of
Rabbinic Judaism. Cf. V 74-75 which describes John's ostensible
concern that the Jews of Caesarea Philippi use only pure oil and
not violate the traditional laws. V labels John's concern a sham,
while the parallel passage in BJ 2.591 omits the religious polemic.
The outlook and concerns of BJ 7 seem closer to those of AJ and V
than BJ 1-6.[12]

No matter what date we adopt for BJ 1-7, Laqueur's idea,
frequent re-edition, may be correct since ancient book production
afforded ample opportunity for changes and corrections.[13] But
BJ provides not a single convincing example of an interpolated
passage [14] and is Josephus' most polished work. Its tone and style
are maintained at a uniformly high level at least through book six.
The central tendentious elements appear quite consistently and the

---

the desecration of the Sabbath is not mentioned in BJ 4-6. What is important
in BJ 7.264 is not only the new interpretation of the theme of the descration
of the temple but also the importance assigned to the theme. John's greatest
sin was the violation of the ancestral laws of purity. On AJ's Halachic
attitude, see chapter five below, section C 2 b. Some passages of AJ can still,
of course, follow BJ's interpretation of ἀσέβεια; cf. AJ 20.166 with BJ 6.110.

[12] On the religious polemic in V 74-75, see below p. 146. It is possible
that BJ 7.254-274 is an addition to the text (in 274 Josephus realizes that
he has interrupted the story) but I see no good evidence for this. Elsewhere
too Josephus is conscious of a digression (e.g. AJ 12.59, 128; 15.372, 379;
17.354; 20.157; CA 1.57; 2.151) even though there is no sign of interpolation.
It is possible that the long account on the Sicarii at Masada (7.275-406) is
an addition or an expansion. The relationship of BJ 7 to BJ 1-6 clearly
needs further study. In particular we should like to know when BJ 7 was
written, and why Josephus wrote it.

[13] H. Emonds, Zweite Auflage im Altertum (Leipzig 1941) 15-17; G. Bardy,
Revue Bénédictine 47 (1935) 356-380. Laqueur's view, endorsed by Eisler,
was rejected by Lewy, Deutsche Literaturzeitung (1930) 487-488, and H.
Schreckenberg, Die Flavius-Josephus-Tradition in Antike und Mittelalter
(Leiden 1972) 63 and 176-177, and Theokratia 2 (1970-72) 87n., because our
Josephan manuscripts descend from one archetype, not two. But this means
that our manuscript tradition provides no proof for a second edition, not
that it provides proof against it. See chapter five below, part D, on the
editions of AJ and V.

[14] Even Laqueur's oft-repeated dictum about doublets (material sandwiched between doublets is interpolated) is uncertain. For example, BJ
2.531-532 seems to be repeated in 2.539 but there is no reason to believe
that the intervening material is an interpolation. Against Weiler, Klio
50 (1968) 144 n. 6, see Yavetz, GRBS 16 (1975) 417 n. 23.

narrative is almost free of explicit contradictions (implicit contradictions are, of course, another matter). In all these respects V and
AJ compare unfavorably, and all these make extensive revision
or re-edition of BJ 1-6, after its initial publication, unlikely. Had
Josephus rewritten, he would not have rewritten so well nor so
consistently. So in BJ 1-6 we have a relatively coherent uniform
work finished as a whole before 81.

B. *Literary Technique* [15]

BJ is a good representative of rhetorical historiography. Everywhere BJ evinces a fondness for colorful detail, anecdotes, exaggerations, drama, and pathos. A few examples of these features
from books two and three will suffice. 100,000 Galileans congregate
against Josephus at Taricheae (2.598). The force of the catapault
is illustrated by some rather amusing anecdotes (3.245-246).
Corpses are hurled about, women shriek, the earth streams with
blood (3.248-249). What could be more dramatic than the scene in
the stadium of Tiberias (2.618-619)? While Josephus is addressing
the crowd, he hears some shouts and turns around—a knife at his
throat! He jumps down and escapes.

One of the major motives of BJ is to blacken John (see below).
Josephus employs both direct pronouncements (e.g. BJ 2.585-589;
4.85, 208, 389-391; 7.263-264), which stop the narrative and describe
John's character (occasionally on the basis of rhetorical commonplaces),[16] and indirect characterization, the deft arrangement of
material so as to produce a desired impression.[17] Thus, the Galileans

---

[15] A fully documented discussion is not necessary; I do not want to
repeat what is already well known. See Niese, *HZ* 76 (1896) 193-237 (204-
208 on BJ).

[16] Thackeray 119-120 compares BJ 2.585-589 and 4.85 (see too his notes
ad locc.) to the portrait of Catiline in Sallust. Baer 141-143 adduces the
portraits of Cleon and Alcibiades in Aristophanes and Thucydides as Josephus' models. But Josephus regularly uses stock formulae in character
descriptions. Not only John (ἀεὶ ἐπιθυμήσας μεγάλων, BJ 2.587) but Jeroboam
too (μεγάλων ἐπιθυμητὴς πραγμάτων, AJ 8.209) is a seditious figure. See
chapter five note 152 below for a long list of Josephan parallels to V's
picture of Simon ben Gamaliel. On all this see Wolff 41-44 and Attridge
109-126 and 172-176. In this respect Josephus is very similar to his contemporary Plutarch who also based his descriptions of many different
individuals on ideal types; see B. Bucher-Isler, *Norm und Individualität
in den Biographien Plutarchs* (Bern/Stuttgart 1972). Josephus' use of rhetorical and historiographical *topoi* needs further study.

[17] The classic discussion of these two methods is I. Bruns, *Die Persön-*

themselves, not Josephus call John "the conspirator against the community" (622). The masses gladly denounce John's followers (624). The Jerusalemites do not believe John's charges (627) and attack those who accepted them (631). In these passages it is not Josephus the narrator but the actors of history who give the desired effect.[18]

We have already discussed (in chapters two and three) BJ's fondness for thematic structure. The description of the Galilean war in BJ 2 is arranged not chronologically but thematically. The lists of those cities which attacked the Jews or were attacked by them (BJ 2.458-460 and 477-480) combine data from different periods and render impossible an exact reconstruction of the events of 66 (see chapter one n. 4 above). The catalogue of fortified cities (BJ 2.573-575) is an obvious parallel. A fourth passage too, the list of generals selected after the victory over Cestius (2.562-568), may be thematic. We shall return to this point in chapter six below.[19]

C. *Aims*

In true Thucydidean fashion the proem to BJ claims that the Jewish war was the greatest of all time. It is no surprise that Josephus presents himself as one of the greatest generals of this war, hence of all time. His vanity is notorious. Vespasian muses before Jotapata that if he could only capture Josephus, "the most sagacious of his enemies", the fall of Judaea (sic!) would be swift and inevitable (BJ 3.143-144; cf. 200 and 340).[20] The Jews too realize Josephus' greatness. They can suffer no ill when he is present (3.193-202; cf. 142). All Jerusalem bewails his reported death (3.436-437). The rebels want to kill him more than anyone else (5.541-542; cf. 3.441 and 6.112).

Josephus displays his greatness by portraying himself as the ideal general. Here is Cicero's description (*De Imperio Cn. Pompei* 13 (36)): [21]

---

lichkeit in der Geschichtsschreibung der Alten (Berlin 1898, repr. Darmstadt 1961).

[18] Josephus' methods of character description—and, indeed, the principles of Josephan historiography—await investigation. I have not had access to the recent Oxford dissertation of T. Rajak.

[19] See pp. 197 and 198 below.

[20] BJ 1.386 is a similar statement (from Nicolaus ?) about Herod.

[21] On which see R. Harder, *Hermes* (1934) 66-67 and 69-71.

> Non enim bellandi virtus solum in summo ac perfecto imperatore
> quaerenda est, sed multae sunt artes eximiae huius administrae
> comitesque virtutis. Ac primum quanta innocentia debent esse
> imperatores! quanta deinde in omnibus rebus temperantia! quanta
> fide, quanta felicitate, quanto ingenio, quanta humanitate!

This list of qualities is elucidated and explained by the orator
(37-48). A general is free of avarice and ignoble passions, always
self-controlled, never cruel to the conquered,[22] readily approachable
by the citizens, a fine speaker, endowed with great *auctoritas*
and *felicitas*. Onasander, an author of the first half of the first
century CE,[23] has a similar description. I excerpt those terms
(from 1.1 and 2.2) which correspond to the dominant elements of
the Ciceronian passage: σώφρων, ἐγκρατής, λιτός, νοερός, ἀφιλάργυρος,
ἱκανὸς λέγειν, ἔνδοξος, χρηστός, εὐπροσήγορος, ἕτοιμος, μὴ οὕτως
ἐπιεικὴς ὥστε καταφρονεῖσθαι μήτε φοβερὸς ὥστε μισεῖσθαι. The origin
and development of this tradition are of no concern here,[24] but
it is clear that Josephus was familiar with this conception. His
Vespasian is an ideal figure [25] and he, like Cicero, calls Pompey a
"good general" (ἀγαθὸς στρατηγός, BJ 1.153) because of the general's
preference for goodwill (εὔνοια) to terror (δέος).

Josephus' greatness is demonstrated by BJ 2.568-584, the
first part of his description of his own actions in Galilee. He and
other nobles are chosen as generals by an assembly (562-568).
To enhance his prestige he omits any mention of his two colleagues
(known from V). His policy in Galilee has two aims: domestic
support and military preparedness. To fulfill his first objective
he strives for the goodwill of the natives (εὔνοια τῶν ἐπιχωρίων, 569),
more specifically, of the well-to-do (δυνατοί, 570). He sets up
a pan-Galilean judicial system with a supreme council of seventy
and local courts of seven judges in every *polis* (570-571).[26] In the

---

[22] Cf. *de Officiis* 1.11 (35) and Vergil's *parcere subiectis*. Onasander 38.1-6
and 42.18-22 recommends kind treatment of captured cities, but purely for
practical reasons. Humanitarian considerations and noble ideals play no
part.

[23] L. W. Daly and W. A. Oldfather, *PW* 18,1 (1942) 403-405; E. Bayer,
Würzburger Jahrbücher für die Altertumswissenschaft 2 (1947) 86-90; A. E.
Gordon, *PW* 8A,1 (1955) 955-959.

[24] I note only that Onasander omits the Roman notions of *felicitas* and
parcere subiectis (see note 22).

[25] See the pages of Wolff cited in n. 16 above.

[26] Perhaps Josephus is portraying himself as a second Moses who also
established councils of seven in every city (AJ 4.214 and 287), i.e., Josephus
ascribes to himself and to Moses the establishment (although κατέστησεν

military sphere (572) he fortifies cities (573-575), recruits a large army (576), and trains it in Roman fashion (577-580). Josephus is concerned about the moral probity of his men. He cautions them to refrain from plunder and rapine; a clean conscience is the best ally (581-582).[27] His forces do not rely on compulsion to obtain their supplies since one half of the recruits provision the other half (583-584).[28] Here we see Josephus not only as a commander of a mighty army but also as a man concerned for *innocentia* and goodwill (εὔνοια).[29]

BJ 2.585-646 describes Josephus' encounter with John of Gischala and the rebellious cities. This section has two motives. The first is to disassociate Josephus from John. The two are generals in the same war fighting against the same enemy in the same province. But since John is the villain, the chief object of Josephus' hatred (BJ 4.85, 208, 389-391; 7.263-264), BJ insists that John was Josephus' enemy from the very beginning (2.593-594, 599, 614-631) and was thwarted only by the brilliant strategems of his rival. Further, in contrast to Josephus, the ideal general, John is mean and despicable. He lacks *fides* (585-586). He is a brigand (λῃστής, 587) who cheats the wealthy (590) and corners the olive-oil market to alleviate his poverty (591-592). John knows how to pretend to be what he is not (614 and 617). He commands only a small band of Tyrian refugees (588, contrast 624-625).

The second motive is to continue the portraiture of the ideal

---

could mean "re-appoint") of a practice widespread in his own time. See Thackeray and Schalit on AJ 4.214; A. Geiger, *Urschrift und Uebersetzungen der Bibel*[2] (Frankfurt 1928) 115 = *Ha Miqra ve Targumav* (Jerusalem 1949) 77; and G. Alon, *Toledot ha Yehudim be Erez Yisrael bi Tequfat ha Mishnah ve ha Talmud* (Jerusalem 1967) 1.107-109. Josephus is thus an ideal figure like the Philonic Moses: priest, prophet, and legislator (in the sense that he presides over a council of seventy which decides questions of law; cf. AJ 4.218). Were καὶ τοὺς ἑβδομήκοντα the object of ἐκέλευσεν he would be a perfect counterpart to Moses—see *Exodus* 18.22 and 26 = AJ 3.72—but the phrase must be the object of ἐπί. However, I wonder if the parallel has real significance; Josephus nowhere makes the correspondence evident and the data on the priesthood, prophetic gifts, and legislative action are presented separately. In any event, the idealizing character of this section is clear. V 79 presents a more sordid, hence a more realistic, picture. Contrast Schürer 2.249 n. 32.

[27] Another *topos*: cf. AJ 6.295 and 12.291.
[28] The proportion is closer to one-third/two-thirds. Josephus recruits over 100,000 men (576) of whom 60,000 (or 60,950 if we include the cavalry and bodyguard) are enrolled in the active infantry (583).
[29] On the prominence of εὔνοια in this section, see p. 70 above.

general. Josephus no longer pretends that he commands a large
and well trained army. He emphasizes instead two aspects of his
own character: *humanitas* and *ingenium*. He restrains his soldiers
and the whole body of Galileans from beginning a civil war against
John. He would rather not kill his opponents (620-623), not even a
conspirator (642). He returns booty to the lawful owners (646).[30]
Josephus is very popular because he courts the goodwill (εὔνοια)
of the Galileans (569, 628, 646). His enemies are motivated by
jealousy (φθόνος, 614, 620, 627). The *demos* of Jerusalem knows
that John's charges are false (627). The loss of four cities is a
testimony not to Josephus' unpopularity but to the delegation's
secrecy (629). We also see Josephus' skill at escaping from dangerous
situations. Onasander would say that Josephus is alert (νοερός)
and prompt (ἕτοιμος).[31] He eludes the wrath of the Taricheaens
by a strategem (στρατήγημα), the adoption of a contrite pose which
provokes the sympathy of the crowd and allows him to deliver a
speech precisely calculated to enable him to escape (601-604).
The vestiges of the disorder are removed by a second trick (610-613).
Josephus boasts that he captured an entire city with but "empty
ships and seven bodyguards" (645).[32] The two themes, humanity
and ingenuity, are united in 630 where Josephus proudly proclaims
that he won back four recalcitrant cities without recourse to arms
and captured the delegates from Jerusalem by his schemes
(στρατηγήμασιν).[33]

The final section of Josephus' account of his own actions is the
extensive narrative of BJ 3. Both Vespasian and the Jews recognize
his greatness (see above). Here we see *virtus bellandi* (151, 205-206,
226-228, 234, 258). Josephus describes with particular pride the

---

[30] This is probably the point of 597 (Josephus intends to return the
Dabaritta booty) but it is possible that Josephus is trying to demonstrate
his concern for Agrippa. See p. 228 below.

[31] Cicero probably means this by *ingenium* although he may mean no
more than "natural ability."

[32] Here V 174 emphasizes not Josephus' skill but his concern for human
life (χωρὶς φόνων). Cf. V 103 (χωρὶς φόνων)//BJ 623 (συνέσει).

[33] BJ 634 refers to Josephus' observance of the Sabbath, but since BJ
has little interest in showing that Josephus was religious, the purpose of
634 is probably to explain the absence of Josephus' army. It had been sent
to collect grain (does Josephus still pretend that he commanded 60,000
men?) and Josephus could not attack on the morrow because it was the
Sabbath. He therefore had to settle for empty ships and seven bodyguards.
Cf. BJ 3.129 which explains why Josephus had to face Vespasian with meager
forces (the entire army had run away).

six tricks he employed while defending Jotapata against the Romans. He speaks as if he invented these techniques although at least four can be illustrated from independent sources.[34] Whether Josephus actually used these tricks or not, is impossible to determine,[35] but he considered it worthwhile to recount them all in BJ because they prove him a great general endowed with *ingenium*. Here are the tricks:

1. Josephus raises the height of the walls to counter the Roman earthworks. He protects the workmen by an awning of fresh oxhide which catches the Roman projectiles and extinguishes the fire brands (BJ 3.171-174). Everyone, especially Vespasian, marveled at his cunning (στρατηγήματα, 3.175-176). Perhaps they marveled, but they should have known that all this is standard procedure in siege warfare. A writer of the Hadrianic period, who apparently does not know Josephus, mentions this use of raw hide as a routine matter.[36] The same techniques were employed five hundred years earlier in the defense of Plataea in the Peloponnesian War, and were then made famous by Thucydides (2.75). Against the Spartan earthworks the townsmen raised the height of their wall while working under a covering of skins to protect them from missiles and fire brands.

2. The Romans know that the Jews are short of water and therefore decide to refrain from storming the fortress while famine and thirst waste the defenders. When, in response to this plan, Josephus hangs out garments dripping with water, the Romans think that the Jews have plenty of water and prepare to attack (3.186-189). This too is an old trick. Herodotus ascribes a similar strategem to Thrasybulus of Miletus (1.21.1-22.3). Reinach appositely cites

---

[34] Detailed discussion follows in the text. Thackeray, following Reinach, adduces Vegetius for parallels to BJ 3.173 and 222-225 but Vegetius may very well be dependent on BJ. See Schreckenberg, *Tradition* 89. Material from BJ entered the Byzantine poliorketic tradition too; see Schreckenberg 123-124.

[35] Since Josephus modeled the earlier part of his account on the textbook description of the ideal general, it is not unreasonable to suppose that these tricks are derived from a poliorketic manual, not historical reality. I see no secure way to separate fact from fiction here. See N. Bentwich, *Josephus* (Philadelphia 1940) 53. G. Misch, *A History of Autobiography in Antiquity* (London 1950) 1.317-318, remarks that BJ 3.129-288 "has the atmosphere of a historical romance written round a hero."

[36] Apollodorus p. 173 line 13-174,7 ed. Wescher, as edited by R. Schneider, "Griechische Poliorketiker I," *Abhandlungen der königlichen Gesellschaft der Wissenschaften zu Göttingen, philologisch-historische Klasse* 10 (1908).

Florus 1.7.15 who draws from Livy 5.48.4 (Manlius hurls loaves of bread from the walls so that the besiegers will not suspect a shortage of food). Other examples are adduced by Frontinus *Strategemata* 3.15.[37]

3. Josephus obtains supplies through unwatched gullies by covering the couriers with fleece so that they will be mistaken for dogs (3.190-192).[38]

4. To blunt the effect of the battering rams, Josephus lowers sacks filled with chaff (σάκκους ἀχύρων πληρώσαντας). The Romans retaliate by cutting the ropes which hold the sacks (3.222-225). Josephus boasts of his inventiveness (σοφίζεται, 222) but this technique is known already to Aeneas Tacticus 32.3 (σάκκους ἀχύρων πληροῦντα) and others.[39]

5. Josephus pours boiling oil on the Romans when they invade the fortress through the broken portions of the wall. The Romans suffer terribly (3.271-275). Josephus again boasts of this strategem (271) but it is well documented from many periods of siege warfare.[40]

6. After recovering from the effects of the boiling oil the Romans press their attack. The Jews pour boiled fenugreek on the gangplanks which render them dangerously slippery. When the Romans stumble the Jews have an easy shot and the attack is foiled (3.277-279). This use of fenugreek is unattested elsewhere and may be Josephus' invention.[41]

Like other ideal Roman generals Josephus enjoys *felicitas*.[42]

---

[37] For a medieval parallel, see G. Pitré, *Biblioteca delle Tradizioni Popolari Siciliane XXII: Studi di Leggende Popolari in Sicilia* (Torino 1904) 175-190. Pitré refers to his *Stratagemmi leggendarii di città assediate* (Palermo 1904) which I have not been able to obtain.

[38] I have been unable to locate a parallel. A "wolf in sheep's clothing" is, of course, a familiar motif of fable and folklore (e.g. *Aesopica* nr. 451 ed. Perry). Jacob covered his arms with goat skin in order to deceive Isaac (*Genesis* 27.16). Odysseus deceived Polyphemus by clinging to the underside of a sheep. But these instances do not seem to be relevant.

[39] The anonymous *De Obsidione Toleranda* 147 (ed. H. van den Berg [Leiden 1947]) quotes this passage from BJ and adds ἀλλὰ καὶ ἕτεροι τῶν παλαιῶν.

[40] See Michel-Bauernfeind's note 67 to BJ 3.271 (but Pliny NH 2.108 is irrelevant and Vegetius 4.8 may depend on BJ). See too Apollodorus p. 146,6 and 183,8-10.

[41] Thus Justus Lipsius, "Poliorceticōn sive de Machinis Libri Quinque," *Opera Omnia* III (Vesalia 1675) 624 = book 5 dialogue 3 (first published in 1599) and Schneider, "Griechische Poliorketiker II," *Abhandlungen ... Göttingen* 11 (1908) 25 note.

[42] On Roman *felicitas* see S. Weinstock, *JRS* 45 (1955) 187.

When the Romans capture Jotapata, Josephus receives aid from some supernatural force (δαιμονίῳ τινὶ συνεργίᾳ χρησάμενος, 3.341) and escapes. In the cave he is nearly killed or forced to commit suicide but, having faith in God's protection (πιστεύων τῷ κηδεμόνι θεῷ, 3.387), he emerges unscathed. Should he speak of chance or of divine providence (εἴτε ὑπὸ τύχης χρὴ λέγειν εἴτε ὑπὸ θεοῦ προνοίας, 3.391)? His prophetic visions, in which God forecast the approaching disasters (3.351), his priesthood (3.352), his prediction to Vespasian (3.399-402), his prophecy that the siege of Jotapata would last forty-seven days (3.405-407), all testify to his special relationship with the divine. Josephus thus possesses almost all the characteristics demanded by Cicero.[43]

Josephus' description of his own actions does not fit one of the main motives of BJ as a whole. It is well known that BJ apologizes to the Romans for the Jews. Not all Jews revolted, only small bands of mad fanatics. These were in no way representative of the Jewish people or bearers of Jewish tradition.[44] Those of them who finally maintained the revolt in Jerusalem and made it necessary for Titus (regretfully) to destroy the city, were a gang formed mainly of refugees who entered Jerusalem from the countryside and Galilee, established a tyranny, and forced the defenseless populace to fight against the Romans. Their motive was the selfish satisfaction of their lust for power, their deeds were execrable and beyond condemnation. They and not the Romans were responsible for the destruction of the temple (thus Josephus apologizes to the Jews for the Romans). Josephus is especially eager to exculpate the members of his own class, the priestly aristocracy and rich nobility. Even in the early stages of the war they opposed the revolutionaries.[45]

---

[43] The only one omitted is the quality called εὐπροσήγορος by Onasander (Cicero says *faciles aditus ad eum privatorum*). Josephus is usually aloof and alone—a testimony, no doubt, to his own vanity and conceit (cf. Nehemiah). Josephus does not need to claim to be fine speaker; he has many grand orations in BJ. Gelzer 325 and Hengel 10 emphasize that BJ exaggerates Josephus' significance in order to make him heroic. The great general motif is sufficient to explain BJ's concern for demonstrating Josephus' mildness and probity, a fact unknown to Drexler 297 and 305, and Schalit, *Klio* 26 (1933) 75-76 n. 2.

[44] The revolutionaries have no connection with any of the "official" representatives of Judaism: Agrippa, the high priests, or the three philosophies. See chapter five below, section C 2 d.

[45] BJ 2.301-304 (the ἀρχιερεῖς and δυνατοί plead with Florus to preserve

But BJ also shows that these reconstructions are false. The masses often fight with gusto and abandon. Many members of the upper classes—including Josephus himself—participate in the war, at least until the winter of 67-68.[46] Josephus realized that he had to separate himself from the process which led to the destruction of the temple and therefore claimed that he was an enemy, not an associate, of John of Gischala, his fellow general in Galilee and one of the most pernicious figures of the entire war. Josephus' conduct, unlike that of almost every other revolutionary leader, was above reproach. He was popular, respected, just, estimable, widely admired, and divinely guided. He was not a tyrant but an ideal general. He was loyal to his cause (thus demonstrating the quality of *fides*) although he knew that with the arrival of the Romans it was doomed to failure (3.130 and 136). His surrender was not betrayal—he would rather die than desert his people (3.137). He, a latter day Jeremiah (5.391-393), had divine authorization to cease the struggle. Inspired by his dreams he knew that he had to cross over to the Romans; Tyche herself already had done so.[47] Josephus went not as a traitor but as God's prophet (3.351-354).

Josephus does not justify his surrender by appealing to the heinous character of the revolt. The tyranny theme is adumbrated in BJ 2.73 (//AJ 17.293) where, in 4 BCE, the Jerusalemites disclaim any responsibility for an insurrection and blame a mob which entered the city and attacked the city populace as well as the Romans. BJ 2 emphasizes that the revolutionaries formed small bands (στῖφοι) separate from, and often opposed by, the *demos* (254-257, 258-263, 264-265). By the arrival of Albinus tyranny was

---

peace), 316 (the δυνατοί and ἀρχιερεῖς persuade the mob to restrain itself), 321-324 (ditto), 332 (the ἀρχιερεῖς and βουλή undertake to maintain calm in the city), 338 (the ἀρχιερεῖς, δυνατοί, and βουλή desire peace), 405 (the ἄρχοντες and βουλευταί collect the back taxes for the Romans), 411-417 (the δυνατοί, ἀρχιερεῖς, and τῶν Φαρισαίων γνώριμοι ask the people to reinstate the sacrifices for Caesar), 418-419 (the δυνατοί ask Florus for aid), 422-437 (defeat of loyalists by insurgents), 556 (many ἐπιφανεῖς flee to the Romans). On the meaning of βουλή and δυνατοί see V. Tcherikover, *IEJ* 14 (1964) 61-78. The apologetics for Agrippa II (343-407, 483, 523-526) and his circle (556) are part of this theme.

[46] See Drexler, esp. 277-281 and 288-289 and our discussion in chapter six below.

[47] On Josephan *Tyche* see Lindner *passim*. Here, of course, Josephus has his closest parallel to Polybius who also explained that Tyche gave Rome world dominion. See Lind, *TAPA* 103 (1972) 253-255.

everywhere (275-276). When the hostilities actually began, the apology becomes more frequent. Menahem was an "insufferable tyrant" (442; cf. 448). The *demos* was helpless in the hands of the revolutionaries (525-526 and 529). Temple and city were polluted (424 and 455), God abandoned his sanctuary (539), the ancestral religion was polluted by illegitimate innovations (414; cf. 118). The priests and aristocrats opposed the war (see note 45). The last occurrence of this motif in BJ 2 is 562a, which says that, immediately after the defeat of Cestius, the revolutionaries won over the peace party, some by force, some by persuasion (τοὺς μὲν βίᾳ τῶν ἔτι ῥωμαϊζόντων τοὺς δὲ πειθοῖ προσήγοντο). But with 562b the situation changes. In an orderly process, generals were chosen, only one of whom (Eleazar ben Ananias) had been involved in the previous action.[48] Josephus points out that Eleazar ben Simon, who, he says, had been prominent in the war against Cestius (although not previously mentioned) and who would later lead the Zealots, received no recognition from the new regime (564-565). From this point until the fall of Jotapata we hear nothing of tyranny, pollution, and coercion. In Galilee Josephus was valiant and popular, an ideal figure (see above). Only after Josephus was in the hands of the Romans does BJ claim that the inhabitants of the Galilean cities were basically pro-Roman but were forced by John and his ilk to participate in the war.[49] Jerusalem was led by Ananus and some aristocrats (δυνατοί) who were anti-Roman (648) but would oppose the fanaticism of the Zealots (651).[50] Ananus was another ideal figure who later receives an encomium worthy of Pericles, as Thackeray remarks (BJ 4.319-322). Ananus prevented Simon bar Giora from tyrannizing over Akrabatene (2.652-653). The Jewish attack on Ascalon (3.9-28) was obviously popular and no compulsion is mentioned. It is significant that even the leaders of

---

[48] Niger the Peraean is not chosen now. His earlier authority is confirmed but subordinated to two of the new generals.

[49] 3.448 and 453-455 (Tiberias), 492-493 and 532 (Taricheae), 4.84, 112-114 (Gischala). Since Josephus is an ideal general, his attacks against the pro-Roman inhabitants of Tiberias and Sepphoris (BJ 2.632-646) do not prove him a tyrant or the Tiberians pro-Roman. A general was expected to suppress dissension in the ranks and Josephus pretends that he regained the loyalty of the city. Sepphoris was a special case. John accuses Josephus of threatening to return to Jerusalem as a tyrant (2.626), but BJ assumes that we know that the charge is false.

[50] There was still a peace party in the city but no compulsion is mentioned (649-650).

Jerusalem who attempted to depose Josephus are not characterized as tyrants although they were opposed by the *demos* (2.627 and 631). The tyranny theme of the first part of BJ 2 returns again at the end of BJ 3 (on the cities of Galilee—see note 49) and especially in BJ 4 which graphically describes the overthrow of the government of Ananus by John and the Zealots.

Thus to explain his own participation in the war, Josephus has created a period of moderation and legitimacy sandwiched between periods of terror and anarchy. It is this apology which has caused so much difficulty for modern historians. Why after the defeat of Cestius, when the revolutionaries were strongest, were generals selected who apparently had not been involved in earlier revolutionary activity? It seems clear that Josephus has intentionally obscured the early course of the rebellion. Ananus et al. must have been prominent in the revolutionary movement even before the defeat of Cestius.[51] But by dividing the early history of the war into two parts, by severing almost all links between the two parts— and we remind the reader that the device used for separation, the list of generals, may be an invention of Josephan literary technique —, by characterizing the first period as tyrannical and the second as legitimate, Josephus was able simultaneously to condemn the fomentors of war and to justify his own involvement. When he needed an excuse for surrender, he invented divine authorization.

BJ explains why Josephus *stopped* fighting the Romans. A crucial issue it never faces is why Josephus *began* fighting the Romans. Why was he chosen as general? Why was he, a priestly aristocrat, a revolutionary? V attempts to provide the answer.

---

[51] See the discussion in chapter six below, note 16. In particular see Drexler's article but even he has not sensed the fundamental tension in BJ 2-3, the tension between Josephus' own involvement in the war and his condemnation of the revolutionaries.

CHAPTER FIVE

VITA: AIMS AND METHODS

A. *V as an Autobiography*

Although the fifth century BCE saw the awakening of auto-biography in both Greece (Ion of Chios, FGrH 392) and Israel (Nehemiah and, perhaps, Ezra),[1] a search for V's antecedents in the Biblical tradition will be in vain because there is no sure sign that the Biblical form exerted any influence on later Jewish litera-ture.[2] We must instead turn to Greco-Roman tradition but here too difficulties obtrude. Autobiography never was recognized as an in-dependent, fixed genre of prose literature; even biography was variously defined.[3] Thus we cannot write an exact history of ancient autobiography nor can we find a precise place for V in the develop-ment of this amorphous genre. The task is further complicated by the loss of so much material. V is the only pre-Christian autobio-graphy extant. Its nearest rival, the autobiography of Nicolaus of

---

[1] Momigliano, *Development* 36, and M. Smith, *Palestinian Parties and Politics* (N.Y. 1971) 255 n. 1.

[2] 1 *Macc.* 16.23-24 (= FGrH 736) refers to the court journal—not auto-biography—of John Hyrcanus. In any event the reference is probably an invention in the author's archaistic style; see the commentary of F. M. Abel (Paris 1949) ad loc. Herod's *Hypomnemata* (FGrH 236 from AJ 15.164-174) must have been in Greek form. Many apocryphal works present Biblical worthies speaking in the first person but I do not know whether their form is due to the Biblical tradition. On the autobiography of Nehemiah see U. Kellermann, *Nehemia: Quellen, Ueberlieferung und Geschichte* (Berlin 1967) 4-8 and 74-88. If Kellermann's theory (135-145) is correct that AJ 11.159-183 is based on the Nehemiah autobiography, we could conjecture that V's form shows the influence of both the Biblical and the Greek tradi-tion. But the theory is uncertain and V's links to Greco-Roman autobio-graphy are so strong that appeal to the Biblical form is unnecessary.

[3] The word *biographia* does not appear until the end of the fifth century CE, *autobiography* not until the end of the eighteenth. See Momigliano 12 and 14. The word *bios* designates not genre but content: deeds, *acta*. The distinction between a biography and an encomium was never very clear nor was the relationship of biography to autobiography. These problems, and the general history of ancient biography, have been treated often and at length. Momigliano 107-116 provides a recent bibliography (109-110 on Greek autobiography). On the amorphous nature of autobiography, see e.g. O. Gigon and V. Pöschl, "Autobiographie," *Lexicon der alten Welt* (Zurich 1965) 416. On biography and encomium see W. Steidle, *MH* 22 (1965) 96 n. 82.

Damascus, is extant in epitomized and excerpted form. The memoirs of Sulla and Augustus must be reconstructed from later sources.[4] Because of this lack we must examine biographies as well as auto-biographies in our analysis of V's structure and content.

Jacoby (FGrH 90) has arranged the excerpts of Nicolaus' autobiography in the following order:

    I. Pedigree (F 131)
    II. Education (F 132)
    III. Activities (F 133-136)
    IV. Character and Virtues (F 137-139)

III is a straight chronological narrative, IV is thematic. This structure was employed in many biographies since IV enabled the author to focus clearly on the character (ἦθος) of the subject, the goal of biographical study. The model was provided by Xeno-phon's *Agesilaus* which presented the king's pedigree (1.2-5), a chronological survey of his actions (1.6-2.31), and a thematic study of his virtues (3.1—end).[5] The most famous exponent of this biographical form is Suetonius. An alternate, equally popular, arrangement was the combination of III and IV into a single chronological description, as in the autobiographies of Sulla [6] and Augustus (followed by Nicolaus in his biography),[7] the *Evagoras* of Isocrates and the biographies of Plutarch.

It is the second arrangement which is found in V: [8]

    I. Pedigree (1-7)
    II. Education (8-12)

---

[4] The Greek autobiographies are collected in FGrH 227-238. On the autobiography of Nicolaus (FGrH 90 F 131-139) see, aside from Jacoby's commentary, the fine analysis of Misch 1.307-315 and the more recent work of Wacholder, *Nicolaus* 37-51. An enumeration of the Roman *commentarii* is in Misch 208-209 (who should have mentioned the military journals of Domitius Corbulo and Suetonius Paulinus). On Sulla's autobiography see F. Leo, *Hermes* 49 (1914) 164-166 = *Ausgewählte Kleine Schriften*, ed. E. Fraenkel (Rome 1960) 1.252-254, and I. Calabi, *Atti della Accademia Nazionale dei Lincei: Memorie* ser. 8, 3 (1951) 245-302. The classic discussion of Augustus' autobiography is by F. Blumenthal, *WS* 35 (1913) 113-130, 267-288; *WS* 36 (1914) 84-103. See too H. Malcovati, *Imperatoris Caesaris Augusti Operum Fragmenta*³ (Paravia s.a. [1947 or 1948]) xlii-xlvi and 84-97.

[5] Omitted here, education became an integral part of political biography only under the influence of Xenophon's *Cyropaedia*.

[6] Leo, *Hermes* 49 (1914) 166 = *Ausgewählte Kleine Schriften* 254.

[7] See Jacoby's diagram, FGrH 2 C p. 262.

[8] The only treatment of this question is Hornbostel 6-12, but my analysis differs somewhat from his.

III. Activities (13-429)
   A. Josephus' early actions (13-27)
   B. Josephus in Galilee (28-413)
   C. Josephus in Roman control (414-429)
IV. Epilogue (430)

Sections I, II, and IV are well suited for an autobiography (see below) but section III causes problems. Its extraordinary length and detail, its near exclusive focus (III B) on a single brief period of the author's life (six months), its inclusion of material tangential to Josephus' affairs,[9] its abandonment of the story before completion (412)—all these seem hardly appropriate to an autobiography. Perhaps these points can be explained by V's origin (at least in section III B) as a *hypomnema* and by V's purpose, autobiographic apology rather than apologetic autobiography. Nevertheless, a contemporary work bears a striking formal similarity to V.[10] Tacitus' *Agricola*, written in 97/8 (V was written somewhere between 93 and 100/1), has the following structure: [11]

   Prologue (1-3)
   I. Pedigree (4.1)
   II. Education (4.2-3)
   III. Career (5-42)
      A. Early career (5-9)
      B. Agricola in Britain (10-40)
      C. Agricola in Rome (41-42)
   IV. Death (43)
   V. Age and Appearance (44.1-2)
   VI. Epilogue (44.3-46)

Here too the disposition of the whole is unremarkable but section III B, long and detailed, concerned with only a brief period of Agricola's life (seven years), and including extraneous material,[12]

---

[9] For example, V 24-27, 32-42, and 43-45, which are not directly relevant but supply helpful background information. Laqueur 37-42 presents his usual array of brilliant conjectures and regards V 32-62 as an interpolation (i.e. by the *Vita* of 100 CE into the *Vita* of 67 CE). V 32-62 may be a secondary addition but Laqueur's arguments are inconclusive; see Helm, *PhW* 41 (1921) 486-487.

[10] Noted by Hornbostel 7 n. 3 who did not elaborate.

[11] Leo, *Biographie* 230.

[12] Notably c. 28 on the Usipi. Chapters 10-12, the ethnography of Britain, and 13-17, the previous history of Roman Britain, are not directly relevant

seems out of place. Its ornate speeches and battle scenes are inappropriate in biography. Some suggest that III B was written by Tacitus as a preliminary draft (*hypomnema*, cf. V) for his *Histories*.[13] Others suggest that the thematic unity of the *Agricola* might justify the procedure of a dutiful son-in-law.[14] But no matter which explanation we accept, the analogy of the *Agricola* shows that Josephus was not the only author in Rome at the end of the first century who was prepared to adapt biographical form to literary or apologetic ends.[15]

The style and content of V are in the Greco-Roman, especially Roman tradition. Since V was originally not a separate work but an appendix to AJ, it probably did not have an independent title.[16] Josephus did, however, twice summarize V's contents: "my pedigree and the deeds (πράξεις) of my life" (AJ 20.266) and "the deeds (πεπραγμένα) of my whole life" (V 430). The emphasis on events or actions (πράξεις) was normal in autobiographies [17] but since Josephus knew that some memoirs (notably the autobiography of Nicolaus of Damascus) and most biographies were really interested in the moral character of their subject, he added "let others judge my character (τὸ ἦθος) from my actions however they wish"

---

to the life of Agricola but they provide helpful background information. Cf. n. 9 above on V.

[13] The suggestion is by G. Andresen. Cf. Leo, *Biographie* 232, "Tacitus [hat] historische Elemente in die Biographie hineingearbeitet."

[14] W. Steidle, *MH* 22 (1965) 96-104 (on the *Agricola*), esp. 96-102, accepted with inadequate acknowledgement by R. M. Ogilvie and I. A. Richmond, *Cornelii Taciti De Vita Agricolae* (Oxford 1967) 11-20, esp. 15, and 245. R. Syme, *Tacitus* (Oxford 1958) 1.122-125, is non-committal on this point. Cf. also Nicolaus' biography of Augustus where the long excursus on the assassination of Caesar (FGrH 90 F 130 c. 58-106) is an integral part of the narrative. This approach will not work for Josephus' autobiography because it lacks any thematic unity.

[15] The larger problem of the relationship between Josephus and Tacitus is not our concern but it is improbable that V has influenced the *Agricola* or vice versa. Laqueur's comparison (34-35) of V 423 and 428/9 to Tacitus *Historiae* 1.1 (*dignitatem nostram a Vespasiano inchoatam, a Tito auctam, a Domitiano longius provectam non abnuerim*) is not significant because the slight resemblance in style is the inevitable result of an insignificant resemblance in content.

[16] The titles provided by our manuscripts were composed when V became independent of AJ. See Niese's apparatus at the beginning and end of V.

[17] Weber 92 n. 1. Weber invokes the Roman *acta* although he knows that V, like almost all ancient autobiographies, would have been considered a *hypomnema* or *commentarius*.

(V 430).[18] Only once in V (80-83) did Josephus interrupt the narrative to analyze and praise his own character (see below). Otherwise, like most autobiographers, he retold his actions, apologetically of course, but did not draw attention to his own character.

Other links of V to ancient autobiography are:

1. The narrative is in the first person. Histories (like BJ) regularly employed the third person when describing the actions of the author (e.g. Thucydides, Xenophon, Polybius (see 36.12), Caesar) while Roman autobiographies usually employed the first person.[19]

2. Unlike a history, V contains no large speeches (contrast BJ 3.361-382).[20] Its inclusion of letters (V 217-218, 226-227, 229, 235) was a normal biographical feature.[21]

3. Personal memoirs were usually nothing more than political apology, at least after Demetrius of Phalerum (FGrH 228).[22] Here V has ample precedent.

4. Section II (V 8-12), on the author's youth, is filled with biographical commonplaces. Josephus was a precocious lad but so were Homer, Aeschines, Apollonius of Rhodes, Nicolaus of Damascus, Ovid, Moses, Jesus, Apollonius of Tyana, Alexander the Great, and Augustus.[23] Great men often begin as *Wunderkinder*

---

[18] Hornbostel 8 n. 1 remarks that this formula sounds like an epilogue from classic Attic oratory. Josephus even addresses Justus as if the Tiberian were the plaintiff in a courtroom (V 340). The similarity is not accidental since apologetic oratory was one of the sources of Greek autobiography; see Jacoby, FGrH 2 B p. 640. In imitation of the Suetonian form (see above), the statement on *ethos* is placed after the chronological survey.

[19] The practice of Greek autobiographies is unknown; Ptolemy VIII Euergetes II used the first person (see Jacoby on FGrH 234 T). Nicolaus wrote in the third person, Roman autobiography normally in the first (Jacoby in FGrH 2 C p. 288 lines 39ff, although the evidence is unsatisfactory). The classic discussion is E. Norden, *Agnostos Theos*[2] (Leipzig 1923, repr. 1956) 313-326.

[20] Hornbostel 12.

[21] Cf. Nepos, Suetonius, Diogenes Laertius, Philostratus, Historia Augusta, the lives of the ten orators, etc. The letters cited in V 365 and V 366 are not part of the main narrative but stand in the digression against Justus.

[22] On the apologetic tone see esp. T 3b and F 28. Aratus' apology (231 T 5 and F 4c) is similar to V's claim of pretense and duplicity but the resemblance is fortuitous.

[23] Herodotean *Vita Homeri* 5; Plutarchean *Vita Aeschinis* 840a (= A. Westermann, *Biographi* [Braunschweig 1845, repr. Amsterdam 1964] 263); *Vita alpha Apollonii* (Westermann 50); Nicolaus, FGrH 90 F 132 c. 1 with which Misch 313 well compares Ovid *Tristia* 4.10.57; Philo *Vita Mosis* 1.20-24 and Josephus, AJ 2.230; Luke 2.46-47; Philostratus *Vita Apol.* 1.7; Plut. *Alex.* 5 p. 666e; Nicolaus, FGrH 90 F 127 c. 4 (cf. Suetonius *Aug.* 8,

but V 8-9 seems more than slightly exaggerated. Josephus now turns to his education (V 10-12), an important feature in all Hellenistic biographies.[24] At age sixteen he decided to try out the three Jewish philosophies, went through the training for all three, then became a devotee (ζηλωτής) of the recluse Bannous in the desert,[25] and after three years returned to Jerusalem and chose Pharisaism (V 10-12). It is well known that Josephus Hellenizes his description of the Jewish sects by converting them into Greek philosophical schools, whose main disputes center on the questions of fate, free will, and immortality of the soul. The Pharisees are close to the Stoics (V 12), the Essenes to the Pythagoreans (AJ 15.371), the Sadducees to the Epicureans.[26] V 10-12 carries the analogy even further. A young aristocrat attends the three academies and chooses a life philosophy. This is normal Hellenistic procedure and seems to bear little relevance to Jewish realia.[27] Thus Nicolaus, after a rigorous propaedeutic, studied all branches of philosophy (φιλοσοφία πάση) and then chose to follow (ζηλωτὴς γενόμενος) Aristotle (FGrH 90 F 132 line 15). We find a similar

---

both from Augustus' autobiography; see Blumenthal *WS* 35 [1913] 123). Jesus' early brilliance is emphasized even more in the NT apocrypha. This motif often appears in conjunction with miraculous births, marvelous infancies, etc., which are not our concern. See L. Radermacher, *RhM* 73 (1920-24) 232-239.

[24] See note 5 above and the list of titles assembled by Jacoby in the commentary to FGrH 134 (vol. 2 B p. 468).

[25] There is no evidence at all for the common view that Bannous was an Essene. Josephus implicitly denies it when he says that he studied first the *trishaeresion* and afterwards with Bannous. Eisler, 1.xxxvi note 3 and 120 note 1, and others, claim that Βαννοῦς is not a proper noun but a simple noun, a Greek transliteration of the Aramaic deformation of the Greek βαλανεύς which they translate "Baptizer" and try to connect with the mysterious *Banna'im* mentioned in Rabbinic literature. This is a needless construct, since Βαννοῦς seems to be the equivalent of Βανναῖος, a name, etymology irrelevant, well attested in the Greco-Roman East. See V. Tcherikover, *Corpus Papyrorum Judaicarum* I (Harvard 1957) 132 n. 1. The Rabbinic *Banna'im* are not "Baptizers"; see J. Heller, "Banna'im," *Encyclopaedia Judaica* 3 (1929) 1021-22 and H. Albeck's supplementary note to M. Miqvaot 9.6 in his edition of the Mishnah. Instead of *Bannous*, Georgius Monachus Hamartolus (I p. 331 ed. de Boor), copied, as usual, by Georgius Cedrenus (*PG* 121.389), writes *Abbas*, perhaps because of assimilation of Josephus' practice to that of Christian ascetics. Medieval Christian tradition regarded Josephus as a Christian cleric, perhaps a hermit; see H. Schreckenberg, *Rezeptionsgeschichtliche und textkritische Untersuchungen zu Flavius Josephus* (Leiden 1977) 46-47.

[26] The last point is never stated explicitly but the intention is clear.

[27] Misch 325, "a Hellenistic rather than a Jewish aspect of education."

educational history for Galen, Justin, and the Philostratean Apollonius.[28] Whether Josephus has modeled V 10-12 on the Hellenistic system or on biographical descriptions of it (e.g. Nicolaus) [29] is uncertain but it is significant that biographies regularly employ ζηλωτής and ζηλοῦν to indicate philosophical, poetical, stylistic, etc. filiation.[30] The impossible chronology in this section may be a sign not of textual corruption but of mendacity: Josephus had three years to study with Bannous because his tour of the academies was imaginary.[31] His claim of adherence to Pharisaism, part of V's religious apologetic, is probably false too (see below section C 2 b).

5. In at least two respects V is similar to the Roman *commentarii*, especially of Sulla and Augustus:

a. Defense of family origins. None of the Greek memoirs shows any interest in the pedigree of the hero; their sole concern is politics. But the Romans regularly parade their ancestors and defend them if necessary: Sulla (frag. 2 Peter = Gellius 1.12.16), Augustus (frag. 1 Peter = frag. III Malcovati = Suet. *Aug.* 2), Nicolaus of Damascus (FGrH 90 F 131), and Hadrian (frag. 1 Peter = SHA *Hadrian*. 1.1). Josephus too boasts of his lineage [32] and defends it against some detractors (V 1-7) who apparently had some basis for their charges.[33] Similarly, Augustus' explanation of

---

[28] Galen *De aff. dign.* 8 (vol. 5 p. 41 line 11ff ed. Kuehn) and *De libris suis* (vol. 19 pp. 12-13 ed. Kuehn); Justin *Dialogus* 2; Philostratus *Vita Apol.* 1.7.

[29] Misch 316 suggests that Josephus appended V to AJ under the influence of Nicolaus of Damascus, but it is unlikely that Nicolaus attached his autobiography to his history; see Jacoby, FGrH 2 C p. 289 and Wacholder, *Nicolaus* 51. See below for other possible examples of Nicolaus' influence on V.

[30] *Vita Arati* p. 54 line 77 Westermann; Marcellinus *Vita Thucydidis* 35-37; Plutarchean *Vita Demosthenis* 844b (p. 281 line 6 Westermann); *Vita beta Platonis* p. 391 line 105 Westermann. Other passages in Hengel, *Zeloten* 62-63 and *Josephus-Studien: Untersuchungen ... O. Michel ... gewidmet* (Göttingen 1974) 185-186 with n. 36. This usage was, of course, not restricted to biography.

[31] Thus Rasp, *ZNW* 23 (1924) 35; Shutt 2 n. 3, anticipated by Whiston ad loc., proposes παρ' αὐτοῖς for παρ' αὐτῷ (V 12).

[32] Josephus boasts of his ancestry from both his mother (V 2) and father (V 7), as did Nicolaus (FGrH 90 F 131; both fathers are honored by the populace and both have a reputation for δικαιοσύνη) and Augustus (Jacoby on FGrH 90 F 126 c. 3).

[33] The genealogy has two problems: 1. The chronology is impossible; 2. how does the list document Josephus' ancestry on his mother's side? If the list is genuine, either it is lacunose or Josephus has misunderstood what he excerpted from his documentary source. Radin suggests that

his divorce from Scribonia (*pertaesus morum perversitatem eius*, frag. 12 Peter = frag. XIV Malcovati = Suet. *Aug.* 62.2) may have been imitated by V 426 (μὴ ἀρεσκόμενος αὐτῆς τοῖς ἤθεσιν).[34]

b. Proclamation of personal virtues. Greek autobiographies show little interest in the *mores* of the hero but the Romans usually refer to their personal conduct. Nicolaus dedicated an entire section to the demonstration of his virtues (see above). Throughout V, Josephus defends his behavior but only once does he explicitly proclaim his moral greatness. That passage (V 80-83) bears a resemblance to an apology in Augustus' autobiography (from Nicolaus FGrH 90 F 129 c. 36): [35]

μητήρ means "female ancestress" but Hebrew and Aramaic usage will not justify such a meaning here since analogous phrases elsewhere show that Josephus intends "mother" (BJ 1.553 and 566//AJ 17.9; BJ 1.557//AJ 17.14; AJ 8.76; we must await the concordance for completeness) and since he seems to be contrasting his mother (V 2) to his father (V 7). Perhaps the reference to Josephus' mother in V 2 is parenthetical and the genealogy applies only to the father. On both of these problems see Schürer 77 n. 4 = Schürer-Vermes 46 n. 3; G. Hölscher *PW* 9,2 (1916) 1935; M. Radin, *CP* 24 (1929) 193-196. The public registers to which Josephus refers (V 6; cf. CA 1.30-31) were stored in the temple (S. Lieberman, *Hellenism in Jewish Palestine* [N.Y. 1950, repr. 1962] 172 and K. H. Rengstorf, *Ḥirbet Qumrân und die Bibliothek vom Toten Meer* [Stuttgart 1960] 67 n. 156) and presumably were destroyed in 70. Did Josephus record the data before the war? According to Africanus, Herod had destroyed all these records (Eusebius *HE* 1.7.13). An exact parallel to this problem is raised by the collection of documents in AJ 14. Josephus claims (AJ 14.188-189, 265-267) that he provides exact transcriptions of documents which were still available for inspection on the capital. But his copies are far from exact and it is unlikely that public copies were still extant. See H. R. Moehring, *Christianity, Judaism and other Greco-Roman Cults: Studies for Morton Smith III: Judaism before 70*, ed. J. Neusner (Leiden 1975) 124-158. In any event, Josephus' Hasmonean ties are probably bogus. When he wrote BJ he claimed only priesthood (BJ 1.3; in BJ 3.352 and CA 1.54 he would have had no need to mention his alleged royal blood), but in AJ 16.187 and V we suddenly discover his Hasmonean forebears. The pro-Hasmonean and anti-Herodian traits of AJ have already been noticed by Laqueur; see chapter two above, notes 102, 110, and 112.

[34] Misch 326 notes the similarity and remarks that it is "no mere chance." Is this a common formula? It does not appear in *Digesta* 24.2 or *Codex Justinianus* 5.17 and 24 (discussions of the grounds for divorce). I do not know whether Josephus consulted the autobiography of Augustus. He probably knew it only through Nicolaus' biography which was based on the memoirs (Blumenthal, *WS* 35 [1913] 115 and Jacoby, FGrH 2 C p. 264) although our excerpts omit Augustus' divorce. On the emperor's apology for his divorce see Blumenthal, *WS* 35 (1913) 285. Josephus may be justifying his divorce on Halachic grounds; cf. *Deuteronomy* 24.1 (LXX ὅτι εὗρεν ἐν αὐτῇ ἄσχημον πρᾶγμα) and M. Gittin 9.10.

[35] Cf. too F 127 c. 12. On the charges to which Augustus was responding

V 80

περὶ τριακοστὸν γοῦν ἔτος ὑπάρχων ἐν ᾧ χρόνῳ, κἂν ἀπέχηταί τις τῶν παρανόμων ἐπιθυμιῶν, δύσκολον τὰς ἐκ τοῦ φθόνου διαβολὰς φεύγειν, ἄλλως τε καὶ ἐπ' ἐξουσίας ὄντα μεγάλης, γυναῖκα μὲν πᾶσαν ἀνύβριστον ἐφύλαξα . . .

Being about thirty years of age, an age when, even if one refrains from illegal passions, it is difficult to avoid slanders caused by jealousy, especially for a man of great authority, nevertheless, I protected every woman from molestation.

Augustus

ὅτι ἔνηφε καὶ ἐγκρατῶς διῆγεν ὁ νέος Καῖσαρ . . . ἐπ' ἐνιαυτὸν γὰρ ὅλον ἐν τοιᾷδε ἡλικίᾳ, ἐν ᾗ μάλιστα σφριγῶσιν οἱ νέοι

καὶ τούτων δ' ἔτι μᾶλλον οἱ εὐτυχεῖς, ἀφροδισίων ἀπείχετο . . .

The young Caesar behaved with sobriety and self control. For a whole year at such an age when young men are rather vigorous,

especially the well-to-do,

he refrained from sexual pleasures.

Cf. too Tacitus *Agricola* 5.1. V 83 ends the passage with the claim that, like all righteous men, Josephus was protected by God and saved from many dangers. This theme, which reappears in V 15, 138, 301, 425, and 208-209 (Josephus' dream),[36] is a standard element in Roman autobiographies which are always filled with dreams, portents, omens, and other signs of divine concern for the subject.[37]

Thus V, although primarily an apology, is also an autobiography in both form and content. The structure of the work is close to the *Agricola* of Tacitus. Many of its themes are derived from the tradition of the Roman *commentarii*, especially the memoirs of Augustus, which Josephus probably knew through the work of Nicolaus.[38]

---

see Blumenthal, *WS* 35 (1913) 123-124. Even if Nicolaus has tampered with the context of this passage (see Jacoby), its ultimate origin probably is the autobiography.

[36] Hornbostel 27 notes that V 402-403 blames not God but a δαίμων for Josephus' fall from his horse. The theme of divine protection is absent from BJ 2 and does not appear until BJ 3.341.

[37] Especially the autobiographies of Sulla (frag. 8 Peter = Plut. *Sulla* 6) and Augustus. See Misch 244-248 and 269-71. Septimius Severus too was convinced by dreams of his great destiny (frag. 1 Peter = Herodian 2.9.3). Are Herod's dream (BJ 1.328//AJ 14.451) and miraculous escapes (BJ 1.331 //AJ 14.455, where he is called θεοφιλής, and BJ 1.340-41//AJ 14.462-63) derived from the royal *hypomnemata* ? The claim of divine protection was not necessarily hybristic; the rhetorically inclined could recommend it as a way to avoid offense when praising one's own deeds. See Plutarch *De Se Ipsum Citra Invidiam Laudando* 11 p. 542e-543a.

[38] See section B for another possible example of the influence of Augustus' autobiography on V.

B. *Literary Technique*

If BJ is Josephus' most polished work, V is his roughest. It is confused and sloppy; its tendentious elements (including the attack against Justus) are inconsistent (see below). At least one pair of statements looks like a factual contradiction (V 177-78 vs. 186). The incorrect cross references (V 66 and 89) have been discussed briefly in chapter one above.[39] In spite of its wealth of detail V's incoherence is so great that the general impression left with the reader is confusion and obfuscation. V 168 is incomprehensible without BJ 2.638-641 (Niese posits a lacuna) and V's version of the Cleitus story (V 173) is near nonsense (cf. BJ 2.642-44).[40] Important bits of information are presented in a casual, hence startling, manner.[41] The course of Josephus' journeys in Galilee is incomplete.[42] Since BJ's fondness for thematic construction is nearly absent, the affair of the *megistanes* is narrated in two places (V

---

[39] See chapter one note 61. Even a short work like V can err in its references, a sign that not all similar errors should be ascribed to lost sources. The καθὼς ἐν ἄλλοις δεδηλώκαμεν is a separate problem which appears in V too (V 61). See below n. 214.

[40] On removing a hand as punishment cf. V 147 (contrast BJ 2.612 which omits it, perhaps to avoid a doublet with the Cleitus story) and B. Sanhedrin 58b (bottom).

[41] E.g., the Sepphorites gave hostages to Cestius, V 31; the Jews of Caesarea Philippi were restricted to the city by Agrippa, 74 (contrast BJ 2.591 which has simplified matters); Josephus received a share of the booty from the Syrian cities, 81; a robber baron named Jesus was active near Ptolemais with a troop of eight hundred, 105 and cf. 200; some Roman cavalry appeared near Tiberias but were mistaken for the vanguard of Agrippa's forces, 157 and cf. 126 (where the parallel BJ 2.595 omits the cavalry); it was believed that a large Roman contingent could suddenly appear at Sepphoris, 378-380.

[42] Josephus begins his tenure in Galilee at Sepphoris (V 30 and 64) whence he proceeds to Bethmaus (64), upper Galilee (67), Tiberias (68), and Gischala (70 and 77). Josephus does not explain how or why he left Gischala for Kana (86). From Kana he went to Tiberias (90ff), Taricheae (96), and Sepphoris (103). After another gap we meet him at Simonias (115), Besara not far from Gaba (118) whence he goes to the Tiberias area (120). Another hiatus and then a series of trips in the Taricheae-Tiberias region (127, 153, 156, 157, 164, 174). The final tour, not connected with the preceding, is the longest, taking Josephus from Asochis (207) through many points (213, 234, 243, 265, 270) back to Tiberias (272) and Taricheae (276, 280, 304). On the arrival of letters from Jerusalem he calls an assembly of Galileans at Arbela (311) from which he returns to besiege Tiberias (323). After the digression against Justus, Josephus mentions only six locations to which he went (Sepphoris, 374; Asochis, 384; Garis, 395; Julias, 399; Kepharnokon, 403; Taricheae, 404) but does not usually explain how or why he went from one to the other. Thus V does not give a single connected account of Josephus' journeys.

112-13 and 149-54) and the story of Gamala in three (V 46-61, 114, 179-86). BJ strove to omit doublets but V tolerates them (see below pp. 124-125).

The uneven method of introducing and re-introducing characters and places is particularly conspicuous in V. Cestius Gallus, the governor of Syria, is mentioned first in V 23 but his title does not appear until V 30. V 49 and 214 record only the name, V 347 and 373 add the title. The village of Dabaritta is mentioned in V 126 but Josephus does not explain its location until V 318. Jesus ben Sapphia is introduced in V 134 as if he were a new character although he appeared at least once before (V 66). We meet Ananias, a member of the delegation, in V 197, but Josephus describes him in V 290 as if for the first time.[43] Elsewhere, too, Josephus employs this same non-technique. The monuments of Helena are mentioned in BJ 5.55 and 119, but Helena is not identified until 147 and 253. John of Gischala appears first in BJ 2.575, but is introduced only in 585. Antioch is described in BJ 3.29 although it was mentioned frequently in BJ 1 and 2. Judas the Galilean, the son of Ezekias, is introduced twice (BJ 2.56//AJ 17.271 and BJ 2.118//AJ 18.4).[44] Antipater the father of Herod is described as if a new character in BJ 1.180-81//AJ 14.121. Any deductions about Josephus' sources based on these inconcinnities are unreliable.[45]

In various respects V is similar to BJ. It employs both direct and indirect characterization. Justus (40), John (70), Jesus ben Sapphia (134), Simon ben Gamaliel (191-192), and Josephus himself (80-83) are described in short sections which stand outside the framework of the story. But, as in BJ, the narrative itself usually gives the desired impression. The actions and motives assigned to the actors are sufficient to delineate their character. Not only Josephus but the Galileans too know that John was a "scoundrel and a perjurer" (V 102). The Galileans themselves often demonstrate their affection for their general (V 205-207,

---

[43] The identity of the two is accepted by Niese, Feldman, and Schalit in their indices and is supported by V 291 which presupposes that Ananias is Josephus' enemy, though it must be admitted that Josephus had more than one enemy.

[44] Assuming the identity of Judas the Galilean with Judas the son of Ezekias.

[45] The sloppiness of Josephan procedure was unappreciated by Schemann 19 (on Helena); Drexler 305 (on John); Marcus, note f on AJ 14.121 (on Antipater). A complete study of this problem is needed.

210-211, 230-231, 233, 243-244, 250-251, 259, 298-299, 306).
Those who try to supplant him know that he is innocent of any
wrong-doing (194-95).

V's fondness for the dramatic and the pathetic is particularly
noticeable in two passages. The first (V 134-144), a portion of
the Dabaritta affair, begins with the dramatic scene of Jesus ben
Sapphia, Torah scroll in hand, haranguing the mob to kill Josephus
(134-35, cf. BJ 2.599). Josephus is left with but one bodyguard
who urges him to die nobly (137). BJ 601 presents a much less
satisfactory scene: four bodyguards remain and they counsel flight.
V 138 and BJ 601 agree that Josephus adopted a suppliant's pose,[46]
but it is V which again is the more dramatic text. Josephus is
nearly killed by the returning soldiers (140). Silence grips the
crowd (141). "If I must die . . . but before my death . . .", he begins
(141).

The second passage is V 204-12. In a pathetic letter Josephus'
father informs him of the deliberations of the Jerusalem council
and pleads with him to return home before his death (V 204). This
scene may have been suggested by Nicolaus' biography of Augustus
which tells of two letters from Atia beseeching the future emperor
to return home (FGrH 90 F 130 c. 38-39 and 51-52). BJ 629 also
mentions a letter but, since the letter is from Josephus' friends,
this account lacks the pathetic elements. A further sign of BJ's
greater reliability here—in spite of its apologetic—is its admission

---

[46] In BJ, Josephus (a) rips his clothing, (b) puts ashes on his head, (c)
places his hands behind him, and (d) hangs his sword from his neck. V omits
(b) and (c), repeats (d), and changes (a) so that Josephus dons black clothing.
Tearing one's garments and sprinkling ashes on one's head (e.g. *Job* 2.12)
as well as wearing black (AJ 7.154 with Marcus' note, AJ 14.172, BJ 1.506//
AJ 16.267, AJ 16.287, BJ 2.1, BJ 4.260, and T. Hagigah 2.9) are old Jewish
customs of mourning. One of the legacies of classical Athens was that a
suppliant at a legal hearing would put on a terrific display in order to arouse
the pity of the tribunal. See Aristophanes *Vespae* 552-575 and 976; Plato
Apologia 34c. The commentaries ad locc. list further passages. Defendants
wore black not only in Greece but also in Rome and Judaea. For Rome see
A. W. Lintott, *Violence in Republican Rome* (Oxford 1968) 16-20, who
provides further references for the Greek practice. For Judaea see, in addition to our passage, BJ 2.237//AJ 20.123 and Y. Rosh ha-Shanah 1.3 p. 57b,
"It is a universal custom for a man who knows that he has a lawsuit to wear
black, to be covered in black, and to let his beard grow long because he does
not know the result of the suit." Cf. Y. Efron, *In Memory of Gedaliahu Alon:
Essays . . .* ed. M. Dorman (Israel 1970) 97 with the notes (Heb.) and S.
Lieberman, *JQR* 35 (1944) 10-11.

that some warning was received.[47] After Josephus announces his decision to depart he is besieged by the Galileans who, with their wives and children, plead with him to stay (205-07, 210-11). Finally Josephus surrenders to their demands (212). This scene, not only dramatic but tendentious as well, seems to be related to the confrontation at Jotapata (BJ 3.193-204). In both cases Josephus deliberates leaving the Galileans but they, with their wives and children, importune him to remain. His presence, they claim, assures their safety (V 205, 207, 210, and BJ 3.193-94, 196, 202). In particular note the similarity in the discussion of the motives of the Galileans:

<table>
<tr><td align="center">V 207</td><td align="center">BJ 3.202</td></tr>
<tr><td>οὐ πόθῳ, δοκῶ μοι, τῷ πρὸς ἐμὲ μᾶλλον ἢ τῷ περὶ αὐτῶν δέει ... ἐμοῦ γὰρ παραμένοντος πείσεσθαι κακὸν οὐδὲν ὑπελάμβανον.</td><td>οὐ φθόνῳ τῆς ἐκείνου σωτηρίας, ἐμοίγε δοκεῖν, ἀλλ᾽ ἐλπίδι τῆς ἑαυτῶν. οὐδὲν γὰρ ἠξίουν πείσεσθαι δεινὸν Ἰωσήπου μένοντος.</td></tr>
<tr><td>Not so much out of affection for me as out of fear for themselves, it seems to me... They assumed they would suffer no harm if I remained.</td><td>Not out of envy for the safety of Josephus but out of hope for their own, it seems to me. They thought they would suffer nothing untoward if Josephus remained.</td></tr>
</table>

Compare too the encounter of the Jews with Petronius at Ptolemais and Tiberias (BJ 2.192-201//AJ 18.263-83).[48] That prefect would agree with Josephus that "it is proper to face even manifest dangers on behalf of so many people" (V 212).

Thus Josephus' inconsistency is well demonstrated. Although the two passages just described show that V too is capable of drama and literary polish,[49] the autobiography as a whole is a sloppy and rough work, stylistically far inferior to BJ.

---

[47] In BJ 629 Josephus' friends inform him that an army is coming but do not know its purpose. Ignorant of what precautions he should take, Josephus lost four cities. Josephus thus implies that 1. he had held the cities; 2. their loss was no sign of unpopularity or incompetence. Even better would have been the claim that he received no warning at all.

[48] The outline is similar: a single official faces thousands of Jews, including women and children. The Jews cast themselves on their faces and plead. The official, adamant at first, at last gives way because he does not want to harm so many people. I do not know whether any of these three scenes took place the way Josephus describes them, but it is clear that all three follow the same literary model. It remains to be determined in which order the three were written.

[49] V rarely uses numerical exaggeration, so frequent in BJ. Cf. V 199 (40,000 pieces of silver); 321 and 331 (10,000 soldiers).

C. *Aims*

1. *Justus of Tiberias and Josephus' Response*

One of the major differences between BJ and V is the frequent mention of Justus of Tiberias by the later work; it is clear that the Tiberian is an important factor for understanding V. The crucial problems are: What did Justus say in his history about Josephus? What was his relationship with Josephus during the Galilean war? Since the non-Josephan sources are of minimal significance, they will be considered only at the end of this section.[50]

a. The Digression Against Justus

The most important passage is V 336-367, the long digression (παρέκβασις, 367) against Justus which has the following structure: [51]

   I. Historiographic introduction (336-339)
  II. Polemic against Justus and Tiberias (340-367)
     A. Justus and Tiberias fought against Rome (340-356)
       1. Justus led the revolt of Tiberias (340-344)
       2. Tiberias willingly fought against Rome (345-354a)
       3. Justus was a revolutionary and a scoundrel (354b-356)
     B. Josephus' history is more accurate than Justus' (357-367)

The digression, allegedly directed against many historians (336), clearly has Justus as its only target.[52] The introduction (336-339), as we would expect (see chapter two above), is a string of historiographic and rhetorical commonplaces. Josephus declares (336) that a historian must strive only for the truth and should not be led astray by enmity (ἔχθρα) or favor (χάρις).[53] Since history must be complete, Josephus contends that BJ's omission of V's

---

[50] The most important works on Justus are: Baerwald; Schürer 58-63 = Schürer-Vermes 34-37; Luther; F. Rühl, *RhM* 71 (1916) 289-308; F. Jacoby, *PW* 10,2 (1919) 1341-1346; Laqueur; Drexler, esp. 293-306; Schalit, *Klio* 26 (1933) 67-95; Jacoby, FGrH 734; T. Rajak, *CQ* 23 (1973) 345-368 (who repeats much of the earlier discussion); B. Z. Wacholder, *Eupolemus: A Study of Judaeo-Greek Literature* (Cincinnati 1974) 298-306. It is unfortunate that Josephus did not cite extensive portions of his opponent's work as he did in CA. Presumably Justus' case was too good and his work too unpleasant for citation.

[51] Hornbostel 8 oversimplifies.

[52] Although obvious, this has been noted only by Laqueur 10 n. 1 and 18 n. 1. But V 336 is correct to the extent that Justus was not Josephus' only opponent.

[53] For many parallel passages see Avenarius 40-44 and 49-54. These *topoi* re-appear in the proem to BJ.

accusatory material was the result not of favor (χάρις), a lapse in the historian's integrity, but of Josephus' own mildness (339).[54] He polemizes now only because he has been attacked (338). The comparison of forgery to false history (337) has the appearance of a rhetorical *topos*.[55] It is particularly appropriate here because in 356 Josephus labels Justus a forger (ῥᾳδιουργός),[56] a charge occasionally levelled against official secretaries (cf. Philo *In Flaccum* 131).

The historiographical argument is resumed in earnest only in the conclusion of Josephus' attack (357-367). Justus has not had the benefit of autopsy, so essential for historical research,[57] nor has he consulted the best sources, the Flavian *commentarii* (357-358). Justus refrained from publication for twenty years [58] because he feared the scrutiny of the knowledgeable survivors of the war (359-360). Josephus' own work received royal attestations of accuracy (361-367).[59] Thus in both the introduction and the

---

[54] Josephus knew that a historian was not supposed to "add or omit anything" (see the beginning of chapter two above) and therefore felt obligated to apologize for omitting this material from BJ. Cf. CA 1.52 where Josephus denies that he omitted anything through χάρις. In biography and encomia an author was allowed more selectivity. See Plutarch *Cimon* 2.5 with the comments of Leo, *Biographie* 148-149.

[55] Cf. Polybius 16.14.8 = FGrH 523 F 4, ἐὰν δὲ κατὰ προαίρεσιν ψευδογραφῶμεν ἢ πατρίδος ἕνεκεν ἢ φίλων ἢ χάριτος, τί διοίσομεν τῶν ἀπὸ τούτων τὸν βίον ποριζομένων; and Philostratus *Vita Apoll.* 2.29 (comparing piracy and forgery to the study of philosophy).

[56] Grant, *The Ancient Historians* 265. V's meaning is the same whether we follow the text of MW, accepted by Naber, ὡς καὶ ταύτας (sc. ἐπιστολάς) σε εὗρε ῥᾳδιουργοῦντα, or of PRA, accepted by Thackeray and Niese, ὡς καὶ (κἂν coni. Niese) ταύταις εὗρε ῥᾳδιουργόν.

[57] See Avenarius 71-85 and G. Nenci, "Il motivo dell' autopsia nella storiografia greca," *Studi classici e orientali* 3 (1953) 14-46.

[58] Luther 68 conjectures that Josephus derived this information from the preface to Justus' history. Perhaps so, perhaps not. The charge may be a Josephan invention ("You could have shown your history to the experts, had you wanted") or a Josephan exaggeration (see Jacoby, *PW* 10,2 [1919] 1343 and Helm, *PhW* 41 [1921] 483). Even if we grant that the figure "twenty years" derives from Justus, we do not know whether it is correct. He too may have exaggerated in order to bolster his claim of accuracy ("My history is not a recent work based on foggy memory; it was written twenty years ago, not long after the war"). See n. 231 below.

[59] On the publication of BJ see chapter four above; on V 363 see below. Of Agrippa's sixty two letters, Josephus has chosen one that praises him as the most accurate of the writers on the war and one in which Agrippa offers to provide some hitherto secret information. No doubt the other sixty were less laudatory and helpful. Josephus' expectation that Justus would try to discredit Agrippa's praise as insincere (V 367) may indicate that the correspondence—including the less flattering letters—was already

conclusion to the digression, Josephus asserts historiographic excellence and accuses Justus of not honoring the primary task of the historian, the transmission of the truth.

From these two sections we learn a few facts about Justus' work. It was an account of the war (336 and 338) [60] which included the Galilean campaign, the actions of both Josephus and the Romans at the siege of Jotapata [61] (357), and the war of Jerusalem (358). Although Justus claimed that he had written a superior (ἄμεινον, 357 and 359) [62] and careful (μετὰ ἀκριβείας, 358 and cf. 360) history,[63] he contradicted the memoirs of Caesar (358). Justus "testified falsely" against Josephus (338). V 357-367 also implies that Justus attacked the accuracy of BJ.

These sections of V's digression are similar to CA 1.46-56 and Laqueur has conjectured that Justus is the target in both texts.[64] CA has just explained why the books of the Bible are more reliable than the works of Greek historians. The Greek do not keep records and are interested only in style, not accuracy (1.19-27), but our Jewish scriptures are venerable, truthful, and carefully preserved (1.28-43). The insouciant Greeks can write history even without knowledge of the facts (1.44-45). Some have written histories of the war without benefit of autopsy (1.46, cf. V 357). I was in the

---

known or that Justus had other letters from Agrippa expressing other opinions. If Justus was Agrippa's secretary when these letters were written, his interpretation carries weight. On the royal vulgarism in 366 (ὅλοι for πάντες), see Marcus' note on AJ 16.132.

[60] The text of 338 is uncertain; it is either peculiar (Shutt 30 n. 4) or corrupt (Jacoby in FGrH 734 T 3b reads περὶ τούτων with most manuscripts and deletes τὸν πόλεμον). The meaning, however, is clear.

[61] This is not absolutely certain because V never discusses the siege of Jotapata or what Justus said about it, but the implication of 357 seems clear. It is mentioned because it shows Justus' mendacity. See below n. 80.

[62] For Laqueur's interpretation of ἄμεινον, see below.

[63] Justus may have claimed to be φιλόπονος (338), or may have referred to his πόνος, words often used to describe a historian at work. Cf. Dionys. Hal. 1.1.2, Nicolaus FGrH 90 F 135, BJ 1.15 (φιλόπονος); Diod. Sic. 1.4.1, Nicolaus ibid., BJ 1.16 (πόνος). See Laqueur 10-11; Thackeray, Josephus 36 n. 27; Avenarius 77-78.

[64] Laqueur 16-21, accepted by Drexler 293. A. Schlatter independently arrived at this conclusion; see Bericht 14-15 = Kleinere Schriften 10-11. Hölscher, PW 9,2 (1916) 1995, assumes that the target is Justus but adduces no proof. The relative chronology of CA and V is obscure. If V was appended to AJ in 93/4, CA is the later work. If we accept the existence of a second edition of AJ or V (see below), CA may be earlier or later. Baerwald's arguments (18) are not decisive. In AJ 8.56 and 20.154-157 Josephus again defends his veracity, but Justus is not involved.

unique position to know the affairs of both sides (1.47-49). After writing my history (1.50a), I received accolades from Vespasian, Titus, Agrippa, and many others, all testifying to my accuracy (1.50b-52, cf. V 361-362). Some have attacked my history—unjustifiably, of course, since both BJ and AJ are based on autopsy or the most reliable sources available (1.53-55). Even if my opponents claim to have read the *commentarii* of the emperors, they cannot have known the true state of affairs on the Jewish side (1.56, cf. V 358). The two digressions are similar not only in theme but also in certain details and phrases.[65] The target(s) of CA 1.53-56 attacked the accuracy of BJ (and AJ?) and appealed to the *commentarii* of the Caesars—is this Justus? The context demands a Greek (i.e. pagan) historian but the victim's anonymity may be deliberate to cover the presence of a Jewish historian among the accused.[66] But identical polemic does not imply identical opponents, especially since many of V's and CA's historiographic arguments are commonplaces which appear even in the proem to BJ.[67] The only particular mentioned in CA 1.53-56, the opponent's appeal to the *commentarii* of the Caesars, does not square with V 358 which accuses Justus of contradicting the *commentarii*, not of pretending to have read them.[68] CA 1.25-27 is so general and so full of commonplaces that it seems unlikely that Josephus has only one specific target.[69]

Whether or not Justus attacked Josephus the historian, the main attack, to judge from the body of the excursus and from V as a

---

[65] Laqueur 16-17 notes ἀναιδεία (V 357)//ἀναιδής (CA 1.46); ἐπέδωκα τὰ βίβλια (V 361)//ἔδωκα τὰ βίβλια (CA 1.51); V 362//CA 1.51; V 361 and 367// CA 1.52. Cf. too ἡ τῆς ἀληθείας παράδοσις (V 364)//παράδοσιν πράξεων ἀληθινῶν (CA 1.53); ἀνδρῶν τῆς Ἑλληνικῆς παιδείας ἐπὶ πλεῖστον ἡκόντων (V 359)// ἀνδράσι καὶ τῆς Ἑλληνικῆς σοφίας μετεσχηκόσιν (CA 1.51); V 357//CA 1.53. There are a few inconcinnities too: V knows of *commentarii* of Vespasian only (342 and 358), CA mentions ὑπομνήματα τῶν αὐτοκρατόρων (CA 1.56). Did Josephus give (V 362) or sell (CA 1.51) his history to Agrippa and the others? (For an amusing attempt to reconcile the two, see Thackeray 27).

[66] Thus Laqueur 17-18 disposes of the objections later raised by Thackeray (note *c* to CA 1.46) and T. Reinach in his note to CA 1.46 in the Budé edition.

[67] The emphasis on autopsy (BJ 1.1 and 3), the opponents' indifference to accuracy (BJ 1.2 and 7-8), the Greek reliance on style (BJ 1.13), not truth (BJ 1.16).

[68] Von Gutschmid 407-408.

[69] On Josephus' pronouncements about rhetorical history, see the discussion at the beginning of chapter two above. With CA 1.26 cf. Philo Byblius, FGrH 790 F 1 (from Eusebius *PE* 1.9.27).

whole, was directed at Josephus the man, his character and actions.[70] Justus contended that Josephus and the Galileans were responsible for the anti-Roman actions of Tiberias during the great revolt (340 and 350). From 353 it may be inferred that Justus accused Josephus of brutality against Tiberias. 340-344 responds that Justus and the Tiberians had attacked the cities of the Decapolis even before Josephus was selected general. Thus it was Justus, not Josephus, who caused Tiberias to revolt. Justus nearly paid with his life for this crime.

345-354a develops the argument by a comparison (σύγκρισις) between Sepphoris and Tiberias, the one pro-Roman although in a good position to revolt (346-348),[71] and the other anti-Roman although in a good position to remain loyal (349-350a). Three arguments maintain that Tiberias was a hot-bed of revolutionary activity. Even after Josephus had been captured Tiberias did not declare loyalty to Rome until Vespasian arrived at the city whereupon the terrified inhabitants had no choice (350b-352).[72] The Tiberians, factious and violent, are contrasted with Josephus who never killed anyone (353). Two thousand Tiberians aided the rebels during the siege of Jerusalem (354a).

The final section in the body of Josephus' attack (354b-356) resumes the theme of 340-44.[73] Vespasian condemned Justus for his

---

[70] Drexler 294-297. V is not concerned with defending the accuracy of BJ as can be seen from the frequent contradictions of the two works. But personal apologetic is found throughout V and is clearly the dominant issue. Schalit, *Zion* o.s. 5 (1933) 184-85 (Heb.), even doubts whether the original work of Justus contained any reference to Josephus the historian, but his appeal to the twenty years of V 360 is in vain; see n. 58. Luther et al. believed that the attack on BJ was a central theme of Justus' work, but their sole evidence was the assumption that the differences between V and BJ were caused by the polemic of Justus.

[71] The phrase περὶ αὐτὴν κώμας ἔχουσα πολλάς (346) is used only in contrast to μηδεμιᾶς πόλεως Ἰουδαίων παρακειμένης (349) and does not imply that Sepphoris legally owned these villages. Sepphoris probably was a toparchic capital and had little territory of its own. See A. Alt, *Kleine Schriften* II (Munich 1953, repr. 1964) 434-435; A. H. M. Jones, *JRS* 21 (1931) 81 and *The Cities of the Eastern Roman Provinces*[2] (Oxford 1971) 274; Sherwin-White 131. Klein, *Galilee* 148, is incorrect.

[72] After the subjugation of Jotapata Vespasian proceeded to Caesarea (BJ 3.409-413) whence he dispatched troops to capture Joppa (414-431). He went to Caesarea Philippi (443) and spent twenty days there (444) before beginning to move against Tiberias and Taricheae. V contends that Tiberias should have surrendered immediately after the fall of Jotapata. For Agrippa's intercession see BJ 3.456 and 461.

[73] Note the ring structure of the digression. Section I (336-39) corresponds

revolutionary activity and even Agrippa, Justus' benefactor, sentenced him to prison or exile.

The argument in the initial portion of the excursus is rather ineffective. Justus' attack against the Decapolis does not prove anti-Roman sentiments (see below). Josephus is badly confused on the number of times Justus was condemned, imprisoned, or exiled. Here are the data:

> V 343: Because of the attack against the Decapolis Vespasian ordered Justus to be punished and turned him over to Agrippa who had the authority to execute. On the intercession of Berenice, Justus was imprisoned and not executed.
>
> V 355-56: After pardoning Justus, Agrippa imprisoned him twice, exiled him twice, and once sentenced him to death. Justus was saved by Berenice. After all this, Justus was appointed royal secretary, but was driven from the king's presence when his forgeries were discovered.
>
> V 410: Because of the attack against the Decapolis, Vespasian turned Justus over to Agrippa who (did not execute him but) secretly imprisoned him.

These three statements can be conflated to produce a single account but confusion and exaggeration seem evident. Did Berenice intercede twice? V 410 omits Berenice and adds the *novum* that Justus' pardon was hidden from Vespasian, although Josephus adds "as we have explained above". V 355-56 presents an incredible picture. The likeliest reconstruction has Justus condemned by Vespasian, turned over to Agrippa for execution,[74] but, on the

---

to II B (357-67), since both deal with historiography. II A 1 (340-44) is balanced by II A 3 (354b-356). In the middle stands II A 2 (345-54a), the polemic against Tiberias.

[74] Why did Vespasian surrender Justus to Agrippa? We may conjecture that Vespasian realized that Justus did not deserve execution, but, to maintain peace with the Decapolis, condemned him and turned him over to Agrippa, knowing that the Jewish king would spare him (contrast Schlatter, *Bericht* 12 = *Kleinere Schriften* 8). We may also conjecture that Vespasian thought Justus did deserve execution but spared him as a favor to Agrippa and preserved the appearance of justice by turning him over to Agrippa "for punishment" which he foresaw would not be inflicted. We may also conjecture, to save Josephus' story, that Agrippa had the right, under the principle of *forum domicilii*, to punish a citizen of his domain, no matter where the crime occurred. But did Agrippa enjoy this privilege? In a previous generation it had been bestowed exclusively on Herod the Great (BJ 1.474). Perhaps in 67 Vespasian wanted to thank Agrippa for his support and therefore honored him with this (temporary?) privilege. On *forum domicilii* see Sherwin-White 28-31 (on *Luke* 23.6-11) and 55-57.

intercession of Berenice, imprisoned instead. The condemnation by
Agrippa and the second intervention of Berenice are a doublet of
this scene.[75] Agrippa may have imprisoned him once or twice—
court officials usually have checkered careers—but Josephus'
interpretation of these events is certainly unsympathetic.

The passage has other difficulties too. The proofs promised
by 344 are not provided.[76] 349 inaccurately depicts the status of
Scythopolis and ignores the existence of Taricheae, an anti-Roman
"city" (97) only thirty *stadia* from Tiberias (157).[77] Josephus
pretends that the internecine strife in Tiberias was not caused by
conflicting political loyalties (353) although he states in 32-36
that the city was torn by three parties of which one was pro-
Roman. The two thousand Tiberians in Jerusalem (354) prove
nothing because Josephus does not say when they arrived in the
capital city. Perhaps they were pilgrims to the Passover feast
(cf. BJ 6.421).[78] But Josephus' argument proves two important
points. The history of Tiberias must have been a crucial issue
between Josephus and Justus since the vehemence of the response
otherwise would be difficult to understand. Why Tiberias' attitude
during the war was still an issue twenty or thirty years after the
event will be investigated below. The second point is that, even
when confuting Justus, Josephus admits that while he was in
Galilee he was no friend of the Romans (346-347). Not a word
here about pretense and pro-Roman sentiment. V regularly
assumes that Josephus was a revolutionary and only seldom claims
that he was secretly planning to submit to Rome. If this claim were
a response to Justus it should have appeared frequently throughout
V and at least once in the long digression.

---

[75] Drexler 295.

[76] Presumably 344 refers to 355 but the scandals retailed in 355 afford
no proof of Justus' revolutionary activity.

[77] The three cities listed in 349 are those attacked by Justus and the
Tiberians (42). Both BJ and V use round numbers to express distances in
Galilee (20, 30, 40, 60, 100, 120, or 140 *stadia*). The only exceptions are V 64
(four *stadia* from Tiberias to Bethmaus) and, perhaps, V 118 (see the reading
of MW). See W. Oehler, *ZDPV* 28 (1905) 72 and Schürer 2.155 n. 236. In
V 349 Josephus wrote τῆς ὑπηκόου βασιλεῖ for τῶν ὑπηκόων Ῥωμαίοις. Is
there a lacuna?

[78] J. Jeremias, *Jerusalem in the Time of Jesus*, trans. F. H. and C. H. Cowe
(London 1969) 77.

b. Josephus' Apologetic

The digression we have just analyzed consists of apologetic and polemic, both directed towards Justus. The beginning and end of the autobiography are determined by these considerations. V's story begins in detail only with Josephus' arrival in Galilee, is taken just far enough for Justus to be arrested by Vespasian (410), and there it abruptly ends with a brief summary and a reference to BJ (411-412).[79] Josephus could afford to ignore Justus' version of the battles of Jotapata and Jerusalem (357-358) because the main charges lay elsewhere.[80] Within the narrative the polemic against Justus recurs in only a few passages (see below) but the apologetic appears throughout.[81] The key passage is V 80-84 which interrupts the story to defend Josephus' character and integrity.[82] At least one of the apologetic elements is directed towards Justus (cf. 82 with 353, on Josephus' frequent capture of, but kindness towards, Tiberias) and so it seems reasonable to conclude that the entire paragraph is a response to the Tiberian.

V 80 proclaims that in spite of his youth Josephus was a paragon of virtue. No woman was assaulted by him (an assertion repeated later by the Galileans, 259). While in Galilee Josephus was accused of living luxuriously (284) and so he insists in his autobiography that he derived no personal profit from the war. He did not accept any gifts, not even the tithes which were his priestly prerogative.[83] His fellow envoys compare unfavorably (63 and 73). Josephus admits (81) that he received a share of Syrian booty, but he asserts that he sent it to his family in Jerusalem.[84] He opposed John's

---

[79] The text of 411 is corrupt but BJ 3.110-128 suggests that not much has fallen out.

[80] Laqueur 8 deduced from V's silence about Jotapata that the factual content of Justus' work was not important to Josephus. For a refutation of this view, see below.

[81] This is the main point of Schalit, *Klio* 26 (1933) 67-95. It weakens Laqueur's thesis only if we maintain (as Laqueur does) that V has added to, but not otherwise tampered with, the *Rechenschaftsbericht*.

[82] On V 80-84 and its parallels in other ancient autobiographies, see section A above. On the apology see Hornbostel 8-9 and 24-27, and Drexler 296-297.

[83] It is well known that Rabbinic literature regularly assigns the tithes to the Levites, while Josephus, Philo, and other sources assign them to the priests. This problem is not our concern.

[84] The μέντοι connects V 81 with V 80. Both sections defend Josephus against the charge of having used the war to make a profit. In V 81 however, his admission in the first half of the sentence (I received a share of the booty) is balanced by his assertion in the second (I did not keep it for myself). For

profiteering (especially since it was at the expense of the pious Jews of Caesarea Philippi, 71-76). The palace at Tiberias was plundered against his instructions (67) and he deposited with responsible custodians whatever booty he was able to recover (68-69), not using it for any illegitimate purpose (295-298). He reimbursed the fleeing *megistanes* for their horses (153) [85] and did not demand redemption money from the captives he liberated after the war (419).

V 82 demonstrates that Josephus did not loot or punish anyone:

> Although I forcefully captured Sepphoris twice, Tiberias four times, and Gabara once, and although I often had John in my power when he was plotting against me, nevertheless I took revenge neither on him nor on any of the just mentioned cities, as the narrative below shall show.

It is amusing that here Josephus claims that he had to capture the leading cities of Galilee no less than seven times although just a few lines before he claims that a peaceful Galilee was his prime objective (78). Since V 82 is part of the answer to Justus, we may have another indication that the claim to have tried to keep the peace (V 78) is independent of his polemic against Justus. We shall return to this point below (pp. 152ff). In any event, sloppy workmanship is evident since V does not entirely support the statements here.[86] Josephus asserts that he did not wreak vengeance on Sepphoris although he captured it twice. The reference is to 373-380 and, apparently, to 394-396, the appeals of Sepphoris to Cestius and Josephus' attacks on the city. The first passage tries to hide the fact that Josephus was scared off by a rumor of the arrival of Roman troops, but it does support the claim of V 82. The second passage shows that Josephus *failed* to capture the city. Its point is not that Josephus was kind to Sepphoris, but that he did his best to prevent it from falling into Roman hands. Another possibility is 104-111, but there too Josephus' concern is to demonstrate his firm stand towards the city. Where is the second capture? [87]

ὁμολογεῖν, to assert or declare, see; *inter alia*, V 168 and the common phrase χάριν ὁμολογεῖν, V 103, 244, 325; AJ 5.30, 17.201, 20.30. The passage is misinterpreted by Schalit, *Klio* 26 (1933) 69 n. 8.

[85] He says nothing of their weapons and possessions (V 112).

[86] Gelzer 323 collects the passages relevant to V 82, but does not discuss the problems.

[87] Perhaps the second capture is that described by BJ 3.59-61 which is probably not a doublet of V 394-396.

We have similar difficulty in identifying the quadruple conquest of Tiberias. Two certain references are 163-173, the sham-
fleet affair, and 317-335, part of the story of the delegation from
Jerusalem. The other two seem to be 97-100 and 381-389 which
describe how Josephus prevented the Galileans from attacking
Tiberias. They confirm that Josephus did not injure Tiberias
but they neglect the reference of V 82 to "forceful capture".

The next city on the list is Gabara [88] but V tells us nothing
else about the capture. In 262-265 the Galileans, assembled at
Gabara, are about to attack Jonathan and the envoys from Jerusalem, but Josephus, seeing that bloodshed would be inevitable,
mounts his horse and flees to Sogane. But what has this to do with
V 82?

V 82 is an example of Josephan vanity and apologetic. He
exaggerates his military significance—shades of the ideal general
motif of BJ—by pretending to have captured cities more often
than he did,[89] but the apologetic element is dominant here. We may
conjecture that Justus adduced Josephus' barbarous conduct as
proof that Josephus forced Tiberias to revolt. Josephus responds
that he treated the cities well. Note especially V 314 where Josephus
denies that he ever threatened Tiberias (although V 317-335, which
describes the capture of the city, makes the denial rather suspect)
and V 67 where he denies that he was present in the city when
Jesus ben Sapphia massacred the Greek population.

V 82 also deals with Josephus' relationship to John. Had Justus
charged that Josephus was not (as BJ claims) John's enemy
but his friend? Or is John introduced here merely as the extreme
example of Josephus' clemency, although Justus had not mentioned
him? We cannot be certain. In any event Josephus here insists that
John was an opponent who often plotted against him (cf. 217).
That he never punished John is evidence not of friendship but of
clementia. This apologetic is found throughout V. John plots against
Josephus: 85-96, 122-125, 189-190, 201-203, 233, 236-238, 246,

---

[88] Γαβαρεῖς or Γαραβεῖς is the correct reading; see Schürer 2.125 n. 231;
Klein 44; Schalit, *NWB* s.v. Γαραβα and Γαραβεῖς; Möller and Schmitt,
s.v. Γαβαρα.

[89] Should we suppose Justus suggested that Josephus was a rather insignificant individual whose career bore no resemblance to that portrayed
by BJ? But Justus also contended that Josephus caused the revolt of
Tiberias and this claim would be difficult to reconcile with an allegation of
Josephus' ineffectiveness and insignificance.

253, 292-304, and 313-316. Josephus restrains an attack against John: 102-103, 305-307, and 368-372. V also emphasizes that Josephus was not a willing associate in John's business plans (71-76). Thus V shares BJ's motive of disassociating Josephus from John, but without the virulence and vituperative rhetoric. Elsewhere too V demonstrates Josephus' *clementia*: 31, his aid to the Sepphorites; 112-13 and 149-154, considerate treatment of the *megistanes*; 418-420, his actions during the capture of Jerusalem.

Many of the passages referrred to by V 82 use formulae and themes which frequently recur in V. Thus in 166 the Tiberians ῥίψαντες τὰ ὅπλα μετὰ γυναικῶν καὶ παίδων ὑπηντίαζον ... καὶ παρεκάλουν φείσασθαι τῆς πόλεως. Cf. 328, οἱ Τιβεριεῖς ... ῥίπτουσιν τὰ ὅπλα μετὰ γυναικῶν δὲ καὶ τέκνων ἱκέτευον φείσασθαι τῆς πόλεως αὐτῶν. Each of these scenes is followed by the imprisonment and punishment of the ringleaders (168-173 and 331-332).[90] With 100, δεινὸν ἡγούμενος ἐμφυλίου πολέμου κατάρχειν, and 377, τοιαῦτα δρᾶν ὁμοφύλους οὐκ ἔστιν ὅσιον, cf. 26, κατὰ τῶν ὁμοφύλων ὅπλα λαβεῖν ὅπερ ἐστὶν ἡμῖν ἀθέμιτον, and 171, ἀποκτεῖναι οὐχ ὅσιον ἡγούμενος ὁμόφυλον ἄνδρα. Related ideas appear in 128, 264, and 321.[91] The Galileans' threats return with dull regularity: 102, ἄρδην ἀφανίσειν ἐπαγγελλόμενοι σὺν αὐτῷ καὶ τὰ Γίσχαλα; 306, ἐπιρέπειν αὐτοῖς ἐλθοῦσιν ... ἄρδην αὐτὸν ἀφανίσαι καὶ τοὺς περὶ τὸν Ἰωνάθην; 375, ὡς ἄρδην ἀφανίσοντες πάντας σὺν τοῖς ἐποίκοις; and 384, ἐπιτρέπειν αὐτοῖς καταβᾶσιν ἄρδην ἀφανίσαι.[92] Josephus' responses are just as monotonous: 103, χάριν ἔχειν αὐτῶν ταῖς προθυμίαις ὡμολόγουν ἐγώ ... παρεκάλουν δ᾽ ὅμως ἐπισχεῖν αὐτοὺς ἀξιῶν καὶ συγγιώσκειν μοι δεόμενος προῃρημένῳ τὰς ταραχὰς χωρὶς φόνων καταστέλλειν; 244, κἀγὼ χάριν αὐτοῖς ἔχειν ὁμολογήσας συνεβούλευον πρὸς μηδένα πολεμεῖν ... θέλειν γὰρ ἔφασκον τὰς ταραχὰς χωρὶς φόνων καταστέλλειν; and 369, προαίρεσιν ἔχων τὰς ταραχὰς χωρὶς φόνου καταστέλλειν. Cf. too 174, χωρὶς φόνων, and the related idea of 31. The apologetic shows little variation. Three times Josephus admits leadership or participation in particular episodes but insists that he fled before anything unpleasant occurred (64-69, 262-265, 373-380). All three accounts are incredible.[93] Twice

---

[90] Another link is ἄνοια in 167 (Thackeray's emendation; cf. BJ 6.310 and 315; 7.4 and 83), 323, and 352. A's reading ἄνοια in 325 is probably incorrect. Cf. also ἀγνωμοσύνη (111 and 174), both as objects of παύω.

[91] Cf. AJ 9.231. BJ lacks the emphasis on ὁμόφυλοι.

[92] ἄρδην appears only once elsewhere in the works of Josephus and there too in the phrase ἄρδην ἠφάνισε (AJ 9.278). See the concordance s.v.

[93] In the first passage, obviously a response to Justus (65), Josephus

Josephus restrains a Galilean attack by stalling for time (305-307 and 385-389). Some of these doublets are propaganda reiterated, others may be relics of the unpolished *hypomnema*.[94] BJ has some of these themes (those of V 100, 102, 103, 166) and some of these phrases (those of V 100 and 166), but, as usual, avoids doublets.

V 83 is the next paragraph in this direct apologetic and claims that Josephus, because of his virtues, was protected by the deity. This theme was common in Roman autobiographies (see above); it reappears in 15, 138, 208-209, 301, and 425. Divine protection implies divine approval.

V 84 boasts of Josephus' popularity in the normal vainglorious manner. Even when cities were captured and women and children enslaved, concern for Josephus' safety was paramount in the minds of the Galileans (cf. BJ 3.435-436). V often emphasizes Josephus' extraordinary popularity: 122, 125, 160, 205-207, 210-211, 230-231, 233, 243-244, 250-251, 259, 279, 298-299, 303, 306, 309-310, and 404.

The delegation episode (V 190-335) in particular is replete with these themes and apparently is directed against Justus [95] (note ἐνταῦθα in 336). Specific charges are mentioned: Josephus was accused of being a tyrant (260 and 302), of living luxuriously while neglecting to soften the effect of the war on the populace (284), of stealing the Tiberian gold (295-298), of threatening Tiberias (314), of administering Galilee incompetently (315). These accusations were raised by the Jerusalem dignitaries and their supporters in 67 CE, and presumably were repeated later by Justus. Josephus responds by having the Galileans themselves hail him as benefactor and savior. His relationship with Tiberias was an important point

---

forces the unwilling members of the senate of Tiberias to assent to the destruction of the palace (65-66), but the demolition itself is carried out only by Jesus ben Sapphia (66). How opportune and inexplicable that Josephus left even the neighborhood (he was never in the city, 64, 67) just before the destruction and returned just after it (68). In 265 Josephus claims that he jumped on his horse and fled to Sogane to prevent an attack on the delegation at Gabara. Presumably either Josephus fought a battle at Gabara and was defeated, or was afraid to fight and fled. After the debacle Josephus realized that a military solution was not readily available and therefore sent an embassy to Jerusalem in search of political support (266-270). 378-380 can hardly hide the fact that Josephus was scared away from Sepphoris by a rumor of the impending arrival of Roman troops.

[94] And none of them, not even 97-103, are signs of interpolation, *pace* Laqueur. See the end of chapter three above.

[95] Drexler 297.

(271-335). Oblivious to an inherent contradiction, Josephus emphasizes that he was popular even in Tiberias (271-312) and that he behaved mildly towards opponents, even Tiberias (313-335).[96] V 62-69 had already disposed of the allegation concerning the Tiberian gold and so V 295-298 could be brief. The major point of V 190-335 is the legitimation of Josephus' tenure. Even his opponents in Jerusalem knew that he should not be replaced (194). Their sole motive was jealousy (204). God himself told Josephus to stay firm (208-209) and ultimately his position was confirmed by the people of Jerusalem (309-312). In contrast to Josephus, popular and noble, the envoys from the capital are liars (217-218, 274-275, etc.) and widely detested (230-233). In his struggle for legitimacy against Jerusalem and against Justus, Josephus is supported by God and the masses. His fine qualities and effective leadership make him superior in every respect (contrast 198 and 278) to the delegation.

   A summary is now in order. Justus wrote a history which attacked (a) the accuracy of BJ (although this is not absolutely certain), and (b) Josephus' character and actions. Josephus refutes (a) with a few historiographical commonplaces and some bold assertions of BJ's accuracy and Justus' mendacity. But the fact that V often contradicts BJ and regularly neglects to defend it, shows that V's main concern was (b). Justus contended that Josephus and the Galileans coerced Tiberias to revolt in the war of 66-67. He supported this claim by specific instances of Josephus' brutality towards Tiberias and the other cities of Galilee. Josephus was a tyrant, an unscrupulous, immoral, unpopular leader, who became rich by his misdeeds. Justus thus revived many of the old charges raised in 67. In addition to the explicit denial of the main accusation, Josephus responded by emphasizing his popularity, his mild and proper conduct, especially towards the Galilean cities. God rewarded

---

[96] In 271-312 Josephus' opponents are Jonathan's party (οἱ περὶ τὸν Ἰωνάθην, 271, 273, 278, 279, 282, 287 bis, 292, 297, 299, 301, 306, 311); his supporters are the Tiberian multitudes (πλῆθος or δῆμος, 279, 289, 298-303). Josephus does admit that the delegation won some adherents (273 and 279) but only once are "the Tiberians" his opponents (305). In 286 (cf. 283) "the Tiberians" are angry at Josephus for not fighting the Romans but are not partisans of the delegation. Contrast 313-335 which assumes that the Tiberians to a man support the delegation. In this section Josephus' opponents are (οἱ) Τιβεριεῖς (314, 317, 319, 321, 323, 327 bis, 328, 333, 335) and οἱ πολῖται (321), citizens of Tiberias (mistranslated by Thackeray, Haefeli, and Pelletier; cf. 42, 135, 278, 353).

him with protection from danger. Unlike BJ, V is not based on a text-book description of the ideal general; Josephus' *virtus bellandi* is nearly absent. He is a general, a *strategos* (97, 98, 123, 135, 176, 194, 205, 230, 250, 341, 380) but his army is usually small [97] and his military actions are skirmishes of minor importance (115-121, 398-406). In one victory, for example, he managed to kill twelve of the enemy while losing only one of his own men (396). V's defense of Josephus' character is so strident that it must be an end in itself, not just an element in a self portrait.

To indicate precisely the border between fact and conjecture, it might be useful to present a list of the charges and counter-charges explicitly mentioned by V.[98]

Explicit charges against Josephus in 66-67 CE

Josephus was preparing to surrender the country to the Romans (V 129-132//BJ 2.598; V 133//BJ 2.599; V 135; V 140//BJ 2.602)
Josephus was preparing to attack Jerusalem and to establish himself there as a tyrant (193//BJ 2.626)
Josephus was a tyrant (260 and 302)
Josephus lived luxuriously but neglected to lighten the effect of the war on the populace (284)
Josephus stole the gold from the palace in Tiberias (295-298, cf. 67-69)
Josephus threatened Tiberias (314)
Josephus administered Galilee incompetently (315)

Presumably all these charges but the first were repeated by Justus.

Explicit charges against Josephus raised by Justus

Josephus and Galileans caused the revolt of Tiberias (340-354)

---

[97] Only in V 321 and 331 does Josephus have 10,000 troops (see n. 49 above). On the numbers of Josephus' forces see chapter six below (pp. 201ff). V often emphasizes Josephus' ingenuity and *strategemata*, but they are not on the same order as those of BJ 3. Josephus outwits his opponents, restrains zealous supporters, and captures a rebellious city, but he is nowhere a field marshal with grand strategies. It is important to note that V would rather emphasize proper behavior than ingenuity, BJ the opposite. Cf. V 103 (χωρὶς φόνων)//BJ 623 (συνέσει) and V 174 (χωρὶς φόνων)//BJ 645 (κενοῖς σκάφεσιν καὶ δορυφόροις ἑπτά). Cf. too V 380 and 389.

[98] To list *all* the charges raised by Justus against Josephus would be impossible. Virtually every sentence of V can be interpreted by the ingenious as an apology or a polemic. In the preceding discussion we have attempted to uncover the main points of Justus' attack and to adduce those examples whose association with Justus seemed secure. In the list here I adduce only those passages where Josephus reports that he was accused, or where he denies something, or where he accuses others. The list is culled only from the central portion of V, the Galilean narrative.

Explicit denials, presumably against Justus

Josephus did not rape any women (80, cf. 259)

Josephus did not accept any gifts (80, cf. 63)

Josephus did not take revenge against or loot Sepphoris, Tiberias, Gabara, or John (82, cf. 97-100, 102-103, 163-173, 305-307, 317-335, 368-372, 373-380, 381-389)

Accusations against Justus

Justus tried to get control of Tiberias and the Galileans (36-39 and 391-392)

Justus was a demagogue (40), a scoundrel (41 and 393), and, with his brother, almost the cause of the disaster (41)

Justus incited the Tiberians to revolt against Agrippa and to attack the neighboring cities (42, 340ff, 354ff, 391)

Justus was condemned by Vespasian and (repeatedly) exiled and condemned by Agrippa (343, 355, 410)

Justus was fired from a secretaryship by Agrippa because of misconduct (356)

Justus claimed to have written the best account of the war (340 and 357) but distorted the truth (40) because he did not know the facts (336ff, 357ff)

Justus contradicted the imperial *commentarii* (358)

Justus did not dare to publish his history while Vespasian, Titus, and Agrippa were alive (359ff)

Josephus accuses the Tiberians

The Tiberians voluntarily rebelled from the king and the Romans and continued to rebel even after Josephus was besieged in Jotapata (345-56).

Our description of Justus' attack and Josephus' response differs in detail from the *communis opinio*, but is in fundamental agreement with it. The major point of contention (the origin of Josephus' assertions of pro-Romanism) will be discussed below (pp. 152ff). A radically different thesis is provided by Laqueur. The factual content of Justus' work could not have been important, Laqueur argues, because Josephus does not even bother to refute his opponent's account of Jotapata. The dispute about Tiberias must have been rather meaningless because a generation after the war the responsibility for the revolt of Tiberias would have been a subject of universal indifference. Even V does not hesitate to admit that Josephus fought Rome (Laqueur 9). Since these questions of content were un-important, Justus' attack must have been on Josephus' style: my history is better (ἄμεινον), i.e. more ornate, more literate, than that priest's history, written in wretched Greek.

Josephus realized that he was outclassed by a man who had a good Greek education (V 40) and so turned to attack Justus' accuracy. How can Justus claim to have written better, i.e. more accurately, than I, since his history is erroneous and he had no opportunity to learn the facts. The history of Tiberias is a spectacular illustration of Justus' unconcern for the truth. Josephus also attacked Justus' character and actions—this was *de rigeur* in ancient polemics—but the feud was primarily literary (Laqueur 10-15). CA's refutation of Justus (see above) confirms that the Tiberian attacked Josephus the writer, not Josephus the politician or Josephus the man (Laqueur 16-21). The virulence of Josephus' response is understandable because Josephus himself had published BJ and the competition from Justus' work meant financial loss (Laqueur 21-23). The pension granted by Vespasian (V 423) had been cut by Domitian and Josephus was now dependent for his livelihood on income from the sale of BJ and on support from his new publisher-patron Epaphroditus. Justus' success not only ruined the market for copies of BJ but also eroded the confidence of Josephus' publisher who now withdrew his support from Josephus' future projects (AJ 20.267-268). Josephus therefore responded in V, CA, and AJ 20.266 with the affirmation of his qualifications (Laqueur 29-35).[99] V's defense of Josephus' character is exclusively from the administrative report of 67 CE and has nothing to do with Justus.

This theory is the usual Laqueurian brew of fact and fantasy. Laqueur utilizes the historiographic digression of CA, which probably does *not* refer specifically to Justus, and slights V's long digression which explicitly refutes Justus. The historian from Tiberias certainly boasted of his superior style and Greek education, but the great digression shows that this was not all.[100] Justus' claim that Josephus and the Galileans were responsible for the revolt of Tiberias provoked a response too vehement for a mere test of accuracy. V 353 agrees with V 80-84 and the delegation story that

---

[99] Laqueur (268-73) assumes that Justus attacked AJ too, not only AJ's style, but also its content. (But BJ's content was ignored?!) This assumption is just as implausible and baseless as the attempt of A. Schlatter, *Der Chronograph aus dem zehnten Jahre Antonins* (Leipzig 1894) 37-47, to show that AJ was based on Justus.

[100] For ἄμεινον in the sense of superior style see Isocrates 4.7ff, cited in chapter three above. Laqueur has no evidence to separate the ἄμεινον of 357 and 359 from the ἀκρίβεια of 358 and 360 and to ascribe the one to Justus and the other to Josephus.

9

Josephus was too noble and well-behaved to have done any of the things of which he was accused. And even if the apologetic elements are derived from a *Rechenschaftsbericht*, why did Josephus use the earlier work as the basis of V unless he needed a detailed apologetic? Laqueur (269) argues that to refute Justus in 100 CE Josephus needed a history, and a history with a nationalistic viewpoint, such as that provided by the administrative report but not BJ. But a much easier procedure would have been to write a special refutation of Justus, since a long and involved history was unnecessary to respond to an attack on style. And why did V not revise BJ just as AJ 14 revised BJ? Such a revision would have produced a "nationalistic" history with a style superior to V's exceptional mediocrity. By basing V on the *Rechenschaftsbericht* Josephus fought back least where he was hit hardest.

Laqueur explains Josephus' vehemence by the theory that Justus' work affected Josephus' financial interests. CA 1.51, which mentions that Josephus sold BJ to many Jews, is supposed to prove that he published his own history,[101] but Laqueur knows that V 362 has "I presented" (ἐπέδωκα) instead of "I sold" (ἐπίπρασκον). Does either text imply that Josephus published his own work? Self-publication was not rare in antiquity, but the normal procedure was for the publisher (often also the patron of the writer) to "buy" the opus from the author and to publish it.[102] Although BJ is not dedicated to anyone, it was produced under royal patronage. Vespasian awarded Josephus a pension and a place to work (V 423) and Titus arranged for the publication of BJ (V 363). Josephus had circulated a few copies in advance among the Roman and Jewish nobility (CA 1.51 and V 361-62) and under the reign of Titus the first six books (see chapter four above) were published. The young emperor signed them with his own hand [103] and ordered

---

[101] Here Laqueur was anticipated by von Gutschmid 410.

[102] T. Birt, *Das antike Buchwesen* (Berlin 1882, repr. 1959) 111-13, and 349-355; idem, *Kritik und Hermeneutik nebst Abriss des antiken Buchwesens* (Munich 1913) 310-22; idem, *RhM* 72 (1917/18) 311-16; W. Schubart, *Das Buch bei den Griechen und Römern*² (Berlin and Leipzig 1921) 149-55. Birt's and Schubart's picture of large scale publication is certainly exaggerated; see R. Sommer, *Hermes* 61 (1926) 389-422, and H. I. Marrou, *Vigiliae Christianae* 3 (1949) 208-224.

[103] χαράξας τῇ ἑαυτοῦ χειρί, "Er versah sie mit seiner Unterschrift oder Chiffre als Imprimatur," Gutschmid 345 and the other translators. Roman emperors often signed documents personally; see F. Millar, *JRS* 57 (1967) 9-19. Titus was famous for his handwriting skills (Suetonius *Titus* 3 and 6).

them to be published (δημοσιῶσαι [or δημοσιεῦσαι] προσέταξεν, V 363). This phrase was interpreted by at least one ancient scholar as a reference to a mere letter of recommendation [104] but the better explanation said that Titus ordered BJ to be published.[105] Thus Eusebius in *HE* 3.9.2. (describing Josephus):

> He was by far the most famous Jew of that time, not only among his compatriots but also among the Romans, so that he was honored by the erection of a statue in Rome and the works completed by him were deemed worthy of the (a?) library (βιβλιοθήκης ἀξιωθῆναι).

Later writers clarify Eusebius' ambiguity: the library meant is the public library in Rome, and the datum is derived from V 361-363.[106] Thus, while the story about the statue may be an invention,[107] the statement that BJ was deposited in the public library is a plausible interpretation of V 363 since such deposit was a form of publication. Purchasers could verify the accuracy of their copies by comparison with the official exemplar.[108]

If Titus sponsored the publication of BJ, the competition with Justus would have had no direct financial impact on Josephus. In any event, it is unlikely that fifteen years after its appearance BJ would still be earning a significant sum for its publisher since the amount of money to be made in ancient book trade was rather

---

[104] Eusebius *HE* 3.10.9-11 quotes V 361-363 and Rufinus translates:
et imperator quidem Titus in tantum probavit ex istis debere libris ad omnes homines rerum gestarum notitiam pervenire, ut manu sua scriberet publice ab omnibus eos legi debere.
Rufinus is copied (with minor variations) by Sicard of Cremona (*PL* 213.458A-B).

[105] See LSJ s.v. δημοσιόω and δημοσιεύω and Birt, *Kritik* 308 n. 2.

[106] Thus Jerome *De viris inlustribus* 13 (Roman veniens septem libros Iudaicae captivitatis imperatoribus patri filioque obtulit, qui et bibliothecae publicae traditi sunt, et ob ingenii gloriam statuam quoque Romae meruit); Suda s.v. Ἰώσηπος (ἑπτὰ λόγους τῆς Ἱεροσολύμων ἁλώσεως τοῖς βασιλεῦσι προσήνεγκεν, οἵτινες τῇ δημοσίᾳ βιβλιοθήκῃ παρεδόθησαν καὶ διὰ τὴν δόξαν τῆς συγγραφῆς ἀνδριάντος ἠξιώθη); Nicephorus Callistus *PG* 145.800B (οὓς [the books of BJ] λόγος ἔχει καὶ τὸν Καίσαρα Τίτον ἰδίαις γεγραφότα χερσί, δημοσιεύεσθαι πανταχοῦ προστάξαι, καὶ τῇ ἐν Ῥώμῃ τῶν βιβλίων ἀναθέσει καταλεγῆναι) and 917D-920A (σοφίαν γὰρ καὶ τὴν τῶν λόγων παιδείαν διαφερόντως [Titus] ἠγάπα. ὡς καὶ αὐτὸν Ἰώσηπον οἷα δὴ λόγου ἄνδρα τιμαῖς ὑπερβαλλούσαις τιμᾶν, τά τε ἐκείνου βιβλία ἰδίαις γράψαι χερσί, καὶ ταῖς βιβλιοθήκαις τῆς Ῥώμης ἐναποτάξαι).

[107] Von Gutschmid 346. A famous author might occasionally be honored by a statue (Pliny *NH* 7.123 = FGrH 680 T 6).

[108] E. J. Bickerman, *JBL* 63 (1944) 352-355, and Lieberman, *Hellenism* 85-86. Birt, *Kritik* 337, misinterprets the passage from Jerome (quoted in note 106) since Titus did not give his copy to the library "as a gift." Eusebius *HE* 2.18 reports that the works of Philo too were deposited in the library.

small.[109] Laqueur's further conjecture that Justus' history com-
promised Josephus' standing with his patron is based on the fact
that the future works which Josephus had in mind when he finished
AJ (20.267f) are not known to have been written. But many other
reasons might have prevented Josephus from writing them.[110]

c. Josephus' Polemic

We turn now to V's polemical passages and to the background
of Justus' work. Why did he criticize Josephus and the Galileans?
Why such a confrontation twenty or thirty years after the war?
All scholars but Laqueur agree that the clue is provided by the
events of 66-67. These we know exclusively from the autobiography
which has two reasons for discussing Justus' past: to show Justus'
(a) wickedness and (b) responsibility for the *katastrophe* (41), i.e.
the revolt of Tiberias and ruin of the city (344).

The most important text is V 32-42, an analysis of the political
scene of Tiberias. Here is a classic Josephan blend of truth, polemic,
and incompetence. His description of the first party (στάσις), the
well-to-do who desired to remain loyal to Rome and Agrippa,
seems accurate (32-34a). The leader Julius Capellus (or Capella
as in 66-69 and 296) was probably a Roman citizen. His brother
Crispus had been a prefect (ἔπαρχος) of Agrippa I.[111] Two Herods
are mentioned. These are men who might well desire peace. After
an obscure sentence (34b) [112] Josephus turns to the second party,
the poor, who are eager for war (35). V 66 will think that the leader
of the party, Jesus ben Sapphia, was named here—another proof of
Josephan sloppiness. So far the account seems trustworthy; we
can readily believe that the political dispute in Tiberias was based

---

[109] See the works of Sommer and Marrou cited in note 102 and R. Feger,
PW Supp. 8 (1956) 517-520.

[110] See AJ 20.267-268 with Feldman's notes. See chapter two n. 116
above.

[111] The μέγας βασιλεύς (V 33) is Agrippa I (cf. AJ 18.110, 142; 20.104
and many coins and inscriptions). Although Agrippa II too is called μέγας
βασιλεύς in some inscriptions, in Josephus he is ὁ νεώτερος βασιλεύς (V 38
and AJ 19.362), in contrast to his father (V 37).

[112] If this Πίστος (γρ Πρίσκος A) is supposed to be the father of the famous
Justus, the text is probably to be understood by the supposition that Pistus'
wealth and connections should have put him in the pro-Roman camp, but
did not, because his son—that villain, Justus—misled him. It is not too
surprising that Josephus does not explain the situation very well. Pistus
re-appears in 88 and 175. Holwerda apud Naber suggests Κρίσπος but this
will not do.

on socio-economic factors. Josephus claims that a third party, headed by Justus, favored revolution for the selfish attainment of power but pretended to be uncertain. The accuracy of this claim is hard to judge. The speech ascribed to Justus in 37-39 is not uncertain at all but advocates revolt against Agrippa. The theme of the address was the old rivalry between Sepphoris and Tiberias. Instead of an attack on Sepphoris or on the territory of Agrippa, the inexplicable result of Justus' oratory is an attack on Gadara and Hippos. Since the speech is in no way connected with the expedition, it may be a Josephan invention to prepare for his comparison between Sepphoris and Tiberias (345-354, see above). Justus himself, incriminated by the comparison, attempts to incite Tiberias against Sepphoris. The point of 32-42 is that Justus incited Tiberias to revolt, sought the aid of the Galileans (39), forced even the supporters of peace to join the war (42), and was despicable (41) [113]—precisely the charges raised by Justus against Josephus and refuted in the great digression (see above). Here Josephus turns around and hurls the same charges at Justus. The speech in 37-39 enforces the polemic here and in the digression.

What is this third party allegedly led by Justus? It may well be a Josephan invention. Josephus would have preferred to make Justus the chief of the revolutionary party, but, since Jesus ben Sapphia already had that title, he had to invent something else.[114] Perhaps Justus did lead an attack against Gadara and Hippos but his Tiberian followers may have been an ad hoc amalgam of citizens (τοὺς πολίτας, 42) eager to avenge the anti-Jewish actions of the Greek cities. Thus Justus may never have been the leader of any party. On the other hand, we could explain that at the beginning of the war Justus may have been the head of a party which was uncertain regarding revolt from Rome but determined to free Tiberias from Agrippa's rule.[115] Justus hoped to lead the Galileans against Sepphoris, but failed because the Galileans hated Tiberias as well as Sepphoris. Instead he led his Tiberian supporters against the neighboring cities (why not against Sepphoris?). The third

---

[113] Another testimony to Josephus' sloppiness is his almost total neglect of Justus' brother, no matter what V 41 promises.

[114] See Luther 44-45.

[115] Baerwald 24-25, followed by A. Schlatter, *Geschichte Israels von Alexander dem Grossen bis Hadrian*[3] (Stuttgart 1925) 343, calls Justus a "zealot of local patriotism." Rajak 352 even says that Justus attacked Sepphoris.

possibility is that Josephus is correct. We simply do not have
enough evidence to settle this question. But no matter which
alternative we adopt, Justus did not have any party or following
worth mentioning by the time Josephus arrived in Galilee. Nowhere
else but V 39 (and 391) does Justus appear as the head of a faction
or group. He was a member of the city council (175) but had no
apparent body of followers or adherents. Unlike Jesus and John,
Justus was not a politician with whom Josephus had to deal and
he soon joined the pro-Roman faction—unless, of course, he had
been a member all along.

Justus' attack on two cities of the Decapolis (42) is probably
true [116] but is misinterpreted by Josephus. The attack is no proof
of revolutionary sentiments. The fighting between pagans and
Jews which accompanied the outbreak of war was, for the most part,
the product of local conditions and was not then conceived as part
of a general Jewish rebellion. Thus the next section in V claims
that John of Gischala was a pro-Roman who defended his homeland
against some gentile [117] marauders (43-45). The attacks of V 42
(against Gadara and Hippos) seem adumbrated in BJ 2.459 (the
Jews attack Gadara, Hippos, and the Gaulan) where their origin is
laid not to anti-Roman action but to revenge after the massacre at
Caesarea (BJ 2.457-58).[118] Josephus' proof has evaporated.

The next important passage is 175-178. Tiberias attempted
to declare loyalty to Agrippa, but Josephus thwarted the plan by
his sham fleet. He sent off to Taricheae the six hundred members of
the city council (BJ 639-641//V 168-169) and punished the instiga-
tor of the plot, one Cleitus, not a member of the city council
(BJ 642-645//V 170-173). At Taricheae Josephus sent for his
captive Tiberians and claimed that he too realized Roman invincibility. He, however, had enough sense to hide these sentiments
from the brigands (λῃσταί) and he recommended to his audience
that they too bide their time for a suitable apportunity to declare

---

[116] Schalit 69-70 n. 8 is the only scholar to doubt V's veracity here, but
his skepticism has no basis. The charges are supported by appeal to public
legal proceedings and an imperial verdict (342f, 410), not likely to have
been invented.

[117] On the identity of the cities see chapter one note 6 above.

[118] On the attacks against the Decapolis see Schlatter *Bericht* 8-24 =
Kleine Schriften 4-20 and H. Bietenhard, *ZDPV* 79 (1963) 42-44, but neither
says anything important about Justus. On these attacks and Justus' politics,
see especially Luther 34-49; Jacoby, *PW* 10,2 (1919) 1342; Rühl 301-302;
Schalit, *Encyclopedia Judaica* 9 (1932) 623; Rajak 352-353; Stein's Hebrew
translation, 100.

for the Romans. This little speech (175-176) was directed towards all the Tiberians present. Justus and Pistus are mentioned individually in a separate sentence which may or may not be a part of the original narrative (see below). Even if we do not accept Josephus' claim that he was secretly anti-war, we may believe that before these Tiberian "doves" he pretended to be sympathetic with their policy. What is significant is that V here considers Justus a pro-Roman,[119] and since this judgment contradicts one of V's explicit aims it is likely to be correct.

Josephus then spoke directly to Justus and reminded him of the death of some of his relatives in Gamala—a not very subtle warning about the consequences of excessive anti-revolutionary agitation (177-178). What actually occurred in Gamala is nearly irretrievable and will be discussed below (pp. 160ff). Justus probably accused Josephus of complicity in the atrocities of Gamala and so Josephus emphasizes (and claims that he emphasized even in 67 CE) that the unpleasantness occurred before he even arrived in Galilee (177). Similarly, the major point of 174-178, the mild treatment of Tiberias (χωρὶς φόνων in 174, om. BJ 645; see note 97) and the Tiberian prisoners, will be a response to Justus who accused Josephus of brutality towards the city.

The last important passage is 390-393. 381-389 describes a defection of Tiberias to the king and Josephus' rescue of the city from the wrath of the Galileans. This was the second time (389) that Josephus saved Justus' hometown,[120] and this defection, like the previous one, was engineered by members of the city council (381). After Josephus regained control, Justus escaped arrest (λαθὼν ἐμέ) and fled to Agrippa (390). We may conjecture that Justus' version of the facts went somewhat as follows. In a second attempt to free itself from Josephus' tyranny, Tiberias called on Agrippa for aid. The king sent his lieutenant Crispus (the same Crispus who was a

---

[119] The alternative would be to suppose that Josephus wished to disabuse Justus of his hope to get control of Tiberias with Galilean support, an ambition attributed to him in 39 and 391. But this is not the natural meaning of the text which does not distinguish between the policy of the pro-Roman members of the city council and that of Justus. V provides no reliable evidence to show that Justus attempted to implement his alleged ambition. Justus' support for John appears only in "Josephan glosses" (see below). On the assertion of V 175-176 see Drexler 302.

[120] The first time is described in 329 and 333-35 whence BJ 646 derived the detail on the return of the booty and conflated it with the rest of the story. See chapter three above.

leader of the pro-Roman party? V 33) but he and some senators were jailed by Josephus and the city was plundered by the Galileans. Crispus and Justus managed to escape (388-90) to Agrippa whereupon Crispus arranged for a meeting between the king and the Tiberian (393).[121] In an apologetic passage (cf. above on V 82) Josephus rejects this version by insisting that he did not touch the city, that he deliberately allowed Crispus to escape (385-389),[122] and that Justus fled not because of political reasons, but because he feared punishment for his wickedness (μοχθηρία, 393 and cf. 354).[123] In 391 Josephus repeats the old litany of V 36-42, how Justus incited a peaceful city to revolt and how he sought to lead the Galileans. Here, however, by ignoring the existence of a war party, Josephus exaggerates the pacific sentiments of the city in order to exaggerate Justus' alleged revolutionary activity. Josephus adds that Justus did not succeed in leading the Galileans because of their hatred of the Tiberians "for what they had suffered from them before the war" (392).[124]

These are the main passages for understanding Justus' actions during the war. He fought the Greek cities, perhaps engaged in suspicious activities at first, but soon preferred the rule of Agrippa to the uncertainties of war. The Galilean war of 67 provided ample opportunity for intense hatreds to arise. Josephus insisted that Tiberias maintain loyalty to him and did not refrain from attacking and plundering the city several times to drive home his point. He imprisoned the pro-Agrippa members of the Tiberian council, including Justus. Another matter entirely was Josephus' alleged complicity in the mistreatment of Justus' relatives at Gamala. Thus a triple tension between the two antagonists: Josephus the

---

[121] The text of 393 is uncertain. AMW read κρεῖσσον for Κρῖσπον. Schlatter *Bericht* 11 = *Kleinere Schriften* 7 n. 1 accepts Κρῖσπον but suggests a lacuna after νομίζων in which Justus' reception by Agrippa would have been described.

[122] A suitable exegesis could be produced to reconcile 388-389 with 393. If we read κρεῖσσον the problem disappears.

[123] Schalit, *Klio* 26 (1933) 79, interprets μοχθηρία as a reference to Justus' political views but the word is a convention of rhetorical abuse and Josephus did not need to have a specific fact in mind when he called his opponent μοχθηρός.

[124] The ὑπ' αὐτοῦ in 392 is most likely a corruption of ὑπ' αὐτῶν. If Josephus had known anything discreditable to Justus he would have reported it. In fact, it is surprising that he did not invent something appropriate. V 42 also implies that Justus did not succeed in leading the Galileans, because he persuaded only τοὺς πολίτας, the citizens of Tiberias (see n. 96).

revolutionary, Justus the anti-war; Josephus the destroyer of Tiberias, Justus the councilman of Tiberias; Josephus the alleged murderer of Justus' relatives.[125] These factors explain Justus' bitterness even twenty or thirty years after the war. BJ could ignore all of these matters, but when the old animosity re-asserted itself, Josephus had to defend himself.

V has several other passages on Justus but their value is dubious because they appear to be "Josephan glosses." If not actual interpolations into a fixed, earlier text, as Laqueur would have it, they are short phrases which have no organic connection with their contexts and seem to intrude on the narrative. V 175 may be an example since its function is only to prepare for 177 (see above). V 65 records that Justus came with other Tiberian senators to meet Josephus and hear his orders to destroy some prohibited artwork. Only under compulsion do the senators consent to the destruction (66). Why Josephus has Justus appear for only that one instant in the story is uncertain; most likely he wanted to implicate him in the negotiations concerning the destruction of the palace. The next such "gloss" is 88 in which Justus eagerly deserts Josephus to support John, thus proving himself an agitator. The same interpretation applies to the mention of Justus in 279. In neither case does Justus do anything substantial or become an active participant in the proceedings. These glosses seem to be the work of polemical imagination. Josephus has fooled some readers but it is striking how little he knows of Justus' actions during the war of 66-67.[126]

d. The Background of Justus' History

If Justus had so many reasons for hating Josephus why did he wait twenty years (V 360) before attacking him in print? Josephus uses this hesitation as evidence of mendacity. You waited for the death of Vespasian, Titus, Agrippa, and all those able to assess the truth of your account because you knew they would not

---

[125] Each of these factors is analyzed by Schalit, *Klio* 26 (1933) 67-95, but he neglected their cumulative effect.

[126] On this point Laqueur 269 is right. Whether the original *hypomnema* mentioned Justus at all is uncertain. If we reject the evidence of the glosses and the initial speech there is no sign that Justus ever did anything to support the war. He advocated peace and never disguised the fact. Schürer 59-60 = Schürer-Vermes 34-35, accepted by Rajak 352 n. 3 and 353-354, believes all of the statements about Justus and determines that Justus played a "double game."

tolerate your lies (359-360). It is not surprising that what Josephus thinks damning, modern scholars think evidence of veracity. Some have deduced that Justus attacked Agrippa and the emperors, restraining the truth until those individuals passed from the scene.[127] But there is no sign that the Tiberian spoke against any royal personage, Jewish or Roman, and it is incredible that, if he had, Josephus should not have made much of the fact. Also there is evidence that the Flavians (even Domitian) tolerated some literary opposition.[128] The polemic against Josephus should not have caused hesitation, at least not after the death of Titus, and CA 1.47-56 shows that Josephus and BJ were widely criticized in literary circles.[129] Because of these problems another explanation has been devised. Justus, who was the imperial secretary at the court of Agrippa (V 356), did not have the time for a literary career until the death of his monarch allowed him to return to private life.[130] If the earlier theories seem too profound, this last seems too facile.

V's peculiar emphasis on the history of Tiberias suggests a different conjecture. Since its founding in 19/20 CE [131] it was the capital of Galilee and received autonomy (with the right of coinage) from Claudius.[132] When Nero bestowed the city as a gift on Agrippa II, its arch-rival Sepphoris (V 37-38) [133] regained the primacy. Although *poleis*, neither Sepphoris nor Tiberias possessed extensive

---

[127] Baerwald 62; Stein 96-97. Against this view see Jacoby, *PW* 10,2 (1919) 1343 and Drexler 312.

[128] Bardon, *Les empereurs* 298-299 and 311-313.

[129] Rajak 355 suggests that the polemic against Josephus would have prevented publication during the lifetime of Agrippa.

[130] Jacoby, *PW* 10,2 (1919) 1342-1343. Nicolaus of Damascus and Suetonius managed to combine literary and court careers.

[131] See chapter two note 129.

[132] For the coins of Tiberias under Claudius (53 CE) see A. Kindler, *The Coins of Tiberias* (Tiberias 1961) 55 nr. 2, with the legend ΚΛΑΥΔΙΟC ΚΑΙCΑΡΟC (sic) LIΓ (obverse) and TIBEPIAC (reverse). G. Hill, *Catalogue of the Greek Coins of Palestine* (London 1914) xiv, thinks that the coin was minted by the procurator but this is incorrect. Hill's catalogue shows that procuratorial coins in Palestine did not bear the name of the city where they were issued. All the Claudian procuratorial coins are dated to year 14, and this to year 13.

[133] Even if Justus' speech (V 37-39) is bogus, it does testify to a tension between the two cities which is inherently plausible and can be paralleled from other areas of the empire (Vienna and Lugdunum, Tacitus *Historiae* 1.65.1; the cities of Asia Minor, Dio Chrysostom, *passim*, with D. Magie, *Roman Rule in Asia Minor* [Princeton 1950] 635-638) and other periods (see Lamentations Rabbah quoted in appendix one below, n. 45). See chapter six below.

municipal territory since they were toparchic capitals.[134] In 68 Vespasian allowed Sepphoris to mint a series of coins bearing the legend *Neronias* (see appendix I). After the war Vespasian continued the urbanization of Palestine by granting municipal territory to many cities: Jamnia, Azotus, Antipatris, Apollonia, Gabara, Joppa, and, perhaps, Sepphoris.[135] The toparchic structure was being replaced by the municipal system. During this period Tiberias had to suffer the ignominy of seeing other cities become the autonomous rulers of extensive territories while it was still subservient to Agrippa and not even the capital of his kingdom. After the death of Agrippa, Tiberias was added to the province of Judaea and, we may, conjecture, immediately sought to be granted a rank equal to or greater than that of its rival Sepphoris. But the purpose of urbanization was to strengthen Roman control by the establishment of a network of pro-Roman bastions throughout the country. Now a large portion of the populace of Tiberias had fought against Rome in 66-67 and Vespasian had torn down part of the city wall as a sign of conquest (BJ 3.460-461).[136] Twenty or thirty years later the Romans probably hestitated before trusting Tiberias with full autonomy. This was the perfect moment for a native son of Tiberias to aid his city. He wrote a history, claiming that Tiberias had desired to remain loyal during the revolt but that Josephus the barbarian (here the author let loose the anger and hatred nursed over a generation) with his Galileans attacked the city and forced it to join the war. Tiberias, Justus concluded, is as worthy as Sepphoris of all municipal privileges and is needed to keep the unruly country peasants (Galileans) in check.

Josephus, whose vanity and arrogance are well known, could not tolerate such an attack. His position in Rome probably was not

---

[134] Jones, *Cities* 265 and 276; M. Rostovtzeff, *Social and Economic History of the Roman Empire*[2] (Oxford 1957) 270; see note 71 above.

[135] Avi-Yonah, *Geographia* 68-69 = *The Holy Land* (Grand Rapids 1966) 110-111; Jones, *JRS* 21 (1931) 78-85. We must admit that the evidence for these grants is not always satisfactory. Vespasian did not actually found any new cities in Judaea (BJ 7.217). Graetz, *MGWJ* 30 (1881) 483-485, deduced from the story in B. Sukkah 27b that Agrippa controlled Sepphoris after 70 but the text implies no such thing. It is possible that Sepphoris received territorial jurisdiction only under Hadrian (Jones, *Cities* 278) or Trajan; see note 141 below. Whether or not Vespasian granted full municipal status to Sepphoris is not a crucial point. After the death of Agrippa, Tiberias and Sepphoris would be competing for honors in Galilee.

[136] See chapter six below, note 78.

threatened, since we may suppose that even the few Romans who
noticed the squabble would regard it with amused indifference.[137]
But it was, perhaps, more than pride that impelled Josephus to
respond. With his unerring eye for a winner, he had been courting
the Yavnean scholars by including Rabbinic propaganda in AJ.
Whether Justus sought the aid of the Rabbis and attacked Josephus'
religiosity is uncertain, but one of V's aims is to portray Josephus as
a religious man, a Pharisaic Jew and friend of Pharisees (see below).
Perhaps Josephus realized that a response to Justus' polemic would
be a good opportunity to address the Rabbis as well. Certainly
Justus had portrayed Josephus as an immoral and self-seeking
tyrant, a charge sufficiently unpleasant even if the religious issue
was ignored.

V speaks directly to the problem: Josephus was not a scoundrel,
Josephus did not force Tiberias to revolt. Tiberias and Sepphoris
cannot be equated since Sepphoris was staunchly pro-Roman and
Tiberias was not. In fact, Justus himself tried to lead an attack
of the Tiberians on Sepphoris! Thus V talks to both the Romans
and the Jews, to the one on the political issue of Tiberias and
Sepphoris, to the other on the religious issue, and to both in defense
of his morality (see below). The anti-Tiberian polemic is not
restricted to V but appears clearly in AJ 18.36-38. The parallel
in BJ 2.168 merely recounts that Herod Antipas founded the city of
Tiberias. But AJ 18.37-38 adds that the populace was an unruly
mob, some of whom had to be drafted to participate in the foundation. Many were poor and of low status, some even slaves freed for
the purpose. Antipas had to offer inducements and apply pressure to
make the new citizens stay. AJ continues: the Tiberians are not
only a motley rabble, they also live in violation of Jewish law.
Their city was founded on the remains of a cemetery where Jews
who fully accept the canons of Rabbinic law would refuse even
to walk, much less to live. (Cf. the indictment of John in BJ 7
which we discussed in chapter four above). Thus Josephus' main
opponents are non-Rabbinic Jews of the basest sort.[138]

---

[137] Schürer 87 = Schürer-Vermes 53 and others claim that Josephus'
position in Rome would have been affected in some way by Justus' work
but they do not say how or why. Josephus responded with a written defense
because he was faced by a written attack. His previous opponents had attacked him orally (V 424-425, 429) or had attacked BJ (CA 1.47-56).

[138] That AJ 18.36-38 has this motive was recognized by Laqueur 117 n. 1;
A. Momigliano, *Richerche sull' organizzazione della Giudea sotto il dominio*

How Josephus fared with the Rabbis is not known.[139] Similarly
we do not know whether Justus' work had any influence. In
99/100 Tiberias was allowed to mint and to call itself "Tiberias the
City of Claudius" (Τιβερι(ᾶς) Κλαυδ(ιόπολις) or Κλαυδ(ιοπολιτῶν)), a
reference to the golden days of Claudius, who had granted it
autonomy, and a pointed contrast to the *Neronias* of Sepphoris,
the city which honored the emperor who had removed Tiberias'
freedom.[140] Thus Tiberias was again in good graces with the Romans,
but its victory was not complete. Its coinage conferred no superior-
ity over Sepphoris because that city too began minting anew under
Trajan. Perhaps it did not receive its territory until the reign of
Hadrian.[141] For Josephus these matters were rather minor; Tiberias'
attainment of municipal rank was not his main concern. He had
refuted the charges about his character and had affirmed his
religiosity.

e. Non-Josephan Sources

We turn now to the non-Josephan sources about Justus. His
name was not unusual in Tiberias and his Hebrew name—if he had
one—may have been Zadoq (a translation of Justus) or Joseph
(or any other name beginning with a "j").[142] Justus is cited several

---

Romano (Bologna 1934, repr. Amsterdam 1967) 74; and Klein, *Galilee* 100-
102. For a discussion of the Halachic problems and the Rabbinic traditions
on the impurity of Tiberias, see G. Alon, *Studies in Jewish History* (Jerusalem 1967) 1.173-174 with n. 105 (Heb.). A cemetery within a city would
offend Greco-Roman sensitivities too (see J. M. C. Toynbee, *Death and Burial
in the Roman World* [London 1971] 48), but Josephus explicitly says that
the foundation of the city violated Jewish law.
[139] See appendix one n. 33 for a Rabbinic story which allegedly describes
a meeting between Josephus and four famous rabbis in Rome.
[140] For these coins see Kindler 55-56 nr. 3 - nr. 6. On the bestowal of the
name Claudiopolis see Rajak 350.
[141] Jones, *Cities* 278. Sepphoris' Trajanic coins read ΤΡΑΙΑΝΟΣ ΑΥΤΟΚ-
ΡΑΤΩΡ ΕΔΩΚΕΝ (Hill 1-4). Whether these coins were minted before or
after 99/100 is unknown. Another uncertainty is the meaning of the legend.
It is probably a reference not to permission for minting (thus Hill xi-xii)
but to a donation of some sort (thus Prof. Peter R. Franke in a letter to the
author). Precisely which Roman official was charged with supervising
municipal issues (the emperor? the local governor?) is one of the central
problems of imperial Roman numismatics. Whoever was responsible allowed
both Tiberias and Sepphoris to mint, perhaps to avoid exacerbating the
tension between the two cities.
[142] Rajak 351 points to two inscriptions for other Justi of Tiberias (Frey,
CIJ I nr. 502 and Vincent, *RB* 30 [1922] 121). A third epigraphical Justus of
Tiberias appears in *IG* V, 1 nr. 1256. On the popularity of this name in

times in patristic and Byzantine literature but, since the information provided is usually meager and, in any case, is either derived from Josephus or irrelevant for our problem, a full discussion is not needed.[143]

The most important text is Photius *Bibliotheca* 33 (= FGrH 734 T 2):

> A chronicle by Justus of Tiberias was read to me. Its superscription was "On the Jewish Kings *en tois stemmasin*, by Justus of Tiberias." Justus hailed from the Galilean city Tiberias. The history begins with Moses and ends with the death of Agrippa, the seventh of the house of Herod and the last of the Jewish kings, who received the kingship under Claudius, was granted additional territory by Nero and even more by Vespasian, and who died in the third year of Trajan, where the history ends.
>
> He has a very succinct style and skips over the majority of the most important events. Because he was afflicted by the illness of Judaism and was a Jew by birth, he made no mention whatever of Christ's coming, of the events which concerned him, and of the miracles which he performed.
>
> He was the son of a certain Jew named Pistos and was, as Josephus says (ὥς φησιν 'Ιώσηπος), the worst possible scoundrel, subservient to money and pleasure. He opposed Josephus. It is said (λέγεται) that he spun many plots against Josephus but that Josephus, although he often had his opponent in his power, only upbraided him verbally and released him without harm. They say (φασι) that the history which Justus wrote is fictitious for the most part, especially where he describes the Roman war against the Jews and the capture of Jerusalem.

Photius refers to two different works. The first is the "Chronicle of the Jewish Kings *en tois stemmasin*" (whatever that means) which covered Jewish history from Moses until Agrippa II who died, according to Photius, in the third year of Trajan (see below). Photius read this Chronicle, summarized it briefly in his normal manner, and noted its most remarkable feature, its silence regarding Christ.[144] The second work is the History, the work which bothered

---

Tiberias, see M. Heilperin in *Sefer Teberyah*, ed. O. Avissar (Jerusalem 1973) 47-48 (Heb.). The name also appears several times in Rabbinic literature. On the equivalence of Justus and Joseph, see *Acts* 1.23 and Leviticus Rabbah 32.5 (p. 748 Margalioth); of Justus and Jesus, see *Colossians* 4.11.

[143] Rajak 358-368 and Wacholder, *Eupolemus* discuss these sources; I see no reason to repeat their remarks. For the Byzantine references to Justus' *floruit*, see note 223 below.

[144] F. Jacoby, *Hermes* 51 (1916) 150-160. On Photius' techniques in paraphrasing and summarizing, see T. Hägg, *Photios als Vermittler antiker*

Josephus. It is apparent that Photius knew this History only through Josephus; everything he says about it is derived from V and is prefaced by "as Josephus says," "it is said," and "they say." The Chronicle and the History must be different works.[145]

The Chronicle of the Kings had some measure of success. Photius read it, Eusebius and several Byzantine writers used it.[146] Even Diogenes Laertius cited it.[147] While the Chronicle had some influence,[148] the History of the war disappeared without a trace. Josephus so dominated Christian historiography that Justus was ignored. There is no sign that any pagan author ever read Justus' History.[149]

Literatur (Uppsala 1975). This brief summary of the *Chronicle* is of the type called *Kurzreferat* by Hägg.

[145] Justus son of Pistos: V 36; Justus a scoundrel, subservient to money and pleasure: V 393 (Justus' μοχθηρία; see n. 123 above); Justus' plots and frequent capture by Josephus: a combination of V 393 and V 82 (on Photius' occasional mistakes and sloppiness in *Kurzreferaten*, see Hägg 198-199); Justus' fictitious history of the war and the capture of Jerusalem: V 357-358. Whether Justus wrote one work or two has been discussed at length; I think it is clear that Photius knew of two distinct works. What the title ἐν τοῖς στέμμασιν (or ἐν τῷ στέμματι) means, I do not know. For the debate on these problems, see Schürer 59-61 = Schürer-Vermes 35-37: Luther 51-54; W. Otto, *Herodes* 14; Jacoby, *PW* 10,2 (1919) 1341-1346; Rühl 293-295; Rajak 358-365.

[146] They quote a synchronization of Moses with some early Greek mythological figures (FGrH 734 F 2 and 3) but it is uncertain exactly what Justus did say; see Rajak 360-361 and Wacholder, *Eupolemus* 123-124.

[147] Diogenes Laertius 2.41 (= FGrH 734 F 1) cites a story about the young Plato at the trial of Socrates which was a standard element in Platonic biographies. See L. G. Westerink, *Anonymous Prolegomena to Platonic Philosophy* (Amsterdam 1962) 9 (section 3) and Olympiodorus *In Platonis Gorgiam Commentaria* 41.6 (p. 211 ed. Westerink = p. 194 ed. Norvin). Historical or not (see W. A. Oldfather, *CW* 31 [1937/8] 203-211 and A. S. Riginos, *Platonica* [Leiden 1976] 56-58), the story is a good sign of Justus' Greek education.

[148] H. Gelzer, *Sextus Iulius Africanus* I (Leipzig 1885, repr. N.Y. circa 1967) 265, suggests that the stories about Jannaeus' conquests and Herod's origin which appear in Syncellus, are derived from Justus through Africanus. The suggestion has some plausibility; see Schürer 62 = Schürer-Vermes 36-37 and Schürer 3.543; Jacoby, *PW* 10,2 (1919) 1345; Rajak 366-367; Wacholder, *Eupolemus* 303.

[149] See appendix one below. H. Gelzer 3-4 suggested that Justus is the source of Africanus' report of a strategem used by the Pharisees (sic) against the Romans but there is no indication which war is intended. For the text see J. R. Vieillefond, *Jules Africain Fragments des Cestes* (Paris 1932) 15, lines 121-125.

2. *Other apologetic aims, perhaps connected with Justus*

Justus was not Josephus' only opponent. In Rome Josephus was subjected to a constant stream of attacks from his fellow Jews (V 424-425, 428-429). Even if the great digression is directed exclusively against Justus, V 336 admits that other figures too are involved. Therefore we cannot assume that V's every apologetic element is a response to the Tiberian. In this section we shall discuss five motives which may or may not be connected with Justus.

a. Josephus' Pedigree

V 1-6 gives Josephus' pedigree and ends with a reference to "those who attempt to slander us." Whether these slanderers include Justus is uncertain. What is certain is Josephus' vanity. He adduces a rather suspect family tree (see note 33 above) in order to prove that he belongs to the Jewish aristocracy. Elsewhere too he emphasizes his social distinction. As a youth (9) he was an associate of the high priests, the leaders of the Pharisees (21), and the foremost men of Jerusalem (28f). He dined (220) and took counsel (305) with the most important men of Galilee. Even his opponents from Jerusalem recognized his rank (198).

b. Josephus and the Pharisees

An important motif in V is the claim that Josephus was a follower of the Pharisees and a strict observer of Jewish law.[150] As a lad he was hailed as an expert in the Law (9), gained first hand acquaintance with all the sects (10) and at nineteen began to live in accordance with Pharisaic teachings (12). He struts about with the Pharisaic chieftains (21). This theme is clear in the beginning of the delegation episode. Since Josephus admits that Simon ben Gamaliel (father of the Yavnean patriarch Rabban Gamaliel II) was the moving force behind the attempt to expel him (190, 193-196) and that three of the four members of the delegation sent from Jerusalem were Pharisees (197), he is careful to emphasize certain things.

---

[150] On V's Pharisaic claims, see Rasp, *ZNW* 23 (1924) 46; M. Smith, in *Israel: Its Role in Civilization*, ed. M. Davis (N.Y. 1956) 75-78; J. Neusner, in *Ex Orbe Religionum: Studia Geo Widengren ... Oblata* (Leiden 1972) 1.224-244 = *From Politics to Piety* (Englewood Cliffs, N.J., 1973) 45-66; Attridge 6-16, esp. 13. On Josephus' claims that he observed Jewish law, see Rajak 357, who cites only a small part of the material. Rajak assumes that this apologetic is directed to Justus.

The attempt against him was instigated by John's jealousy (189). The Pharisaic delegation chosen by Simon knew that he was learned in the Law (198). Most amazing of all is the description of Simon ben Gamaliel (191-192). This man, who was an "old" friend of John of Gischala,[151] who arranged to have the high priest bribed to consent to Josephus' removal (195), who should therefore have been painted in the blackest colors—this man receives an encomium. 191 seems reasonably accurate (Simon is a Jerusalemite, of outstanding lineage, and a Pharisee) but 192 ("This man, highly gifted with intelligence and the power to reason, was able, by his intellectual powers, to set aright an unfortunate situation.") is an ideal portrait of no value for our knowledge of the historical Simon ben Gamaliel.[152] The parallel passage in BJ 2.626 did not consider Simon worthy of mention. Spelled Symeon, he appears in BJ 4.159 as one of two named leaders who urged the people to resist the Zealots, but nothing more is said of him. BJ adheres to its apologetic and does not even label him a Pharisee (see chapter four above). Between BJ and V Simon's stock rose spectacularly, as did the fortunes of the Pharisees. Their heirs were now established and influential at Yavneh and Josephus wanted their friendship. This suggests that they were also influential at Rome but of that we know nothing. The results of the new attitude are clear: glorious Simon was only temporarily (τότε, 192) ill-disposed towards Josephus. Therefore Josephus' dispute with Simon and some Pharisees in 67 should not disqualify the historian in the eyes of the Pharisees of a later generation.

V also emphasizes that Josephus observed the laws, even if it does not explicitly say that the laws were Pharisaic. He was

---

[151] φίλος παλαιός 192; παλαιός om. MW haud male, says Niese. Cf. our English colloquialism "old friend" reflected in Greek by ἀρχαῖος φίλος (AJ 19.276; Ecclesiasticus 9.10). Nouns modified by ἀρχαῖος may have an inherent quality which has existed for a long time and continues to exist; παλαιός rarely indicates this. LSJ s.v. ἀρχαῖος and παλαιός are inadequate. φίλος καὶ συνήθης (192) is a standard Josephan expression (cf. V 180 and 204) and is another example of Josephus' predilection for two words where one would suffice. See chapter two above note 3.

[152] Cf. the portraits of Abraham (AJ 1.154 and 167), Joshua (AJ 5.118), Ahitophel (AJ 7.202), David (AJ 7.391), Uzziah (AJ 9.216), Josiah (AJ 10.50), Ezekias (CA 1.187), and Eleazar (BJ 4.225). On these and similar passages see Attridge 109-126 and 172-176. The only important element missing is Simon's rhetorical ability. Baer 140-141 suggests that the Josephan Simon is modeled on the Antiphon of Thucydides 8.68.1 but this is not necessary. On Josephus' use of ideal portraits see chapter four note 16.

particularly moved to aid the two prisoners sent to Rome when he learned that they, like Daniel and Tobit, refused to eat non-kosher food (V 14). He ordered the destruction of the palace at Tiberias because it was decorated with prohibited representations of living creatures (V 65). BJ says nothing of either episode. BJ 597 does not have the religious motive of V 128 for the return of the Dabaritta booty. In V 159 Josephus claims that he had no troops available because he had sent them home for the Sabbath; he did not wish the Taricheaens to be disturbed on the day of rest.[153] In BJ, which does not attempt to present Josephus as an observant Jew, the parallel passage (2.634) mentions the Sabbath only in a secondary role; troops were not available because they had been sent to collect grain.[154] In V 161 Josephus is afraid of starting a military operation of Friday afternoon lest he desecrate the Sabbath when to fight even for compelling reasons is forbidden.[155] BJ omits these fine points. The delegation story makes clear that not Josephus but the Jerusalemites behave impiously. They violate the most fearsome oaths (V 275), their piety is but a sham (V 291, cf. 75). Josephus excuses himself for wearing arms to synagogue on a public fast day (293). His opponent, however, not only interrupts the sacred service (295) but even attempts to kill Josephus right in the synagogue (302). Again, BJ has nothing of all of this. Similarly, V 74-76 demonstrates that John fleeced the pious Jews of Caesarea Philippi. They were attempting to observe the laws of purity—they were afraid they might have to use pagan oil and thus violate the laws— but John was interested only in profit, not piety. BJ 591-592 skips the religious dimensions of the episode. It is BJ 7, not BJ 2, which attacks John's religiosity (see above pp. 87-89).

The religious apologetic appears most clearly in the last part of V. Since he knows that a priest is not allowed to marry a woman who has been taken captive (CA 1.35; AJ 3.276; AJ 13.292), Josephus insists that the emperor ordered him to take a wife "from the captives" and that the woman was still a virgin when he married her (414).[156] After the destruction of the temple Josephus knew

---

[153] Cf. V 275 for the same argument advanced by the delegation.
[154] See chapter four note 33. Laqueur 84 misinterprets the passage.
[155] On Jewish attitudes towards fighting on Sabbath see M. D. Herr, *Tarbiz* 30 (1961) 242-256, 341-356 (Heb.) and S. Lieberman, *Tosefta Ki-Fshutah: Moed* (N.Y. 1962) 342-343 and 1362 (Heb.).

no greater consolation than the rescue of some Jews and scrolls of the Law (418).[157] Again, BJ provides no parallel.

Hence it is clear that Josephus was expecting a Jewish audience to read V. He wanted to show his co-religionists, especially the Rabbis, that he had always been a religious Jew by Pharisaic standards. But V also has unmistakable signs that a non-Jewish readership was intended.[158] Many Jewish customs are elucidated and bear an explanatory ἡμῖν, "for us Jews" (1, 26, 128, 275, 279; cf. 65, 161). Josephus has to remind the reader about the *trishaeresion* and the Pharisees (10, 12, 191). He assumes that V will come to the hands of those who know little about Palestinian geography (31, 42, 115, 118, 123, 157, 230, 232, 269, 318) and who must be told that Jerusalem is the country's largest city (348, cf. 20).[159]

The expectation of a pagan audience is understandable. Justus' work on the history of Tiberias in 66-67 was directed to the Romans (see above) and the response to it therefore presumes a Roman audience. But is the anticipated Jewish readership also the result of Justus' work? Did the Tiberian try to discredit Josephus before the court of Jewish (or Pharisaic/Rabbinic [160]) opinion? [161] The religious apologetic, like the anti-Justus polemic, appears throughout V. The prohibition of slaying or harming one's fellow Jews (ὁμόφυλοι) appears several times (26, 128, 171, 377; cf. 100, 264, 321) as part of Josephus' personal apologetic and is phrased in

[156] This point was noted by Whiston. Reland apud Havercamp suggests that the prohibition will explain the divorce recounted in 415 but Josephus does not imply this.
[157] On these scrolls see Lieberman, *Hellenism* 23, and J. P. Siegel, *The Severus Scroll* (Missoula 1975) 53.
[158] A few of the following passages were noted by Gelzer 302.
[159] Part of the story of the refugees from Trachonitis (112-113 and 149-154) is directed towards Roman readers. Josephus was no narrow minded fanatic but a believer in the philosophical monotheism popular among contemporary intellectuals (φάσκων δεῖν ἕκαστον κατὰ τὴν ἑαυτοῦ προαίρεσιν τὸν θεὸν εὐσεβεῖν, 113). All worship the same God (τὸν θεόν) but each in his own way. It is remarkable that in spite of its religious apologetic V allows Jesus ben Sapphia to attack Josephus on religious grounds (134-135—one of the few passages where the revolutionaries are said to fight for the Torah, as noted by W. R. Farmer, *Maccabees, Zealots, and Josephus* [N.Y. 1956] 62-65).
[160] Even though Galilee did not come under Pharisaic-Rabbinic influence until after the Bar Kokhba war (132-135 CE), Justus may have sought the aid of the Rabbis in his campaign. We may presume that the Jewish opinion which Josephus (and Justus?) sought to influence will have been Roman as well as—if not more than—Palestinian.
[161] Laqueur assumes that Justus did attack Josephus' treatment of the Bible as untraditional, but this is a baseless assumption. See note 99 above.

apparently religious terms, usually with the indication that Josephus piously observed it. But this evidence is insufficient to justify an affirmative answer. Nowhere in the great digression does Josephus emphasize his piety. He calls Justus a revolutionary, a liar, a scoundrel, but not irreligious. V 80-84, directed against Justus, likewise omits Josephus' religiosity. God protects Josephus not because of his observance of God's law but because of his *clementia* (διὰ τοῦτο, 83).

This religious-Pharisaic viewpoint is not a new element in Josephus' output since it is found in AJ and is related to AJ's "nationalistic" outlook.[162] On the whole the Pharisees are treated much better by AJ than BJ. In particualr AJ emphasizes their power and influence.[163] Herod is condemned for his violation of the traditional laws (AJ 15.267-276, 326-330; 16.1-5) and so is his son Archelaus (AJ 17.341). AJ 18-20, whose motives will be discussed below, also passes judgment on the basis of adherence to the ancestral law. It condemns revolutionaries (AJ 18.9), princesses and kings (AJ 20.143, 191, 216-218), and the city of Tiberias (AJ 18.38; see above). It praises the religious behavior of Agrippa I, especially his concern for purity (AJ 19.331). All of these passages are unique to AJ (BJ 2.118 is but a faint parallel to AJ 18.9). BJ condemns the revolutionaries for lawless behavior (παρανομία), i.e. for committing capital crimes and interfering with the temple cult, but denunciation for the violation of specific Halachic norms rarely appears. Even in vocabulary AJ can be more Jewish than BJ. In two passages it omits BJ's (Nicolaus'?) references to spirits (δαίμονες) and avenging deities (ἀλάστορες); it studiously avoids BJ's pagan and fatalistic terminology for the divine.[164]

---

[162] The second half of Laqueur's book demonstrates this bias in great detail (though only for AJ 14). Thus AJ's treatment of Herod is much less fulsome than BJ's. See chapter two above. Laqueur does exaggerate, but his thesis has gained widespread acceptance. See e.g. Hengel 15 who notes some of the passages we shall discuss here. Our primary concern is AJ 18-20.

[163] See the works cited in n. 150 above.

[164] Cf. the decline and fall of Antipater in BJ 1.582b-647//AJ 17.61-148. The Hades and *alastor* of BJ 1.596 disappear in AJ 17.75. The demons of BJ 1.599, 607, 613, and 628 do not trouble AJ 17.77-78, 82, 87, and 98. The comparison of BJ 1.607//AJ 17.82 and BJ 1.613//AJ 17.87 is particularly instructive. Cf. too BJ 1.593//AJ 17.71. Thackeray, *Josephus* 65, observed the same relationship between BJ and AJ on the death of Mariamme. AJ and V occasionally ascribe misfortune to a δαίμων or to τὸ δαιμόνιον but these words are more characteristic of BJ. See A. Schlatter, *Wie sprach Josephus von Gott?* (Gutersloh 1910) 38-43, reprinted in *Kleinere Schriften zu Flavius*

AJ's religious-Pharisaic bias will explain some of the differences between AJ and BJ. In an offhand remark Josephus informs us that he had friends in Samaria (V 269). Since at least the times of Nehemiah the priests of Jerusalem had allied themselves with the nobles of Samaria and V 269 shows that this legacy was maintained in the first century. Therefore it is no surprise that BJ evinces no hostility towards the Samaritans. BJ 3.308 mocks some Samaritan revolutionaries not because they are Samaritans but because they are revolutionaries who persist in their folly despite Roman success and Jewish catastrophe.[165] AJ, however, is decidedly anti-Samaritan (e.g. AJ 9.290-291; 11.114, 346; 12.257). The shift in attitude, from neutrality to hostility, is clear from the comparison of BJ 2.232-246 to AJ 20.118-36 on the conflict between the Jews and the Samaritans under Cumanus.[166] Not one Galilean (BJ 2.232, 237, 240) but many (AJ 20.118 and 127) were slain by the Samaritans. BJ 2.233 mentions the Galilean preparations for war suppressed by AJ 20.119. Only BJ 2.235 points out that in their reprisal the Galileans killed many of their enemies, showing no compassion (om. AJ 20.121). AJ emphasizes that collusion between the Samaritans and the Romans prevented the Jews from attaining a fair hearing. Cumanus was bribed by the Samaritans and therefore was ineffective (AJ 20.119 and 127, contrast BJ 2.233 and 240). At Rome Cumanus and the Samaritans had so much influence upon Claudius' freedmen that the Jews would not have attained an impartial trial had not Agrippa asked Agrippina to intervene with the emperor (AJ 20.135, cf. BJ 2.245). Finally, AJ increases the guilt of the Samaritans and decreases that of the Jews by reporting that Quadratus found the Samaritans to have been the cause of the trouble and crucified Samaritans as well as

---

Josephus, ed. K. H. Rengstorf (Darmstadt 1970) 98-103, and Cadbury 167 n. 14. εἱμαρμένη, τύχη, and χρέων characterize BJ, not AJ; see Attridge 154.

[165] Thackeray and Ricciotti (the latter copied by Michel-Bauernfeind) miss the point in their notes on BJ 3.308.

[166] Some of the following observations were made by G. Hölscher, *Die Quellen* 70-71 and M. Aberbach, *JQR* 40 (1949/50) 1-14, esp. 7-12. Only here (AJ 20.122) does AJ represent the *Sebasteni* troops as supporters of the Romans against the Jews. Cumanus is prejudiced in their favor and it is not surprising that they aid him. All of the references in BJ 2.52, 58, 63, 74, to the *Sebasteni* as loyal supporters of Rome are omitted by AJ. The *Sebasteni* appear in AJ 19.356-366 where they are censured by Rome and in AJ 20.176 where their actions are inglorious and not conspicuously pro-Roman. For a different interpretation see Hölscher, *PW* 9,2 (1916) 1987 note.

Jews (AJ 20.129; BJ 2.241 omits Samaritans).[167] AJ also cuts
down the number of Jews beheaded from eighteen to five, and
spares Jonathan and some other nobles the dishonor of being
sent as prisoners to Rome (AJ 20.130f, contrast BJ 2.242f).

Besides the above, other discrepancies too between AJ and
BJ can be explained by AJ's religious-Pharisaic bias. Tiberius
Julius Alexander, a nephew of the philosopher Philo, had a resplen-
dent equestrian career. He was prefect of Egypt and the chief of
Titus' staff during the war. BJ refers to him several times, always
with respect and once with moderate adulation (BJ 5.45-46). AJ
mentions him in only one passage (AJ 20.100-103) but says what
BJ never said: Alexander was an apostate (τοῖς γὰρ πατρίοις οὐκ
ἐνέμεινεν οὗτος ἔθεσιν).[168] Another figure whose repute declined
between BJ and AJ is the high priest Jesus ben Gamala (or Gamaliel).[169] BJ 4 praises his oppostition to the Zealots and bestows upon
him a few words of approval (BJ 4.322). Its favorable attitude is
understandable if V 204 correctly informs us that Jesus was
Josephus' friend. But in AJ 20.213 Jesus appears more as a mob
leader than a high priest. The reason is clear: Pharisees never did
like high priests. An even more spectacular shift in opinion affects
Jesus' colleague Ananus. BJ 4.319-321 is an encomium which
makes Ananus a worthy counterpart of the Pericles of Thucydides
(thus Thackeray). But AJ 20.199 condemns Ananus as brash,
reckless, and a follower of the Sadducees, "who are more savage in
their legal decisions than any other Jews." V 193-196 shows that
Josephus had a personal reason to dislike Ananus because the high
priest had supported the attempt to have Josephus removed from
office (V adds that Ananus' consent was bought by a bribe). What
is important, however, is the pattern. High priests are treated

---

[167] Feldman, note c to AJ 20.129, does not realize that BJ omits any
mention of the Samaritan prisoners. The Epitome and the account in Tacitus
agree with BJ in saying nothing of Quadratus' crucifixion of Samaritans,
but Naber is probably mistaken in relying on the Epitome against the
manuscripts for the original text of AJ. Having added the statement that
Quadratus found the Samaritans guilty, AJ had to support it by having
him execute some of them.

[168] E. G. Turner, *JRS* 44 (1954) 63. BJ's account of Alexander's tenure
as procurator differs from AJ's (BJ 2.220//AJ 20.100-102), but the explanation is probably not to be sought in the shift in attitude towards Alexander.
See below.

[169] On the identity of Jesus ben Gamalas with Jesus ben Gamaliel, see
appendix one n. 36 end.

much better by BJ than AJ, partly because AJ has its own political apologetic (see below), and partly because AJ was written by an adherent of the Pharisaic view.[170]

Thus V's presentation of Josephus as a devout Jew, observant of the Pharisaic rules, learned in the laws, a loyal admirer of Simon ben Gamaliel, fits well with AJ which criticizes the religious behavior of kings, cities, governors, and revolutionaries, but which, on the whole, is favorable to the Pharisees. Intense antipathy towards the Samaritans is characteristic of AJ but not BJ. Of course V's inconsistency should not be overlooked.[171] Josephus is not embarrassed to admit (in short asides, to be sure) his friendship with some men of Samaria and with a high priest whom he elsewhere treats in unflattering terms. More significantly he nowhere hides the fact that he led Galileans (Γαλιλαῖοι), country peasants of Galilee and 'ammei ha arez all.[172]

c. Josephus fought the Romans

Another theme directed to V's Jewish audience is the insistence that Josephus fought the Romans to the best of his ability and, specifically, tried to regain Sepphoris for the revolutionary cause. BJ, of course, portrayed Josephus as a great general heroically and ingeniously fighting the Romans. It even has an explicit defense against the charge of betrayal (BJ 3.137). On this point V is much more subtle but the motive is clear nevertheless. Josephus was appointed a *strategos* by the *koinon* of Jerusalem (341) and fought the Romans and the forces of Agrippa whenever they

---

[170] E. M. Smallwood, *JTS* 13 (1962) 30, comments that the two portraits of Ananus are "not necessarily irreconcilable" because by 68 Ananus was older and wiser than he had been in 62. Perhaps Ananus did change his views, but the question is why each portrait is so stark and one-sided. Similarly we understand why BJ omits the stories of high priestly misdemeanors (Smallwood 31), but why does AJ include them? See below. The Rabbinic traditions about the high priests need not be discussed here. On AJ's dislike of high priests and Sadducees, see Rasp, *ZNW* 23 (1924) 32 and 46, and Baumbach, *Kairos* 13 (1971) 24.

[171] Nor should we overlook AJ's inconsistency. It has several passages which are quite nasty to the Pharisees (e.g. AJ 13.410ff) and which are understated by the works cited in n. 150 above. Whether AJ's legal and exegetical material is Pharisaic or sectarian in any way, requires investigation; for a provisional statement see Attridge 176-179.

[172] For Josephus and his *Galilaioi*, see chapter six below. Rabbinic literature has many references to the 'ammei ha arez of Galilee, those who do not observe the Rabbinic laws of purity and tithing. See e.g. S. Baron, *Social and Religious History of the Jews* I[2] (N.Y. 1952) 278-279.

threatened (114-121, 398-406). He even broke his wrist in one engagement (403). During the delegation episode he had to demonstrate his military preparedness (281-289). Although V does not pretend that Josephus is a great general leading thousands of well-armed and well-trained troops, it is clear that the reader is expected to receive the impression that Josephus fought Rome.

The autobiography emphasizes that it was not a dereliction of duty which allowed Sepphoris to become pro-Roman. The citizens were afraid of Josephus (104) and he sternly threatened them (111, cf. 314). He almost captured the city twice. The first time he had to break off the assault because of the ferocity of the Galileans (373-380, apologetic vs. Justus; cf. 31). By the time of his second attempt the Sepphorites had succeeded in receiving a garrison and Josephus was unable to retake the city (394-396). Again it is unnecessary to conjecture that specific accusations prompted these statements. If Justus is the culprit, his rhetorical education permitted him to attack Josephus for compelling Tiberias to join the revolt while simultaneously attacking Josephus for not compelling Sepphoris to join the revolt.[173]

d. Josephus was pro-Roman

In spite of the unabashed admission of his anti-Roman actions and in spite of V's overall account, in a few passages Josephus insists that he was only pretending to be a revolutionary. He really wanted peace with the Romans and Agrippa but was afraid to admit this publicly. He pretended to side with the revolutionaries and thus became involved in a war he opposed. The following are the key texts.[174]

> 17-23: After his return from Rome, Josephus together with the high priests and chiefs of the Pharisees opposed the war. When they realized it would be dangerous to make their true policy

---

[173] Niese, *HZ* 76 (1896) 228 n. 2, conjectured that Josephus was accused of allowing Sepphoris to fall to the Romans and Luther 80 ascribed the accusation to Justus. V 347, a portion of the anti-Justus digression, appears to be an apologia for the fortification of a pro-Roman city but it may be an invention to aid the contrast of Sepphoris to Tiberias. See appendix one below, part B.

[174] Another set of passages (68, 130-131, 388-389) asserts loyalty to Agrippa but this does not imply loyalty to Rome. Thus BJ alleges fidelity to the king (2.597-598) although it never disguises Josephus' revolutionary activity. These passages will be discussed in chapter six below.

known, they instead advised the Jews to refrain from attacks on their enemies so that they could claim they had taken arms in self defense.

28-29: When the chiefs of Jerusalem saw that the revolutionaries were well-armed, they feared for their lives and sent Josephus with two other priests to Galilee in order to keep the country as peaceful as possible and secure arms for the Jerusalem leaders.[175]

72: Josephus did not permit John to carry off the grain of upper Galilee because Josephus wanted to keep it either for the Romans or for himself.

77-78: After sending back his fellow envoys, Josephus procured arms and fortifications. He then made an arrangement to keep the brigands satisfied and peaceful. Josephus made them promise to attack neither the Romans nor the Galileans because he wanted, above all else, to keep Galilee peaceful.

175-176: Josephus told the members of the Tiberian council that he too realized Roman invincibility but that he had to pretend support of the war because of the brigands. He recommended that they too adopt a policy of duplicity and await the proper moment to declare loyalty to Rome.

None of these statements is paralleled in BJ and all seem to contradict, some more sharply, some less, BJ's picture of Josephus as a general sent to Galilee to conduct the war against Rome and whole-heartedly devoting himself to this task. Most investigators agree that Justus is responsible for the pacific pretensions of V. He had accused Josephus of being a revolutionary, an enemy of Rome, and responsible for the war, and Josephus therefore responds that he was sent to Galilee to maintain the peace, a commission which he faithfully executed.[176] But this explanation is untenable. If the assertions of peacefulness and passivity were directed against Justus, their omission from the digression, which is explicitly and exclusively aimed at Justus, is inexplicable. Not only does the great digression refrain from any mention of this claim, it pictures Josephus as actually fighting the local Roman authorities and resisting the attempts of Sepphoris to submit to Rome. Hence we are led to suppose that Justus' political charge focused only on Josephus' relationship with Tiberias, nothing more.[177]

The explanation of V's pacific claims must be sought elsewhere.

---

[175] This apparently is what is meant by ἔστιν ἄμεινον τοῖς κρατίστοις τοῦ ἔθνους αὐτά (i.e. τὰ ὅπλα) τηρεῖσθαι but this motif wholly disappears in the sequel.

[176] Thus e.g. Baerwald 22-26; Luther 70; Drexler 302; Rajak 355-356.

[177] Well noted by Drexler 294.

BJ had claimed that the Jews as a whole did not revolt in 66-70, only a small number of fanatics who tyrannized over the populace. Some Jews were compelled to join the struggle but most remained passive. Josephus never denies that these revolutionaries were Jews, i.e., that the Jews themselves produced the cause of their own disaster, but he does try to show that these internal enemies of the Jews were not an integral part of the Jewish people or of Jewish tradition. The revolutionaries had no connection with, and were not supported by, the "official" representatives of Judaism: Agrippa, the high priests, and the three philosophies. King Agrippa delivered a magnificent oration in opposition to the war (2.345-404). The high priests and aristocrats unequivocally supported Rome (see chapter four note 45 above). The founder of the Fourth Philosophy, one of the revolutionary movements frequently castigated by Josephus, had nothing in common with any of the other "sophists" —i.e. religious teachers—of the time (2.118). BJ never attributes any revolutionary activity to the Essenes, Sadducees, or Pharisees. An isolated individual, John the Essene, fights the Romans (2.567; 3.11 and 19) but the Essenes as a whole do not appear in BJ after BJ 2.120-161. Even 2.152-153, a description of the tortures inflicted on the Essenes "in the war against the Romans", does not say explicitly that they participated in the war.[178] The Sadducees disappear after BJ 2.166. The Pharisees appear only once after BJ 2.166 and there they oppose the war (2.411).[179] Thus on the Jewish side full and exclusive responsibility lies with the revolutionary fanatics who, although Jewish, in no way represent Judaism or the Jewish people.

BJ admits that external factors, notably the malfeasance of two Roman governors, played a part too. Albinus prepared the city for its destruction (BJ 2.276). Florus, even worse than his predecessor (277-279), deliberately provoked war (280-283, 287-288, 292ff). But not even Albinus and Florus can efface the guilt of the revolutionaries (see Agrippa's remarks, BJ 2.352ff).

---

[178] Nor does it say that the Romans inflicted the tortures. Of course, both are implied but it may be important that Josephus does not actually say so. In an author so slovenly it is hard to be sure how much importance should be attributed to exact form of expression. The Essenes are mentioned in a geographical aside in 5.145.

[179] O. Holtzmann, *Neutestamentliche Zeitgeschichte*[2] (Tübingen 1906) 206, echoed by Farmer 32 and S. G. F. Brandon, *Jesus and the Zealots* (N.Y. 1967) 37-38, conjectures pro-Pharisaic bias but this is to ignore BJ's apologia as a whole.

In AJ and V this thesis is modified substantially. Yes, we Jews did rebel, admits Josephus, but we had no choice; we were assailed both internally and externally by powers beyond our control. Isolated Jewish fanatics are not the only ones to blame. Their guilt is joined by the guilt of the "official" Jewish leadership. The pernicious actions of the high priests and of king Agrippa were significant steps on the way to war. Similarly Josephus no longer hides the connection of some revolutionaries with the Pharisees, one of the "official" sects. And yet the war is not the product of Jewish activity alone. In the new theory Josephus emphasizes the deleterious effects of external causes. The procurators were incompetent and immoral, Nero was unfair to the Jews, the *Sebasteni* were virulently anti-Jewish, the pagans of the neighboring cities attacked without cause. Thus Josephus admits that the people as a whole fought the Romans, but, he insists, the Jews were compelled by an irresistible concatenation of circumstances.

The new thesis is epitomized by the words "necessity" (ἀνάγκη) and "unwilling" (ἄκοντες): "the war of the Jews against the Romans was caused more by necessity (ἀνάγκη) than by deliberate choice" (προαίρεσις, V 27) and "they fought the Romans unwillingly" (ἄκοντες, AJ 1.6). BJ agrees that the Jews did not voluntarily fight the Romans but it denies any national participation. Only the tyrants and some of their unfortunate victims fought the war. In BJ "unwilling" (ἄκοντες) describes the Romans (e.g. Titus unwillingly destroys the temple, 1.10 and 6.266), never the Jews. Similarly BJ never uses "necessity" (ἀνάγκη) to explain why the Jews fought the Romans. Once the war has begun necessity forces men in particular circumstances to do things they otherwise might not do (e.g. 6.197) or might not do so well (e.g. 3.149), but it does not govern history on the national level.[180]

To return to AJ's new theory: let us consider first the internal factors which led to the war. For all of its "nationalistic" and

---

[180] See the concordance s.v. ἄκων and ἀνάγκη. For other contrasts of προαίρεσις and ἀνάγκη see BJ 6.230 and AJ 6.219. Farmer 14 n. 7 realizes the difference between the theories of BJ and V 27 but does not notice the overall pattern. S. Applebaum, *JRS* 61 (1971) 157, notes that AJ spreads the guilt more broadly than BJ. Rajak 355 misses the point entirely. Josephus' conception of historical causation requires further analysis. On his usage of Tyche and Eimarmene see H. Lindner 85-94, and G. Stählin in *Josephus-Studien: Untersuchungen ... Otto Michel ... gewidmet*, ed. O. Betz et al. (Göttingen 1974) 319-343.

religious bias, AJ dislikes the revolutionaries as much as BJ does. AJ 18.6-10 is a severe critique of the Fourth Philosophy lacking in BJ. In this section AJ still adheres to BJ's apologetic that Judas (and Saddok the Pharisee, omitted by BJ) founded an "intrusive" school without any legitimacy (AJ 18.9). This is not contradicted by the fact, which here Josephus admits, that the Fourth Philosophy agrees with the Pharisees in all matters but one (AJ 18.23). The one difference was of such importance in its consequences that it made of those who accepted Judas' teaching a separate "philoso-phic" (i.e. legal) school and also a peculiar revolutionary party. But, unlike BJ, AJ had no reason to hide the similarity of the sect, in *other* respects, to the Pharisees, and the participation of a Pharisee in its formation. Similarly V speaks of the Pharisees' actions in the war and of John's friendship with Simon ben Gamaliel.[181] The condemnation of the revolutionaries which appears in AJ 20.166 and which ascribes the destruction of the temple to God's anger at the *Sicarii*, is not in BJ. AJ emphasizes more than BJ the presence of brigands, revolutionaries, and charlatans in the country (AJ 20.5, 97-98, 160, 188, 208-210, all omitted by BJ). But, in spite of all this, because AJ does not assign exclusive guilt to these groups, it does not need the vituperative rhetorical con-demnations so characteristic of BJ. We hear nothing of their heinous crimes or their tyranny. John, that arch villain of BJ, appears in V in more favorable light. He is still a villain but he is no brigand (λῃστής); the defamations of BJ 2.585-589 are absent.

In addition to these revolutionaries AJ condemns the highest echelons of Jewish society, the high priests and the aristocracy. They boldly usurped all the priestly tithes so that some of the poorer priests, devoid of any income, starved to death (20.181 and 206-207). The high-priests fought with each other, with the common priests, and with the aristocracy.[182] Each of the contenders as-sembled a mob of supporters (described as "reckless revolutionaries", θρασύτατοι καὶ νεωτερισταί) and proceeded to the fray (20.179-180 and 213). Even Costobar and Saul, relatives of Agrippa, participated in the fighting, and, from that time, "our city became diseased,

---

[181] The prominence of the Pharisees fits AJ's aim of demonstrating Pharisaic influence and power. On the alleged contradiction in AJ, see n. 236 below.

[182] Feldman understands AJ 20.180 a bit differently, as if there were a μέν ... δέ to contrast the high-priests with the regular priests and the leaders of the *demos*.

everything proceeding from bad to worse" (AJ 20.214). BJ has little of this.[183]

Even Agrippa contributed his share. The king's first dispute with the priests ended with a victory for the priests (AJ 20.189-196), but the second had catastrophic consequences. Agrippa allowed the Levites to wear the priestly robes and allowed those who had menial functions in the temple to learn the hymns by heart, two innovations contrary to the traditional laws "the violation of which made punishment inevitable" (AJ 20.216-218). BJ has none of this.

Let us turn now to the external causes of the war. The incompetence and immorality of the procurators is increased by AJ. BJ's short optimistic account of Cuspius Fadus and Tiberius Alexander (they kept the nation in peace by disturbing none of the local customs, BJ 2.220) is ignored rather than contradicted. We have noted above that AJ blackens both the Samaritans and Cumanus in AJ 20.118-136 (cf. BJ 2.232-246).[184] Felix in particular does not fare well in AJ. Both works admit that Felix captured many brigands (BJ 2.253//AJ 20.161) but only AJ 20.162-164 adds that the procurator hated Jonathan to the extent that he arranged for the high priest to be murdered by some brigands. BJ 2.256 mentions the assassination but not the complicitly of Felix. The Roman attacks against the false prophets are justified more by the account of BJ 2.258-263 than AJ 20.167-172a.[185] Felix' selection of two embassies from Caesarea, representing both sides of the *stasis* (BJ 2.270), is ignored by AJ 20.182-184 and replaced by two separate delegations, one sent by the Jews to accuse Felix (who is acquitted because of his influence at court) and the other by the Greeks to maintain their claim against the Jews. Thus AJ suppresses

---

[183] BJ 2.274-276 apparently refers to the activities described by AJ 20.213-214 and even mentions δυνατοί (274) and ἴδιον στῖφος (BJ 275, cf. AJ 20.180). But the identity of the mobsters is not indicated by BJ. BJ's final clause is similar to AJ 20.214, but BJ blames all revolutionaries, not just aristocrats. See above pp. 60-61.

[184] See pp. 149ff. Several small touches blacken Cumanus even more. His attack on a crowd of Jews is justified more by BJ 2.225 (the Jews hurl stones at the soldiers) than by AJ 20.108-110 (the Jews hurl curses). In BJ 2.229 Cumanus orders the arrest of some local villagers, in AJ 20.114 he orders the villages to be plundered too.

[185] AJ omits BJ's characterization of these prophets as revolutionaries (BJ 2.258-259; AJ omits ἐλευθερία). Only BJ 262 emphasizes the threat of the Egyptian prophet to capture the city with its Roman garrison and to tyrannize over the populace. Note BJ's apologetic in 263: the entire people joined the defense.

the even-handed action of the procurator in order to show Roman inequity. AJ forgets to mention Festus' vigorous campaign against the *lestai* (AJ 20.185//BJ 2.271). The tenure of Albinus (AJ 20.204 and 215//BJ 2.272-276) is the only exception to this pattern and has been analyzed above in chapter two. AJ 20.252-256 repeats BJ's estimate of Florus (BJ 2.277-279) and then adds: "It was Florus who compelled us (καταναγκάσας ἡμᾶς) to raise war against the Romans" (AJ 20.257, cf. 18.25). The reader is referred to BJ for a full account of what the Jews were compelled (ἠναγκάσθημεν) to do (AJ 20.258).

AJ also puts some of the blame for the war on Nero. As we have just remarked, in BJ Felix behaves properly in the Caesarea affair. BJ also shows no hostility towards Nero for deciding against the Jews. It does imply (BJ 2.284) that his decision caused the outbreak of the war, but the implication is very gentle; BJ 2.285ff proceeds to a story which has no connection whatever with Nero's decision. Contrast AJ, which has Felix behave improperly and has Nero favor the Greeks on account of bribery (AJ 20.183-184). Nero's decision was one of the causes of the war, and here AJ is explicit, "Nero's decision was the cause of the troubles which affected our nation afterwards. Once the Jews of Caesarea learned of the decision, they persisted all the more in their strife with the Syrians until they ignited the war."

The Romans are not the only ones to blame for the riots in Caesarea. The troops in the city were *Sebasteni*, men of Samaria, who hated the Jews and, according to AJ, who should have been transferred from Caesarea even in 44 CE. They managed, however, to persuade Claudius (note again AJ's insistence on the evil consequences of Samaritan influence at the Roman court!) to let them remain (AJ 19.366). BJ and its parallel in AJ 20 (see note 166) recount the participation of these troops in the disturbances, but it is AJ 19.366 which indicts them, "The *Sebasteni*, also in the succeeding period, were the source of the greatest disasters for the Jews, sowing the seeds of the war under Florus". They, too, share in the guilt.[186]

Thus AJ shows that many diverse factors converged to make war inevitable. The Jews, assailed from within and without by powers beyond their control (from within by revolutionaries, high priests,

---

[186] With σπέρματα βαλόντες of AJ 19.366, cf. BJ 2.276.

aristocrats, and Agrippa; from without by procurators, Nero, and *Sebasteni*),—the Jews were forced to fight a war they did not want. V develops the theory further; it too condemns brigands, revolutionaries, and fanatics (V 17-24 and 28), but it adds the inhabitants of the pagan cities of Syria and Palestine to AJ's list of external aggressors. The numerous attacks of the Jews against the Greek cities (BJ 2.458-465) are not mentioned. V 25f instead recounts how the Jews of Syria were massacred although they were loyal to Rome and to their native cities. Only with reference to Scythopolis does V mention Jewish initiative (V 26) but again it is to show how some Jews became involved in the war against their will. According to V the Scythopolitans forced the local Jews to bear arms against their coreligionists. Contrast BJ 2.466 and 7.364-366 in which the Scythopolitan Jews voluntarily participate. Like AJ, V concludes that these facts, i.e. the actions of the brigands and the attacks of the pagans, prove that the war was the product not of intention but necessity (V 27).

In the context of this new apologetic theory, two puzzling claims of V make sense. The first is the remarkable statement that even John tried at first to remain at peace but had to react after he was attacked by pagans from neighboring cities (V 43-45). We have already noted several times that John is treated better by V than by BJ; this will explain why John's initial participation in the war is apologetically explained. We also understand that Josephus wants to show that Justus (V 36-42) was more militant than John (V 43-45). But V 43-45 is still remarkable—why should V admit (or claim) that John was an innocent victim of circumstances beyond his control? The answer is that the claim of V 43-45 is part of a larger conception: like his fellow Jews John was compelled to fight.[187]

The second feature of V explained by V 27 and the new apologetic

---

[187] Whether V 43-45 is reliable or not is uncertain. It certainly does not prove that John was ever a "moderate" or pro-Roman; see chapter six below n. 80. On the contrast intended by the juxtaposition of V 36-42 to V 43-45, see Drexler 299. As a part of this anti-Justus polemic, Josephus separated Justus' attacks on Gadara and Hippos from their larger context of Jewish reactions to the pogroms in the Greek cities (see chapter one above n. 4 and the text above at n. 118). Thus one could argue that the polemic against Justus caused Josephus to suppress the Jewish attacks in V 25-27 and to invent John's initial pacificity, both to highlight Justus' militancy. I do not think that this polemic sufficiently explains V's silence in V 25-27, the extraordinary claim of V 43-45, or the concluding phrase in V 27.

theory is Josephus' claim of pro-Romanism. Josephus too did not
want to fight Rome. He and the aristocrats opposed war and were
terrified of the well-armed *demos* (V 20-22, 28). He was sent to
Galilee to promote peace (V 29) and he tried to execute this commission (V 77-78). He intended, at the appropriate moment, to
surrender to the Romans (V 72, 175-176). Unfortunately, V never
explains the necessity which caused Josephus to fight the Romans at
Jotapata; the narrative breaks off before that point.[188] Nor does V
rigorously adhere to this theory. Once Josephus arrives in Galilee, he
is busy fighting the Romans, attacking pro-Roman cities, and
fortifying towns long before any *ananke* might have intervened and
without any pro-Roman pretense. Perhaps in the projected brief
history of the war (AJ 20.267) Josephus planned to develop the
theory further. At all events, the passages in V which claim that
Josephus was sent to Galilee to keep the peace, and that he intended
to submit to the Romans as soon as possible, are to be explained as
products of the general apologetic claim of his later period, that the
Jews desired peace but were pushed into a war they did not want.

e. Philip son of Jacimus

One of the most enigmatic features of V is the account of Philip
son of Jacimus.[189] BJ mentions him only a few times. After Eleazar

---

[188] Whether the *ananke* was to be internal or external we do not know.
Perhaps it is provided by Josephus' dream (V 209), "Remember that it is
necessary (δεῖ) for you to fight the Romans too." The dream is part of a
section of V which resembles the BJ 3 description of Josephus at Jotapata
(see section B above), and, in fact, the Asochis dream and the Jotapata
vision have analogous functions: they justify an ostensible change in Josephus' political life. Jotapata explains why Josephus stopped fighting the
Romans, Asochis explains why he began. The primary objection to this
interpretation is that V does not explicitly use the dream for this purpose;
the main point of Asochis is to provide an unimpeachable response to the
demand that Josephus return to Jerusalem (Rajak 357). On prophetic
dreams in Josephus, see J. Blenkinsopp, *JJS* 25 (1974) 246, who notes a
parallel between Josephus' dream at Asochis and Paul's at Corinth (*Acts*
18.9-10). Cf. too *Acts* 19.21; 23.11; 27.24. I have treated V 175-176 with
the other passages which show Josephus' pro-Romanism even though it
differs from them in one important respect. Josephus may well have claimed
before the Tiberian senate to be a pro-Roman even if we regard the claim
as false. See above. But, even if the speech is historical, presumably it was
included in V because it agreed with the *ananke* theory. V's statements
about the Jerusalem aristocracy in V 17-23 and 28 do not contradict AJ's
condemnation of *some* high priests and aristocrats.
[189] The best discussion of the Philip material is Drexler 306-312; see too
Baerwald 37-40 and Schlatter, *Bericht* 24-35 = *Kleinere Schriften* 20-31.

ben Ananias had instigated the priests to refuse the sacrifices of gentiles, the peace party (BJ 2.411), to obtain aid, sent Simon ben Ananias to Florus, and Saul, Antipas, and Costobar to Agrippa (BJ 2.418-419). Florus, of course, desired war and gave no response (BJ 2.420), but Agrippa sent a force of two thousand cavalry under Darius the hipparch and Philip son of Jacimus (BJ 2.421). Saul et al. apparently returned to Jerusalem with this contingent. Philip and his troops (the βασιλικοί), first from the upper city (422-424 and 426) and later from the royal palace (431-432), fought against the rebels based in the lower city and temple. After the attacks of Menahem (433-437) the royalists and the peace party surrendered on the condition that their lives would be spared (437) and left the Roman garrison to its fate (438-440, 449-457). But Philip did not yet leave Jerusalem. He was still there when Noarus began causing trouble in Agrippa's kingdom (BJ 2.481-483) and when Cestius' expedition was repulsed (BJ 2.499-555). Only then (after 8 Dios = Marḥeshvan, 66 CE, BJ 2.555) did Saul and Philip flee from the city to Cestius (BJ 2.556). The legate sent them to Nero, then in Greece, to explain what happened and to blame Florus (BJ 2.556-558). Philip appears only once more in BJ and there (BJ 4.81) not as an active character but as a point of reference (see below).

V has a different version of the facts. After the surrender of the king's troops in the royal palace (which, according to BJ 2.440, took place on 6 Gorpiaios = Elul) Philip nearly was executed by Menahem (V 46), but was lucky enough to escape. For four days he was protected by a contingent of "Babylonian" Jews (see below). On the fifth (about 11 Gorpiaios) he donned a disguise and fled to a village near Gamala (V 47). Here he fell sick and wrote to Agrippa and Berenice. He sent the letters to Varus (Noarus in BJ) who was then Agrippa's representative in his kingdom (V 48-61).[190] Varus, who wanted no competitor, impounded the letters and killed the messengers so that Philip's whereabouts remained unknown and rumor reported that he had gone over to the revolutionaries. After Varus was removed (V 61 and 180), Philip was able to contact

---

Since neither these authors nor Schalit (n. 206 below) appreciate all the problems, I have discussed this material at some length although I am unable to reach many definite conclusions.

[190] V often refers to Agrippa and Berenice as οἱ βασιλεῖς (e.g. V 49 and 126), a usage which may have epigraphical attestation (see Schwabe, *Journal of Juristic Papyrology* 4 [1950] 309-315).

Agrippa (V 180-181) and the king was glad to discover the falsehood
of the rumors about him (V 182). Agrippa displayed Philip to the
Roman governors, apparently Cestius and his council (τοῖς
ἡγεμόσιν),[191] as proof of his minister's loyalty (V 183). The king sent
him back to Gamala with instructions to pacify it (V 183-184).
Later, when Philip was accused before Vespasian by the Tyrians of
having, on Agrippa's orders, betrayed the Roman garrison in
Jerusalem, Agrippa was exonerated of any wrong doing, but
Vespasian recommended that Philip be sent to Nero (V 407-408).
By the time Philip actually reached Nero, the political situation in
Rome was so precarious that he returned home immediately
(V 409).

There are two important contradictions between V and BJ. The
first is: who sent Philip to Nero? Was it Cestius (BJ 2.558) or
Agrippa on the recommendation of Vespasian (V 408)? Here V seems
to be more reliable. First, since Philip was Agrippa's man he would
presumably have gone to Agrippa, as V reports, not to Cestius,
as BJ. Second, BJ's description of Philip's mission—to turn Nero's
anger upon Florus and away from Cestius—is implausible since
Philip was a suspected revolutionary and it was his own conduct
that needed explanation. BJ assumes that Philip was an un-
assailable pro-Roman, a false assumption. BJ has simplified and
condensed in its normal manner by joining Philip to Saul et al.

The second contradiction concerns the date of Philip's departure
from Jerusalem. In BJ Philip flees shortly after 8 Dios = Marḥeshvan (late October), in V about 11 Gorpiaios = Elul (late August
or early September), a difference of about two months. Since
both accounts seem to be apologies for Philip it is difficult to
determine which is more accurate. Perhaps, in order to protect
Philip from the charge of revolutionary activity (known from V 182,
407-08), V advances the date of his departure from Jerusalem,
thus minimizing his stay in a city (Jerusalem) controlled by
revolutionaries. Perhaps, in order to protect Philip from allegations
raised by his suspicious conduct in Gamala (allegations which we
can reconstruct from V's tendentious account), BJ postponed
the date of his departure from Jerusalem, thus minimizing his stay
in a city (Gamala) controlled by revolutionaries.

---

[191] Cf. BJ 2.334. Although Drexler 310 knows that the chronology is
against it, he suggests that τοῖς ἡγεμόσιν means Vespasian and Titus (V
407-408).

I see no way of solving this problem because arguments can be advanced for both accounts. According to V (the "early" chronology) Philip fled on 11 Gorpiaios, a week before the massacre of the garrison (17 Gorpiaios or later).[192] When Philip arrived north, there were rumors that Agrippa was going to be executed because of the crimes of the Jews (V 52, reading ἁμαρτίας). Even if these crimes do not include any alleged misdeeds of Philip after the betrayal of the garrison, the chronology is difficult because until the massacre the Jews committed no unpardonable error.[193] A better argument against V's chronology is its clear motivation. The problem BJ ignores, V removes. Philip could not have been in Jerusalem fighting the Romans because he was elsewhere. Where? Not in Gamala itself—that city was about to oppose Agrippa's legate. Not in another city—why did Philip not contact Agrippa earlier than he did? V therefore immobilizes Philip with sickness and hides him in a small village near Gamala. Since his letters were intercepted by Varus, no wonder that no one heard from him for a few months! In contrast, the motivation of BJ is not so definite nor is its chronology so problematic. BJ manages to tell the story of Varus (Noarus) without once mentioning Philip or Gamala. BJ is consistent and clear.[194] V's claim that Philip succeeded in pacifying

---

[192] After 11 Gorpiaios, the alleged date of Philip's departure, occurred Menahem's tyrannical behavior and his murder by the partisans of Eleazar. The date 17 Gorpiaios is derived from Megillat Taʿanit; see chapter one above, note 3.

[193] See Drexler 308-309. Perhaps to support the "early" chronology V claims that Agrippa was not in Antioch (BJ 2.481) but Beirut (V 49). In BJ the massacre had already occurred and Agrippa must have been discussing Cestius' war plans. Antioch was the staging point of Cestius' expedition (BJ 2.500). But in V the massacre was still in the future and so Josephus has Agrippa go to his favorite city (V 181 and 357; AJ 20.211-212; M. McCrum and A. G. Woodhead, *Select Documents of the Principates of the Flavian Emperors* [Cambridge 1966] nr. 244).

[194] The only chronological problem may be BJ 4.83, which says that the revolt of Gamala began (τῆς ἀποστάσεως ἀρξαμένης) on 24 Gorpiaios. Simhoni, in his Hebrew translation, notes that this date could possibly refer to either 66 or 67 CE. If the former, Gamala revolted even before the defeat of Cestius (8 Dios) and only two weeks after Philip's departure from Jerusalem (11 Gorpiaios, according to V). Thus this date may confirm V. But it is more likely (as Simhoni says) that the date is 24 Gorpiaios 67 and refers to the beginning of the revolt *against Vespasian*, when the city refused to surrender and the Roman siege began. Even before the fall of Jotapata Vespasian must have known that Tiberias and Taricheae were in revolt but in BJ 3.445 their hostility is reported to the general as if it were something new, i.e. he now hears that they refuse to surrender and that their revolt is begun.

Gamala (V 59-60) may be an apologia for anti-Agrippa activity or may be sheer invention, inspired by Philip's later, allegedly pacific, activity there (V 183-184).[195] V thus seems to be a tendentious correction of BJ.[196]

But it is precisely BJ's consistency and clarity which is suspicious. We have seen that BJ often simplifies chronology and, since its statement that Cestius sent Philip to Nero is mistaken (see above), its chronology too may be mistaken, whether a result of compression and simplification (treating Philip with Costobar and Saul) or of apology for Philip (removing him from Gamala). At least one detail of V's account does not appear invented: Philip's flight in a wig (V 47). V's extensive description of Philip's relations with Gamala presumably hides his revolutionary activities there which may well have taken place before the defeat of Cestius.

No matter which account we follow, the actions of Philip must be understood in conjunction with the history of Gamala and here too absolute certainty is beyond attainment. In the following reconstruction I consider the chronology of both BJ and V.

The conflicts between the Jews and Greeks in the cities of Syria form the background. Varus or Noarus,[197] who was of royal lineage (BJ 2.481//V 52), thought the time was ripe for an assault on Agrippa's throne. He attempted to curry the favor of the Greeks of Caesarea Philippi [198] by turning upon the Jews (V 53). Similarly he attacked the Babylonian Jews of Ecbatana [199] but here the problems begin. In BJ seventy noble Jews of Batanaea come to Noarus of their own accord and request a contingent to prevent an anti-Roman outbreak. Noarus slays them all, and BJ's only

---

On 8 Gorpiaios 67 Vespasian was at Tiberias-Taricheae (BJ 3.542) and he may well have approached Gamala on or about 24 Gorpiaios.

[195] On Josephus' duplication of events, see chapter three above, pp. 81-82.

[196] This is the conclusion of Drexler 309. Baerwald 40 and Luther 88 follow V.

[197] On these names see chapter one note 16.

[198] V frequently mentions Caesarea Philippi: V 52, 53, 55, 57, 59, 61, 74, and 75. The more famous Caesarea is mentioned only in V 414. Schalit, NWB s.v., confuses them; Möller and Schmitt 113-116 are correct.

[199] Ecbatana (V 54-57) was a settlement in Batanaea, otherwise unknown. Havercamp notes that Herodotus 3.62 and 64 refers to an Ecbatana in Syria, but that story is not reliable because a suitable location had to be discovered or invented to verify the prophecy that Cambyses would die in Ecbatana. See the commentary of How and Wells on Herodotus 3.62 ("the religious coincidence is more than suspicious") and Marcus' note on AJ 11.30.

explanation, "on account of greed", is not elucidated (BJ 2.482-483). V is more detailed and more hostile to Varus. The legate, using the services of twelve prominent members of the Jewish community of Caesarea Philippi (and this after the attacks of V 52-53?), persuaded the Jews of Ecbatana to send to him a delegation of seventy to attest their innocence of any plan to revolt. These delegates, together with the envoys from Caesarea, were mostly massacred (V 54-57). Varus then turned upon Ecbatana, but the Babylonians, warned by some who had escaped the massacre, fled to Gamala. V claims that Philip, who had left Jerusalem shortly after the fall of the palace and had since then been lying sick in a village near Gamala,[200] now arrived in the city and restrained the Jews from battling against Varus and the Greeks of Caesarea. There were rumors that Agrippa had died but Philip nevertheless remained loyal and maintained the peace (V 58-61). Finally, Agrippa replaced Varus with Aequus Modius (V 61).

According to BJ, Philip's intervention at this point in Gamala is impossible because Philip did not leave Jerusalem until after the defeat of Cestius. Modius became legate before Josephus arrived in Galilee (V 74) and so the events of V 58-61 must have occurred before Cestius' defeat. Another problem with V's account is that we seem to have another reference to the *ananke* theme. The poor Jews of Ecbatana desperately wanted to remain at peace (V 56), but were provoked by Varus beyond endurance. Even so, Philip managed to restrain them.[201] I see no way to determine what actually happened in Gamala and Ecbatana. The only sure point here is that Gamala and its Babylonian immigrants evinced sentiments hostile to Agrippa's lieutenant who had to be replaced.[202] The Jews of Caesarea Philippi, too, were restive after this affair (V 74).

---

[200] Schlatter *Bericht* 27 = *Kleinere Schriften* 23 well notes that neither V nor BJ explains what became of Darius and the 2000 cavalry that were sent by Agrippa with Philip to Jerusalem. Presumably they joined the revolutionary forces in Jerusalem or went to Gamala with Philip and helped him to take the town.

[201] With Philip's speech in V 60, cf. Josephus' in V 17 and 175. The progenitor of all three speeches is Agrippa's magnificent oration (BJ 2.345-401).

[202] Luther 88 deduces from BJ 2.568 that the authorities of Jerusalem believed that Gamala sided with the revolution. But the deduction is not cogent because legates may have been sent to organize and incite peaceful areas. Alternatively, BJ 2.568 may be exaggerating the scope of Josephus' command or telescoping the events.

The next installment is V 114 which says that Modius besieged
Gamala. The chronology here too is very obscure. Was Philip
in Gamala when Modius attacked it? It is possible that V 179-187,
which describes the revolt of Josephus (not the historian) in Gamala,
belongs before V 114 (see below). Another uncertainty.

The story resumes with Philip's final successful attempt to
contact Agrippa at Beirut (V 180-183). According to the chronology
of BJ this will have occurred shortly after the defeat of Cestius.
The king greeted his minister warmly and demonstrated to the
Romans that all the rumors about his disloyalty were false (V 183a).
Agrippa then sent Philip to Gamala with instructions to take the
Babylonians back to Ecbatana and to guard the peace (V 183b-184).
Whether any of this is true is impossible to determine. Perhaps
Philip fled from Jerusalem directly to Gamala, there engaged in
revolutionary activity, and fought Modius (V 114) before becoming
reconciled with the king (V 180-183). Did Agrippa send him back to
Gamala? V 184 does not say when or why Philip left Gamala. V 177
suggests that Philip did not execute his instructions to remove the
Babylonians from Gamala, but the suggestion is not wholly con-
clusive, since "feuding" (στασιάζοντες) can refer to quarreling
between neighboring districts. The statements that *after* Philip's
departure the men of Gamala, fighting with the Babylonians,
killed relatives of Philip and of Justus of Tiberias (177) and that
this was done when Gamala revolted from the king (185-187) are
intended to indicate that as long as Philip, his men, and his Babylonian allies were on hand, Gamala was kept in line, but once they
withdrew (on the king's orders!) the revolt broke out. This may
or may not be true.

The leader of the revolutionaries was Josephus ὁ τῆς ἰατρίνης.[203]
He attacked the aristocracy (πρῶτοι), persuaded some to abandon
the king, and compelled or killed the others (V 185). A few victims
are mentioned by name (V 186). Josephus sent aid to the revolutionaries, a contingent of soldiers for defense and workmen to
construct the walls of the city (V 186). Not only Gamala but all of
Gaulanitis as far as Solyme (location unknown) revolted from the
king (V 187).

This section too has many problems. It is impossible to reconcile
V 177-178 with V 185-186. V 177 mentions *stasis* between the

---

[203] Or τις 'Ιαίρου παῖς; see Schalit, *NWB* s.v. 'Ιώσηπος nr. 7.

Gamalites and the Babylonians, but in V 185 the struggle is between the revolutionaries and the aristocrats of the city. In V 186 the Gamala revolutionaries kill Chares, his relative Jesus, and a brother (or sister) of Justus. V 177-178, however, has the following account: the Galileans (not the Gamalites) [204] maimed (not slew) a brother of Justus before Josephus arrived in Galilee (the chronology of V 186 is not clear); the Gamalites slew Chares (with V 186), here identified as a relative of Philip, and his brother (not merely "one of his relatives" as in V 186) Jesus, here identified as Justus' brother-in-law. BJ 4.81 mentions a sister of Philip and her two daughters who were in Gamala during the final siege by the Romans and evidently were on good terms with the rebels. In BJ 4.18 and 68 Chares and Josephus (presumably the ὁ τῆς ἰατρίνης of V) are busy fighting the Romans, a bit of information rather difficult to reconcile with V 177 and 186 (Chares is killed by the Gamalites). (Were there two leaders in Gamala named Chares?) [205] If we knew where Solyme was (V 187), we should know whether V 187 contradicts BJ 4.4 which says that Sogane and Seleucia, two towns in Gaulanitis, went over to the king at the beginning of the revolt. Or does BJ 4.4 describe an event which took place after V 187?

The revolution in Gamala was a great success. If we postpone V 114 to this point, Modius now attacked the city. The siege lasted seven months (BJ 4.10). Agrippa's forces tried to prevent supplies from reaching the city (V 398), but it held out until Vespasian captured it after a fierce struggle (BJ 4.11-53, 62-83). Only Jotapata, Jerusalem, and Masada could claim greater loyalty to the cause.

Why are the stories of Gamala and Philip important to V? Are they responses to Justus? V 177-178 (on the massacres in Gamala) yields the plausible conjecture that Justus accused Josephus (and Philip?) of complicity in the deaths of his relatives in Gamala. Josephus denies any responsibility and labels the Gamalite revolutionaries as the culprits. He even suggests that Justus' brother was harmed "before the war" but here V 177 is refuted by V 186. It is not hard to reconstruct an account less flattering to

---

[204] Cf. the confusion on Judas the Galilean and Judas the Gaulanite. V 186 implies that these relatives were killed because of their pro-Roman views but V 177 says nothing to suggest this. Schalit, *Klio* 26 (1933) 82-83, does not appreciate this distinction.

[205] Niese, Feldman, and Schalit agree in their indices that there was only one Chares in Gamala.

Josephus,[206] but it is obvious that we cannot hope to recover exactly what Justus said or what transpired in Gamala in 66-67.

Philip's relevance is harder to estimate. The simple demand for background information to the history of Gamala [207] cannot explain the extraordinary amount of detail. Perhaps to defend Agrippa V had to defend Philip. Although Vespasian absolved Agrippa of any guilt and excoriated the king's traducers (V 408), the future emeror (and his son) did not develop a personal relationship with Agrippa. They accepted Agrippa's support but without enthusiasm. Agrippa was not allowed to take an active role in the war.[208] Was his loyalty suspect?[209] BJ defends the king by assigning him a magnificent speech and showing his strong support for the peace party. But why should V have been concerned about Agrippa, now dead? The appeal to Agrippa's testimony (V 364-367) cannot be the only reason. It is difficult to see how Justus' case would have been aided by allegations of royal anti-Romanism, and, in fact, there is no sign that Justus accused Agrippa.[210] If Justus indicted Philip too for the death of Justus' relatives, why does Josephus defend him at such great length? He could have ignored the entire matter or he could have sundered Philip's activities from Agrippa's aegis. If Justus ignored Philip V becomes even more, puzzling.

Laqueur suggests that Josephus had written a history of Gamala and Batanaea (or a history of Agrippa's kingdom) which, naturally, included a full discussion of Philip. V needed material on Gamala to refute Justus and so Josephus simply transcribed (that is, paraphrased in the normal manner) the relevant sections which happened to contain much irrelevant information.[211] The fragments of this work are: (1) AJ 17.23-31, Herod's foundation of a colony of

---

[206] Schalit 78 and 83-90 makes a valiant attempt to recover Justus' version, but many of his conjectures are baseless.

[207] As suggested by Schalit 90 n. 1.

[208] Schlatter, *Bericht* 31 = *Kleinere Schriften* 27.

[209] Some scholars question Agrippa's loyalty (Baerwald 37-40 and Drexler 311-312) but the actions of Philip are the only evidence and there is no way to determine what Agrippa's instructions were to his minister. After the war Vespasian bestowed additional territory on Agrippa (see Photius quoted on p. 142 above).

[210] Jacoby, *PW* 10,2 (1919) 1343 and Drexler 312. If V is trying to draw a parallel·between the trials of Philip (V 407-408) and Justus (V 410), I do not understand the significance.

[211] Laqueur's thesis (see Laqueur 42-45 and 270) is considerably modified and expanded here.

Babylonian Jews in Batanaea and the dynasty of Zamaris, grand-father of Philip; [212] (2) V 46-61, on Philip, Varus, Caesarea Philippi, Gamala, and the Babylonian Jews; (3) V 179-187, on Philip, Agrippa, and Gamala; (4) V 114, Agrippa sends Aequus Modius against Gamala. In addition, V 74, on Modius' siege of the Jews of Caesarea Philippi, and V 407-409, on Vespasian's trial of Philip, may derive from this work. There are several indications that these passages belong to an independent whole. Sections (2), (3), and (4) follow one upon the other without break.[213] AJ 17.28 promises fuller treatment of the theme, a promise nowhere honored in AJ. V 61 has "as we have explained elsewhere".[214] V 177-178 contradicts V 186 in several details (see above), a sign of incompetence, but a bit more understandable if V 177-178 is the product of memory and apologetic and V 186 is drawn from a previously written source which Josephus did not peruse carefully. The intrusion of V 187a ("Gaulanitis too, as far as the village of Solyme, revolted from the king"), a short statement which interrupts the connection between 186 (Josephus' aid in the fortification of Gamala) and 187b-188 (the list of fortified cities), is hard to explain according to Josephus' normal principle of thematic composition. These indications are scarcely compelling, but, in any event, AJ and V have great interest in Gamala, Batanaea, and Philip, greater than what simple refutation of Justus would require.

f. Summary

In this section we have studied several features of Josephus' autobiography which have no direct connection with Justus of Tiberias and his polemic. Even if we except the enigmatic sections on Philip and Gamala, no dominant theme can be discovered which would unite the autobiography's disparate elements. Josephus

---

[212] J. Neusner, *A History of the Jews in Babylonia* I (Leiden 1965) 38-41; G. M. Cohen, *TAPA* 103 (1972) 83-95; S. Applebaum, in *Studies in the History of the Jewish People ... in Memory of Zvi Avneri*, ed. A. Gilboa et al. (Haifa 1970) 79-89 (Heb.).

[213] It is uncertain whether (4) should be transposed. If it is not transposed, the three sections do not fit well together at all. V 180-181 is hardly the natural result of V 114.

[214] Niese could repeat his suggestion that ὡς ἐν ἄλλοις ἐδηλώσαμεν is a meaningless phrase, a device for punctuation (see chapter two above, note 78). I doubt that it refers to BJ 2.483 (thus Niese in his apparatus and Drüner 83) because BJ is much less detailed—it does not even mention Aequus Modius—and such a cross reference would be useless.

tells the Jews and Romans that he was of noble lineage, an aristocrat who always associated with aristocrats. He was a religious Jew who followed Pharisaic rules and maintained piety throughout his life. As a loyal Jew, he fought the Romans in the great revolt and, in particular, tried his best to suppress pro-Roman sentiments in the Galilean cities. This claim does not prevent Josephus from advancing the theory that the Jewish people, Josephus included, were forced to fight a war they did not want. They were compelled by a wide variety of circumstances and incidents. Josephus, for example, was sent to Galilee to oppose the war and pacify the revolutionaries, yet somehow became involved in the conflict.

Three of these aims are not new to V but appear already in AJ, showing that, at least to some extent, V really is an appendix to AJ. Josephus' Hasmonean lineage, religious outlook and Pharisaic bias, and compulsion theory are all integral parts of AJ 18-20. It is unlikely, therefore, that any of these motifs owe their origin to Justus.

D. *Date*

An unsolved problem is the date of V's publication. Although it is an appendix to AJ (AJ 20.266), apparently written in or shortly after 93/94 CE (AJ 20.267), V refers to the death of Agrippa (V 359-360) which, according to Photius,[215] occurred in 100 CE. Therefore either we separate V from AJ and affirm that they were written seven years apart, or we discount the testimony of Photius. All the evidence which bears on this question is ambiguous and at present we cannot reach a definite conclusion.[216] Before we turn to the Josephan text, we must first consider the non-Josephan sources.

The literary evidence for the death date of Agrippa II, V's *terminus post quem*, is worthless. The earliest statement is by R. Yosi (mid-second century):

> Rabbi Yosi says, Persia (ruled) during the (second) temple (period) for 34 years, the Greek kingdom for 180 years, the kingdom of

---

[215] The patriarch says clearly that Agrippa τελευτᾷ δὲ ἔτει τρίτῳ Τραιανοῦ (the entire text is reprinted above). One of the two chief manuscripts of the *Bibliotheca* omits the phrase, no doubt by dittography (Οὐεσπασιανοῦ/ Τραιανοῦ), and emendation is not justifiable.

[216] A good statement of the problem with bibliography is Schürer-Vermes 54 and 480-483.

the house of Hasmonaeus for 103, the kingdom of Herod for 103. From that point compute the date according to (the era of) the destruction of the temple [217]

Elsewhere R. Yosi says that the second temple existed for 420 years and here we see how he divided the total (34 + 180 + 103 + 103 = 420).[218] R. Yosi assumes that Agrippa II directly succeeded Agrippa I and thus treats the Herodian rule as an unbroken continuum lasting 103 years. The assumption is false because at least five or ten years intervened between the death of Agrippa I (44 CE) and the ascension of Agrippa II (49 CE in Chalcis, 54 CE in Gaulanitis). It is unclear whether R. Yosi committed a second error and synchronized the death or retirement of the last of the Herodian house with the destruction of the temple. He merely says that after the Herodians had ruled for 103 years the temple was destroyed and a new chronographic era was begun. Later Jewish writers, however, accepted R. Yosi and deduced this false synchronization. According to some Agrippa II reigned just twenty years; according to others, he was executed by Vespasian during the war against the Romans.[219]

In an astounding coincidence (?) Eusebius agrees with these Jewish writers. Although he knows that Agrippa II was not elevated to the throne immediately after the demise of Agrippa I (*HE* 2.9.1-2.10.10, 2.19.2), his *Chronicle* counts the years of Agrippa II from 45 CE and assigns 103 years to the Herodian house. Thus Eusebius has Agrippa II reign until 70, for a total of twenty

---

[217] Seder ʿOlam Rabbah 30 (p. 71a Ratner, p. 66 Neubauer) and B. ʿAbodah Zarah 8b.

[218] Seder ʿOlam Rabbah 30 (p. 65b Ratner, p. 63 Neubauer); cf. R. Yohanan in B. Yoma 9a. J. Lauterbach, *PAAJR* 5 (1933-34) 77-84, gives unconvincing apologetic for the 34 year Persian period and ignores R. Yosi's explicit statement of 420 years.

[219] The author known as Yerahmiel (ed. Neubauer in *Medieval Jewish Chronicles*, vol. 1, p. 170) allocates the 103 years among the Herodian kings and assigns Agrippa II twenty years. Josippon 77 p. 291 ed. Hominer = Abraham ibn Daud, *Book of Tradition* 1 (p. 14 in the English translation, p. 9 in the Hebrew text, of G. D. Cohen) know the figure 420 but, under the influence of *Daniel* 9.26, they have Vespasian execute Agrippa three and a half years before the destruction. Thus Agrippa reigned twenty years but the total of the Herodian period is 100, not 103 (Josippon 63, p. 228 ed. Hominer). See too Joseph Kimhi, *The Book of the Covenant*, trans. F. Talmage (Toronto 1972) 51 and Rashi on *Daniel* 9.26. A glossator on the Aramaic *Megillat Antiochus* (ed. S. A. and A. J. Wertheimer, *Batei Midrashot*[2] [Jerusalem 1968] 1.330) thinks that the Hasmoneans reigned 206 years (103 + 103).

six years.[220] This section of the *Chronicle* is theologically motivated. It states that all the Herodians were "foreigners", i.e. non-Jews (ἀλλόφυλοι), who ruled in fulfillment of *Genesis* 49.10 that after the arrival of the messiah no son of Judah shall again reign over Israel.[221] It was theologically convenient for Eusebius to remove these kings, the last vestige of Jewish independence, at the destruction of the temple, the definitive sign of divine rejection. This Eusebian scheme was adopted with but minor modifications by later Christian writers.[222]

Neither the Rabbi nor the Father wins praise for accuracy. Eusebius and his followers also assign a date to Justus but the information is contradictory (the guesses range from the first year of Nerva to the second year of Trajan) and uncertain (what exactly is

---

[220] See the Armenian version p. 154 and 214 ed. Karst, and Jerome's Latin version p. 179 ed. Helm. The Armenian and the Latin agree on the computation: Herod, 37 years; Archelaus, 9; Herod Antipas, 24; Agrippa I, 7; Agrippa II, 26; total 103. If Eusebius needs an apology, we could explain that Tacitus *Annales* 12.23.1 puts the death of Agrippa I (in a thematic context) in 49 CE, the same year which BJ 2.284 considers the first of Agrippa II. The parallel between Eusebius and R. Yosi has not hitherto been noted and a comparative investigation of Jewish and Christian chronography is needed.

[221] This is stated first, to the best of my knowledge, by Justin *Dialogus* 52.3-4 (who is repeating Jewish anti-Herodian propaganda). Even where theology is irrelevant Justin can display surprising ignorance. In *Apologia* I 31.2 he thinks that Ptolemy Philadelphus was a contemporary of Herod the Great.

[222] See *Chronica Minora*, ed. Mommsen I 639 line 306 and III 283; Marianus Scotus, *Chronicon* III 48 (in *PL* 147.644); Nicephorus Callistus, *PG* 145.897c; *Epitome Syria* in *Eusebi Chronicorum Canonum*, ed. A. Schoene (Berlin 1866) 211; *Chronographeion Syntomon* in *Eusebi Chronicorum*, ed. A. Schoene (Berlin 1875) Appendix 4, p. 96; and the following texts in the editions of the *Corpus Scriptorum Historiae Byzantinae*: Chronicon Paschale p. 460 line 18; Syncellus p. 629 line 19; p. 636 line 16 (corrupt); p. 648 lines 2-3; Georgius Cedrenus p. 343 line 17. These texts assign 23, 25, 26, or 27 years to Agrippa II. A few of them round off Eusebius' 103 years to 100 (cf. Josippon above). A completely independent tradition is preserved (mutilated is the better term) by the chronicler printed by C. Frick, *Chronica Minora* I (Leipzig 1892) 110 = *Chronica Minora*, ed. Mommsen I 140. Carl Erbes, "Das Todesjahr Agrippa's II," *ZWT* 39 (1896) 415-432, tried to reconstitute the text by the very dubious assumption that the chronicler was an accurate historian. After positing and filling a lacuna, and tampering with two numbers whose correctness was guaranteed by the grand total, Erbes has the chronicler declare that Agrippa II died in 86 CE. The date is obviously incorrect, despite Erbes' protestations (see below), and so Schürer 598 n. 45 = Schürer-Vermes 481 n. 45 modified the theory. The text is too uncertain to indicate anything.

the given date supposed to indicate?).[223] These literary sources do not help us.

We turn now to the archaeological evidence. Almost all the coins and inscriptions of Agrippa II bear a date, some bear a double date.[224] The problem is the definition of the era or eras. Some numismatists proposed complicated schemes of three or four different eras, used simultaneously, but Seyrig's view, that all the inscriptions and all but a few of the coins are dated from 56 CE, has gained wide support.[225] Therefore Agrippa's last coin, bearing "year 35", dates from 90/91 CE and his last inscription (OGIS 426 = IGRR 3.1127), bearing "year 37", dates from 92/93. Thus we have no evidence that Agrippa was alive after 92/93 and some evidence that he was dead by 95/96 when an inscription from Agrippa's territory was dated "the sixteenth year of Domitian".[226] Another inscription from the area is dated "the first year of Nerva" (IGGR 3.1176). Both inscriptions omit any mention of Agrippa.

---

[223] Eusebius *Chronicon* p. 218 Karst and p. 193 Helm, first year of Nerva; Prosper Tiro in *Chronica Minora* ed. Mommsen I 419, immediately after the death of Nerva; Syncellus p. 655, after the accession of Trajan; Marianus Scotus III 104 (*PL* 147.660), second year of Trajan. These authors contradict each other on the absolute date of years A.D. for Justus' *floruit* (or whatever this date indicates) and also disagree with our accepted chronology, which places Nerva's accession in 96 and Trajan's in 98. It is useless to try to save Photius by conjecturing that his "third year of Trajan" was not 100 CE but, with Syncellus, 92 CE, a date which fits neatly with our computation of AJ 20.267 (13th year of Domitian = 93/94 CE); if the conjecture were correct, AJ 20.267 for Photius would not indicate 93/94 CE but a much earlier date. Using our computation of years A.D. as a medium of exchange to move an item from one chronological system to another is unjustified. This point is not appreciated by T. Frankfort, *RBPh* 39 (1961) 53, copied by Rajak, *CQ* 23 (1973) 362 and PIR² I 132.

[224] For a list of the inscriptions mentioning Agrippa II, see PIR² I 132 to which add M. Avi-Yonah, *IEJ* 16 (1966) 258-264 = *L'année épigraphique* (1967) 525 = *Bull. épigraphique* (1970) 633; H. Seyrig, *Syria* 42 (1965) 31-34 = AE (1966) 493 = *Bull. épigr.* (1966) 473; IGLS 6.2759; J. P. Rey-Coquais, *Mélanges de l'université saint-Josephe de Beyrouth* 47 (1972) 87-105. The best collection of the coins is by Meshorer 141-153, whose omissions and inaccuracies do not affect our discussion. For some recent literature on these coins see B. Kanael, *Jahrbuch für Numismatik und Geldgeschichte* 17 (1967) 177-179.

[225] H. Seyrig, *Revue Numismatique* 6. ser. 6 (1964) 55-65, endorsed by Meshorer 81-87 and Avi-Yonah in the prolegomenon (p. xxxiii) to the reprint of F. W. Madden, *History of Jewish Coinage* (N.Y. 1967). See Schürer-Vermes 480 n. 43.

[226] M. Dunand, *Mission Archéologique au Djebel Druze: La Musée de Soueida* (Paris 1934) 49-50 nr. 75. The exact site of discovery of this inscription is not known.

Tiberias was minting coins in its own name in 99/100 (see above). Here, then, is good evidence that Photius' date is incorrect and that Agrippa may have been dead even before AJ was completed in 93/94.[227] An inscription from the Hauran or Djebel Druze which has a soldier pass directly from the service of Agrippa II to Trajan cannot upset this conclusion.[228]

Let us turn now to Josephus. Does V have any passages, aside from the reference to the death of Agrippa, which might date the work? V 429, which lists Domitian's benefactions towards Josephus and omits any reference to Nerva and Trajan, makes it probable that Domitian was the reigning emperor when V was completed. Because of the general hatred in Rome for Domitian after his death, it is unlikely that Josephus would then have boasted of—or even mentioned—the favors received from him.[229] Two other passages often invoked are ambiguous. Josephus' patron (V 430) may or may not have been the Epaphroditus executed by Domitian in 95.[230] The figure of twenty years in V 360 cannot supply any sound deductions.[231]

---

[227] Of course, we must not overstate our case. Seyrig's theory is plausible but not certain. The most popular opposing view dates all the coins from 61 which would have Agrippa alive and well in 97/98. The advantage of this view is that 61 CE is an era which explicitly appears on one issue of coins whereas the era of 56 CE has to be deduced from the double dates. But there are as many chronological inconcinnities with the era of 61 CE (see Schürer-Vermes 480 n. 43) as with the era of 56. If we accept the era of 56, Agrippa's Flavian coins begin precisely in 70, which makes perfect sense, and end in 90/91, just in time for AJ which was completed in 93/94 and seems to presume Agrippa's death (see below). To solve this problem we need a detailed study of the coinage of Agrippa II (including an investigation for possible die-links) and/or some new archaeological discoveries. The inscriptions from Agrippa's domain dated by Roman emperors are not decisive because Agrippa's kingdom might have been dismembered piecemeal by the Romans (see note 248 below). For a history of Agrippa's kingdom and a map locating the sites of the inscriptions, see T. Frankfort, "Le royaume d'Agrippa II et son annexion par Domitien," *Hommages à A. Grenier*, ed. M. Renard (Brussels 1962) 659-672. See too the important article by J. P. Rey-Coquais mentioned in n. 224 above.

[228] H. Seyrig, *Syria* 42 (1965) 31-34.

[229] See e.g. Vincent, *RB* 8 (1911) 373; Helm, *PhW* 41 (1921) 484; Schalit, *Zion* o.s. 5 (1933) 186 (Hebrew).

[230] The arguments for identifying him with the *a libellis* of Nero or with the grammarian M. Mettius Epaphroditus are inconclusive.

[231] See notes 58 and 70 above. Since Josephus may have invented the figure, since Josephus or Justus may be miscalculating or exaggerating, since we do not know exactly when BJ appeared, V 360 is not helpful for determining the dates of V and Justus. Contrast the attempts of Laqueur 3;

Is V an appendix of AJ completed in 93/94? In AJ 20.266 Josephus promises to write "about my pedigree and the events of my life," a promise fulfilled by V.[232] There are several indications of a close connection between the two works: V's inceptive δέ and abrupt opening; V 430, which announces the completion of AJ; the manuscript tradition, which almost unanimously juxtaposes V to AJ;[233] V's continuation of several important themes of AJ 18-20 (see above). Thus, although our manuscripts and editions separate the two works and assign V its own title, it is likely that V was originally but an appendix to AJ.

The problems begin when we analyze AJ's final paragraphs (AJ 20.259-268). Laqueur suggests that AJ was published in two different editions, the first in 93/94, ending with AJ 20.258 and 267-268, without V, the second after Agrippa's death in 100, ending with AJ 20.259-266, with V as an appendix. Later editors combined the two conclusions. This theory is based on the unnecessary duplication of 259 (παύσεται δ' ἐνταῦθα μοι τὰ τῆς ἀρχαιολογίας) by 267 (καταπαύσω τὴν ἀρχαιολογίαν) and solves our problem by maintaining V's connection to AJ while simultaneously vindicating Photius.[234] But this analysis assumes that Josephus was a careful craftsman, never prolix and always well organized. Since the assumption is incorrect, the analysis fails to prove Laqueur's theory. Even according to Laqueur, V 430 (... τὴν πᾶσαν τῆς ἀρχαιολογίας ἀναγραφήν ... καταπαύω) repeats AJ 20.259. Laqueur does not explain why the first conclusion was split in half and the second inserted in the middle.[235] But even if AJ has only one ending, the

---

Helm, *PhW* 41 (1921) 483; A. Schalit, *Zion* o.s. 5 (1933) 183-184 (Hebrew); idem, *Encyclopedia Judaica* 9 (1932) 625 and *Encyclopedia Judaica* 10 (1971) 479-480, s.v. Justus.

[232] See above p. 104. AJ 20.267 has nothing to do with V; see Feldman's note *b* ad loc. and Schürer 87-88 (who ignores AJ 20.266).

[233] Schreckenberg, *Tradition* 11. The manuscripts used by Eusebius *HE* 3.10.8 (copied by Nicephorus Callistus *PG* 145.801B) and Photius cod. 76 (where a summary of V is sandwiched between paraphrases of AJ 20.257-258/9 and AJ 20.267) still linked V to AJ.

[234] Laqueur 1-6. H. Ewald, *Geschichte des Volkes Israel VII* [2=3] (Göttingen 1868) 108, also suggested that V was published as part of a new edition of AJ.

[235] The parallel adduced by Laqueur 5 from Dio Chrysostom 11.22-24 (vol. 1 pp. 120-121, ed. von Arnim) is of no assistance. See Emonds 339. (Emonds somehow manages to fill 402 pages about multi-editions in antiquity without mentioning Josephus once.) A better parallel is provided by Tertullian's *Adversus Judaeos*. Chapters 9-12 and 13-14 are different treatments of the same theme, the former supposed to replace the latter, but

existence of two (or more) editions is quite plausible. AJ is so long, so uneven, so discursive, and so diverse (contrast BJ) that we can readily imagine that Josephus returned to his work several times with additions, corrections, etc. Many passages and stylistic peculiarities can, conjecturally, be assigned to this activity but certainty is never attainable.[236] To conclude this portion of the argument: we cannot be sure that V was appended to AJ in 93/94. Laqueur does not have enough evidence to support his view, but the possibility remains that AJ was revised after 93/94 and V written after 100.[237]

our texts contain both versions and thus sunder 13-14 from its original connection with 7-8. See H. Tränkle, *Q.S.F. Tertulliani Adversus Judaeos* (Wiesbaden 1964) lii-liii. The *Historia Ecclesiastica* of Eusebius is another work whose current text is the result of many different editions. When the *De Martyribus Palaestinae*, originally an independent work, was appended to the *HE*, various passages had to be shifted and the resultant confusion is similar to Laqueur's reading of AJ 20.259-268. See E. Schwartz' introduction in the third volume of his edition of *HE* (Leipzig 1909) xlvii-lxi, with the remarks of G. Bardy, *Revue Bénédictine* 47 (1935) 368-369. These parallels show that Laqueur was correct to raise the possibility that V was appended to a second edition of AJ but his case is weak. The evidence for multiple editions of the *Adversus Judaeos* and the *Historia Ecclesiastica* is far better than the evidence Laqueur cites for AJ.

[236] Ancient editions were not as rigid as their modern counterparts; see chapter four above, note 13. Farmer 33-34 n. 23 suggests that the first edition of AJ, like BJ, denied any connection between the Fourth Philosophy and the Pharisees (AJ 18.9), but that the second edition admitted the truth (AJ 18.23), thus producing a contradiction. An equally implausible explanation is that Josephus first paraphrased his source (BJ? Nicolaus?), with the addition of some new data, and then proceeded to state his own view. See Hengel 83-84 with 84 n. 1 and 90-91. But no explanations are needed because there is no real contradiction; see above n. 181. On AJ 17.23-31 see below n. 248. The numerous stylistic peculiarities of AJ have been blamed either on Josephus' assistants or on secondary tamperings with the text by the author. See G. C. Richards, *CQ* 33 (1939) 36-40. But I do not see that these stylistic inconsistencies need indicate anything more than the inconsistency of the author; see Schreckenberg, *Rezeptionsgeschichtliche ... Untersuchungen* 173-174 n. 8. (Other lists of Josephus' uneven word usage are in Thackeray's preface to his *Lexicon* and to volume four of the Loeb Josephus; Naber, *Mnemosyne* n.s. 13 [1885] 360; N. G. Cohen, *JQR* 54 [1963/64] 312-318.) A full study of this problem is needed and should be facilitated by the concordance. Richards and Shutt, *CQ* 31 (1937) 172, conjecture that AJ 16.187-199 and 16.395-404 originate in the second edition because they are absent from the Latin translation, but the first omission, at least, seems to have been caused by the loss of a page from the Greek text used by the translator since the story resumes *in medias res* in AJ 16.200. Attridge 52 n. 2, who cites further literature on this subject, has not convinced me that doublets in the proem to AJ confirm Laqueur's theory.

[237] On the theory that V appeared in two editions, see chapter three

Do CA and AJ imply that Agrippa was alive when they were written? CA 1.51 ("most excellent king Agrippa") has been cited as proof of Agrippa's continued existence but since Josephus there needs Agrippa's testimony, it is no surprise that he flatters him.[238] AJ's attitude towards the two Agrippas is a more significant indication. Josephus always treats Agrippa I with great respect. AJ recounts the long saga of his rise to glory and even the much shorter account of BJ is adulatory.[239] But the children of Agrippa I, notably Agrippa II and Berenice, fare much better in BJ than AJ.[240] BJ recounts at great length how Agrippa and Berenice did their best to prevent outbreak of war (BJ 2.309-314, 342-407). Not a word of condemnation.[241] At the beginning of AJ 20, Agrippa's reputation is still intact:[242] he convinces Claudius to allow the Jews to maintain control of the high-priestly vestments (AJ 20.9-12; cf. AJ 15.407) and he convinces the emperor to favor the Jews rather than the Samaritans (AJ 20.135; cf. BJ 2.245 which lacks the statement that without Agrippa the Jews' case would have been lost). But the situation quickly changes. Agrippa's sister Drusilla marries Felix and thus violates the ancestral laws (AJ 20.143).

---

above, notes 24-26. Rühl 296 argued that V must have been written several years after AJ because AJ 20.266 writes that people are still alive who can verify Josephus' autobiography while V complains that Agrippa et al. are already dead. This argument is not cogent because AJ 20.266 is a rhetorical phrase, part of the polemic against Justus, and probably not accurate. V argues that Justus waited for the death of all those able to convict him of mendacity and contrasts this ignominious behavior with Josephus' publication of BJ. V neglected to mention that the death of those able to convict Justus was also the death of those able to convict Josephus. AJ 20.266 was supposed to remedy this problem and if it contradicts V we should not be surprised. V often contradicts itself.

[238] Contra Hölscher, PW 9,2 (1916) 1941n. and 1987. On the relative chronology of V and CA, see above note 64.

[239] Perhaps AJ more than BJ exaggerates Agrippa's importance (and Claudius' incompetence) but both works are favorable. See V. M. Scramuzza, The Emperor Claudius (Harvard 1940) 12-18 and 58-59; D. Timpe, Historia 9 (1960) 502; and O. Henning, "Römische Stücke aus Flavius Josephus" (diss. Tübingen 1922) 34-42. This Agrippa saga needs a full investigation; Henning's conjectures require further analysis.

[240] G. Hölscher, PW 9,2 (1916) 1987.

[241] BJ demonstrates Agrippa's loyalty not only to the Romans but also to the Jews. Agrippa scolds the Jews not out of a callous disregard of their sufferings, but out of a desire to keep the peace (BJ 2.337). He cares for both Romans and Jews (BJ 2.421). Thus Agrippa's support for the Romans does not show unconcern for the Jews.

[242] The casual references to Agrippa II and Berenice in AJ 18-19 can be omitted here.

There were rumors that Agrippa's sister Berenice was having sexual relations with her brother (AJ 20.145). She reportedly deserted her second husband "out of licentiousness" (146). The king violated tradition and offended the people by his construction project (AJ 20.189-196). Like Herod, Agrippa was hated by his subjects for spending Jewish money to decorate foreign cities (AJ 20.211-212). Members of the royal house terrorized the people (AJ 20.214). Like Herod, he violated the ancestral laws and made divine punishment inevitable (AJ 20.216-218).

The nationalistic religious viewpoint evident here typifies AJ in contrast to BJ which has none of those unfavorable items.[243] Many Jews could admire Agrippa I who was ostensibly faithful to the ancestral traditions (AJ 19.331, not in BJ) and made an effort to attain some independence from Rome (AJ 19.326-27, contrast BJ 2.218-219; AJ 19.338-342, not in BJ). Rabbinic tradition too preserves stories favorable to Agrippa I.[244] Thus AJ criticizes Agrippa II, an irreligious Roman lackey, for his donatives to Beirut (AJ 20.211-212) but not Agrippa I, who also was a benefactor of the city (19.335-337).

Many have argued that Josephus could not have written these unfavorable statements during the lifetime of Agrippa II.[245] This is inherently plausible; therefore we may suppose that Agrippa II was dead before AJ 20.143 and later passages were written. What makes the conclusion uncertain is the possibility that Josephus might have been willing to sacrifice Agrippa II to his new nationalistic religious bias even when the king was still alive. Laqueur conjectures precisely that and interprets AJ 16.187 as a declaration of independence from the king, still reigning (βασιλεύοντας ἔτι). The text is corrupt but the meaning is clear: "Unlike Nicolaus, I shall not distort the truth to protect anyone nor am I afraid of entering into disputes with royal Hasmoneans although I respect them." Josephus speaks as if many Hasmoneans were still on their thrones and available for disputation; Laqueur assumes that Agrippa II is the real target. But a sentence from Nicolaus' auto-

---

[243] Laqueur 261-262.

[244] On the identity of the Agrippa of the famous story of M. Sotah 9.7, see S. Lieberman, *Tosefta Ki-Fshutah: Nashim* (N.Y. 1973) 683 (Hebrew). There is no trace of any memories favorable to Agrippa II.

[245] Erbes 426; Luther 54-59; Hölscher, *PW* 9,2 (1916) 1941n.; Macurdy, *AJP* 56 (1935) 250; Frankfort, *RBPh* 39 (1961) 54.

biography explains this rhetorical exaggeration [246] as well as the intent of the entire passage. The Damascene also boasted of his dedication to truth (FGrH 90 F 137 c.2):

πρὸς γε μὴν τὸ δίκαιον ἀκλινὴς οὕτω καὶ ἀθώπευτος, ὥστε καὶ ἀπειλὰς ἐνεγκεῖν τινων ἡγεμόνων ποτὲ δικάζων ὑπὲρ τοῦ μὴ τοῦτο παραβῆναι.

His loyalty to justice was so unswerving and incorruptible that, in order not to violate this principle, when he once was serving as judge, he had to bear the threats of certain monarchs.

AJ 16.187 is an implicit contrast between Nicolaus and Josephus. In spite of his protestations Nicolaus was not prepared to bear the ill-will of rulers; his distorted history shows this clearly (AJ 16.183-186). He claimed he was threatened by kings but he shamelessly apologized for Herod. I too claim to have borne the anger of kings but my assertion is correct because I respect truth more than he. If this interpretation is correct, AJ 16.187 is a rhetorical response to a passage from Nicolaus' autobiography, should not be taken at face value, and has little to do with Agrippa II.[247]

Even if AJ 16.187 does not support his conjecture, Laqueur may be right. Perhaps Josephus was willing to insult Agrippa when the king was still alive. Another alternative is that all the anti-Agrippa passages were added in a later edition after the king's death.[248]

---

[246] It is possible that some descendants of Mariamme were still reigning in the 80's or 90's but we have no definite information. Aristobulus of Armenia Minor (AJ 20.158) may or may not be the Aristobulus of Chalcidice (BJ 7.226)—and even if he is, his dates are still unknown. Alexander III of Ketis was another Hasmonean (AJ 18.140) but we know nothing about him.

[247] Against Laqueur 262. Otto, *Herodes*, used the reference to πολλοί as one of his proofs that AJ 16.183-187 was cribbed from an anonymous source. Before Laqueur, Schürer 599 n. 47 had conjectured that Agrippa and Josephus quarreled, which would explain AJ's unfavorable attitude, but Schürer forgot to cite AJ 16.187.

[248] AJ 17.28 describes how the two Agrippas ruled Batanaea harshly and how the Romans, succeeding them (δεξάμενοι τὴν ἀρχήν), crushed the inhabitants with their fiscal exactions. If Agrippa II died in 92/93, it is difficult to see how by 93/94 the Roman rule could have been so oppressive. Therefore either AJ 17.28 is a later addition or Agrippa lost Batanaea before his death. Schürer 598-599 chose the latter alternative, Laqueur 45 the former. AJ 17.28 is a fragment of the history of Gamala and Agrippa's kingdom which we discussed above and it is not implausible that the entire section (AJ 17.23-31) was added to the text. Laqueur did not attribute the other anti-Agrippa passages to the second edition because they do not appear to be additions to the text and Laqueur assumes that Josephus generally adds

But the simplest explanation, surely is that Agrippa was dead before AJ was completed in 93/94.

Although the evidence is meager and ambiguous, we must attempt a conclusion. If it were not for Photius no one would think that Agrippa was alive after 93. According to the most plausible interpretation of his eras, Agrippa's Flavian coinage begins in 70 and ends in 90/91. His last inscription is from 92/93. AJ, completed in 93/94, condemns him. Inscriptions from his territory are dated by Domitian and Nerva. Tiberias is minting on its own in 99/100. If it were not for Photius no one would think V was completed under Trajan. V has close connections to AJ and boasts of benefactions of Domitian. It is unjustified to reject all this in favor of elaborate theories of second editions, piecemeal dissolution of Agrippa's kingdom, etc., whose only purpose is to defend the honor of a tenth century patriarch.[249]

Thus our tentative conclusions are as follows. Agrippa died in 92/93, leaving Josephus a full year in which to display his hostility to the king.[250] Justus pleaded for his native city and attacked Josephus not long after Agrippa's death. The former general of Galilee responded with his *Vita*, certainly before 96. Whether he had planned to write an autobiography even before Justus' attack is uncertain.[251]

---

to, but does not change, his first edition. This assumption is false (see chapter two) and so we have the third possibility that innocuous statements of the first edition became the hostile ones of the second.

[249] The simplest explanation of Photius' error is that Justus' *Chronicle of Kings* ended with the death of Agrippa II but was not completed or published until 100. Photius erroneously identified the two dates. On Photius' occasional errors in *Kurzreferaten* (see n. 144 above), see Hägg 198-199.

[250] Would it be rash to conjecture that Agrippa died while Josephus was composing AJ 20? This would explain why the first part of AJ 20 is still favorable to the king.

[251] Our conclusions agree with those of Frankfort, *RBPh* 39 (1961) 58. Smallwood, *Jews* 354 and 572-574, also follows Frankfort.

CHAPTER SIX

JOSEPHUS IN GALILEE

By now it should be clear how little we know of the events of 66-70. Because Josephus is our only extensive source and because he is so unreliable our knowledge is very defective. That Josephus provides enough data to refute his own account is a sign of sloppiness and incompetence rather than conscientiousness and objectivity.[1] The narrative is always tendentious and, because we have no external control, we can never be sure of the underlying events. He can invent, exaggerate, over-emphasize, distort, suppress, simplify, or, occasionally, tell the truth. Often we cannot determine where one practice ends and another begins. Thus it is easy to destroy Josephus' account, but nearly impossible to construct a more truthful one.

I. *The Problems*

In this chapter we attempt to determine the events in Galilee and Jerusalem during the first part of the war, 66-67 CE. Here the fundamental difficulty just described manifests itself in several secondary problems. Although we have two long accounts, we do not have enough data to reconstruct the events in detail, because not even V gives a full description of the crucial months in Galilee. Josephus never gives clear definitions of the Fourth Philosophy, the *Sicarii*, and the Zealots. Are they separate groups or identical with one another? What was their position at the outbreak of the war—if they were all in existence at that time—and what was their relationship to John of Gischala, Eleazar ben Ananias, etc? The fact that an enormous literature has been devoted to these questions shows Josephus' failure to answer them clearly. An even greater problem is the organization of the revolutionary government. How was the *koinon* of 66-70 related to the *synedrion* of the pre-war period? Is there a difference between *koinon*, *boule*, and *synedrion* during the years 66-70? [2] What was the source of authority of the

---

[1] Cf. G. E. M. de Ste. Croix, *Historia* 3 (1954) 3, "Thucydides was such a remarkably objective historian that he himself has provided sufficient material for his own refutation."

[2] The study of C. Roth, "The Constitution of the Jewish Republic of

leaders of the city, for example Ananus and Simon ben Gamaliel? The motives of individuals and groups form another dark area. BJ never admits that the actors, even in those tumultuous times, may have changed their minds. The people always wanted peace, the revolutionaries always wanted war. Ananus and the "moderates" (as modern scholars call them) always wanted *rapprochement* with Rome. The conflicting emotions and shifting loyalties are rarely indicated. Here V represents a significant improvement, but whether its portraits are true is another matter. Both V and BJ model some characterizations on literary types and use rhetorical common-places, whence great doubt of their veracity.

Thus we are confronted with insurmountable obstacles. Since certainty is unattainable, we must be satisfied with what is most plausible. We should not try to decide between various possibilities without good evidence. Most historians have satisfied themselves with a "critical" paraphrase of Josephus' account, but what is needed is a critique based on the fundamental point that we really know very little about the war of 66-70.[3]

In chapter four above the dominant motives of BJ 2-3 were discussed. They are: since only small groups of fanatics and tyrants fought the Romans, the Jews as a whole do not bear the responsibility for the war; the aristocracy actively sought peace; although Josephus fought in the war and was an ideal general, he was not a revolutionary because the period from the defeat of Cestius until the fall of Jotapata was an oasis of legitimacy and temperance in the struggle. In chapter five we mentioned BJ's attempt to apportion some of the guilt to Florus, the last procurator. Before we present

---

66-70," *JSS* 9 (1964) 295-319, is predicated on the premise that Josephus "uses his Greek terms consistently and precisely" (296 n. 1) but Roth himself admits that this premise is false (307 and 313 n. 4). The status, organization, and authority of the Sanhedrin before 70 are some of the most difficult problems in Jewish history. See H. D. Mantel, *Studies in the History of the Sanhedrin* (Harvard 1965). I assume here that there was only one council in Jerusalem which, at least during the war, claimed authority over the entire country. See Schürer 2.245-246; H. Dessau, *Geschichte der römischen Kaiserzeit* II,2 (Berlin 1930) 809 n. 1; Kennard, *ZNW* 53 (1962) 28; Tcheri-kover, *IEJ* 14 (1964) 67.

[3] As the subsequent footnotes show, my discussion is indebted to Drexler. I do not understand why Drexler's healthy skepticism and acute obser-vations have had little influence. Hengel and Michel-Bauernfeind know Drexler's work but ignore his central thesis. Schürer-Vermes hardly mentions him at all. I do not accept all of Drexler's conjectures.

our reconstruction, we must consider the veracity of these statements.

Surely Josephus is right that the number of members of the organized revolutionary groups was relatively small. The masses may have sympathized with certain views or followed certain leaders, but were fundamentally uncommitted and unreliable. And surely he is right that some of the populace opposed the war. But Josephus too often oversimplifies and writes as if there were a clean dichotomy between the advocates of war and the advocates of peace. There must have been a wide variety of opinions between the two extremes, the desire to surrender to the Romans as soon as possible and the readiness to die in a blaze of glory. Intermediate positions are mentioned but only rarely and inconsistently. Thus Ananus' policy as described by BJ 2.651 (Ananus was temporarily cooperating with the war effort because he wanted to be able to control the revolutionaries and force them to a more "salutary" view) may or may not be the same as that described by BJ 4.320-21 (Ananus wanted peace but, forced by necessity [4] to provide for war, he made military preparations to the best of his ability). V's portrayal of Josephus' secret pro-Romanism (V 28-29 and 175-176) can—but need not—be reconciled with either of these views. Although Josephus never says that these sentiments were widespread, many people may have supported the war, especially in its early successful stages and especially in Jerusalem, without being fanatic or extreme. Even more must have supported protests and other actions which turned out in the long run to have been steps, and sometimes important steps, towards war, but which were not seen as such by many of the people involved, because they did not foresee the consequences.

It is therefore somewhat misleading though convenient, to write of "the peace party" and "the war party". Very few of "the peace party" were consciously determined on "peace at any price"; any repetition, say, of the attempt to place an imperial statue in the temple, would probably have met military resistance from an overwhelming majority of the Jewish population. On the other hand, probably few of the revolutionaries counted on war, and even fewer wanted it for its own sake. Many of the eschatological groups

---

[4] This statement is similar to AJ's and V's theory of *ananke* (see chapter five), but in BJ *ananke* compels specific men in specific circumstances (as here), not the Jewish people as a whole.

expected that war would be avoided—the End would come first. For others the war would be some supernatural conflict of which they would merely be spectators cheering for the winners. The more practical may have seen in the insecurity of Nero the chance for a negotiated peace—a fatal mistake, but a possible one. It is impossible to list, even in speculation, the vast number of different possible policies that the many different revolutionary groups may have conceived. For convenience, we shall go on writing of "the peace party" and "the war party" but it should be understood that by these terms we do not mean single or organized parties, nor even groups of persons determined on peace or war. Our "peace party" is that class of persons who thought Roman military intervention all too likely and were seriously concerned, and ready to make major sacrifices, to prevent it. Our "war party" is made up of all those who wanted an end to direct Roman government and taxation, and were ready to risk military reprisals, if necessary, for these ends. And most numerous of all will have been the people who never conceived of any policy but merely lived from day to day and expressed their political feelings with little or no concern either for consistency or for consequences. For them, especially, the situation was very fluid. BJ repeatedly insists that the "revolutionaries" (στασιασταί, etc.) were a small minority of the Jewish population, but, on the other hand, BJ 2, the book which is of special concern to us, occasionally admits that the populace (πλῆθος: 315, 320, 325; δῆμος: 294) was hostile to the Romans.

The attitude of the aristocracy is a special problem. BJ frequently refers to its adamant opposition to war (see chapter four note 45). No doubt many of the wealthy wanted nothing more than the preservation of the status quo (BJ 2.338) [5] but Josephus again is guilty of exaggeration when he implies unanimity. Eleazar ben Ananias, who provided the spark for war by refusing the sacrifice of gentiles (BJ 2.409-410), was the *strategos* of the Temple and the son of a high priest. BJ 2.443 mentions his aristocratic colleagues and shows that he was not acting alone. According to BJ 2.429 his father Ananias was a member of the peace party and, therefore, his opponent, but AJ 20.208-210, which describes an

---

[5] Drexler 283 (top) assumes that the entire aristocracy was anti-Roman but this view is as extreme as Josephus' and, like Josephus', demonstrably false.

incident involving the two men, implies no such thing.[6] The emissaries of the peace party to Agrippa (BJ 2.418), aristocrats all, remained for two months in a city allegedly dominated by extemists. So far as we know they made no attempt to save Cestius from his embarrassing defeat. Only after the failure of Cestius' expedition did Saul and Costobar leave Jerusalem (BJ 2.556). Antipas did not leave even then but waited a full year until he and two other nobles of royal blood were slain by the Zealots (BJ 4.140).[7] Philip ben Jacimus, the leader of the royal troops, presumably was involved in revolutionary activities, whether in Jerusalem or Gamala (see chapter five, section C 2 e). Since his 2000 cavalry are not mentioned after their initial dispatch (BJ 2.421), they probably aided the revolutionaries. Who else are the soldiers (στρατιῶται) of BJ 2.450?[8] Silas the "Babylonian", a deserter from Agrippa, was prominent in the battles against Cestius (BJ 2.520) and Ascalon (BJ 3.11 and 19). Thus three prominent aristocrats of Jerusalem, Saul, Costobar, and Antipas, all relatives of the king and all leaders of the peace party were, it seems, not wholly peaceful. Philip, the general sent to aid the peace party, aided the revolt. In 67, and even in the summer of 70 (BJ 6.114), there were still many wealthy aristocrats in Jerusalem who could be attacked by the Zealots.

Many of these revolutionary aristocrats were primarily interested in self-aggrandizement. Saul, Costobar, many of the high-priests, priests, and lay aristocracy formed gangs which fought with each other (AJ 20.180 and 213-214). John of Gischala, a wealthy man (V 71-76) with a following of several hundred, and Philip ben Jacimus with his Babylonians, are similar figures. These men might occasionally support peace or war but they would always look out for their own interests.

The most serious effect of BJ's apologetic was the thorough distortion of the history of the war from 66 until late 67, the irruption of the Zealots into the city. The crucial passage is BJ 2.562-568, the selection of the generals after the defeat of Cestius. BJ does not pretend that these aristocrats were members of the

---

[6] Drexler 278 and 281.

[7] Drexler 279 understands BJ 4.140 to mean that Antipas was in charge of the treasury of the revolutionaries but πεπιστεῦσθαι probably is pluperfect. Michel-Bauernfeind translate "dass ihm sogar die öffentlichen Gelder anvertraut worden waren."

[8] Drexler 279.

peace party. Modern scholars regard these men as "moderates",
supporters of the policies of Ananus as outlined by BJ and of the
chief men (πρῶτοι) as outlined by V (see above), but BJ does not
agree with this view. It never calls Ananus a "moderate" (μέτριος) [9]
and never considers him an archetypal figure. Ananus is a crypto-
pacifist only when opposing the Zealots in the winter of 67-68;
BJ 2.651 is anticipatory.[10] Thus, although BJ normally apologizes
for the aristocracy, here it does not. BJ's statements about the
actions of these men are more credible than V's statements of their
intentions. Ananus fortified the walls of the city and prepared
weapons (BJ 2.648). John the Essene (BJ 2.567) was a leader in the
battle at Ascalon (BJ 3.11 and 19).[11] Eleazar ben Ananias (BJ
2.566, as emended) is the same hothead who refused the sacrifices
for the emperor. True, he was given a minor position, a testimony
to the power struggle which took place within the revolutionary
leadership after the defeat of Cestius (see below), but he was
included in this allegedly "moderate" government.[12] Finally,
Josephus in Galilee was a war leader, not a "moderate" (see below).
During the reign of Felix he went to Rome to rescue some revolutionaries (V 13-16),[13] not the task of an opponent of war. After

---

[9] BJ 2.648 implies that Ananus was not a μέτριος since his associates are
τῶν δυνάτων ὅσοι μὴ τὰ 'Ρωμαίων ἐφρόνουν and what he and they do in 648
causes consternation to the μέτριοι in 649. The μέτριοι are the peace party
(BJ 2.275, 306, 455), not the moderates often described by modern scholars.
The concordance is awaited for a full list. As far as I know, Josephus has no
term for an intermediate party between the war and peace parties.

[10] Ananus feuds with the revolutionaries and succumbs to their violence
only in book four of BJ, not in books two and three. BJ 2.651 describes an
event which will unfold "little by little" (κατὰ μικρόν). The entire paragraph
is a forecast and does not refer to the content of BJ 2. Indeed some exegesis
is required to reconcile 651 with 647-650, which assumes that Ananus was
busy preparing for war, apparently with all sincerity, and was not a member
of the peace party (see n. 9). Therefore BJ 2.651 should not trouble those
who consider that the Zealot party came into existence only in the winter
of 67-68. BJ 2.564-565 may be anticipatory too. On BJ 3.130-131 and 135-
140, see below.

[11] The military activities of Niger the Peraean (BJ 3.11, 20, 25, 27) also
presumably indicate the policies of the government of BJ 2.562-68 under
which he was acting although he was not appointed to a generalship.

[12] C. Roth, JSS 4 (1959) 341, considers Eleazar a "moderate." Roth
apparently believes that only a "moderate" would refuse to sacrifice for
the emperor.

[13] Josephus pretends that they were sent to Rome διὰ μικρὰν καὶ τὴν
τυχοῦσαν αἰτίαν (V 13) but this phrase is a cover-up for revolutionary activity
(cf. AJ 20.215). See chapter two above, pp. 61-62. Not only citizens but
important criminals too, especially revolutionaries, were sent to Rome.

returning to Jerusalem he fled from Menahem into the temple (V 20-21), the seat of Eleazar ben Ananias' strength—there Menahem was overthrown (BJ 2.445ff)—and the center of revolutionary activity (see below).[14]

Although BJ does not deny the revolutionary actions of these generals, at least in the fall of 66, it distorts the history of the war by saying nothing of any connection between the initiators of war and the leaders of BJ 2.562-568. Josephus wants to blame the outbreak upon a small group of extremists, but he also wants to show that during his tenure as general the war was led by aristocrats and was legitimate. But the party in power after the defeat of Cestius was presumably the party that defeated Cestius.[15] The generals were elected at the temple (BJ 2.562). The reference of BJ 2.566 to Niger's governorship (ἄρχοντι τότε) perhaps indicates that an aristocratic government may have been formed even before the defeat of Cestius (see below). But Josephus wanted to say as little as possible of the connection between the "new" government and the revolt that led to it. The success of his apologia can be gauged by the fact that most modern scholars, oblivious to the problems, accept what he suggests. These scholars do not explain how their alleged "moderates"—or anyone else for that matter—could have wrested control from the "extremists" in the hour of extremist victory.[16]

E.g. Felix dispatched Eleazar ben Deinaeus and his followers to Rome (BJ 2.253//AJ 20.161).

[14] This has been noted only by Prager 6 and was omitted even by Drexler. Contrast Hengel 371.

[15] Prager 7; Baerwald 15; Drexler 287. The use of πλείονας (BJ 2.562) reinforces Josephus' theory that these generals did not previously participate in the war. Similarly in the English, American, and French revolutions, the "moderates" gained control only because they had been prominent in the revolutionary movement all along. See C. Brinton, *The Anatomy of Revolution* (N.Y. 1959), esp. c. 5, "The Rule of the Moderates."

[16] All the standard texts agree that the war was begun by extremists and that after the defeat of Cestius the "moderates," including Ananus and Josephus, came into control. Thus Schürer 606 and 617 = Schürer-Vermes 489 and 496; A. Momigliano, *Cambridge Ancient History* 10 (1934) 850-858; Hengel 365-383. Recent statements of this position are: R. Mayer and C. Möller in *Josephus-Studien: Untersuchungen ... O.Michel ... gewidmet*, ed. O. Betz et al. (Göttingen 1974) 271-284; and Rhoads passim. The notable exceptions, aside from Drexler, are A. H. M. Jones, *The Herods of Judaea* (Oxford 1938) 248 ("it is somewhat surprising that they [the aristocrats] should have been able to oust the extremists from power"); S. G. F. Brandon, *Jesus and the Zealots* (N.Y. 1967) 138 n. 2 ("the situation seems rather

The treatment of Florus is just as tendentious. When Florus plunders the Temple and claims that the money is for Caesar, Josephus blames his greed (BJ 2.293, cf. 288 and 331) and forgets to mention that the Jews were behind in their payment of tribute (BJ 2.403-407). Florus wanted to incite the war in order to cover up his crimes (BJ 2.282-283, cf. 293, 420, and 531), as if a Roman governor who failed to keep the peace in his province would not have to answer for his conduct.[17] Florus, unprovoked, attacks the Jews who tried to remain peaceful (BJ 2.297-300, 305-308, 325-327). His conduct towards Berenice was inexcusable (BJ 2.309-314). But if the city was so peaceful why did Florus need to bring in more troops from Caesarea (BJ 2.318)? The confrontation with the new troops (BJ 2.325-327) is suspiciously similar to an earlier incident (BJ 2.297-300). Josephus cannot hide the fact that neither the Caesarean troops, entering the city from the north (BJ 2.328, near Bezetha), nor Florus and his soldiers, attacking simultaneously from the royal palace in the west (BJ 2.328), were able to break through the opposition, reach the Temple, and relieve the garrison in the Antonia (BJ 2.330-333). It is obvious that Florus had good reason to attack the city since much of the population was willing to resist him actively—no matter what Josephus says.[18]

2. Florus and the Jews

We now pass from historiography to history. It is typical that the two causes of the war most often invoked by modern historians, the economic abuse of the country and the widespread apocalyptic speculation, are almost entirely omitted by Josephus. Even he, however, is aware of the hostility caused by the incompetent, in-

---

inexplicable"); and H. Kreissig, *Die sozialen Zusammenhänge des judäischen Krieges* (Berlin 1970) 138, who claims that the nobles of BJ 2.562-568 did not usurp control from anyone because they opposed the Zealots and were the peace party (Kreissig follows V). The problems were sensed by Graetz, *Geschichte* 484-485 with 485 n. 1, and G. Ricciotti in his note on BJ 2.563. Drexler was anticipated to some extent by G. Hölscher, *Der Sadduzäismus* (Leipzig 1906) 71-75. Most of these scholars failed to do what Drexler did: to analyze the motives of Josephus' statements about the aristocracy. A distinguished example of this is Brunt, *Klio* 59 (1977) 149-153, who believes practically everything Josephus says and does not realize the differences between BJ and V.

[17] Drexler 282. Ancient historiography often attributed the origins of wars to personal, even silly, reasons. See A. Momigliano, *Studies in Historiography* (N.Y. 1966) 125.

[18] Drexler 281-283.

sensitive Roman rule. These and other factors affected all levels of society and the conflagration broke out under Florus.[19]

Florus' tactless assault on the temple treasury (BJ 2.293-296), combined with the incident at Caesarea (BJ 2.285-292), provoked the populace to riot. That Florus' action was justified by the Jewish failure to pay taxes was irrelevant. It seemed a classic case of the profanation of the temple by a gentile, but unlike Heliodorus (2 *Macc.* 3) Florus was not struck down by a heavenly apparition. Perhaps the riots began as a protest against Florus (BJ 2.294, 315, 340, 342, 402), but they soon were directed against Caesar and Rome. The entire city was in an uproar. In another tactless maneuver Florus sent troops to clear the way (BJ 2.297-300) and he arrived (from Sebaste, BJ 2.292) at the royal palace (BJ 2. 301). He then summoned the notables and ordered them to hand over the leaders of the demonstrations. When they refused he sacked the upper market (BJ 2.305-308), the area immediately to the east of the royal palace, Florus' headquarters (16 Artemisios, BJ 2.315). Josephus, of course, pretends that the Jews were the peaceful victims of Florus' soldiery. Florus next day (?) received reinforcements (which he must have ordered previously) from Caesarea (BJ 2. 318). Josephus claims that the population went out to greet the troops, but began to abuse Florus when the troops failed to respond, and so touched off a riot in which many were trampled. Florus would probably have said that revolutionaries jeered and attacked the troops as they were coming in, and so produced the trouble. In any event it is clear that the city authorities did not openly try to keep the troops out; had they wanted to do so they could have shut the gates. The troops were permitted to enter the city in the northwest corner, Bezetha, while Florus was in the west at the royal palace. From these two positions Florus and the new troops made

---

[19] For a survey of the causes of the war, see Rhoads 80-87. On M. Aberbach, *The Roman-Jewish War (66-70 A.D.): Its Origin and Consequences* (London 1966), see the review of L. Levine, *Judaism* 20 (1971) 244-248. Modern scholars tend to assign bona fide religious, social, and nationalistic motives to the revolutionaries, in marked contrast to Josephus. See Applebaum, *JRS* 61 (1971) 155-170; Borg, *JTS* 22 (1971) 505; and L. Levine, *Cathedra* 1 (Sept. 1976) 39-60 (Hebrew). The extent of economic abuse suffered by the aristocracy has not been investigated. Most scholars assume that only the lower classes were affected; see e.g. M. Rostovtzeff, *Social and Economic History of the Roman Empire*[2] (Oxford 1957) 664 n. 32. The fact that the conflict was also a civil war between the upper and lower classes does not imply that only one class had economic grievances.

a coordinated effort to force their way through the city to the Antonia fortress at the northwest corner of the Temple. Both attacks failed, a clear sign of the massive popular resistance which Florus had to face. The revolutionaries reigned in the temple (BJ 2.320) and the Roman garrison in the Antonia was cut off (BJ 2.330).

Thus, in spite of Josephus' distortions, the outline of events is reasonably clear. In this section BJ refers only to revolutionaries (στασιασταί, BJ 2.295, 325, 330; τὸ στασιῶδες, 320) and wicked men (πονηροί, 304). By whom were these revolutionaries led? Since the temple was the center of unrest, it is reasonable to conjecture that some priests were in the forefront. Certainly false is the claim that "every priest" (BJ 2.321) tried to quiet the crowd, since many priests would soon support Eleazar ben Ananias (BJ 2.409-410). Perhaps some of the wealthy (δυνατοί) and the high priests (ἀρχιερεῖς) too were among the leaders. Although we have no way of knowing how much of Josephus' apology for these aristocrats is true, we should not doubt the existence of a peace party. Florus' treatment of Berenice (BJ 2.309-314) and some Roman citizens (BJ 2.308) is problematic. Is it wholly an invention of Josephus, or did something of the sort occur? And if it occurred was it a testimony to Florus' barbarity (as Josephus claims) or to the anti-Roman conduct of the victims?

Finally Florus left Jerusalem. He realized that he could not recapture the city with the forces at his disposal and so he withdrew, hoping that the peace party ("the high priests and the council") would be able to restore calm (BJ 2.331-332). At Caesarea Florus sent to Cestius and accused the Jews of revolt, but Berenice and the magistrates (ἄρχοντες) of Jerusalem accused Florus (BJ 2.333). Are these magistrates the peace party with which Florus had just made an agreement? Or are they the leaders of the anti-Florus (= anti-Roman) movement? Perhaps both. Cestius dispatched a legate to Jerusalem (BJ 2.334-335) who, Josephus insists, found a peaceful city loyal to the Romans (BJ 2.339-341). Even if this is true, it is not difficult to see why the Jews wanted also to appeal to the emperor against Florus and against the accusations of Jewish revolt. Florus had sacked one district of the city and a considerable number of people had been killed. The families of the victims wanted revenge. Moreover, since Florus was certain to accuse the Jerusalemites of revolt, the wisest thing was to accuse him first.

But, besides these immediate matters, the central concern probably was the tribute. Because of his attempt on the temple treasure, the Jews wanted Florus removed. After that was done they, including, perhaps, the war party, would be willing to discuss the payment of tribute. Neapolitanus presumably informed the Jews that the Romans could not accept this blackmail. When some Jews (who?) decided to appeal to Nero, Agrippa addressed the Jews from the Xystus and implored them to pay their tribute (BJ 2.344-404). Agrippa also requested them to rebuild the porticoes which would re-establish Roman control over the temple by linking it with the Antonia. Josephus claims success for the king (BJ 2.405), but admits that it was only temporary. Upon advocating obedience to Florus, Agrippa was ousted from the city (BJ 2.406-407).

The "war party" was in control of the temple throughout this period but, given our preceding remarks about the internal diversity of "the war party" and the variety of its members' goals, we find in this no reason to doubt the report that Neapolitanus addressed the people and did obeisance in the temple (BJ 2.341). The apologetic for Agrippa and Berenice (BJ 2.336-38, 343-407) is hard to assess.[20] We may assume that Agrippa will not have been foolish enough to engage in overt hostile activity. Otherwise he surely would have been replaced, as expected by Varus (V 52). He may have nurtured secret hopes for a Jewish victory or for a Jewish success that would lead the Romans to consider placing him on the throne of Judaea,[21] but he must have known that direct action would be suicidal. Agrippa's magniloquent oration is obviously Josephus' composition, but whatever Agrippa told the revolutionaries, whether pacific or conspiratorial, was unsolicited and unappreciated. BJ 2.405 presumably exaggerates the success of Agrippa's speech.[22]

3. From Florus to Cestius

After the expulsion of Agrippa, war breaks out. The temple

---

[20] On the apologetic for Agrippa see chapter five note 241.

[21] Baerwald 37-40 and Drexler 311-312. BJ implies (2.343) that Agrippa opposed the war because he saw he had nothing to gain from it.

[22] An indication of the exaggeration may be found in BJ 2.407 where Josephus says that the tribute remained uncollected and tribute collectors undesignated. See Drexler 282, but contrast Thackeray's note *a* to BJ 2.407. We are never told what became of the ἄρχοντες and δυνατοί who were sent to Florus by Agrippa.

must be purified of all foreign contagion. Florus' attack on the temple treasury was the last time a gentile would be allowed to profane the holy. Eleazar ben Ananias, son of a high priest and a captain of the temple, persuaded his fellow priests to reject all offerings by gentiles, including the emperor (BJ 2.409).[23] The inevitable appeals of the high priests, the nobles, the wealthy, and the Pharisaic nobles inevitably were in vain (BJ 2.410-417). Whether Eleazar only now attained prominence or had been a revolutionary leader for some time, is unknown. Eleazar was not acting alone but had for support an entire multitude (πλῆθος), i.e. of priests and Levites, and the most vigorous of the revolutionaries (τὸ ἀκμαιότατον τῶν νεωτεριζόντων, BJ 2.410). Those priests and high priests first mentioned by Josephus after the defeat of Cestius must have been important figures even before that point but exactly when they became active is unknown. Perhaps they were the associates of Eleazar.[24] In any case, the control of the war party was not yet so complete, nor was its policy so uniform, as to prevent the peace party from assembling for one last time within the temple precinct (BJ 2.411).

After failing to persuade Eleazar ben Ananias, the peace party sent requests for aid to Florus and Agrippa (BJ 2.418-419). Florus did not reply (BJ 2.420), presumably because he had already failed once before to capture the city and had no reason to expect a better result. Also, as far as he was concerned, the fat was now in the fire. The authorities now appealing to him may have been the same ones who had recently accused him to Cestius and to Nero. Should he now lay himself open to further charges of brutality, looting, etc. in order to save their necks? He had already defended himself by accusing the Jews of revolt. Now let them prove he was right. This is the account of his actions Josephus indicates and is not implausible. Although Florus did not reply, Agrippa sent 2000 cavalry (BJ 2.421). Two Roman garrisons were still in the city, one in the Antonia (430) and the other near the royal palace (438-39). Thus fortified, the peace party, based in the upper city,

---

[23] On the rejection of the offerings of gentiles and on the purification of the temple, see Hengel 204-211 and 223-226; Rhoads 169-170.

[24] Hengel 366 searches for the motives of Eleazar and ascribes to him the realization that the revolutionaries would attain control in Judaea and the hope that he would share in the leadership of the movement. Hengel ignores the fact that many aristocrats fought Rome and not only from a selfish desire for power.

fought the war party (i.e. Eleazar) based in the lower city and the temple. After seven days neither side was victorious (BJ 2.422-24).

The situation soon changed. While Eleazar had been purifying the temple from the sacrifices of gentiles, some revolutionaries (τινὲς τῶν μάλιστα κινούντων τὸν πόλεμον) were capturing Masada (408). Josephus does not specify who these revolutionaries were. In 433-434 Josephus recounts again the capture of Masada, this time by Menahem, who broke open the arsenal and armed his followers.[25] Since later passages speak of Masada being in the hands of the *Sicarii* (BJ 4.400, 516; 7.253, 275, 297, 311), most scholars identify Menahem as the leader of the *Sicarii*.[26] Who then are the captors of 408? A related problem is that the *Sicarii* enter Jerusalem in 425 but Menahem does not arrive until 434. We have two choices. Perhaps 408 and 433-34 refer to the single capture of Masada by the *Sicarii* under Menahem while 425 and 434 refer to the single irruption of the *Sicarii* into Jerusalem under Menahem. 408 and 425 are in their correct chronological position, 433-34 is a thematic passage focusing on Menahem. The difficulty is that the details of these passages do not mesh smoothly.[27] The alternative is that we are dealing with discrete events. The captors of 408 were, perhaps, the priests of Jerusalem who could have feigned loyalty to Rome and thus have captured an otherwise almost impregnable fortress. In 433-434 Menahem took the fortress not from the Romans, but from the priestly war party, which would make his swift assassination in Jerusalem even more understandable. If Menahem and the *Sicarii* entered the city separately, that shows only that the *Sicarii* were composed of different bands. This problem is not our main concern but it does show our ignorance and Josephus' lack of concern for accuracy.

To return to the narrative: the situation changed when many *Sicarii* entered Jerusalem on the day of the wood-carrying and,

---

[25] Josephus calls him Judas' son but he probably was Judas' grandson. See J. S. Kennard, *JQR* 36 (1945-46) 281-286.

[26] Josephus never says this explicitly but Eleazar ben Jair, an associate of Menahem (BJ 2.447), is a *Sicarius* in BJ 7.253, 275, 297.

[27] The suggestion is Drexler's (280-281) who, however, omits the distinction between chronological and thematic. Menahem's arrival as a king in 434 does not match the entrance of 425. Possible support for this theory is provided by BJ 7.297 which describes Eleazar's capture of Masada by a trick (δόλῳ). Unless this refers to BJ 2.408 (λάθρα), the reference is unclear.

joining forces with Eleazar (425),[28] succeeded in driving the royal troops from the upper city (426a) and enclosing them in the royal palace (429a). The poor of the "lower city" and perhaps some peasants who had come in for the wood-bringing festival (425), as soon as they got into the upper city, began to loot the houses of the wealthy, notably Ananias (Eleazar's father), Agrippa, and Berenice (426b). They also burned the archives and record office in the hope of obliterating their own debts and arousing a general rebellion of the poor (427). Needless to say, the aristocrats (οἱ δυνατοὶ καὶ οἱ ἀρχιερεῖς) fled—Eleazar had been no threat to them— and many, including Ananias, found refuge with Agrippa's troops in the royal palace (428-429). Eleazar, we may suppose, was safely fortified within the temple where he was accompanied by his supporters, among them Josephus (V 20). Soon the Antonia fell to the rebels (BJ 2.430), but for a while the royal palace held firm (431-432, 435-437a). It is only now, according to BJ 434, that Menahem and his forces from Masada arrived on the scene and took over the siege of the palace. Finally Agrippa's troops yielded and were allowed to depart under truce (437b). Philip, Agrippa's general, would later be accused of treachery (V 407) for abandoning the Roman garrison to its fate (BJ 2.438-440, 449-454). Whether Philip departed now for Gamala (with V 46-47) or remained in Jerusalem not to depart until after the defeat of Cestius (with BJ 556) has been investigated in chapter five above. Since the question is unsettled, we cannot make any firm deductions based on Philip's whereabouts.

The truce did not, of course, end the hostility of Menahem to his rivals. Philip was protected by his Babylonians (V 47), Josephus was still hiding in the temple with Eleazar (V 20-21). Ananias, the father of Eleazar, and Ezekias were not so fortunate. They were caught by Menahem and executed (BJ 441). Menahem thought he was master of the situation (442), but when he went to the temple, the stronghold of Eleazar, he was assassinated (444-448) by Eleazar's aristocrats (443). Josephus claims that the *demos* participated in the assassination, hoping thereby to quell the war (445 and 449), but the historicity of this apologetic is hard to judge.

With the removal of Menahem we hear again of the leadership of Eleazar (450-453) who, with some soldiers (στρατιῶται, 450),

---

[28] The Greek does not justify Thackeray's translation "forced their way in."

apparently the soldiers of Philip, continued the assault on the Roman garrison. Although three envoys arranged for the garrison's safe withdrawal (451), it was massacred by Eleazar's forces (451-453). Only the commander was spared (454).[29] The moderates (i.e. the peace party) were dejected by these events and felt that the destruction of the city was imminent (454-456).

4. The Defeat of Cestius and the Selection of Generals

"On the same day and same hour" as the massacre of the garrison (17 Gorpiaios?), the Jewish community of Caesarea was slaughtered (457). As a result of these events all of Syria was ablaze with fighting between Greeks and Jews (BJ 2.458-480; V 25-26). BJ pretends that a single wave of Jews attacked the Greek cities but names no Jewish leaders. V provides some assistance: Justus attacked Gadara and Hippos (V 42), John attacked the Tyrians (V 43-45).[30] Thus we have local conflicts and local chieftains, not a centrally directed movement. At this time Varus (or Noarus) attacked the Jews of Caesarea Philippi and Ecbatana (BJ 2.481-483//V 46-61). The revolutionaries (οἱ στασιασταί, BJ 484)—Josephus does not give their origin—seized Cypros while the Jews of Machaerus captured their fortress from the Romans (485-486). The troubles in Alexandria are not our concern (487-498).

The account of Cestius' expedition (499-555) provides no solid information on the internal political developments in Jerusalem. Cestius' forces plundered Jewish districts on their way to Jerusalem —ancient armies were expected to finance themselves largely by loot—and we cannot be sure that the towns and areas looted (Chabulon and its territory, Narbatene, Joppa, Aphek, Lydda, BJ 2.503-509, 514-515) were centers of revolutionary activity. But there was some discrimination. A column dispatched into Galilee was welcomed at Sepphoris, killed some 2000 "rebels and brigands" in the neighboring hills, found the rest of the country quiet, and rejoined the main force at Caesarea (510-512). On approaching Jerusalem, Cestius was attacked at Gibeon by "the Jews" from the metropolis (516-521). Josephus says the attack was made on a Sabbath during the Feast of Tabernacles (517), but says nothing of any group's abstaining from or opposing it.

---

[29] See appendix I for the statements of Suetonius and Megillat Taʿanit which apparently refer to this event.

[30] On the text of V 44 see chapter one note 6.

On the other hand, two or three days later (522), when Agrippa, who was with Cestius, sent a delegation to offer terms, the revolutionaries, "fearing lest the whole multitude, with the hope of a pardon, would go over to Agrippa" (525), attacked the emissaries, killed one of them, wounded another, and drove the protesters from their own ranks back into the city. Four days later (528) Cestius occupied the new city and the upper city (at least the section near the royal palace) without difficulty, the people, "guarded by the insurgents" (529), having withdrawn to the lower city and temple. These Cestius besieged for six days, without being able to force an entrance. Many of the distinguished citizens were persuaded by Ananus ben Jonathan (533) to get in touch with Cestius and to offer to open the gates to him, but were discovered by the revolutionaries and driven from the walls (533-534). On the sixth day Cestius began his retreat, first to Scopus (542), next day to Gibeon (542, 544), and then to Beth Horon (546) and Antipatris and beyond (551ff).[31] In this retreat Cestius was pursued first by "the brigands" and then by "the Jews" as a whole.

Nowhere in this long account does Josephus name the generals of the Jews. The Jews distinguished for valor in the first attack were Niger of Peraea, Silas the Babylonian, and two relatives of the king of Adiabene (520). Simon ben Giora attacked the Roman rear while the army was approaching Jerusalem and captured much baggage (521). Eleazar ben Simon, not mentioned by Josephus in the fighting, managed to get control of most of the loot (564). We may conjecture that each of these aristocrats had his own body of followers. Priestly groups must have been prominent. Perhaps the one to which Josephus belonged was still under the leadership of Eleazar ben Ananias. (Had Eleazar been replaced already by higher ranking priests, e.g. Ananus ben Ananus?) If Philip was still in Jerusalem, he too with his followers may have fought Cestius. Other aristocrats as well may have participated. Cestius was opposed not by a single unified block of revolutionaries but by numerous different groups led by different aristocrats, Which of these groups, if any, was dominant at this time, is not clear. After the great victory, however, their relative positions can be deduced to some degree.

---

[31] On Cestius' defeat at Beth Horon, see Bar-Kochva, *PEQ* 108 (1976) 18-21.

The evidence is provided by the selection of generals as described by BJ 2.562-568. The account as it stands in BJ is suspect. It is motivated by apologetic considerations (see above and chapter four). It assumes (a) that all the generals were chosen at the same time in one orderly process and (b) that all the generals executed their assignments to the best of their ability (BJ 2.569). (a) may be the result of thematic compression and we can conjecture an alternate context for the mission of at least one of these generals.[32] The most likely explanation of the reference to Niger's governorship (ἄρχοντι τότε, 566) is that even before the defeat of Cestius, perhaps after the fall of the royal palace, a revolutionary government had been formed and representatives sent to various parts of the country. Other generals on this list may have been similarly designated. (b) is suspect because many of these generals do not appear at their posts. True, Ananus fortifies the walls of Jerusalem (BJ 2.648) as he was instructed to do (563). Joseph ben Gorion reappears, perhaps, as Gorion ben Joseph, at the side of Ananus when the Zealots are searching for victims (BJ 4.159 and 358). Josephus is busy in Galilee (see below). John the Essene, however, did not go to his toparchy but joined with Niger and Silas in an attack on Ascalon where he was killed (BJ 3.19).[33] None of the other generals is mentioned again, even when BJ describes the Roman conquest of their districts.[34] Thus we could argue that some of these generalships are the products of Josephus' industrious and apologetic imagination. Josephus would want a glorious war to have a full complement of generals.

Nevertheless, even if Josephus has exaggerated and simplified, we have some reason to follow his account. It is inherently plausible: with the defeat of Cestius the last vestige of Roman control disappeared and the revolutionaries would want to set up an administrative structure of their own. Since Josephus was interested in the actions of no one but himself (BJ 2.569), it is not surprising that he provides little data on the other generals. The marginal resistance

---

[32] John ben Ananias, the governor of Gophnitike and Akrabatene (568), was perhaps the leader of the army sent by Ananus to Akrabatene in order to remove Simon ben Giora (653).

[33] Niger's participation in the expedition against Ascalon is reconciliable with our list since the attack may have been staged from Idumaea. When the attack failed the Jews took refuge in a town in Idumaea (BJ 3.20).

[34] BJ 3.414-431 (Joppa); 4.2-83 (Gamala); 4.444-450 (Idumaea, Jericho, Peraea, Thamna, Lydda, Emmaus); 4.551 (Gophna and Akrabatene).

encountered by the Romans in all these districts testifies not to the non-existence of these generals or to their incompetence and insincerity, but to the general disinclination of the country (outside of Judaea) to fight Rome. The chronological problem is more difficult, but most of these generals must have been sent not long after the great victory over Cestius. The revolutionaries could gain nothing by postponement and much by promptitude. In the following discussion I assume that all the generals were selected at one time although I admit that this is uncertain.

As stated above BJ 2.562-568 demonstrates the importance of priests in the revolt. Of the eleven generals (omitting Niger and including Josephus' two companions) selected in the temple (562-568), one (Ananus) was a former high priest, two (Jesus ben Sapphias [35] and Eleazar ben Ananias) were of high-priestly families, and three (Josephus and his two companions who are suppressed in BJ because of Josephus' vanity [36]) were priests. Two others (Joseph ben Simon and John ben Ananias) bear priestly names. None of the remaining four can be classified. But although priests thus predominated in positions of command, it cannot be supposed that they were all members of the party of Eleazar ben Ananias whose action touched off the revolt. On the contrary, it is presumable that once the resistance got under way, various priestly grandees joined in, each with his own forces. And this presumption is confirmed by the fact that Eleazar ben Ananias does not now get control of Jerusalem but is shunted off to Idumaea, a testimony to the party struggles within the priesthood. Similarly, although Eleazar ben Simon had been successful enough to obtain control of the Cestian booty and much else besides, his fellow priests mistrusted him and removed him from power (564). He would get his revenge later.

It is important to note the omissions from this list. We shall discuss below the absence of Simon ben Gamaliel and Jesus ben Gamala. If Philip remained in Jerusalem after the assassination of Menahem (thus BJ) and fought Cestius, he nevertheless did not receive a commission. He went north to stir up trouble in Agrippa's kingdom, ultimately to be reconciled with the king. We do not know what Costobar and Saul had been doing in Jerusalem, but

---

[35] Not the Jesus ben Sapphia whom Josephus confronts in Tiberias!

[36] Drexler 302 is the only scholar to doubt Josephus' admission that he was accompanied by two other envoys. I do not understand Drexler's reasons since the presence of the envoys does not aid the polemic against Justus.

they now joined Cestius, advancing the claim of loyalty to Rome (BJ 2.556 and 558). Antipas (BJ 2.557 and 4.140) and Silas (BJ 2.520; 3.11 and 19) remained in Jerusalem, but neither was appointed to office. Other revolutionaries were excluded too. Monobazus and Cenedaeus, the relatives of the king of Adiabene, do not re-appear in BJ (cf. 4.567). Niger of Peraea was retained but in a subordinate role (BJ 2.566). Simon ben Giora left (or was ejected from) Jerusalem and set himself up in Akrabatene as an opposition leader. His appeal to the lower classes was similar to that of the *Sicarii* and it is no surprise that, when attacked by the Jerusalem aristocracy, he fled to Masada (652-654). Whether Simon had this radical tendency even in Jerusalem is unknown. It is significant that none of these men, except for Jesus ben Gamala (see below), was, as far as we know, a priest.

What was the task of these generals? Obviously to organize the war against Rome. These men hated Rome for seizing the temple treasure, curbing the traditional aristocracy, and denigrating the high-priesthood. Some of them, presumably, believed with apocalyptic fervor in the imminent arrival of the End. Of course they feared the hostility of the peasants and urban poor recruited by the *Sicarii* and, later, the Zealots. Hence the bitter animosity between them and these groups (*Sicarii* in BJ 2, Zealots in BJ 4).[37] Perhaps some of them would have been willing to come to terms with Rome had they succeeded in exacting certain concessions, but after the defeat of Cestius the focus was on war. The pacifist policy Josephus ascribes to Ananus resulted from Ananus' encounter with the Zealots and probably indicates nothing about the situation in fall 66 (see note 10). Some of the districts to which the generals were sent had already manifested anti-Roman sentiment: Jericho (Cypros had been captured, BJ 2.484), Peraea (Machaerus, BJ 2.485-486), Joppa (BJ 2.507: note the fighting at Aphek, a village between Joppa and Thamna, BJ 2.513), Galilee (suppression of brigands, plundering of Chabulon, 503-505, 511-512). The other districts were, apparently, still peaceful and the generals must have been told to incite them to join the war.

---

[37] I have emphasized the social factor as the chief source of tension between the *Sicarii* and the aristocrats, but other factors played a part too; see Hengel 371. Kreissig 132-134 is too one-sided.

5. The Mission of Josephus

Josephus claims that he was one of these generals. This claim provided Josephus the legitimation that he needed, not only to gratify his vanity but also to refute charges of tyranny (see chapter five). BJ disposes of the problem by stating once for all that Josephus was a general appointed in Jerusalem and granted authority over lower Galilee, upper Galilee, and Gamala. V is much more strident in its insistence that Josephus was chosen by the *koinon, synedrion,* or the leaders (πρῶτοι) of Jerusalem (28-29, 62, 65, 72, 267, 310, 341, 393). V, like BJ, emphasizes that Josephus' jurisdiction included upper Galilee (72). Local leaders recognize him as a man whose authorization they need before embarking on certain projects (V 71-72//BJ 2.590; V 75-76; V 85-86//BJ 2.614-615; V 106). We could reject all of this as apologetic and conjecture that Josephus placed himself at the head of the revolutionaries in Galilee.[38] Perhaps he was a native of Galilee, an associate of John of Gischala. John organized upper Galilee, Josephus lower Galilee. The two companions described by V were perhaps the "legitimate" emissaries whom he sent home just as he later would defeat another delegation from Jerusalem. Perhaps ... but there is no justification for throwing out a report, even when it comes from a known liar, if it is plausible and there is no evidence against it. Admittedly, Josephus *may* have made up the whole story. But if so it is amazing that some things suggested by the reported course of events, but left unsaid by his narrative (for instance, his association with the party of Eleazar ben Ananias) explain and make plausible the things he does report (for instance, his appointment as general for Galilee). Therefore I reject this conjecture although I am not sure it is wrong.

Josephus and two companions were sent to Galilee. Tripartite leadership was bestowed on Idumaea too (BJ 2.566). V 28 claims that Galilee was not yet fully committed to revolution from Rome (τὴν Γαλιλαίαν οὔπω πᾶσαν ῾Ρωμαίων ἀφεστάναι) and this claim seems to be correct. When Cestius was on his way to Judaea he looted a district on the western border of Galilee and encountered only mild resistance. The Jews of Chabulon fled (BJ 2.503-505) and did not return to their homes until Cestius withdrew (506). Later Cestius detached a column to hold down central Galilee. Once

---

[38] Drexler 302 considers this possibility.

Sepphoris declared loyalty to Rome the other cities too remained quiet. All the rebels of the area fled to Mt. Asamon and were killed by the Romans (BJ 2.510-512). Cestius had no further trouble in Galilee. Even after his defeat, there is little evidence of active hostility to Rome. If the Galileans harrassed the retreating Romans, Josephus does not mention it. Sepphoris, the largest city of Galilee, never wavered from its pro-Roman stance (after surrendering hostages to Cestius [V 30-31] it had little choice). The second largest city, Tiberias, was torn by factional strife. In this district the social tensions between city and country were stronger than anti-Roman sentiment (see below). Galilee was not ready for war.

Neither Josephus nor John ever attained a large following among the populace. All the fighting in Galilee was on a small scale until the siege of Jotapata. Of course Josephus does exaggerate. BJ tosses off recruitment figures of 100,000 (BJ 2.576) or 60,000 (BJ 2.583) [39] and even V, which is not prone to numerical exaggeration, mentions 10,000 troops (V 321 and 331)—if μυρίους is to be taken literally. Josephus apparently had an army of about 3000 (V 234) which, he claims, was augmented on occasion to 8000 (consisting of 3000 regulars and 5000 reinforcements, V 212-213), or 5000 (3000 regulars plus 2000, V 399). Once Josephus refers to 2000 soldiers (V 118). Twice he was able to spare 500 men to accompany an embassy to Jerusalem (V 268 and 332): once he sent 800 (V 240-241). We receive the clear impression that these forces were not stable but appeared and disappeared with ease—precisely what we would expect in a period of tumult and crisis. In one encounter Josephus had only 200 men (V 90), in others his only support came from a few friends who had weapons (φίλοι καὶ ὁπλῖται, V 144, 161, 164; cf. BJ 2.600//V 132). Once Josephus had no cavalry (V 116) but later he had 80—or at least so he says (V 213). Thus Josephus may have had a pool of about three to five thousand from which he could draw, but for normal day-to-day activities he never had more than a few hundred men. If we omit the fantastic 60,000 from BJ 2.583, our conclusion is confirmed. Josephus had 250 or 350 horse (probably exaggerated), 4500 soldiers—probably brigands—in his pay (μισθοφόροι), and 600 bodyguards. The casualty figures that we have also fit well. In one battle the Galileans lost

---

[39] W. Bauer, *Festgabe für A. Julicher* (Tübingen 1927) 23-24. See too F. X. Malinowski, "Galilean Judaism in the Writings of Flavius Josephus," (diss. Duke University 1973) 62-66.

one man, their opponents not many more than twelve (V 396-397).
In another the Galileans lost six men (V 406).

The numbers of Josephus' opponents are of the same caliber.
John of Gischala had 400 (BJ 2.588, perhaps a deliberate distortion),
1000 (V 95), 3000 (V 233), or even 5000-5500 men, of whom 2000-
1500 stayed with him in spite of Josephus' threats (BJ 2.625//V
371-372). Other groups have 600 (V 145 [cf. BJ 2.610] and V 200)
or 800 (V 105). The Jerusalemites send 1000 (V 200-201) or 2500
men (BJ 2.628). One of the two Roman contingents in Galilee
musters 200 infantry and 100 horse (V 115), and the other a total
slightly over 1000 (V 214). Except for the two wild exaggerations
in BJ these figures are all well within the bounds of probability
and look like the work of an author who, although not concerned
about precision (as the discrepancies between BJ and V prove),
was not indulging in fantastic invention.

Thus the total number of Galileans armed and ready for combat
with Rome could not have exceeded 10,000 or so. Josephus and
John could never count on more than about 5000 each and most of
these will have been *lestai*, bandits, not all of whom were revolutionaries, who picked up some easy money by enrolling themselves with
one or another commander. Roman contingents of a couple of
hundred men are a full match for these Galileans. Of course, once
Vespasian arrived with the full panoply of Roman might, the 10,000
disappeared. Josephus' troops melted away (BJ 3.129), leaving
their field marshal the choice of surrender or refuge in one of his
fortresses (BJ 3.130-140). When Titus approached Gischala John
put up no resistance and fled to Jerusalem (BJ 4.84-120).[40] The
population total of Galilee at this period is not known [41] and we
cannot even guess how many revolutionaries there would have been
had every able-bodied man raised a spear in defense of his home-

----

[40] In BJ 4.115 Titus killed 6000 of those who were fleeing with John and
captured 3000 women and children, whom John had persuaded to flee with
him and then abandoned (4.106-111); this is of course a "pathetic" and
polemic passage, and the figures are probably exaggerated.

[41] Malinowski 62-63 gives an inventory of the guesses which range from
100,000 to 1,200,000 or higher. Josephus himself implies a population of
more than 3,000,000 (BJ 3.43 with V 235). The modern guesses partly
depend on Josephus' own figures of the soldiers he recruited and so it would
be circular, not to say futile, to ask what percentage of the total population
supported the war. The most recent study reaches a conclusion of 630,000
for the population of first-century Galilee; this guess does not depend on
Josephus' recruitment figures. See A. Byatt, *PEQ* 105 (1973) 51-60.

land. But both BJ and V seem to agree that Galilee was no hotbed of revolutionary activity. BJ 3.41-42 (on the courageous and freedom-loving Galileans) rhetorically idealizes the constituents of an ideal general.[42]

Josephus and his two companions arrived in Galilee. The three functioned together (V 73) and whether Josephus was the leader, as he implies (V 62), is uncertain. Their task was to organize the country for war. We do not know whether they were preparing for a life-or-death struggle with Rome or whether, as Josephus claims for Ananus faced by the Zealots in early 68 (BJ 2.651 and 4.320-321), they really desired a negotiated peace, but were preparing for war as a basis for negotiation. In the fall of 66 the envoys themselves probably were unsure of their ultimate objective. They knew that war was imminent and that preparations had to be made. Presumably these preparations included attempts to solidify revolutionary control of the country and to eliminate pro-Roman centers that might serve as bases for the Romans later on. Perhaps they were instructed to prevent the Galileans from fighting among themselves and to obtain arms for the Jerusalem government (V 28-29) but V's interpretation of these instructions is presumably false. It is unlikely that the envoys were sent to preserve the peace and to do nothing but "wait and see" what the Romans would do.[43]

Did they fulfill their mission? Since we know next to nothing about the activities of Josephus' two companions, the question really focuses on Josephus' own attitude. Was he a traitor to his

---

[42] The exaggeration is evident in BJ 3.43 which provides an absurd figure (although defended by Sherwin-White 130-132); see n. 41. Hengel 322, Brandon 54, and other authors, including many on the "Galilee of our Lord" (e.g. G. Vermes, *Jesus the Jew* [London 1973] 46-48), write of Galilee's almost traditional militancy in opposing the yoke of all foreigners. But Josephus has very little to report on anti-Roman disturbances in Galilee after 4 BCE. The troubles are in Judaea and the Greek cities. Judas the Galilean and John of Gischala, the two most famous revolutionaries produced by Galilee, gained their fame in the south, not their homeland. This fact was pointed out by M. Smith, *HTR* 64 (1971) 15 and has been recognized recently by two students of W. D. Davies (Malinowski 41, 271, 291-296, and Rhoads 175 n. 1). See n. 51 below.

[43] Laqueur is the most strident defender of V here. He contends (97-107) that when Josephus arrived in Galilee, and even months later when he wrote his administrative report, he did not yet know of an impending war with the Romans. This view is untenable. After the capture of the Antonia, the massacre of the Jerusalem garrison, and the defeat of Cestius (during which an *aquila* was captured, as Suetonius says), the Roman reaction could not have been in doubt. Josephus is fighting the Romans throughout V.

mission? Even if we discount all of BJ's inflated rhetoric about the recruitment and training of an enormous army, about the ideal general fighting huge and ingenious battles at Jotapata, about the single-minded devotion to the cause, the siege of Jotapata remains.[44] This was not the act of a man who was only pretending to be anti-Roman. Josephus explains why he remained at Jotapata. He says that after Vespasian's arrival he realized the invincibility of Rome (BJ 3.130-131 and 136) and saw only two possibilities, defeat or surrender (BJ 3.137); he therefore wrote to Jerusalem requesting either authorization to negotiate or reinforcements (BJ 3. 138-140). The alternative is hard to explain. If he realized that the Romans were invincible why did he try to draw more men into the defeat? He justifies at least his own decision to fight by rhetoric: he had been sent to fight a war and this is what he would do unless instructed otherwise. Although these paragraphs are apologetic to the Romans for his actions ("I fought the Romans although I knew I would lose"), the outline of the narrative is plausible. Generals are often motivated by rhetoric rather than reason. But if this explanation is true, then Josephus had been sent to prepare for war and if Ananus already wanted peace Josephus knew nothing of it. So the passages of V that imply the contrary will be secondary falsifications. What exactly Josephus expected to achieve by his resistance at Jotapata we do not know. Perhaps he really did hope that the reinforcements from Jerusalem would be sufficient to defeat Vespasian. Perhaps he was naive or vain enough to believe that he alone was a match for the best of the Roman generals. Perhaps he simply wanted to give Jerusalem more time to prepare its defenses. Perhaps he hoped that his stiff resistance would induce the Romans to seek a settlement. There are other possibilities too.

Throughout his tenure in Galilee Josephus was active in the anti-Roman cause. He aided the revolutionaries in Gamala (V 186).

---

[44] We could doubt the veracity of the entire Jotapata account and conjecture that Josephus surrendered to Vespasian without a struggle. The reference in Suetonius *Vespasianus* 4.5 (see appendix I below) does not guarantee the authenticity of this siege because propaganda reiterated is not history verified. BJ's account is propaganda not only for the Jewish general but also for the Flavian who conquered him. But not all stories that serve Josephus' propaganda are false, and to reject the entire narrative is unjustified in the light of Josephus' usual methods. Josephus does exaggerate but he does not normally engage in large scale invention.

He boasts that he fortified many "cities" and villages (V 186b-188//BJ 2.573-575). Of course he exaggerates his own importance by increasing his share in the fortification of these places. He even contradicts himself several times,[45] but the underlying policy is clear. He attacks pro-Roman cities (V 155-173, 373-380, 381-389, 394-396; BJ 3.61) and skirmishes with the forces of Rome (V 115-121, 397; BJ 3.60) and Agrippa (V 398-406). His attacks on the Syrian cities fit the pattern well (V 81) although by themselves they would not indicate anti-Roman sentiment. Significant too is his early friendship with Jesus ben Sapphia and John of Gischala, both anti-Roman (see below). Once a struggle for power erupted among them he was accused of betraying the country to the Romans (BJ 2.594, which is anti-John polemic; cf. too V 129 and 132//BJ 2.598), but he was accused of many things by his political opponents and it is nearly impossible to determine where polemic ends and truth begins. The autobiography throughout emphasizes the personal factor which separated Josephus from his opponents and this emphasis seems correct.[46] The choice of leaders which faced the Galileans was not a choice of policies. John, the delegates from Jerusalem, and Josephus are at odds with each other, but are

---

[45] Since Josephus was in Galilee for only six months or so and since he commanded only limited resources, the list of fortified cities must be a great exaggeration. The contradictory evidence on the fortification of Sepphoris will be treated in appendix I part B below. It is plausible that John fortified Gischala after the troubles he had with his neighbors (V 45). Josephus handles this datum in two ways. First he tries to give himself some of the credit (BJ 2.575 and 590; cf. V 71 which does not state whether John built the walls). Second, he pretends that John fortified Gischala only as an aid to remove Josephus (V 189). It is unlikely that Josephus fortified any settlement in upper Galilee; see below. Josephus claims to have fortified Tiberias and Taricheae (V 188//BJ 2.573) but contradicts himself about the order of events. Clearly he had fortified neither before the Dabaritta affair, when he was still promising fortifications to both cities (V 142 and 144; BJ 2.606 and 609). BJ 3.464-465 states that Tiberias was fortified "at the beginning of the revolt" before Taricheae, whereas V 156 states that Taricheae was fortified before Tiberias. I can see no tendentious motive in either passage. The archaeological discoveries in Galilee do not affect this discussion; see appendix one part A. That Josephus has exaggerated his role in these fortifications was recognized by Bar-Kochva, *IEJ* 24 (1974) 116.

[46] Laqueur 113-114 notes the frequency of ἀπόστασις from, and προστίθεσθαι to, a specific individual (V 87, 88, 123, 124, 155, 158, 167, 271, 273, 277; cf. 333). Laqueur deduces that Josephus did not yet have an official position as *strategos* but this is false. Loyalty even to Agrippa is stated in personal terms (e.g. V 155) although Agrippa was an "official" king. BJ has similar terminology in BJ 2.615 and 629.

all anti-Roman. The issues were: who would be a better leader (V 230-231, 249, 277), who could minimize the effects of the war on the populace (V 284), who could best protect the country from the Roman invaders (281-289, cf. 227). In their first letter the delegates said they hoped to reconcile Josephus to John (V 217-218), showing again that the two men were not separated by fundamental political differences. The Galileans criticize the delegates not for supporting the Romans, but for disturbing the country and creating dissension (V 250). The evidence seems clear. From his arrival in Galilee Josephus did what a general of the revolution should do. He fortified cities, fought the Romans, befriended other revolutionaries. The numerous disputes which soon erupted between him and the others were the result of personal factors and the desire for power. The local leaders resented the intrusion of outsiders into their domain.[47]

The details of Josephus' tenure need not detain us. We have no way of resolving the minor discrepancies between V and BJ. V's order of the events deserves preference since it reflects the structure of the *hypomnema* more accurately than BJ (see chapter three above). We need to investigate instead the powers in Galilean society with which Josephus had to deal and which he tried to reconcile to his rule. Some supported him, some remained neutral, some opposed him, and some vacillated. They are: the Galileans, the local aristocracy, the brigands, the large cities (Gabara, Sepphoris, and Tiberias), John of Gischala, the delegates from Jerusalem, and Agrippa.

6. *The Galileans and the Galilean Aristocracy*

Josephus' main source of strength was the peasantry, the Galileans (Γαλιλαῖοι). CA 1.48 states this explicitly and the Galileans appear throughout V. Only once (113) does V refer to the inhabitants of Galilee as "Jews" ('Ιουδαῖοι), and this in a passage where they are contrasted with gentiles. Although BJ 2 never calls Josephus' followers "Jews" ('Ιουδαῖοι), it avoids *Galilaioi* (which appears only once in 2.622) in favor of "the natives" (ἐπιχώριοι, 569), "those from the countryside" (οἱ ἀπὸ τῆς χώρας, 602), "the others", (οἱ ἄλλοι, 608; is this a corruption of οἱ Γαλιλαῖοι?), and "those in the surrounding countryside" (οἱ ἀνὰ τὴν πέριξ χώραν,

---

[47] Luther 33-34 and Laqueur 111-114.

621). We may see here the hand of the Greek secretary who edited Josephus' Greek for Roman readers and eliminated barbarous names. BJ 3 admits more readily that Josephus was supported by *Galilaioi* (BJ 3.61, 199, 233—was the secretary getting tired?) but, more significantly, BJ 3 regularly uses the term *Ioudaioi* (BJ 3.130, 142, 147, 149, etc.). *Ioudaios* can mean "worshipper of the God of Israel", which the *Galilaioi* certainly were, and "a native of Judaea", which the *Galilaioi* certainly were not.[48] It is in contrast to this latter sense of *Ioudaioi* that Josephus employs *Galilaioi* and *Idumaioi* and even calls each of them a tribe or nation (ἔθνος: BJ 2.510 and 4.105 for *Galilaioi*, 4.243 and 272 for *Idumaioi*).

Josephus is fairly clear and consistent on the identity of these Galileans. They come from the countryside and the villages (V 230-32 and 243), not the cities (cf. V 102 with BJ 2.622).[49] They are distinguished from the men of Sepphoris (V 30, 39, 375, 379), Tiberias (V 39, 99, 107, 143, 302, 305, 381, 383, 384, 385, 391, 392) and Gabara (V 125), that is, from the citizens of the three largest settlements of Galilee (V 123) who are never called *Galilaioi* by BJ and V. Josephus based his power on the old tension between city and country. The Galileans wanted nothing more than to sack Sepphoris (V 30, 39, 373-380), Tiberias (V 98-100 and 381-389), and Gabara (V 263-265). Sepphoris was, and Tiberias had been, the administrative capital of Galilee; this would exacerbate the tension. The Galileans had suffered at the hands of the Tiberians before the war (V 392)[50] and wanted revenge. Their hatred of the cities undoubtedly included hatred of Rome, the defender of the established order, but it was one thing to attack and plunder Sepphoris or Tiberias, quite another to face the imperial legions. The Galileans were eager for the former, but were afraid of the latter. It is no surprise that their enthusiasm for war waned when the Romans arrived.[51]

---

[48] See W. A. Meeks in *Christianity, Judaism, and Other Greco-Roman Cults: Studies for Morton Smith*, ed. J. Neusner (Leiden 1975) 1.181-182 and the abstract of an unpublished article by Morton Smith in the *Association for Jewish Studies Newsletter* nr. 14 (June 1975) 9.

[49] But remember that Josephus often uses *polis* as a synonym to *kome*.

[50] Read ὑπ' αὐτῶν (to agree with Τιβεριεῖς) instead of ὑπ' αὐτοῦ which is unexplained and makes little sense. See chapter five note 124 above. Thackeray's reference to V 341 is irrelevant.

[51] Josephus pretends that the only reason for the Galileans' hostility is the pro-Roman policy of Sepphoris and Tiberias (V 30, 39, and 340), but the cause is obviously deeper than that as V 375, 384, and 392 (even retain-

Josephus claims that even the Galilean aristocracy supported him. He dined with the chief men of Galilee (οἱ τῆς Γαλιλαίας πρῶτοι, V 220), summoned them (οἱ πρωτεύοντες τῶν Γαλιλαίων) to a conference (V 305), and sent one hundred of them (πρῶτοι) to Jerusalem (V 266). The BJ account of the formation of an aristocratic council and judicial system is obviously false (BJ 2.570-571) but even V 79 claims that, at least outwardly, Josephus and the Galilean authorities (οἱ ἐν τέλει τῶν Γαλιλαίων) were friends. True, he wanted the aristocrats more as hostages than as judges, but the passage makes sense only if Josephus and the aristocrats were on good terms. We could deduce more from V 79 if we knew whose good faith (πίστις) the aristocrats were guaranteeing: of themselves and the others of their class, or of the Galileans? The only sign of tension is V 228 where Josephus claims that he sent thirty of the most distinguished citizens (δοκιμώτατοι), each accompanied by a soldier, to greet the delegation. These thirty are never mentioned again and the motivation for sending them is unclear. Perhaps they deserted Josephus for the delegation, but were afraid to denounce the general because of his tyrannical behavior. This silence Josephus converted to an instruction "to say nothing" (μηδὲν λέγειν). If this conjecture is correct, we see that at least some Galilean aristocrats could not tolerate Josephus' rule. Most of them, however, apparently supported him.[52] The reference in V 386 to the pro-

---

ing αὐτοῦ) show. On city-country tension in Judaea during the war, see Hengel 371; Smith, HTR 64 (1971) 17-18; Applebaum, JRS 51 (1971) 167f; R. MacMullen, Roman Social Relations (New Haven 1974) 53; Rhoads 161; Brunt 151. MacMullen's entire chapter on rural-urban relations (28-56) has much useful comparative material. The socio-economic situation in the Galilean countryside is not clear. Did most of these peasants till their own land, or were they sharecroppers and laborers on large estates, perhaps belonging to the emperor or to Agrippa? See S. Klein, "Notes on the History of Large Estates in Palestine," Bulletin of the Jewish Palestine Exploration Society 1 (1933) nr. 3, pp. 3-9 and 3 (1936) 109-116 (Heb.); A. Alt, Kleine Schriften II (Munich 1953, repr. 1964) 435; Sherwin-White 139-142; Kreissig 28-31, 43-44, 82-86; S. Applebaum, EI 12 (1975) 125-128 (Heb.); M. Avi-Yonah, The Jews of Palestine (Oxford 1976) 21; D. J. Crawford in Studies in Roman Property, ed. M. I. Finley (Cambridge 1976) 63. Peasants of both types had ample cause to hate the neighboring large cities, the seats of the tax collectors and the large landowners (cf. V 33). On the inclination of the Galilean peasants towards peace with Rome, cf. BJ 4.84.

[52] οἱ πρῶτοι τῆς Γαλιλαίας (cf. Mark 6.21) probably are the moderately wealthy men of the countryside, men like John of Gischala in upper Galilee, and there is no need to posit an official district council (or Sanhedrin) of which they would have been members (Bammel, JJS 12 [1961] 160 n. 19).

Romanism of some of the leading citizens (δοχιμώτατοι) is plausible but the passage is part of a "strategem" and does not pretend to tell the truth.

The largest settlement which supported Josephus was Taricheae (V 160). (Other sizable towns may also have sided with him, as Jotapata did, but he barely mentions them.) Taricheae often served as his headquarters (V 96-97, 127, 157-168, 174, 276, 304, 404) and would later resist the Romans (BJ 3.462-542). Its anti-Roman orientation was furthered by the numerous Jewish refugees from Trachonitis, Gaulanitis, Hippos, and Gadara (BJ 3.463, 492-493, 500-501, 532, 542) who crowded the town and hated Rome. Although "outside agitators" serve BJ's apologetic purpose by demonstrating that Taricheae itself wanted to remain peaceful, their existence is confirmed by V which agrees that the town had resident aliens (ξένοι, V 142-143 and 162). Although Josephus does distinguish, as he should, between the Galileans and the Taricheaens (V 143), the city-country tension probably did not hamper the relationship of the two groups, not only because of these refugees and their anti-Roman militancy, but also because of Taricheae's hostility to Tiberias (V 142-144//BJ 2.606-609 and V 156; cf. 162). Before the foundation of its rival, Taricheae had been the most important settlement on the western shore of the Lake of Gennasaret. The loss of this distinction must have been hard to bear. In addition, Taricheae was a native Galilean town while Tiberias was settled in part by outsiders. Therefore the Galileans and Taricheaens cooperated in operations against Tiberias (V 98-100 and 304-306).[53]

Why they supported Josephus is not clear. (In an earlier period the δυνατοί of Galilee supported Herod, AJ 14.450//BJ 1.326). Here are some possibilities. Perhaps they too hated the big cities and the Romans. Perhaps they too were afraid of the brigands. Or we could suggest that they were afraid they would lose control of the Galileans if they opposed their wishes. Perhaps Josephus bought their support.

[53] Most investigators have simply equated *Galilaioi* with Zealots or revolutionaries. Thus Gelzer 311-312; Hengel 57-61; Klausner 173. Recently S. Zeitlin has proposed that *Galilaios* is neither a geographic term nor a general synonym for revolutionary, but designates a particular, hitherto unrecognized, group of revolutionaries. See his "Who were the Galileans?" *JQR* 64 (1974) 189-203. His main argument is the contrast between "Galilean" and the residents of the Galilean cities. Therefore, concludes Zeitlin, "Galilean" cannot be a geographical term. But Josephus tells us that the Tiberians were only in part of Galilean stock (AJ 18.37). The people of Sepphoris were even more suspect: the original inhabitants had been sold as slaves by a lieutenant of Varus (AJ 17.289//BJ 2.68) and the city had

14

The Galileans also threaten John and Gischala (V 102 and
368//BJ 2.622)—at least this is what Josephus says, perhaps
rightly. Josephus' source of support was lower Galilee and John's
was upper Galilee. Only for the very beginning of his tenure does
Josephus even claim a venture into upper Galilee (V 67) and Gischala
(V 70 and 77). Whatever may be thought of these claims, it is sure
that after his power struggle with John, Josephus lost all influence
in the north and never returned there. The delegation from Jerusalem concentrated its attention on lower Galilee but won over only
the city of Gabara which was soon attacked by the Galileans
(V 263-265). Therefore Josephus' assertion to have fortified four
villages of upper Galilee is suspect.[54] Some manuscripts of BJ
2.645 add Gischala to Josephus' conquests but this reading is
worthless since it is either Josephan rhetoric or an unintelligent
gloss.[55] BJ 2.629, too, is worthless (see below).

It is striking that both BJ 2.568 and V 72 emphasize Josephus'
authority in upper Galilee. Josephus knows that de facto he had
little influence in that region and therefore insists that at least
de iure he was the leader there too. But the reference to John's
"province" (ἐπαρχία, V 73) is strange. Perhaps John had some
legal status in his district, similar to the status of Niger who had
been the governor of Idumaea and was confirmed in his post by the
revolutionary government (BJ 2.566).[56] We shall return to this
point below.

---

been rebuilt by Antipas as *Autokratoris*, presumably with a cult of Augustus
(AJ 18.27). So the distinction between the inhabitants of these new royal
cities and the native Galileans is probably justified. Another justification
of the distinction is the political situation. The Sepphorites, Tiberians, and
Gabarenes belonged to recognizable political units, in contrast to the mass
of the country population which did not. See note 51 above. As for the
notion that the Galileans were a special class of revolutionaries, they are
conspicuously absent from the catalogue of revolutionaries (BJ 7.259ff).
The arguments of F. Loftus, *JQR* 65 (1975) 182-183, do not help Zeitlin
much. Against Zeitlin see too Rhoads 48 n. 2.

[54] BJ 2.573//V 188 (V omits Seph.). See note 45 above.

[55] Bauer 24-25 realized that Josephus succeeded only in lower Galilee,
but did not cite all the evidence. Bauer theorizes that it was because of this
failure in the cities and upper Galilee that the Jerusalem government decided
to replace Josephus, but this theory misses the mark; see below. Klein,
Galilee 50, notes that Josephus is much better informed about lower Galilee
than upper Galilee. On the distinctions and tensions between upper and
lower Galilee, see E. M. Meyers, *BASOR* 221 (1976) 93-101.

[56] Klein 42 has a similar conjecture.

7. The Brigands

In addition to the *Galilaioi* Josephus had to deal with *lestai*, brigands. Because this term can indicate both revolutionaries and highway robbers,[57] the context of every occurrence must be investigated. Our conclusion is that in the Galilean narrative of both V and BJ *lestai* usually refers to men who were primarily brigands, only secondarily, and not always, revolutionaries. Sepphoris, a staunchly pro-Roman city, could hire a brigand-chief (ἀρχιλῃστής) and his troops against Josephus, an anti-Roman general (V 104-111).[58] The citizens made the chieftain an offer he could not refuse: much money (V 105). Josephus says he retook the city by striking an alliance with the brigands, i.e., he paid the chieftain even more money (V 110). It was perhaps not wholly a matter of indifference to these *lestai* whether their victims were Jews. Since most of them were Jews themselves and not without feeling for their co-religionists, they probably preferred to rob Romans although they would rob anybody who was available. Business was business, and they were primarily interested in money, not politics or nationality.

One of the most important passages of the autobiography is V 77-78 in which Josephus admits that he bought the support of many *lestai*. Of course, he adds that he would have preferred to disarm them because he wanted to keep Galilee peaceful (V 78 fin.). But this claim is part of the *ananke* theory and without it the passage makes sense. Josephus arrived in Galilee with the backing of the revolutionary government of Jerusalem, but without troops or money. He found a peasantry which would support him against the cities, but which was victimized by hordes of bandits. He could have organized the peasants to destroy the bandits, but this—as he says—would have filled the country with civil war (no doubt many of the peasants had relatives who were bandits) and might have failed. After all, the bandits were experienced, fulltime fighters who did not have to return to their farms for a livelihood. Facing this problem, Josephus proposed a brilliant solution:

---

[57] Hengel 46. For comparative material from Greco-Roman sources, see Hengel 25-42 and R. MacMullen, *Enemies of the Roman Order* (Harvard 1966) 255-268.

[58] Hengel 44 and 378-379 identifies all of V's *lestai* (including those summoned by Sepphoris!) with the revolutionaries. The same mistake appears in Klausner 173. See Rhoads 160.

he would persuade the peasantry to provide him with funds to hire the bandits as mercenaries, making it a condition of their employment that they should not harass the peasants. He thus attempted to build up a sizable force of bandits loyal to himself. That Josephus ordered his troops not to plunder the peasants, and talked much of brotherly love, is therefore not merely plausible, but essential. That he also prohibited his men from attacking the Romans is not impossible. Josephus may have been vain enough to instruct his *lestai* to do nothing without his command, not even to harrass the Romans. And, apart from vanity, he probably realized the insecurity of his profitable position and did not want to precipitate the inevitable attack. His work was not yet complete.

Such was Josephus' plan according to V 77-78. The actual events, however, did not follow the plan. We have seen above that the total number of men under Josephus' command, including his peasants and his brigands, never exceeded a few thousand. For normal day-to-day operations he never had more than a few hundred, probably brigands. Josephus failed.

The presence of brigands in Josephus' forces is confirmed by other passages not only in V but in BJ. In V 244, after succeeding to repress the enthusiasm of the Galileans, Josephus tells them not to fight anyone (i.e. without his instructions), not to stain their hands with plunder (μήτε ἁρπαγῇ μολύνειν τὰς χεῖρας), but to tent peacefully on the plain and subsist on their rations.[59] These troops obviously had been accustomed to plunder. The Galileans plead with Josephus not to desert them because, without him, they would be prey to the brigands (V 206 and 210). Even BJ, with all its talk of 100,000 troops trained in Roman fashion, is unable to conceal that Josephus' forces were *lestai*. The general has to warn his forces to refrain from their customary crimes (συνήθη ἀδικήματα): theft, brigandage (λῃστεία), plunder (ἁρπαγή), deception and "the consideration of the losses of their friends as profit for themselves" (τὸ κέρδος οἰκεῖον ἡγεῖσθαι τὴν βλάβην τῶν συνηθεστάτων, BJ 2.581). They should wage their war justly because a good conscience is the best ally (BJ 2.582).[60] The next paragraph refers to these soldiers as mercenaries (μισθοφόροι, BJ 2.583-584), a term borrowed from V 77-78. The scheme for extortion and bribery,

---

[59] Havercamp notes a good parallel in *Luke* 3.14. The text of V 244 is uncertain but the meaning is clear.
[60] A *topos*; see chapter four note 27.

described by V, is transmuted in BJ to the claim that one half of the "army" supported the other half. Here we see clearly how BJ has modified the *hypomnema*.[61] One group of his followers was supposed to support the other because one group, the peasantry, was supposed to finance the other, much smaller, but militarily far more efficient, group, the body of hired bandits (μισθοφόροι and δορυφόροι), but this fact is so described as to suggest a more edifying arrangement.

Josephus was not the only leader of *lestai*. BJ (but never V!) calls John of Gischala a *lestes* (BJ 2.587) and adds that at this stage John was so desperate that he would attack anyone, even the Jews of Galilee (BJ 2.589). In BJ 2.593 John knows that Josephus' task was to protect the citizenry from the *lestai* and therefore sends out his *lestai* to pillage the country. These passages are part of BJ's anti-John polemic and do not appear in V 122-125.

In the two remaining passages where the word *lestai* appears, the anti-Roman attitudes of the brigands are prominent. The brigands of V 145, who have just accused Josephus of betraying the cause to the Romans and are dissatisfied with his excuses, certainly appealed to revolutionary sentiment, but their primary concern was the booty (V 146), not Josephus' politics, and they discoverd his political unreliability only after he expropriated their loot. V 175 indicates that the brigands in general were violently anti-Roman and this is plausible. Josephus got his position, after all, as a revolutionary leader and his supporters would have dropped him if they thought him otherwise. So Josephus' claim to the Tiberian councilors—that he recognized Rome's invincibility and was only waiting for a safe moment to surrender, but didn't dare do so yet because of the *lestai* (i.e. his followers)—would have been, in the circumstances, perfectly credible. As to whether or not Josephus evei made such a claim to the Tiberian city council, we have no way to discover; if he did, he was probably lying, since when the chance to surrender came he chose, instead, to stand siege in Jotapata (see above). But to suppose that Josephus did occasionally lie does not strain belief and this lie, if he used it, would have been a plausible one.[62]

---

[61] See the discussion in chapter three above. Perhaps the numbers in BJ 2.583, except for the first which is incredible (60,000 infantry), derive from the *hypomnema*. V 77-78 omitted these figures because Josephus was using the passage for apologetic purposes.

[62] Although it supports the *ananke* theory, V 175 need not be an addition

Therefore we have some information on Josephus' supporters. They were the citizens of Taricheae, who hated Tiberias; the refugees in Taricheae, who hated Rome; the Galileans, who hated Sepphoris, Tiberias, and secondarily, the Romans; and the brigands, who would plunder anyone worth plundering though they probably enjoyed Roman victims more than Jewish. Some Galileans supported Josephus because he was the only man who could keep the brigands under control. Josephus tried to set himself up as the intermediary between the populace and the brigands and to gain the loyalty of both.[63] It was his difficult task to unify these diverse groups and create a single anti-Roman force. He failed, not necessarily because he was incompetent or disloyal, but because his supporters were for the most part not interested in fighting Rome itself. Their primary concerns lay elsewhere.

8. *Josephus and the Cities*

Josephus was supported by the countryside but was opposed by the three cities of Galilee: Gabara, Sepphoris and Tiberias. BJ 2.629 states that these cities and Gischala supported the delegation, but were reconquered by Josephus without recourse to arms. The latter claim is absolutely false, part of the grandiose description of a grandiose general, and does not appear in V 203. Josephus never conquered Gischala, by force or otherwise. Gabara supported John and never was under the control of John's opponent. Sepphoris was pro-Roman and wanted nothing to do with Josephus, John, or the delegation. Tiberias had to be retaken in a pitched battle. We shall now investigate in detail Josephus' relationship to these cities and shall ignore the testimony of BJ 2.629.

a. Gabara [64]

Although Gabara was anti-Roman,[65] it did not favor Josephus. Simon, the chief of the city, convinced the citizens to support

---

of the *Vita* of the nineties to the early *hypomnema*. See chapter five above n. 188. We cannot be sure that the word *lestai* appeared in the *hypomnema*.

[63] Laqueur 108-120 and 247-253 makes this point the basis of his historical reconstruction, but one of his errors is the assumption that all *lestai* were primarily revolutionaries.

[64] The name is variously corrupted in Josephan manuscripts; see Schalit, *NWB* s.v. Γαραβα, and Möller and Schmitt, s.v. Γαβαρα.

[65] The city was sacked by Vespasian (BJ 3.132-134). It was devoid of fighting men (μαχίμου πλήθους ἔρημον) because they all had fled, to Jerusalem, to the hills, to Taricheae, etc.

John, his friend and associate, but from fear of Josephus' Galileans
(V 124-125), they did not immediately proclaim their loyalty
to John. With the arrival of the delegation Gabara was instructed
by Jerusalem to support John (V 203//BJ 2.629), and obeyed.
The delegates established their headquarters in the city and there
met with John (V 229, 233, 235, 240). Its support for John and the
delegates was unquestioned (V 235 and 313). The most important
text is V 242-265, which describes the attack of Josephus and the
Galileans on Gabara. The Galilean forces encamped outside the
city while the delegates retired to a fortress-like mansion.[66] Finally
a confrontation took place in the camp. Here the Galileans en-
thusiastically applauded their general and threatened the delegates.
Josephus admits that he instructed his soldiers to have their
weapons ready (V 253), but claims that the Galileans attacked
the delegates without his instructions. In fact, he tried to restrain
them (V 262-264) but, after losing control of the situation, fled
to Sogane in order to avoid any imputation of initiating a civil
war (V 265). This account is obvious apology and we cannot
determine exactly what happened at Gabara. We can be sure only
of Gabara's unhesitating support for John and the Jerusalem
envoys. We may conjecture, however, that Josephus led a Galilean
attack on Gabara but was defeated and defeated badly. After
beating a hasty retreat to Sogane, he realized that he could not
defeat the delegation by military means and therefore sent ambas-
sadors to Jerusalem in quest of a political solution (V 266-270).

b. Sepphoris

Sepphoris opposed Josephus not only because of the Galileans,
but also because of its pro-Roman policy. It luxuriated in its
status as capital of Galilee and in its surname *Autokratoris* (AJ
18.27). When Cestius invaded the country, it welcomed the column
he dispatched to pacify Galilee (BJ 2.511), but nevertheless was
required to give hostages (V 31). During Josephus' tenure the
Sepphoretis requested (V 373) and ultimately received (V 347 and

---

[66] V 246 says εἰς τὴν Ἰησοῦ οἰκίαν but this Jesus is unknown. It is unlikely
that he is Jesus ben Sapphia, as Schalit, *NWB* s.v. Ἰησοῦς nr. 2 claims and
the indices of Niese (s.v. Ἰησοῦς nr. 16) and Feldman (s.v. Jesus nr. 19)
suggest, because that Jesus is never otherwise found in or near Gabara.
Perhaps Josephus was confused and meant Σίμωνος, the leading man of
the city (V 124).

394) another Roman garrison which was reinforced (replaced?) by Vespasian (V 411; BJ 3.30-34 and 59).[67]

Josephus at first tried the soft approach. He says he restrained the Galileans from attacking the city, "permitted" the Sepphorites to communicate with their compatriots who were being held hostage at Dor (V 30-31), and "permitted" them to fortify their city (or was tricked into fortifying it himself).[68] If these claims are true we may suppose that Josephus was trying to moderate their loyalty to Rome. Whether Josephus entered the city at this point is unclear. While V 30 and 64 are ambiguous, V 103-111 clearly states that Josephus was in the city, at the *agora* (V 107) and near the city gates (V 108), and this although the Sepphorites feared him (V 104). The narrative is obscure and presumably false, so we do not know what really occurred. Perhaps Josephus and his soldiers (V 107) attacked the city, the Sepphorites invoked the aid of an *archilestes*, the general and the brigands came to an agreement, and the city was left defenseless. If Josephus did capture it once, that would account for his claim, in V 82, to have captured it twice. But it is more likely that he never had any chance of winning the city and was excluded from it, as he later admits (V 346). He tells of assaulting the city on at least three occasions, but never with success. Once he was scared away by a rumor of Roman reinforcements (V 373-380),[69] twice he was beaten back (V 394-396 and BJ 3. 59-61).[70] Unlike Gabara which opposed Josephus but befriended John, Sepphoris rejected the advances of John (V 124) and the delegation (V 232-233).

c. Tiberias

Josephus' relationship to Tiberias and its archon Jesus ben

---

[67] Our manuscripts constantly confuse Caesennius Gallus with Cestius Gallus, but since Caesennius was the lieutenant of Cestius the sequence is clear. See Niese's apparatus to V 30, BJ 2.510, and 3.31; see too PIR² C 170.

[68] On the pro-Roman viewpoint of Sepphoris and on Josephus' claim to have fortified the city, see appendix I part B.

[69] This section has the double purpose of demonstrating both that Josephus did his best not to allow Sepphoris to remain pro-Roman and that he did not treat the city harshly. See the discussion in chapter five, p. 122 and 151-152. BJ 2.646 has conflated the story of the revolts of Tiberias and Sepphoris (narrated by V 373-389) with the details of another incident (V 328-335).

[70] Although these two accounts are suspiciously similar, they need not be doublets. Josephus may have attacked Sepphoris several times.

Sapphia is more complicated and defies rational exegesis.[71] Tiberias, divided socially and politically, seems to have supported alternately Josephus, John, the delegation, and Agrippa. Unfortunately Josephus is not interested in the political machinations which lay behind these shifting loyalties. He wants only to demonstrate his popularity in the city and his mild behavior towards his opponents. These motives have been investigated in chapter five above. A crucial figure here is Jesus ben Sapphia who was archon of the city and leader of the popular party. He appears first as an opponent of the city council (V 66-67) although later he is supported by it (V 300). Josephus does not explain why Jesus sometimes is apparently absent from Tiberias. Once he is found in Taricheae (V 134//BJ 2.599). Did he lose power in Tiberias and flee to Taricheae to continue his activities? Or was he still in control of Tiberias, but eager to overcome the mutual rivalry of the two cities and to unite them against Rome and against the general from Jerusalem? Josephus and Jesus at first were on good terms and why they became enemies is not explained. Although the council of Tiberias is occasionally characterized as pro-Roman (V 167-168//BJ 2.638-641 and V 175-176; V 381), it also supports John and the delegates (V 313). We do not know whether the same men were willing to pursue any policy which would free them from Josephus' tyranny, or whether the membership of the council varied as different parties vied for power. Twice (V 89//BJ 2.616 and V 272) an official appointed by Josephus [72] warns him about the affairs of Tiberias but on several occasions Josephus has to rely on other sources of information (V 158//BJ 2.634; V 276; V 383). Thus we really know little about the internal history of Tiberias during 66-67, although V talks more about this city than any other.

The wealthy of Tiberias, the men with names like Herod and Julius, desired peace (V 32-34). This statement is inherently plausible but we should remember that Josephus has a habit of apologizing for the aristocracy. The archon of the city, Jesus ben Sapphia, was the leader of the lower classes and advocated war (V 35 and 66). Undoubtedly there was a middle ground between

---

[71] I have not found any detailed discussion of the history of Tiberias in 66-67 CE.

[72] Called a *strategos*. Cf. the *strategos* appointed by Agrippa I to supervise his interests in Jerusalem (AJ 19.333). The two episodes which refer to Josephus' *strategos* in Tiberias are similar and may be doublets; see the discussion at the end of chapter three above.

these positions, but what V says about Justus (V 36) is polemic and unreliable (see chapter five above). When Josephus and his two comrades first came into Galilee they approached, but did not enter, the city. Josephus says that when the *protoi* and the members of the council came to see him, he urged them to destroy the palace erected by Antipas, because of its illegal representations of animals (V 64-66). How much of all this is correct, as always, is uncertain,[73] but the following narrative is certainly false. Josephus claims that he did not touch the palace at all but was away from the city when Jesus and some Galileans destroyed the building and massacred the Greek population of the city (V 66-67). How did he and the council come to control the booty if they had nothing to do with the actual pillage? He pretends that he simply took it from the criminals and gave it to Julius Capella to safeguard for Agrippa (V 68-69). What really happened is unknown and the complaint assigned to Jesus in V 295-296 does not provide an alternate version. We may conjecture that Josephus and Jesus at first cooperated in the destruction and the massacre. Either Capella too participated and his leadership of the peace party (V 32) is suspect,[74] or Josephus used some of the loot in an attempt to buy the loyalty of the city aristocracy (V 69). V 295-296, in which Jesus is satisfied when told that Capella still has the property, implies that Capella and the ten *protoi* were the treasurers. Perhaps greed alone induced Capella to join with these revolutionaries. It is most unfortunate that we do not know what occurred here because the next time we meet Jesus he is opposing Josephus. Was he cheated out of his share of the booty? The final point we note is that Jesus was helped by a contingent of Galileans (V 66). Presumably the country folk reserved their hatred for the city aristocracy more than for the city plebs. And, besides, Galilean peasants surely enjoyed plundering the palace of Antipas.

Thus Josephus tried to gain the support of the city aristocracy and the plebs, but his bid did not go unchallenged. John soon arrived, with or without Josephus' permission, and won some

---

[73] Many scholars have connected V 64-66 with the Rabbinic tradition about the "Eighteen Decrees." See C. Roth, *HTR* 49 (1956) 169-177. Similarly, John's concern about kosher oil (V 74-76//BJ 2.591-592) may be related to these decrees; see Roth 175-176; Hengel 204-211; S. Hoenig, *JQR* 61 (1970-71) 63-75; Baer, *Zion* 36 (1971) 135 (Heb.).

[74] V wants to clear Capella in order to heighten the guilt of Justus. All the Tiberian aristocrats supported Rome—all except Justus.

followers (V 85-103//BJ 2.614-623). Josephus nearly was killed in the city, but was saved (V 96) by his bodyguard and by a native of the city, Herod (an aristocrat?).[75] He got away to Taricheae, and there rallied the Galileans[76] for an attack on Tiberias. At this point John departed. We do not know who was in control of Tiberias, since Josephus does not specify whom John brought over to his side. The absence of Jesus from both Tiberias and Taricheae at this time is remarkable. But whoever was in charge of the city apparently supported the war, preferred John to Josephus, ejected (?) Jesus (still Josephus friend?), yet tolerated the presence of Josephus' *strategos* Silas (V 89). When Josephus fled, some Tiberians, perhaps followers of Jesus, fled with him (V 99) and later aided the Galileans in the operations against Sepphoris (V 107).

But the situation soon changed. A new regime (?) came to power which turned down a request from John for support (V 123-124).[77] During the Dabaritta affair Jesus and his followers were at Taricheae where they denounced Josephus as a traitor (V 134//BJ 2.599). Josephus managed to escape, however, by driving a wedge between the Taricheaens and the Tiberians. It is surprising that some Galileans supported the latter over the former (V 143; BJ 2.608 has τοῖς ἄλλοις), a testimony to the popularity of Jesus among the lower classes of city and country.

Soon Tiberias invoked the aid of Agrippa (V 155-173//BJ 2.632b-645). The aristocratic peace party (which included Justus) was in control (V 168//BJ 2.638-641 and V 175-176) and it is no surprise that neither Jesus nor Silas (see V 158//BJ 2.634) was in the city. The recapture by Josephus meant, of course, (temporary) eclipse of the peace party. The next we hear of the city is its support of the delegation. Silas is there (V 272), having been reappointed after Josephus' conquest, but so is Jesus, who promises that he will bring the city over to the camp of the delegation (V 271-278). Silas must have been ejected shortly thereafter, because in V 276

---

[75] BJ 2.619 simplifies and talks of two bodyguards. Here BJ, more than V, emphasizes Josephus' popularity because Josephus is alerted by the shouts of τις τῶν οἰκείων in V 94 but of the δῆμος in BJ 2.619. Laqueur's deductions (pp. 80-84 and 257) from this difference are far fetched.

[76] Only V 97 mentions the Taricheaens; BJ 2.620 thinks of Josephus the general supported by his soldiers (στρατιῶται), forgetting that he was on a boat in the middle of the lake.

[77] Even if we do not accept Naber's conjecture (οὐδέ for αὐτοῦ δέ), V 124 has the Tiberians give only lukewarm support to John.

Josephus must rely on anonymous informants. The Tiberians support the war (V 281-289) and even demand that Josephus aid the Galileans, their "fellow countrymen" (ὁμοεθνεῖς, V 286)—confirmation that Jesus is in control. Throughout this section Josephus claims widespread support among the populace (πλῆθος and δῆμος) of the city (V 279, 289, 298, 299, 300, 301, 303) but this is false, as is shown by the account of his attack on a city united against him (V 327-330). His supporters in Tiberias must have been few. The peace party obviously would have nothing to do with him. The war party (led by Jesus) preferred the delegation. The council and *protoi* of the city also opposed him (V 300-301, 313, 331). What happened to Jesus' Galilean followers during Josephus' attack on the city is unclear.

After these events Josephus was faced by another pro-Agrippa movement, again led by the council (V 381). Jesus must have fled the city when Josephus captured it from the delegation. Perhaps Josephus imprisoned him (cf. V 332). Silas too would not have been safe in a city controlled by the peace party and so Josephus has to rely on his *Galilaioi* to be told what is taking place (V 383). Whether Josephus really forestalled an attack on the city is not clear (V 385-388). When Vespasian arrived in the country, the Jewish general fled to Tiberias and was accepted by the citizens. His opponents, Jesus and the peace party, are nowhere in sight (BJ 3.131, 135, and 142). We may conjecture that the peace party soon prevailed and that Vespasian had no reason to turn upon the city. But when Josephus was besieged in Jotapata, a violent struggle took place in Tiberias (V 353) during which Jesus returned to power. When the Romans captured the city (BJ 3.445-461), the peace party ("the elders and distinguished members of the populace", γηραιοὶ τοῦ δήμου καὶ προύχειν δοκοῦντες) could claim with some justification that Jesus did not represent the policy of the majority (BJ 3.453-455).[78] Jesus fled to Taricheae (BJ 3.457) where, as we

---

[78] This is part of BJ's apology. BJ 3.460 pretends that a section of the city wall was removed only because the entrance was not wide enough for Vespasian's troops. But BJ 3.461 claims that the remainder of the wall was spared only because Agrippa interceded for the city and this is surely correct. Part of the wall was destroyed as sign of conquest of a hostile city; cf. BJ 4.117 and 418. Vespasian knew of Tiberias' past and was not misled by the peace party. We have conjectured that Tiberias' ambiguous behavior was still remembered in Rome in the nineties (see chapter five). Alon, *Studies* 1.230 n. 42, does not understand BJ's apologetic.

have already seen, the war party was in firm control and Jesus had a large following.

In sum, although we do not have enough information to understand the details, the outline is clear. Josephus, John, and the delegation courted the city, each with some success. Jesus at first supported Josephus, later John and the delegation. The city had a peace party too which sought aid from Agrippa. Not all the aristocrats and members of the council were unimpeachable loyalists. Some apparently aided Josephus and Jesus in plundering the palace and some supported Jesus in his struggle against Josephus (although it is possible that Jesus and the peace party, in a marriage of convenience, joined together to oust their common enemy). The conflicting motives of these groups are beyond conjecture. Two points, however, are beyond dispute. (1) Because many Tiberians disliked him, Josephus never had a firm grasp on the city. Some Tiberians may have so hated him that they did not care whether they invoked John or Agrippa.[79] At least one prominent citizen preserved this hatred for over twenty years. (2) Josephus attacked the city whenever any group was in power which did not owe loyalty to him. It made no difference whether his opponents were pro- or anti-Roman.

9. *John of Gischala and the Delegation*

Josephus' major opponent was John. Each had his own sphere of influence, Josephus in lower Galilee and John in upper. Josephus pretends that John's followers were mostly refugees from the Syrian cities (BJ 2.588 and 625, V 372), but it is apparent that John had considerable support, not only in Gischala (V 76) but also in the villages of lower Galilee (V 237). John's greatest success in lower Galilee was in Gabara (V 124) and occasionally even Tiberias supported him. He was not yet the radical friend of the Zealots, as he appears in BJ 4. He was an enemy of the Romans but a friend of aristocrats, notably Simon ben Gamaliel (V 192). We have conjectured above that John was the "official" governor of upper Galilee much as Niger was the archon of Idumaea (BJ 2.566). If this is true it would confirm John's connections with the Jerusalem aristocracy. John was not appointed general of Galilee, probably

---

[79] Laqueur 117-119 assumes that Tiberias had a stable government whose only aim was to be free of Josephus' control. But this explanation is inadequate to explain the actions of Jesus ben Sapphia.

because he was not a priest and not a native of Jerusalem. Niger too was subordinated to the Jerusalem generals. Simon was not in a position of influence when the generals were chosen (see below) and so was unable to aid his friend. John's association with Ananus (BJ 4.208-215) probably began later and was not a factor when the priestly party met at the temple. Thus both John and Josephus moved in high social circles and opposed Rome.

John's career begins for us with his defense of Gischala against the Tyrians and Greeks (V 43-45). V contends that John wanted to maintain the peace but could not because of the gentile attacks. This claim may be true or it may have been invented to fit V's theory of *ananke*.[80] The next time John appears he is a war leader. BJ's portrait of John is modeled on the traditional descriptions of trouble-makers and demagogues. John in BJ is a *lestes* (BJ 2.587) who readily attacks Jewish property (BJ 2.589 and 593), i.e. he is a brigand rather than a revolutionary. Although V has no affection for John these extreme characterizations are nearly absent.[81] John is never called a *lestes* and never attacks Jewish territory. V assumes throughout that John was a revolutionary rather than just a brigand, and this assumption seems correct.

That John and Josephus at first were on good terms is barely disguised by BJ 2.590-592//V 71-76. The "approval" of John's two schemes is probably a Josephan euphemism for cooperation although it is uncertain why John needed Josephus' cooperation, let alone approval, for transactions between upper Galilee and Caesarea Philippi.[82] Josephus had recently arrived in Galilee, did not yet command a large force, and never did control the north. Perhaps the story merely intends to exaggerate Josephus' importance and to discredit John to Jewish readers, by telling how he gouged

---

[80] Some have accepted V 43-45 at face value and theorize that these attacks converted John from a pro-Roman to a "moderate" anti-Roman. See Alon, *Studies* 235-236 n. 54; Hengel 381; Kingdon, *NTS* 17 (1970) 72; and Rhoads 124 (who, notwithstanding his caveat on p. 3, oversimplifies the dichotomy between "moderates"—not a Josephan term!—and "revolutionaries"). Luther 75 rejects V 43-45 as an apology for Josephus' friendship with John, but since both V and BJ try to deny this friendship, this interpretation is improbable.

[81] See BJ 2.585-589; 4.85, 208, 389-391; 7.263-264. V 70 calls John νεωτέρων ὀρεγόμενον πραγμάτων and V 87 characterizes John's supporters as νεωτέρων ἐπιθυμοῦντες αἰεὶ πραγμάτων. Both phrases are similar to BJ's rhetoric (BJ 2.587) and AJ 8.209. See chapter four note 16.

[82] Caesarea-Philippi (V 74) is more likely than Syria (BJ 591).

the pious Jews of Caesarea. In any event, enduring cooperation between the two leaders was impossible. John resented the intrusion of a rival into his domain and Josephus was too vain to accept anyone as an associate. John made repeated attempts to win over the cities of lower Galilee (V 85-101//BJ 2.614-621 and V 123) but without great success. Only Gabara supported him, and that only because the chief of the city was his friend (V 124). Finally [83] John realized that he was making no progress and therefore wrote to his old friend Simon ben Gamaliel (V 190).

While Josephus, John, and the Galileans were struggling in Galilee, another struggle was taking place in Jerusalem. Three leaders of Jerusalem appear in V 190-198 and 309: Ananus, Simon ben Gamaliel, and Jesus ben Gamala.[84] Of these only Ananus is mentioned in the list of BJ 2.562-568. The conjecture seems irresistible that the priests who had predominated after the defeat of Cestius faced competition from a Pharisaic party. The Pharisees did not have a uniform policy regarding the war (or anything else). BJ 2.411 mentions the pacific actions of the nobles, high-priests, and Pharisaic chieftains and we may suppose that R. Yoḥanan ben Zakkai was not the only Pharisee to flee Jerusalem. But other Pharisees disagreed and stayed in the city to pass the Eighteen Decrees and fight Rome.[85] There is no trace of this war faction until Simon ben Gamaliel appears in V 190. None of the figures active in the early stages of the war is identifiable as a Pharisee.[86] The only one of the generals in BJ 2.562-568 who is said to have been a follower of the Pharisees is Josephus himself, but his Pharisaism is of the most dubious variety, and he did not discover it until the

---

[83] BJ 2.599 pretends that John participated in the Dabaritta affair but this claim is a "Josephan gloss" and part of BJ's anti-John polemic. See the discussion in chapters three and four above.

[84] Or Jesus ben Gamaliel. See appendix I note 36 below.

[85] I mention the Eighteen Decrees although I am uncertain of their significance. See above n. 73. "The Pharisees" perhaps were not a unified political group, at least not after the reign of Herod, but during the power vacuum created by the war, it is probable that some Pharisees formed a political party. Graetz was the first to conjecture a split in Pharisaic opinion regarding the war but his characterization of Beth Shammai as militant and Beth Hillel as pacifist is without adequate evidence; see G. Alon, *Scripta Hierosolymitana* 7 (1961) 53-78, esp. 73-76; C. Roth, *JSS* 7 (1962) 63-80; and J. Neusner in *Ex Orbe Religionum* 1.243-244.

[86] See n. 88 below. BJ had an apologetic reason not to mention the Pharisees or any other sect in the war narrative. See chapter four.

nineties of our era. In the sixties he was a Jerusalem priest and, in all likelihood, not a Pharisee (see chapter five above).

Simon's unexpected prominence in V 190 may have been the result of a power struggle between the priests and the militant wing of the Pharisees. Simon managed to force his way to the top and there he remained until ousted or assassinated by the Zealots. The position of Jesus ben Gamala in these developments is unclear, but it is suggestive that he was remembered kindly by Rabbinic tradition.[87] A further sign of Pharisaic power at this point is the composition of the delegation sent to Galilee. Two of the four envoys were priests, but three of the four were Pharisees (V 197).[88]

John was apprised of these developments and decided to write to his old friend Simon for assistance (V 190).[89] John hoped that Josephus would be removed and that he (John) would be appointed in his stead. Personal rivalry between the two leaders is a sufficient explanation for this ploy and recourse to political differences is not necessary. We do not know whether John relied only on his

---

[87] B. Baba Bathra 21a. See J. Neusner, *The Rabbinic Traditions about the Pharisees before 70* (Leiden 1971) 1.396-397.

[88] Since V tries to demonstrate that Josephus sided with the Pharisees, it will not have invented the Pharisaism of these envoys. The names of the delegates pose a problem:

V 197	BJ 2.628
'Ιωνάθης	'Ιούδης 'Ιωνάθου
'Ανανίας	'Ανανίας Σαδούκι
'Ιώζαρος	'Ιώεσδρος τοῦ Νομικοῦ
Σίμων	Σίμων

Since 'Ιώζαρος is the same as 'Ιώεσδρος (see Schalit, *NWB* s.v. 'Ιώζαρος nr. 1; all the manuscripts of V have a corrupted form of the name here, but not in 324, 325, and 332), three of the four names are identical in BJ and V. Our text of BJ 628 identifies Judas and Ananias with the envoys of BJ 2.451 who were sent to arrange the surrender of the Roman garrison. But instead of 'Ιούδης 'Ιωνάθου, V writes 'Ιωνάθης no less than fifty times (see Schalit, *NWB* s.v. 'Ιωνάθης nr. 14). Therefore Schlatter conjectured that 'Ιούδης and Σαδούκι should be deleted from BJ 2.628, explaining that they were interpolated here under the influence of BJ 2.451. See Schlatter, *Die hebräischen Namen* 54-55 = *Kleinere Schriften* 194-195; Stein 112; Baer, *Zion* 36 (1971) 139. This conjecture is probably right and therefore we have no reason to regard 'Ιούδης 'Ιωνάθου and 'Ανανίας Σαδούκι of BJ 2.451 as Pharisees.

[89] There is no evidence to support Hengel's conjecture that John was a Pharisee "perhaps of the school of Hillel" (Hengel 381). Did Simon befriend only Pharisees? He was said to have lived near a Sadducee in Jerusalem (M. Erubin 6.2; see Neusner, *Traditions* 1.379-380). On φίλος καὶ συνήθης (V 192), see chapter five above, note 151.

friendship with Simon or whether he also tried to convince him of the appropriateness of this action. Perhaps John advanced the charges of tyranny and malfeasance which later were repeated by the delegation (V 249, 260, 277, and 302). Perhaps what is ascribed to Simon in V 193 was first stated by John. In any event, John did not receive what he requested. Ananus at first defended the integrity of a member of his party but, after being bribed (so V claims), he reluctantly consented to have Josephus replaced (V 193-196).[90] After more political maneuvering, doubtless, Simon and Ananus agreed to send a delegation, but not for the purpose John had requested. The delegates were to kill or remove Josephus (V 193 and 202) and John's assistance was requested in the attainment of this goal (V 203), but the delegates were never told to establish John as governor of Galilee. Simon hoped that the delegates themselves would replace Josephus (V 198)[91]—they did, in fact, attempt to kill him (V 302)—and thus establish Pharisaic control over the district.

The tension between the delegation and John is apparent in V's narrative. The Galileans were offered a choice between Josephus and the delegation, not between Josephus and John (V 267, 271, 278, 287, cf. 324). We therefore understand why John's support for the delegation was lukewarm. John met the delegates at Gabara with 3000 men (V 233), but there is no sign that he did anything when

[90] The role of Jesus ben Gamala here is obscure. He is approached by Simon ben Gamaliel in V 193 (whether or not we accept the gloss of MW which adds καὶ Ἰησοῦν τὸν τοῦ Γάμαλα after the second Ἄνανον) but reappears only in V 204. Did he approve of Josephus' dismissal? The phrase τῶν ἐν αὐτῇ τῇ βουλῇ γενομένων εἷς (V 204) is ambiguous. Thackeray translates "who had been present at the conference" (thus too Haefeli and Pelletier). Thackeray's *Lexicon to Josephus* s.v. βουλή (2) apparently translates "a member of the Sanhedrin" (thus too Stein) but that leaves αὐτῇ unexplained. Another possibility is "who had assented to the plan" (cf. AJ 17.243). The description of the letter in V 204 is intended to be pathetic and may be modeled on a passage from Nicolaus of Damascus. BJ 2.629 seems more plausible; see chapter five above, section B.

[91] In V 198 Josephus makes his opponents sing his praises: he is from Jerusalem, learned in the Law, and a priest. These features would alienate rather than attract the populace of Galilee. Thus in V 278 Jesus praises the delegates not because they are from Jerusalem but because they are four in number, not because they are priests but because they are pedigreed, not because they are learned in the Law but because they excel in understanding. But the qualities of V 278 are not those which the autobiography wanted to emphasize and therefore V 198 has the Jerusalem-Pharisees-priests admit that Josephus is their equal. Malinowski 101-104 follows V 198 uncritically.

Jonathan and his friends descended to the plain to address the Galileans (V 249ff). John apparently remained in Gabara and Josephus feared a possible attack (V 253) but whether John participated in the fighting at Gabara, which resulted in defeat and flight for Josephus (V 262-265), is uncertain. If John really supported the delegation why did he return to Gischala right after the victory (V 271)? His assistance would have been useful in Tiberias. Perhaps there had been a confrontation in Gabara between John and the delegation during which the differing assumptions of the two sides were made clear. Their only link was their mutual hatred of Josephus. Thus Josephus' meeting with Jonathan in Tiberias (V 273-275) may have been an attempt to work out a settlement and to alienate the delegation still further from John. But a settlement was out of the question and Josephus was told to leave the city. John and the delegation agreed that Josephus must be eliminated (V 292, 301 and 304), but, again, after the attempt miscarried, John immediately departed for Gischala (V 308). He returned to Tiberias for another meeting (V 313-316), but when he was needed most, when Tiberias was struggling against Josephus (V 319-335), he was back in Gischala (V 317).[92] Soon after capturing Tiberias Josephus rounded up all of John's followers in lower Galilee [93] and John no longer ventured outside of his stronghold in upper Galilee.

Why did the delegation fail? These Pharisees from Jerusalem were unable to win the loyalty of the Galileans, Josephus' main supporters. The Pharisaic movement was centered in Jerusalem and did not become influential in Galilee until after the Bar Kokhba war (132-135 CE). What affection could these Pharisees expect to receive from Galileans, most of whom they regarded as sinners (ʿammei ha areẓ)? If their alliance with John had been more sincere perhaps they would have been able to succeed. But John apparently made no attempt to turn his following in Tiberias and lower Galilee towards the delegation. Hiis military assistance was minimal. Josephus claims that the Jerusalem government realized the error

---

[92] V was not eager to make clear the disagreement between John and the delegation because it claimed that the delegation was sent only on account of John's jealousy (V 189).

[93] Only in lower Galilee did Josephus have sufficient strength to threaten burning and confiscation (V 370//BJ 2.624; V tones down the language). The πολῖται of V 372 (not ὁπλῖται as in PRA) are the citizens of Gischala who remain with John.

of its ways and confirmed him at his post, thus removing the legal authority of the delegation (V 310). Whether this is true is impossible to determine. BJ omits it. If true, it would indicate the realization of Ananus and Simon that Josephus was too strong to be dislodged without a major military undertaking (cf. BJ 2.653). Whether or not Josephus was a self-seeking tyrant, it was easier to let him stay in power. Josephus' claim of extraordinary popularity with the people of Jerusalem (V 266, V 309-310 //BJ 2.631, and V 315) certainly is exaggerated, but it is not impossible that some of the people may have rioted in his support, especially since the plot to remove him was hatched in secret by the high priest and the aristocratic leader of the Pharisees.[94] Josephus had begun his career as a member of Eleazar's party which had considerable support from the lower priesthood and the *demos*.

The delegation episode helps solve a few problems raised by the later history of the war. Because John lost all support in lower Galilee and because he and Josephus were determined opponents, he made no move to aid his rival at the siege of Jotapata. We may conjecture that John was annoyed with Simon for sending a delegation instead of appointing John to the governorship. Therefore when John arrived in Jerusalem he associated not with Simon, his old friend, or with Jesus, Josephus' friend, but with Ananus (BJ 4.208-215). Of course his friendship with any of these men is difficult to understand if they confirmed Josephus at his post. Will the delegation episode explain why John turned against the aristocrats and joined the Zealots? Finally, whether or not Josephus was confirmed, the delegates who returned to Jerusalem probably did not speak highly of the man caused the failure of their mission. Their reports would explain why Josephus received no answer to his letters to Jerusalem before the siege of Jotapata (BJ 3.138-140). He was abandoned to his fate.[95]

---

[94] BJ 2.627, 629; V 194 (emphasizing ἀρχιερεῖς, i.e. the priestly party), 196 and 309. The claim of secrecy is plausible since the Pharisees were not yet sure of their position when they pushed for Josephus' dismissal.

[95] He would have been abandoned anyway since Jerusalem had no troops to spare and the revolutionaries must have realized that any troops they would send north could not defeat Vespasian. If Josephus did receive an answer to his letters, it is unlikely that he would have omitted mentioning it. In fact, we should not have been surprised had he invented something appropriate.

10. *Agrippa*

Although Josephus fought with Agrippa's troops (V 398-406), attacked Tiberias which had declared loyalty to the king (V 155-173//BJ 632-645 and V 381-389//BJ 645-646), and aided Gamala in its revolt (V 186),[96] both V and BJ seem to claim that he tried to benefit Agrippa. Josephus preserved the booty of Dabaritta (V 130-131//BJ 2.597-598) and Tiberias (V 68) for Agrippa. He also treated the personnel of the king in a laudatory manner (V 112-113, 149-154, and 388-389). All of these passages are unadulterated apology but their primary intent, apparently, is to demonstrate not loyalty to the king, but financial probity. Josephus admits that he and his associates kept some loot—but it was not for themselves. It was for Agrippa. In fact, one of V's aims is to show that Josephus did not use his office to become wealthy (see chapter five). Justus (or someone else) had accused him of plundering the *megistanes* and of maltreating Agrippa's emissary, and he retorted that he did none of these dastardly deeds. Thus not only do we have no indication of any real friendliness for Agrippa, we also have little evidence that Josephus claimed such friendliness.[97] Neither when ruling Galilee nor when writing about his Galilean tenure did Josephus consider it necessary to woo Agrippa.

11. *Jotapata*

So far we have not uncovered anything treasonous. Perhaps Josephus was cruel, brutal, self-seeking, tyrannical, vain, intolerant, etc., but he was no traitor to his cause. The rumors that he was betraying Galilee were begun by political opponents or disgruntled supporters and deserve no credence without some evidence. Why, then, was he so much hated by the Jews during and after the war (V 424-425//BJ 7.437-450 and V 428-429)? Even the Romans regarded him as a traitor to his people as the καί shows in V 416 (καὶ αὐτῶν προδότην).[98] The siege of Jotapata must be the

---

[96] On Philip and the history of Gamala, see chapter five above. Although we do not know what happened in Gamala, Josephus and Philip certainly were involved in the revolutionary activity there.

[97] BJ suppresses some of Josephus' activities against Agrippa, notably the fighting with Sulla (V 398-406) and the supply of troops to Gamala (V 186; BJ 4.9 mentions only fortifications), but neither omission seems significant. BJ omits all the minor battles because a great general should fight only another great general or his legate.

[98] The Roman soldiers ask Titus to punish Josephus, because, they say,

cause. When Vespasian arrived in Galilee, he sent a garrison to Sepphoris. Josephus put up a brief resistance (BJ 3.29-34, 59-63, 110-131) until he entered Jotapata after Vespasian attacked it (BJ 3.141-142). The mighty battles and heroic resistance (BJ 3.143-288 and 316-339) are obvious exaggerations and convert Josephus from a guerilla leader with a small following to a field marshal equal to the best Rome could muster (see chapter four). To doubt the existence of the siege may be unreasonable (see note 44) but to accept the account of BJ is impossible. The narrative about Josephus' own surrender is equally famous and suspect (BJ 3.340-408). Obviously we shall never know what happened at Jotapata.

In the nineteenth century voices were raised accusing Josephus of betrayal. How else did he know that the siege would end on the 47th day (BJ 3.316 and 406)? Who was that mysterious deserter who informed the Romans of the Jews' weakness (BJ 3.317-322) and how did Josephus hear about him? [99] More important than this conjecture is the fact that Josephus' conduct after his surrender was such as to arouse suspicion (BJ 3.438-39). He hailed Vespasian as Messiah and king. He served the Romans as interpreter, guide, and propagandist. Later, while ensconced in Vespasian's house, he wrote a history which was approved by the emperor. Whether or not Josephus did anything treasonous at Jotapata, both Jews and Romans considered him a traitor.

It is not our task to condemn or excuse. Two points need to be emphasized. (1) We have no indiction of treasonous conduct in all of Josephus' actions in Galilee before Jotapata. He was sent to Galilee to prepare the country for war and this commission he executed. His vanity could brook no opponent and so much energy and time was wasted on internal squabbles that effective organization for war was impossible, but this complaint cannot be confused with the accusation of treachery. (2) Rather than die at Jotapata Josephus surrendered; he sold his services to the Romans as the price for his life. Josephus' vanity probably played a part here

---

"he has betrayed us *too.*" This point, missed by Thackeray, was well noted by Stein ad loc. and in his *The Relationship between Jewish, Greek and Roman Cultures* (Israel 1970) 57 (Heb.).

[99] See especially F. Lewitz, *De Flavii Josephi Fide atque Auctoritate* (Königsberg 1857) 14; Graetz, *Geschichte* 485 n. 1; and Baerwald 16, 42-45, and 59-62. Josephus mentions the deserter to explain how Jotapata was taken: but for him the fortress would have held out even longer.

too. He considered himself much too important for a death in a cave near an obscure fortress in the country district of a small province. He must have been born for greater things.[100]

12. *Conclusion*

66-67 CE was a period of great confusion. The war, not the premeditated result of a series of actions, began spontaneously. Plans had yet to be made, no one was in command. Many aristocrats gathered about themselves groups of followers and prepared to participate in the conflict. Their motives varied and V incorrectly regards them all as crypto-pacifists.[101] Many of these aristocrats were involved in the war from its inception and BJ 2 deliberately distorts matters by positing a clean separation between the periods before and after the defeat of Cestius.

Josephus was an adherent of one of these aristocrats (Eleazar ben Ananias) and, with two other priests, was sent to Galilee. Their mission was to prepare the district for the Roman onslaught. This was a difficult task because the local population on the whole did not want war. Not that the natives loved the Romans—they simply were not inclined towards war. The peasants reserved most of their fear for the brigands and most of their hatred for the cities. The brigands plundered anyone worth plundering. As for the cities, Sepphoris was staunchly pro-Roman, Tiberias was torn by factional strife, Gabara supported John. Josephus attempted to unite these disparate elements. He tried to set up an arrangement between the brigands and the peasants, to impose his will upon the cities, to arouse the apathetic to prepare for war.

He tried but failed. Many of the brigands refused to cooperate. John of Gischala not only closed off upper Galilee, he also competed with Josephus for followers in lower Galilee. A delegation was sent from Jerusalem to put itself in charge of lower Galilee. The cities persisted with their political feuding. But, most fatal of all to

---

[100] Josephus' vanity is an important ingredient of his character and has been emphasized by von Gutschmid 340 and J. Salvador, *Histoire de la domination romaine en Judée* (Paris 1847) 2.45-49. Recent writers have generally not appreciated this factor sufficiently.

[101] Recent English, American, and Israeli scholarship emphasizes that there were many different revolutionary groups, each with its own slogans, techniques, and history, and that we cannot impose an organic unity or a single title on this diversity; see Borg, *JTS* 22 (1971) 504-512; Smith, *HTR* 64 (1971) 1-19; M. Stern, "Zealots," *Encyclopedia Judaica Yearbook 1973* (Jerusalem 1973) 135-152; Rhoads passim; L. Levine (n. 19 supra).

Josephus' plans, was that the Galilean population was in no mood to fight Rome. It was pre-occupied with other matters and neither Josephus, nor John, nor Jesus ben Sapphia, nor the delegation, nor anyone else, was able to incite it to a war it did not want. Vespasian's arrival caused the desertion of most of the meager forces which Josephus had succeeded to recruit. Josephus was compelled to enter Jotapata where, after a resistance of sorts, he was captured.

The delegation episode gives us a brief glimpse into the political developments in Jerusalem while Josephus was in Galilee. Priests had been prominent in the struggle from the beginning and had consolidated their power after the defeat of Cestius. Before very long, however, a Pharisaic party, headed by Simon ben Gamaliel, entered the scene. Simon and his allies somehow forced their way to the top and, when John asked Simon, his old friend, to oust Josephus, the Pharisees had their first opportunity to benefit from their success. Simon agreed that Josephus, who, in all probability, was not a Pharisee, must be replaced, but, instead of appointing John, he and Ananus sent a delegation to Galilee. Two of the four delegates were priests, three of the four were Pharisees. Josephus managed to outmaneuver these envoys and send them back to Jerusalem. The episode is of interest not only because it sheds light on the history of the Pharisees, but also because it may explain why Josephus was thenceforth ignored by the Jerusalem aristocracy, and why John abandoned his old friends to become a radical. All this is conjecture but seems likely.

CHAPTER SEVEN

CONCLUSION: JOSEPHUS IN ROME

After his capture Josephus served the Romans as propagandist, guide, and interpreter. He viewed himself not as a traitor but as a Jeremiah *redivivus* (cf. BJ 5.391-393) who announced God's will. The prophecy had revealed divine truth: further fighting against the Romans was not only foolhardy but impious. God and Tyche were on the side of the Romans (BJ 5.367, 412, etc.). Whether all of this theology was developed by Josephus during the war or was merely subsequent apologetic, we cannot tell. No matter how Josephus justified his conduct, he served the Romans, with the result that both Romans (V 416) and Jews (BJ 3.439) regarded him as a traitor to his people. After the war Josephus went to Rome with the young Caesar (V 422). He recounts at length all the benefits and privileges bestowed upon him by the Flavians (V 423, 425, 429). He also mentions the incessant attacks of his fellow Jews but how, in the classic manner of the genre *de mortibus persecutorum*, his opponents came to an inglorious end (V 424-425, 428-429). Unfortunately he rarely specifies the nature of these attacks and so we know neither the charges raised against him (except in the affair of Jonathan of Cyrene) nor why they caused him such concern. The substance of Justus' attack is known, but there too we cannot be certain why Josephus felt impelled to respond.

It was while in Rome,[1] while enjoying the munificence of the Caesars, and while being subjected to constant harrassment by his fellow Jews, that Josephus embarked on a literary career. Under the impetus of Titus and Epaphroditus he produced three works without which almost nothing would be known of the political history of the last two centuries of the second temple period. Before we turn to the aims of these works, let us first review their methods.

Josephus normally revises the language of his source. Occasional words and phrases are retained but, on the whole, the result is Josephan Greek, not a mechanical crib of the source. This procedure is documented not only by the treatment of *Aristeas*, *Esdras*, and 1 *Maccabees*, but also by the relationship of AJ 13-14 to BJ. Scholars

---

[1] We have no indication that Josephus ever left Rome.

who attempt to reconstruct lost sources from Josephus' text (e.g. the work of Nicolaus of Damascus or the source of BJ's description of the Essenes) must reckon with this fact.

With revision of language some revision of content is inevitable. Details are added, omitted, or changed, not always with reason. Although his fondness for the dramatic, pathetic, erotic, and the exaggerated, is evident throughout, as a rule Josephus remains fairly close to his original. Even when he modifies the source to suit a certain aim he still reproduces the essence of the story. Most important, he does not engage in the free invention of episodes. Of course his imagination is at work to enliven the narrative but, unlike other authors, he has not invented sagas for Biblical heroes. We may assume that he has not invented sagas for Alexander Jannaeus, Herod, or—himself.

Regarding the sequence of his source Josephus is even more faithful. The most common reason for rearrangement is the desire for a thematic narrative. This principle not only explains many of the deviations from the Biblical order, it also is the key for understanding the relationship of AJ 15-16 to BJ and V to BJ. In both cases AJ (which includes V), arranged chronologically, follows the disposition of the source which BJ rearranges thematically. When analyzing Josephan chronology we must always keep in mind the possibility that Josephus deliberately departed from the historical sequence for this literary reason.

In all these points Josephus followed standard Greek practice. An author was expected to vary the diction of his source, to embellish the narrative, to create something new. The preference for thematic organization to strict chronology has many antecedents in Greek historiography beginning with the fourth century BCE. Furthermore, all of Josephus' statements on the duties and methods of the historian are rhetorical or historiographical commonplaces which confirm our conclusion that Josephus did and said what a historian was expected to do and say. Not all of these pronouncements fit their Josephan context too well but this is to be expected when an author repeats traditional formulae.

We have emphasized another aspect of Josephus' work: his inveterate sloppiness. Texts suitable for tendentious revision as well as passages which contradict his motives are sometimes left untouched. The narrative is frequently confused, obscure, and contradictory. Legal and technical terms are used very loosely.

These inconcinnities do not necessarily provide any reliable evidence about Josephus' sources since the confusion can be caused by Josephus himself.

But while Josephus' methods nearly prohibit the precise reconstruction of his sources, they make reasonably clear the different motives prominent in the different portions of his work. Laqueur realized that these shifts in opinion indicate the changing conditions which Josephus had to face and therefore are valuable not only for the biography of Josephus himself but also for the history of the last quarter of the first century.[2]

In Rome Josephus continued his career as Roman apologist and propagandist, a career on which he had embarked while still in Palestine. The war was a recent event, fresh in everyone's mind, and a new peace between Jews and Romans had to be established. In the *Bellum Judaicum*, begun under Vespasian but not completed until the reign of Domitian, Josephus attempted to provide the basis for the new relationship. He argued that there was no fundamental antipathy between Romans and Jews. Herod the Great, in spite of his madness and his murders, symbolized the Roman-Jewish symbiosis and therefore received lavish praise with hardly a word of criticism.[3] The war was the unfortunate result of the misdirected actions of a few individuals on both sides. On the Jewish side, the war was begun by small groups of mad fanatics in no way representative of Judaism or the Jews. The priests, the three sects, and Agrippa, i.e., the "official institutions" of Judaism, opposed them. Except for a brief hiatus the fanatics were in command throughout, tyrannizing over the populace, and it is they who bear the responsibility for the war and its catastrophic conclusion. Therefore the Romans should not bear ill will towards the Jews since the Jews as a nation are innocent. On the Roman side, the war was begun by a few corrupt or incompetent procurators. The "official" Roman government had no desire to fight the Jews. Titus offered the Jews many opportunities to surrender, all adamantly rejected. At a meeting of his council the future emperor decided not to

---

[2] My debt to Laqueur's eighth chapter, "Der Werdegang des Josephus," is large although I disagree with him on many points and have substantially modified some of his theories. I do not attempt to sketch here all the motives of all of Josephus' works.

[3] H. R. Moehring discussed some of these points in "Josephus' Attitude toward the Roman Empire," an unpublished lecture delivered at Columbia University on 25 April 75. See too Yavetz, *GRBS* 16 (1975) 421.

destroy the temple and, when a recalcitrant soldier tossed a torch into the holy precincts, Titus attempted to extinguish the blaze—but in vain. In the Biblical manner, God was using a foreign host to purify his temple and chastise his people. Thus neither the Romans nor the Jews are responsible for this disastrous turn in Roman-Jewish relations.

Before writing his history (or dictating it to his *amanuenses*), Josephus prepared, in the normal manner of ancient historiography, a *hypomnema*, a detailed outline or series of notes. The *hypomnema* was arranged in chronological order and was, perhaps, basically truthful—although it would have been an extraordinary feat for Josephus to record the unvarnished truth about anything. Since the *hypomnema* was meant to be revised and edited, we cannot hope to recover its exact content or language. Only for the last part of BJ 2, which is paralleled by the *Vita*, can we determine how Josephus treated the *hypomnema*.

BJ abandoned the *hypomnema's* chronological sequence in favor of a thematic arrangement (much as BJ thematically revised Nicolaus' chronological account of Herod's reign). The Galilean narrative was constructed around two themes: Josephus the ideal general and Josephus the conqueror of sedition. Josephus the ideal general established a Galilean judicial system, won the loyalty of the populace, fortified the cities, recruited and drilled a large army. His troops were not brigands or Galilean peasants but well-trained and well-behaved professionals. Since a general of this caliber could not be troubled with small encounters and minor skirmishes, the fighting did not begin until Josephus (in BJ 3) confronted Placidus, a lieutenant of Vespasian. Soon the inevitable confrontation took place between the two ideal generals, the Roman and the Jew. Josephus embellished the account with some ingenious tricks which he cribbed from a poliorketic manual.

Josephus the conqueror of sedition was opposed primarily by John of Gischala. John was from the start an unscrupulous brigand and there was no possibility of cooperation between him and our hero. He embarked on a series of attempts to kill or remove Josephus: the Dabaritta affair, the episode at Tiberias, and the delegation from Jerusalem. Josephus also had to overcome the revolts of Tiberias and Sepphoris. This theme is really part of the portrait of Josephus as an ideal general because ideal generals should know how to escape from difficult situations and should behave mildly towards opponents.

The account in BJ 2-3 is more than a concession to Josephus' vanity. It also explains how Josephus was different from the nefarious tyrants whom he blames for the war itself and the destruction of the temple. The tyrants and extremists began the war, against the wishes of aristocracy and populace, but after the victory over Cestius, a new government gained control which had no connection with the preceding events. These men were not fanatic revolutionaries but aristocratic and noble, ideal figures like Josephus and Ananus. Once Josephus the general was safely in the hands of the Romans, Josephus the historian could again contend that the people wanted peace but were overpowered by the extremists. When Ananus succumbed to the Zealots, all shred of legitimacy was lost and the war proceeded to its inexorable conclusion, now as before, under the rule of the tyrants. Thus Josephus and his aristocratic colleagues fought in the war but had no connection with its outbreak or the destruction of the temple.

BJ 1-6 was completed in the reign of Titus. During the reign of Domitian, many of Josephus' opinions and attitudes began to change. Why this happened is not entirely clear. Josephus was becoming more "nationalistic", more conscious of religious considerations, less concerned about flattering Rome.[4] He had enough sense to realize that Roman-Jewish symbiosis was necessary for Jewish survival, but his new attitude was more ambivalent. AJ still has nice things to say about Herod, some of them not found even in BJ, but the earlier panegyric is absent. Herod is condemned for his crimes, notably his violations of religious law. His Maccabean opponents are more sympathetic figures in AJ than BJ—it was when writing AJ that Josephus discovered his Maccabean forebears. The two Agrippas, further symbols of Roman-Jewish symbiosis, had both been treated well by BJ but AJ distinguishes between them. Agrippa I, loyal to his people and his religion (qualities which BJ omitted or de-emphasized), is praised while Agrippa II, a Roman lackey and a desecrator of traditional Judaism (again ignored by BJ), is damned. BJ had contended that isolated individuals from both sides were responsible for the outbreak of the war, although it assigned far greater guilt to the Jewish bandits

---

[4] The usual explanation is that the autocrat Domitian threatened the status of the Jews and that Josephus rose to his people's defense. See S. J. Case, *JBL* 44 (1925) 10-20, and E. M. Smallwood, *CP* 51 (1956) 1-13. Laqueur conjectured that Domitian suspended Josephus' pension.

than to the Roman procurators. AJ redistributes the guilt more equitably between the Jews and Romans and more broadly within each group. On the Jewish side, the fanatics are no longer the only culprits as they were in BJ. The high priests and even Agrippa himself are assigned some of the responsibility. AJ, unlike BJ, has no reason to hide the fact that the fourth philosophy is related to one of the three sects. Similarly, V speaks of the Pharisees' active participation in the war. AJ never restricts Jewish guilt to the revolutionaries alone; it never denies that "the Jews" fought the Romans. On the Roman side, AJ increases the guilt of the procurators beyond what BJ had done. It also blames the Sebastene soldiers in Roman employ and even the emperor Nero himself. AJ agrees with BJ that there is no fundamental tension between Jews and Romans but its theory is much less apologetic. The great war erupted as the result of the confluence of many diverse causes which made war inevitable. Part of this theory is V's claim that the Jews were the innocent victims of attacks by the pagan cities and that Josephus and John at first opposed the war but somehow became involved by factors beyond their control.

Related to AJ's nationalism is its religious outlook. AJ uses loyalty to the ancestral traditions as a criterion in judging kings, cities, and governors. V demonstrates that Josephus carefully observed the *Halachah* and that his opponents, including the Pharisees from Jerusalem, did not. In BJ this religious outlook is noticeable only in BJ 7, which, like AJ, was completed under Domitian. The other six books of BJ practically ignore this criterion.

With this religious outlook comes a pro-Pharisaic bias. AJ still has a few nasty things to say about the Pharisees, but, on the whole, these sectarians do better in AJ than BJ. Their importance and influence are much increased; AJ alleges that not only the masses but even the Sadducees obey them. The war had destroyed the religious establishments of the country, and, we may conjecture, many groups were attempting to fill the vacuum. Josephus allied himself with the Rabbis, the heirs of the Pharisees, who were then becoming influential and may have already attained some measure of official recognition for their academy at Yavneh. Perhaps they were becoming important in the Jewish community of Rome too. We may conjecture that Josephus realized that they would emerge as the leaders of the Jewish scene and imagined himself as their representative in Rome who would intercede on their behalf with emperors and empresses. In any event, Josephus contends in AJ that the Pharisees had always been prominent and therefore deserve Roman support. Their rivals, the Sadducees, the high priests, and the Samaritans, are all denounced by AJ although they had been treated mildly by BJ.[5]

V makes the ultimate commitment to this Pharisaic bias and declares that Josephus had always been, since his youth, a loyal follower of the Pharisees. Josephus' relationship with Simon ben Gamaliel and the Pharisaic delegation appointed by him is recounted in painstaking detail (not, however, painstaking accuracy). In the seventies or early eighties BJ could afford to glide over the entire incident but in the nineties Josephus had to explain to the Rabbis why he was so opposed by the Pharisees of Jerusalem. He blamed his arch enemy, John of Gischala, a friend of Simon, as the moving spirit behind the effort to supplant him. Simon was only "temporarily" disenchanted with Josephus and V's description of the father of the patriarch shows that the historian claimed to be his enthusiastic admirer. The Pharisees who were sent to Galilee were not Pharisees of the best sort, says Josephus. They swore false oaths, used sacred occasions for nefarious purposes, and violated the sanctity of the synagogue. Josephus, popular and religious, had no choice but to remain at his post and oppose these delegates. A divine figure appeared to him in a dream and ordered him to stand firm because he had also to fight the Romans. Thus Josephus pleads that his squabbles with Simon and the Pharisees during the war should not disqualify him from friendship with Simon's son and the Rabbis of Yavneh.[6]

We do not know whether Josephus' "nationalistic" viewpoint and Pharisaic bias were provoked in any way by Justus of Tiberias and his polemic. After the death of Agrippa II, Justus was concerned primarily with the status of his native city which was attempting to regain the position of honor it had enjoyed under Claudius. Justus exonerated Tiberias of any war guilt by accusing Josephus of forcing the city to support the revolt. Josephus was a

---

[5] On the opposition of the priests to the activities of the Rabbis at Yavneh, see J. Neusner, *A Life of Yohanan ben Zakkai*[2] (Leiden 1970) 215. Vespasian bestowed a city, Flavia Neapolis, upon the Samaritans (Jones, *Cities* 276-277) and this sign of royal favor must have caused the Rabbis some uneasiness.

[6] It is possible that the legal and exegetical material of the first half of AJ was supposed to convince the reader of Josephus' Pharisaic loyalty. I hope to return to this point elsewhere.

cruel, rapacious tyrant, and if certain segments of the Tiberian population fought the Romans, the blame lies not with the Tiberians themselves but with Josephus and the unruly country peasantry. Therefore, concluded Justus, Tiberias is worthy of trust and recognition.

Why Josephus felt it necessary to respond to these charges, is unclear. Perhaps his vanity could not tolerate a well written indictment—Justus' is the only known written attack on Josephus' character. Josephus responded with an apologetic account of his whole life, beginning with a brief survey of his youth and activities before he was sent to Galilee, then reporting fully his actions in Galilee, and concluding with a rapid resume of his subsequent career. This new composition he published as his autobiography in order to demonstrate his popularity, morality, and proper behavior. He was an "official" general, not an illegitimate tyrant, and compelled neither the Tiberians nor anyone else to join the revolt. These concerns are similar to BJ's but the emphasis is different, because in BJ they merely contribute to a desired effect, the picture of Josephus as a great general, while in V these concerns are paramount, not just parts of a larger whole. Since the autobiography does not subscribe to BJ's apologetic theory, it does not need to pretend that Josephus was a great general; he was not fundamentally different from the other revolutionaries. V mentions those insignificant battles which BJ considered unworthy of mention. Josephus' ubiquitous ingenuity appears in V only in connection with petty affairs while in BJ it determines the course of mighty battles. Since the image of the ideal general is absent, V's frequent reiteration of Josephus' popularity, moderation, propriety, etc., must be a response, presumably a response to Justus.

With the absence of the ideal general motif, much of the anti-John polemic is gone. John and Josephus are not friends but V admits at least grudging approval of (i.e., participation in?) John's two profit-making schemes. John is no longer the seething radical, the brigand attacking Jews and Jewish territory, but a fellow revolutionary and politician. He and Josephus are comrades in another respect too. In a continuation of AJ's theory, V claims that both John and Josephus entered the war unwillingly (see above).

To return to the apologetic: in order to refute Justus, Josephus needed a detailed account of his actions and this he found in his old *hypomnema* which he had prepared before writing BJ. He retained the chronological structure of this document but added, omitted, and modified material *ad lib*. Perhaps these revisions were not as thorough as those done in order to produce BJ, but they were still thorough enough to prevent us from reconstructing the *hypomnema* in detail. We can see fairly clearly what BJ has added (the fierce anti-John polemic, including the statement that John participated in the Dabaritta affair; the recruitment and training of an army), omitted (the numerous minor skirmishes with Romans and Jews), and changed (Josephus' brigands become professional soldiers), but exactly what V has done, aside from adding some references to Justus, is not as clear. Even the original *hypomnema* may have had apologetic material.

Josephus ended his career with the *Contra Apionem*, an apologetic for BJ and a retort to the antisemitism of the day. Although the roots of this work lie in Alexandria, Josephus' religious outlook and nationalistic bias are evident. The Jewish legal system is praised while the religious behavior of other nations is ridiculed. The book defends the thesis that the ideals of Hellenism find their best expression in the Mosaic polity, not contemporary Greco-Roman culture.[7]

Our analysis of the shifts in the motives of the works of Josephus has allowed us to trace the development of the historian from a Roman apologist to a religious nationalist. Students of ancient Jewish history must bear these different motives in mind and must realize the distinction between BJ and AJ and between BJ and V. Those sections of the Josephan narrative which support these motives should be regarded with suspicion. They may, of course, be true and may derive from unbiased sources—tendentiousness and falsity are not necessarily synonymous—but the historian cannot ignore their historiographic purpose. Similarly those elements of the Josephan narrative which contradict these motives may be accepted as, in all likelihood, the unedited report of Josephus' source but that is no sign of veracity.

We have discussed the following motives of BJ:

1.   Not all Jews revolted, only small bands of mad fanatics.
2.   The revolutionaries have no connection with any of the "of-

---

[7] I hope to return elsewhere to CA and its place in the Josephan corpus.

ficial" representatives of Judaism (the high-priests, Agrippa, and the three philosophies).

3. The revolutionary leaders, especially John of Gischala, were evil tyrants.
4. Josephus in Galilee was an ideal general, ingenious, popular, self-controlled, lucky, and an enemy of John of Gischala.
5. The aristocrats, the masses, and Agrippa strenuously opposed the war.
6. From the defeat of Cestius until the rise of the Zealots the war was directed by aristocrats who were noble figures and had nothing to do with the beginning of the revolt.

Some of the motives of AJ are:

1. The Pharisees always were powerful and influential. Related to this motive are the following:
    (a) The Samaritans are scoundrels who have always caused trouble for the real Jews.
    (b) Various figures are condemned as untraditional (Herod, Archelaus, Judas the Galilean, the Tiberians, Tiberius Julius Alexander, Drusilla, Agrippa II), one (Agrippa I) is praised for his religiosity.
    (c) High-priests are denounced.
2. The Jews as a whole participated in the revolt but were compelled by necessity; the responsibility lies with the revolutionaries, the procurators, the high-priests, Agrippa II, Nero, Sebastene troops, and, V adds, the neighboring pagan cities.
3. Agrippa I was a loyal Jew and a good king but his children, notably Agrippa II and Berenice, violated the traditional laws.

The motives of V are:

1. Justus the man, the politician, and the historian was (or is) a scoundrel, a revolutionary, and a liar.
2. Tiberias was a revolutionary city.
3. Josephus is a reliable historian.
4. Josephus was a popular and well-behaved general in Galilee who harmed no one and did not use his office to become wealthy.
5. Josephus was an opponent of John of Gischala.
6. Josephus restrained his Galileans from wreaking vengeance on John and three Galilean cities.

16

7. Josephus did his duty and attacked pro-Roman cities, notably Sepphoris.
8. Josephus has a fine pedigree and has always moved in high society.
9. From his youth on, Josephus lived as a Pharisee, was widely known as a legal scholar, and always observed the Law. His dispute with Simon ben Gamaliel was a temporary aberration.
10. The war was a product of compulsion; both Josephus and John, at least at first, wanted peace.

Thus our study of Josephus' minor work, the *Vita*, has led to a clearer picture of the aims and methods of his larger works, BJ and AJ. Naber's warning (see the introduction) has proved incorrect.

NON-JOSEPHAN DATA

This appendix considers all the non-Josephan data on the war, from its beginning in 66 CE until the surrender of Jotapata in mid-67, and confirms the old conclusion: on the whole Josephus is our only source for the history of the war. In the preceding chapters we have attempted to show that even with Josephus we know very little about the war, but at least we know how much we don't know; without Josephus even that level of knowledge (ignorance?) would be beyond us. Thucydides too is our only source for much of what he writes but our problem is that Josephus was no Thucydides.

A. *Archaeological and Epigraphical Evidence*

The silence of these sources is remarkable. The richest site, Beth Shearim (Besara), testifies to a revolt of the fourth century CE (see below) but provides nothing for 66-70. The numerous synagogues are late.[1] Fortifications have been discovered at several Galilean villages which Josephus claims to have fortified, and some of the fortifications may date from the second half of the first century CE, but archaeology cannot tell us *who* fortified these villages, whether Josephus, John of Gischala, or someone else.[2] One excavator claimed that Sepphoris was pro-Roman (see below) because it depended on an external water supply which could be

---

[1] E. K. Vogel, "Bibliography of Holy Land Sites," *HUCA* 42 (1971) 1-96, and M. Avi-Yonah ed., *Encyclopedia of Archaeological Excavations in the Holy Land* (Englewood-Cliffs, N.J., 1975ff). On the remains of the synagogues see e.g. E. R. Goodenough, *Jewish Symbols in the Greco-Roman Period* I (N.Y. 1953) 178-267.

[2] Prof. Eric Meyers has informed me that first century walls have been discovered at Gamala, Jotapata, and Taricheae (on which see V. C. Corbo, *Studii Biblici Franciscani Liber Annuus* 24 [1974] 5-37). The fortifications of Meron which have been discovered date not from the first century (as stated in *BASOR* 214 [April 1974] 2-25) but from a later period, as Prof. Meyers will show in a second preliminary report. A gate and two towers have been found at Tiberias but they apparently pre-date Josephus and are part of Antipas' establishment of the city. See M. Heilperin in *Sefer Teberyah*, ed. O. Avissar (Jerusalem 1973) 46-49, and the report in *Hadashot Archeologiot* 48-49 p. 39.

blocked easily by a besieging army.[3] The explanation may or may
not be correct. Many cities had cisterns within the municipal
limits but we do not know how many or how large the cisterns of
Sepphoris were. If, however, the theory were correct, the pro-Roman
attitude of the city would testify to the relative ineffectiveness
of the Galilean revolutionaries. Why did they not besiege the city,
cut off the water supply, and demand capitulation? Their impotence
could be attributed to Josephus' ambiguous leadership (see V
30-31: Josephus prevents an attack on Sepphoris) or to the weakness of the revolutionaries (although V 373-380 represents them
as able to take the city by a surprise attack but scared away by a
rumor). But other explanations too are possible.[4] The important
point—the pro-Roman policy—could never have been divined
from the archaeological remains.

The lack of epigraphical evidence is even more disappointing.
Inscriptions might have helped us solve the historical problems
analyzed here, but all the inscriptions from Galilee are late. Pre-70
texts are seldom encountered in Palestinian epigraphy.[5]

---

[3] S. Yeivin in *Preliminary Report of the Univ. of Michigan Excavations
at Sepphoris, Palestine, in* 1931 ed. L. Waterman (Ann Arbor 1937) 23-24.

[4] Schürer 2.210-211 suggests that the population was mixed gentile and
Jewish, but there is no evidence for this. Schürer 2.210 n. 494 admits that
BJ 3.32 (ὁμόφυλοι) speaks against his theory. So does V 376-77 (ὁμόφυλοι).
M. Kiddushin 4.5 shows that, in the opinion of R. Yosi (mid-second century),
the old regime or record office (ערכי הישנה) of Sepphoris enrolled only
pedigreed Jews. It does not follow that the new regime enrolled even gentiles.
And in 150 the "old" regime was probably that of 70-132. Contra Schürer. S.
Klein, *Ma'amarim Shonim la Ḥaqirat ʾEreẓ Yisrael* (Vienna 1924) 54-56,
accepts (without acknowledgment) Schürer's theory of mixed population
but explains the pro-Roman stand of the city as the result of the anti-
Pharisaic attitude of the local priests who formed a large percentage of the
population and had Sadducean sympathies. How Klein knows that the
priests were numerous and influential in pre-70 Sepphoris is not stated.
Alt, *Kleine Schriften* II (Munich 1953, repr. 1964) 434 n. 3 and Alon, *Toledot* 1.90, are certain that pre-70 Sepphoris was predominantly Jewish.
Another explanation for Sepphoris' pacificity is that the city was the
capital of Galilee and did not want to lose this jealously guarded privilege
(V 37). Sepphoris was surely not going to side with its arch rival Tiberias
against its Roman benefactors. On the rivalry of the two cities, see chapter
five above, note 133.

[5] The standard but lacunose and inaccurate collection is J. B. Frey,
Corpus Inscriptionum Judaicarum II (Rome 1952). See Schürer-Vermes 15-16.
From several scrappy inscriptions M. Schwabe was able to reconstruct some
details of the inner life of Tiberias of the Talmudic period. See "On the
History of Tiberias," *Commentationes Iudaico-Hellenisticae in Memoriam
Iohannis Lewy*, ed. M. Schwabe and I. Gutman (Jerusalem 1949) 200-251

B. *Numismatic Evidence*

Although the coins of the revolutionary government were minted at Jerusalem and contain no reference to the Galilean conflict,[6] a series of coins of Sepphoris provides important evidence. In 1936 M. Narkiss published the following in his *Coins of Palestine I*: *Jewish Coins* (Jerusalem 1936) III (in Hebrew):

Nr. 56. Aes. 24 mm.

Obv. two crossed cornucopiae with a caduceus between them. Legend around rim:

[   ] ϹΕΠ ΦΩΡΗΝΟΥΕϹΠΑ

Rev. wreath encircling the legend

LΔΙ/ΝΕΡΩΝΟ/ΚΛΑΥΔΙΟΥ/ ΚΑΙϹΑΡΟ/Ϲ

Nr. 57. Aes. 19 mm.

Obv. large letters S C and, in smaller letters

ϹΕΠΦΟ[Ρ]ΗΝΟϹΙΡΗΝΟΠΟΙ

Rev. circle and wreath around the legend

LΔΙ/ΝΕΡΩΝΟ/ΚΛΑΥΔΙΟΥ/ ΚΑΙϹΑΡΟ/Ϲ

The legend of nr. 57 was interpreted as Σεπφωρηνῶ(ν) Εἰρηνόποι(ος). Nr. 56 has a clear allusion to Vespasian (ΟΥΕΣΠΑ). In 1950 H. Seyrig, unaware of Narkiss' work, discussed the same coins in *Numismatic Chronicle* 10 (1950) 284-289. Seyrig's specimen of nr. 57 had the large S C with ΝΙΛϹ above, ϹΕΠΦΩΡ below, and ΝΟΛΙΡΗΝΟΠΟΛΙ around. Seyrig interpreted the inscription as Εἰρηνόπολι(ς) or Εἰρηνοπολι(τῶν) and [Νερω]νιάς. The ΝΟ was left unexplained. His reconstruction of nr. 56 from some previously known but misattributed coins yielded Εἰρηνόπολι(ς) Νερωνιά(ς) Σεπ(φωρηνοί). Narkiss reacted in a confused and confusing article in which he affirmed his reading Εἰρηνόπο(ιος) and instead of Seyrig's Νερωνιά(ς) he proposed [ἔτ]ο(υς) δι' Νέρων(ος) ιαʹ Σεπφωρη-ν(ῶν).[7] In an additional note in *Numismatic Chronicle* 15 (1955) 157-159, Seyrig was still unaware of either of Narkiss' contributions but he now discovered what Narkiss knew all along—the coins bear the name of Vespasian. Seyrig claimed that his new specimen of nr. 56 had a "complete and legible" inscription (he did not publish a photograph) which reads:

(Heb.). But even scrappy inscriptions from first century Tiberias are non-existent.

[6] L. Kadman, *The Coins of the Jewish War of 66-73 C.E.* (Jerusalem 1960).

[7] M. Narkiss, *Bulletin of the Israel Exploration Society* (= *BIES*) 17 (1953) 108-120 (Heb.). Narkiss did not read Seyrig's article carefully.

ΕΠΙ ΟΥΕΣΠΑΣΙΑΝΟΥ ΕΙΡΗΝΟΠΟΛΙ ΝΕΡΩΝΙΑ CΕΠΦΩ

We may accept Seyrig's final reading and summarize the results. In the fourteenth year of Nero, which ran from 13 October 67 to 12 October 68,[8] the city of Sepphoris issued coins declaring fidelity to Vespasian (Οὐεσπασιανοῦ with and without ἐπί) and the senate (S · C).[9] It was granted the titles Neronias and Eirenopolis,[10] a fact of great importance. The city must have been a bastion of pro-Roman sentiment even before 67-68 if Vespasian allowed it the titles "City of Nero" and "City of Peace".[11] V frequently (30, 38, 104, 124, 232, 346-348, 373-380, 394-396, 411) mentions Sepphoris' support of the Romans. V 38 claims that even under Felix Sepphoris was conspicuously pro-Roman (ἐπειδὴ ʽΡωμαίοις ὑπήκουσεν). It supported Cestius Gallus on his approach to Jerusalem (V 30). BJ usually agrees (2.511; 3.30-34 and 59).[12] Combined with the numismatic evidence this testimony establishes Sepphoris' loyalty to the Roman cause.

In three locations, however, BJ alleges Sepphorite revolutionary activity. BJ 2.629 claims that the Jerusalem delegation wrote to Sepphoris, Gabara (the correct reading), Gischala, and Tiberias, thereby winning them over to the anti-Josephan banner, but that Josephus managed to regain them all without recourse to violence.

[8] See Schürer-Vermes 488 n. 16.

[9] Seyrig, NC 15 (1955) 158, notes that the provincial coins of Syria often bear S C. The initials do not necessarily refer to the juridical authority by which the coins are minted; they indicate that the coinage is 'official' and valid. Thus Seyrig explains the S C on one set of coins of Agrippa II.

[10] Narkiss' εἰρηνόποιος is disposed of by Seyrig's reading. Seyrig, NC 10 (1950) 288-289, conjectures that the title Eirenopolis was granted in 64 BCE but it seems more likely that it was bestowed in 68 CE as recognition of Sepphoris' loyalty. Narkiss tried to avoid Νερωνιάς because nowhere else does Sepphoris have that title, but the title presumably was short-lived because Nero was. Narkiss' proposal δι' Νέρωνος ια' Σεπφωρηνῶν is ingenious but, I think, impossible. The era of 56/7 is attested only for the coinage of Agrippa II, not Sepphoris. IA should be AI (as it is on the coins of Agrippa II). Seyrig's legible coin has no room for a double date. Seyrig gives the references to all previously published specimens of these coins (except, as I mentioned, for those published by Narkiss). Other specimens are published in the Sylloge Nummorum Graecorum: Royal Collection of Coins and Medals, Danish National Museum: Palestine-Characene (Copenhagen 1961) plate 1 nr. 1 and by Hamburger, IEJ 20 (1970) 85-86. I have examined a specimen at the American Numismatic Society, New York (where it is shelved with the coins of Agrippa II). The crucial legend is illegible in all these exempla.

[11] Caesarea, another pro-Roman city, minted similar coins. See Hill, BMC Palestine 16, cited by both Narkiss and Seyrig.

[12] On these garrisons see chapter six with note 67.

This statement is false and has already been discussed above in chapter six.[13] Gischala was the headquarters of John's activity and never was won over by Josephus peacefully or otherwise. V 327 mentions a battle at Tiberias which does not quite fit the claim to have captured the city "without arms" (δίχα τῶν ὅπλων). V 203, the parallel to BJ 2.629, says that the delegation wrote to John, Sepphoris, Gabara, and Tiberias, and ordered them to fight their opponent. We are not told whether the cities obeyed. In fact V 232 describes how the envoys approached Sepphoris but achieved nothing except a meeting with the inhabitants; this, at least, is credible.

The other two BJ references to an anti-Roman Sepphoris concern the fortification of the city. BJ 2.574 says that Josephus had only to permit [14] the Sepphorites to build their wall because they were wealthy and eager for war (προθύμους ἐπὶ τὸν πόλεμον δίχα προστάγματος)—on which side, he does not say, but he implies the anti-Roman. BJ 3.61 presents a different story. Josephus fortified Sepphoris before it had abandoned the Galilean cause (πρὶν ἀποστῆναι Γαλιλαίων). Implication: in the early stages Sepphoris supported the revolt. V too claims that Josephus fortified Sepphoris, but, unlike BJ, it does not pretend that the city was anti-Roman. V 188 merely states the fact of fortification while V 347 offers the claim with an excuse: Josephus fortified the city but only because the Sepphorites pretended to be anti-Roman and so tricked him (ἠπάτησαν). Which account is true? The numismatic evidence makes the claim of BJ 3.61 rather dubious. Josephus was a leader of the resistance against Rome, Sepphoris had long been pro-Roman (V 38). V 188 at best is an exaggeration or a simplification. In the fortification list Josephus repeatedly claims credit for projects over which he had no control (see chapter six, especially note 45). This leaves us with the choice between V 347 (Josephus was tricked) and BJ 2.574 (the Sepphorites fortified the city themselves and Josephus merely "permitted" them). It is plausible that the Sepphorites, surrounded by hostile Galileans, fortified their city for their own protection. Thus BJ 2.574 seems correct

---

[13] See above p. 214. Smallwood, *Jews* 305, believes BJ 2.629.

[14] ἐφῆκε is Bekker's emendation; the manuscripts read ἔφη or ἀφῆκε. Simhoni and Michel-Bauernfeind translate "permit." Thackeray translates "the inhabitants of Sepphoris . . . were authorized by him." See his textual note and the concordance s.v. ἀφίημι and ἐφίημι.

(except for the suggestion that Josephus "permitted" what he
simply could not prevent) but it is surprising to find Josephus
admitting that he was tricked (V 347). We remain in doubt. What
is beyond doubt, however, is Sepphoris' pro-Roman orientation.[15]

C. *Literary Evidence*

Extant literary accounts know little of the Jewish war. Pagan
authors ignored Josephus the historian and knew only Josephus
the prophet (Suetonius *Vespasianus* 5.6; Appian Ἑκατονταετία
fragment 17, p. 534 Viereck-Roos; Dio Cassius 66.1.4). Neither
pagan nor Christian bothered with the preliminaries of the war
because what mattered was the siege of Jerusalem and the destruction of the temple. Pagan writers were interested in the rise of a
new dynasty, its victories and *omina imperii*. Suetonius mentions
Vespasian's and Titus' battles in Galilee only to demonstrate
imperial heroism. When Vespasian and Titus leave the scene, the
war is over. The capture of Masada and the other battles described
by BJ 7 are omitted. For Christians the destruction of the temple
marked the fulfillment of prophecy, the final sign of the rejection
of the old Israel. The war in Galilee was theologically irrelevant.
And for a description of the horrors of Jerusalem in its final hours,
who could ask for a more rhetorical, more embellished, more
moving narrative than BJ? Christian writers had no incentive
to look for other accounts.[16] Rabbinic material has problems of its
own, discussed below. The history of Justus of Tiberias has been
discussed in chapter five above.

1. *Pagan Literature*

All extensive descriptions of the Jewish war other than Josephus'
are lost or extant only in fragments. The following pagan writers
provide or may have provided non-Josephan data.

a. BJ 1.1-2 and 6-8 refer to numerous writers who delighted
in depreciating the Jews and belittling their courage. (CA 1.46
also castigates inaccurate historians of the revolt but we know
nothing about them). If the *commentarii* of Vespasian and Titus

---

[15] Luther 84-85 reached this conclusion without knowing the numismatic
material. Contrast Baerwald 47-48 and, more recently, Smallwood, *Jews*
302 n. 34. See Schürer 2.212 n. 502.
[16] G. Bardy, *Revue d'histoire ecclésiastique* 43 (1948) 179-191, and especially
Schreckenberg, *Tradition* and *Rezeptionsgeschichtliche ... Untersuchungen*.

were ever published, they must have appeared after Josephus wrote this proem.[17] The *commentarii* presumably described at great length the victories of the Flavians, including those in Galilee, but all details are uncertain. The writers of the events of 69 CE, such as Cluvius Rufus and Vipstanus Messala, may have touched on the war in Palestine but probably only in the manner of Tacitus— a sentence or two on the early stages and then an account of the siege of Jerusalem.

b. Sometimes in the 70's Pliny the Elder wrote a history *a fine Aufidii Bassi*, i.e. from 32 CE. It must have dealt with the Flavian triumphs in the East—Pliny feared that his history would arouse the accusation of servile flattery—but to what extent is unknown. The notion that Pliny served in Judaea under Vespasian is erroneous.[18]

c. Antonius Julianus is known from a corrupt passage in Minucius Felix *Octavius* 33.4 as an author of a work *De Judaeis*. Nothing is known beyond what Minucius says: Antonius described the disasters which befell the Jews. Even if the author is identical with the Antonius Julianus of BJ 6.238, it seems unlikely that he devoted any space to the Galilean war.[19]

d. Domitian wrote an epic on the Jewish war in which he celebrated the exploits of Titus. Our sole source is Valerius Flaccus *Argonautica* 1.12-14 (the poet addresses Apollo):

> versam proles tua pandet Idumen [20]—
> namque potest—Solymo ac nigrantem pulvere fratrem
> spargentemque faces et in omni turre furentem.

It is unfortunate that we do not know the content of this poem, written by the man who was to be the emperor when Josephus wrote V and quarreled with Justus. When the poem was written is another uncertainty. The *Argonautica* was composed during the Flavian principate, but the exact date, which provides the *terminus ante quem* for Domitian's epic, is the subject of controversy.[21]

---

[17] On these *commentarii* see Laqueur, *PhW* 41 (1921) 1107-1109; H. Bardon, *La littérature latine inconnue II: L'époque impériale* (Paris 1956) 209-210 and *Les empereurs* 271-272; Lindner 16; Schürer-Vermes 32-33.

[18] M. Stern, *Greek and Latin Authors on Jews and Judaism* I (Jerusalem 1974) 465-501.

[19] See Schürer-Vermes 33-34 and Stern 458-461. The crucial text of Minucius is reprinted as FGrH 735. Jacoby seems to accept the view that Julianus wrote on the Bar Kokhba war.

[20] *Idumae* is a synonym for Judaea; see Stern 316 n. 1.

[21] K. Scott, *Rivista di Filologia* 62 (1934) 474-481, suggests a Domitianic

It is likely, however, that Domitian celebrated the exploits of his brother while Vespasian was still alive, since such admiration would be inexplicable at a later period when Titus and Domitian were enemies.[22] If the epic focused on Titus and Jerusalem, Galilee was probably ignored.

e. Tacitus' *Historiae* originally contained an extensive description of the Jewish war but only a portion survives. We notice immediately the focus of Tacitus' account: *Sed quoniam famosae urbis supremum diem tradituri sumus, congruens videtur primordia eius aperire* (5.2.1). The famous discourse on Jewish manners and history (5.2.1-13.4) is but an introduction to the narrative on the fall of Jerusalem.[23] The details Tacitus gives on the situation in Jerusalem do not affect us. But he does confirm the Josephan account of the early stages of the war. 5.10.1 is the important passage:

> Duravit tamen patientia Iudaeis usque ad Gessium Florum procuratorem: sub eo bellum ortum. et comprimere coeptantem Cestium Gallum Syriae legatum varia proelia ac saepius adversa excepere. qui ubi fato aut taedio occidit, missu Neronis Vespasianus fortuna famaque et egregiis ministris intra duas aestates cuncta camporum omnesque praeter Hierosolyma urbes victore exercitu tenebat.

All the essentials agree with BJ: outbreak of war under Florus, *varia proelia* and ultimate defeat of Cestius Gallus, and Vespasian's subjugation of the entire country outside of Jerusalem in two seasons of campaigning. Note that Jotapata is not mentioned. The idea that Gallus was dead when Vespasian began his activities is new but reconcilable with Josephan data. Gallus was active throughout the winter of 66-67 (V 214, 373, and 394) but with the arrival of Vespasian he disappears from the scene. Tacitus supplies the explanation, "fato aut taedio occidit."

f. Suetonius' biographies of the three Flavian emperors contain several items on the war. *Vespasianus* 4.5 describes Vespasian's appointment and his initial success. Two items are of interest:

---

date. The most recent discussions, by E. Lefèvre, *Das Prooemium der Argonautica des Valerius Flaccus* (Mainz/Wiesbaden 1971) 60-64 and J. Strand, *Notes on Valerius Flaccus' Argonautica* (Goteborg 1972) 31, date the *Argonautica* to the reign of Vespasian. See too Stern 502-503.

[22] Suetonius *Titus* 9.5 and *Domitianus* 2.6. See too *Domitianus* 20. This date is defended by Bardon, *Les empereurs* 282 and Lefèvre 33-37.

[23] An archaeological excursus was often prefixed to the description of a famous city, people, or building. See H. Lewy, *Studies in Jewish Hellenism* (Jerusalem 1969) 118 n. 5 and 140-141 (Heb.).

> Iudaei ... rebellarunt caesoque praeposito legatum insuper Syriae consularem suppetias ferentem rapta aquila fugauerunt.

The consular legate is Cestius Gallus. Who is the murdered *praepositus*? The natural assumption (thus Ailloud ad loc.) is that Gessius Florus is meant. But neither Tacitus nor Josephus mentions the death of Florus at the hands of the revolutionaries and they surely would have mentioned it. Perhaps Suetonius refers to the head of the Jerusalem garrison (τῶν Ῥωμαίων ἔπαρχος), a certain Metilius. Josephus says that when the garrison was massacred by the Jews in violation of a truce, Metilius alone was spared because he promised to be circumcised (BJ 2.450-54). Metilius may have been executed soon after or Suetonius preserves the (apparently erroneous) report which reached Rome.[24] Perhaps Suetonius refers to the commander of the garrison of the Antonia who presumably was killed with the rest of the garrison (BJ 2.430). The other new feature here is the mention of the *rapta aquila*. Suetonius proceeds to describe the composition of Vespasian's army, which does not concern us, and Vespasian's fortitude in battle:

> Unoque et altero proelio tam constanter inito, ut in oppugnatione castelli lapidis ictum genu scutoque sagittas aliquot exceperit.

Ailloud notes that the *castellum* is Jotapata where Vespasian was wounded (BJ 3.236-239). But this dry narrative pales beside the vivid and dramatic description of BJ. Vespasian's foot is struck by an arrow and begins to bleed. Titus runs to his father, the army is thrown into terror, etc. The general masters his pain and encourages his army to fight all the more vigorously. All of the characteristic traits of BJ are present: drama, pathos, flattery of Titus and Vespasian, the fierce resistance of the Jews. This is too good to be true. Another important passage is *Titus* 4.3:

> Ex quaesturae deinde honore legioni praepositus Tarichaeas et Gamalam urbes Iudaeae validissimas in potestatem redegit, equo quadam acie sub feminibus amisso alteroque inscenso, cuius rector circa se dimicans occubuerat.

BJ 3.470-503 agrees in ascribing to Titus the lion's share of the capture of Taricheae. Gamala too owed its capture to the heroism of Titus (BJ 4.70-83). The story about Titus' horse shows that

---

[24] Weber 35 suggests that in Rome the report was received that the entire garrison had been wiped out.

Titus, like his father, did not hesitate to enter the thick of the battle.

g. Appian wrote a work called Ἐκατονϰετία which probably covered the century of 30 BCE to 69 CE although this is uncertain. It mentioned Josephus' prophecy to Vespasian but whatever else it said about the Jewish war is unknown.[25]

h. Dio Cassius has a rather extensive description (66.4.1-7.2) of Titus' siege of Jerusalem. It supplements and contradicts BJ in several points, large and small.[26] But not a word on the Galilean war.

2. Christian Literature

Christian writers delighted in describing the sufferings of the Jews. The number of works which may contain relevant material is enormous; I do not claim to have checked them all.[27] But Josephus so dominated Christian historiography that non-Josephan data are seldom (only caution prevents the declaration: never) encountered. Our texts of Josephus contain Christian matter—even aside from the notorious Testimonium—but who can declare with certainty what is a Christian interpolation? [28] The Galilean war, however, was

---

[25] *Appiani Historia Romana I: Prooemium ... Fragmenta*, ed. P. Viereck et A. G. Roos, addenda et corrigenda adiecit E. Gabba (Leipzig 1962) vii and 534 fragment 17.

[26] The most significant supplement is the fact that many Jews, not only of the Roman empire but also of πέραν Εὐφράτου, went to Palestine to help the revolutionaries (66.4.3). BJ mentions that the Jews of Palestine hoped for aid from across the Euphrates (1.5; 2.388; 6.343) and a handful of fighters from Adiabene is mentioned. But only much interest, if not intervention, in the war could explain why Josephus had to write an Aramaic BJ for the Jews of the East. Since the purpose of BJ was to restrict guilt, BJ never hints that the Jews of the Roman empire assisted the revolutionaries. If BJ is correct, why was the *fiscus Judaicus* levied on all the Jews of the empire, not just Palestine? The importance of Dio's remark was realized by Weber 21 but ignored by Schürer-Vermes 501 n. 83. See Smallwood, *Jews* 356-357. The passage is unknown to Neusner, *History of the Jews in Babylonia* 1.64-67. Another interesting addendum is that some Roman soldiers deserted to the Jews (Dio 66.5.4). See M. Stein, *The Relationship between Jewish, Greek and Roman Cultures* (Israel 1970) 56-57 (Heb.).

[27] I have perused all the important Fathers, especially the *Adversus Judaeos* literature. The indices to Migne *PG* and *PL* were consulted. For Byzantine literature the classic guide is still K. Krumbacher, *Geschichte der byzantinischen Literatur*[2] (Munich 1897). Cf. also M. E. Colonna, *Gli storici Bizantini dal IV al XV secolo: I storici profani* (Naples 1956).

[28] V. Ussani, *Rivista di Filologia* 42 (1914) 417-440; Eisler *passim*; E. M. Sanford, *TAPA* 66 (1935) 127-45; and Schreckenberg, *Tradition* 172-174.

theologically too insignificant to warrant much interpolation.

Some Byzantine accounts teem with blunders. A good example is Johannes Lydus *De Mensibus* 4.109 (p. 149 Wuensch):

> Cestius, the consular governor of Jerusalem, set up by night an image of Nero in the temple of the Hebrews, in order that Nero might share in the honor given to God. They (the Hebrews), being very upset, slew Cestius and all the Romans found in the east, and openly proclaimed war against their masters.

Petronius has become Cestius, Caligula has become Nero. All the Romans in the East are massacred in Mithridatic fashion. The war breaks out after the failure of the attempt to desecrate the temple, i.e. in 40-41 CE. The datum that the revolutionaries killed Cestius is opposed by Tacitus and Josephus; its context indicates that it is historically worthless. Such confusion is not rare in Byzantine literature.

3. *Rabbinic Literature*

Rabbinic historiography too excels in confusion, especially for the pre-70 period. The Talmudic sages were not historians. For them history was a branch of Aggadah: *nihil illicitum*. Neusner has shown that the Rabbis knew little about pre-70 Pharisaism, let alone Palestinian history, and what they report is usually untrustworthy.[29] The stories about the war of 66-70 CE and about Bar Kokhba too are an insoluble compound of fact and fantasy (mostly the latter). Optimistic scholars may search for historical "kernels" but to assume the existence of such kernels is often unjustified.[30]

Christian authors quote many passages which they ascribe to Josephus but which cannot be found in our texts. Revision and interpolation are not the only explanations. The book of *Jubilees* is occasionally confused with AJ (especially by Syncellus). See Eisler 1.521-527. Whether other fragments of "pseudo-Josephus" can be attributed to extant apocryphal works needs to be investigated.

[29] E.g., Alexander Jannaeus and John Hyrcanus are identified (B. Berakhoth 29a); Simon the Just heard a heavenly voice announcing the death of Caligula (B. Sotah 33a); the trial of Herod is distorted almost beyond recognition (B. Sanhedrin 19a-b). See Neusner, *Traditions*. On history as a branch of Aggadah, see I. Heinemann, *Darkhe ha Aggadah* (Jerusalem 1970) 17-18.

[30] J. Derenbourg, *Essai sur l'histoire et la géographie de la Palestine I: Histoire de la Palestine* (Paris 1867) 264-265, realizes the fantastic nature of most of the Rabbinic stories but he excels in searching for kernels. Thus on 291 he discusses Lamentations Rabbah on *Lamentations* 1.5. The vulgate text has, "Vespasian besieged Jerusalem for $3\frac{1}{2}$ years and with him were

Fortunately, we need not become entangled in this net. Fantastic stories about the Galilean war are lacking because, for the Rabbis too, the center of interest was the capture of Jerusalem and the destruction of the temple (almost the sole topics of the famous passage in B. Gittin 55b-58a).

Even when the Rabbis are at their historical best, they are fundamentally not interested in history. Their primary concern was Halachah; historical anecdotes, often of great value, usually were narrated only when the data impinged on some contentious point of law.[31] Consider T. Parah 9 (8).2:

> And thus was R. Judah accustomed to say, "The stream of Selame [32] is forbidden (to provide water for the red heifer ceremony) because it failed in the time of (the) war (*polemos*)." They said to him, "All the waters of creation failed in the time of (the) war (*polemos*). An ant was able to walk in Siloam."

R. Judah (floruit mid-second century) probably refers to the war of 66-70 since Galilee did not revolt with Bar Kokhba. Unfortunate-

---

four generals (*duces*, דוכסין), the *dux* of Arabia, the *dux* of Africa, the *dux* of Alexandria, the *dux* of Palestine (פלסטיני)." Buber's edition (p. 33a) has "Vespasian spent 3½ years at Jerusalem and with him were four generals (*duces*), the *dux* of Arabia, the *dux* of אפניקא (a mistake for Africa or Phoenicia), the *dux* of סיביתיני (a mistake for Sebastene or Palestine), the *dux* of Alexandria." Derenbourg sees here Tiberius Alexander (Alexandria; cf. ὁ τῆς πόλεως ἡγεμών, BJ 2.492), Agrippa II (Palestine), Malchus (Arabia; cf. BJ 3.68). The *dux* of Africa is left unexplained. If Derenbourg had seen Buber's edition (which was not published until 1899) he probably would have accepted the reading Phoenicia instead of Africa and identified the *dux* with Sohaemus king of Emesa (which for an Aggadist is close enough to Phoenicia), mentioned in BJ 2.501 and Tacitus *Historiae* 5.1.2. But is this procedure legitimate? The text is a late recension of a late story and is supported by nothing. Four *duces* were needed for the end of the story (each is assigned the destruction of one wall of the temple), so four were provided from the territories uppermost in the mind of the seventh century Palestinian story teller: Palestine itself, Alexandria, Arabia (whence the conquest of 640), and Africa (the genuine and unhistorical reading)—the province from which Heraclius had come as conqueror. The whole is worthless. See Neusner, *Development* 162-167 (a reprint of A. Cohen's translation with Neusner's comments) and 232. Many literary problems in this story still need investigation.

[31] E.g., the execution of R. Judah ben Baba by Roman legionaries is mentioned only to show the details of *semikha* (B. Sanhedrin 13b) or of the laws of fines (B. ʿAbodah Zarah 8b); the trip of R. Gamaliel to the governor of Syria is adduced only because the story has information on the intercalation of the calendar (B. Sanhedrin 11a).

[32] On the form צלמון for Σελάμη, see Schalit, *NWB* s.v. Σελάμη and *Sepher ha Yishub* I,1, ed. S. Klein (Jerusalem 1939) 165 with references.

ly, the only thing Josephus says about Selame is that he fortified it
(BJ 2.573//V 188). He provides no indication that there was a
stream in the vicinity, whether it failed or not. Although R.
Judah's bit of non-Josephan data is not particularly helpful or
significant, this passage is important for two reasons. (1) It exem-
plifies the Rabbinic tendency to narrate historical matter only
when Halachic consequences were involved. (2) It documents that
varied possibilities exist in the relationship of Rabbinic to Josephan
tradition. R. Judah's statement shows that some Rabbis had
access to detailed traditions about the war which do not derive
from Josephus. I shall argue elsewhere that the statement of R.
Judah's disputants is similar to BJ 5.409-410 and seems to derive
from it. Similarly, the story of Yohanan ben Zakkai's prophecy
to Vespasian seems to have been inspired by BJ's account of
Josephus' prophecy. Some Rabbis apparently knew BJ. This
entire problem requires further study.[33]

To return to our concern: because of its love for fantasy and
its general neglect of reliable historical material, Rabbinic literature is not the important source of non-Josephan data it could have
been. That aspect of V for which Rabbinic literature is most valuable is the aspect in which we are least interested here: the study
of Josephan *realia*. The Rabbis help us to identify many of V's
Galilean settlements [34] and provide information about buildings,

---

[33] There are numerous studies of the Yohanan saga. See e.g. Neusner,
Development and *Life*²; A. Schalit in *Aufstieg und Niedergang der antiken
Welt* II,2, ed. H. Temporini (Berlin 1975) 208-327; and A. J. Saldarini,
Journal for the Study of Judaism 6 (1975) 189-204. If the Talmudic Rabbis
did not know Josephus, then the earliest known Jewish reader of Josephus
(apart from Justus of Tiberias), is I think, the author of Josippon (tenth
century). Josephus is never mentioned by Talmudic literature. H. Graetz
thought he could identify Josephus in one passage and his opinion has gained
adherents: S. Rappaport, *Agada und Exegese bei Flavius Josephus* (Vienna
1930) xvi note 1 and L. Finkelstein, *Akiba* (1936, repr. N.Y. 1970) 141 and
150-152 (who list earlier literature). The text, from the treatise *Derekh Erez*
ed. Higger p. 183-188 = treatise *Kallah* ed. Higger 316-317, describes the
reception in Rome of four famous *Tannaim* by a philosopher (see the translation in Finkelstein). Graetz proposed that פילוסופוס is not *philosophus* but
Flavius Josephus. In fact in one—but only one—textual tradition פילוסופוס
is the man's name (והיה להם חבר אחד ופילוסופוס שמו, see Higger's apparatus). The tenuous nature of the whole matter is evident. Some medieval
rabbinists (the two treatises are medieval) did not know what פילוסופוס was
(cf. Tosaphoth to B. Shabbath 116a) and one scribe took it for a proper
name.
[34] A convenient collection of Rabbinic testimonia arranged alphabetically
by place name is *Sepher ha Yishub* (see note 32). The numerous but repetitive

synagogues, Halachic practices, and other such matters mentioned by Josephus.[35] Some individuals are mentioned by both Josephus and Rabbinic literature but the Rabbis know nothing about the revolutionary activities of any of the central figures of V.[36]

Only four texts need consideration here. The first (*Shir ha Shirim Zuta*, end) has been treated extensively by Lieberman and there is no reason to repeat his remarks.[37] Here is Lieberman's translation:

---

works of S. Klein dominate the field. See too M. Avi-Yonah, *Geographia* and *The Holy Land* (Grand Rapids 1966).

[35] E.g. the palace in Tiberias (V 65) perhaps appears in B. ʿAbodah Zarah 50a (and Epiphanius *Panarion* 30.12). See S. Lieberman, *JQR* 36 (1945) 366-367 and Klein, *Galilee* 41 n. 10. See too Stein ad loc. The olive oil of Gischala (V 74-75//BJ 2.591-592) was proverbial in Rabbinic literature. See *Siphre Deuteronomy* 316 and 355; T. Menahoth 9.5. Further passages are listed in Strack-Billerbeck, *Kommentar* 1.155-156 and L. Finkelstein, *The Pharisees*[3] (Philadelphia 1966) 52 and 192 with the notes. The synagogue of Tiberias (V 277) may be that of M. ʿErubin 10.10. Stein's commentary is particularly rich with such references.

[36] Derenbourg 267 suggested that the famous *Qamza* and *Bar Qamza* of the legend of the destruction of the temple are derived from Κομψὸς ὁ τοῦ Κομψοῦ (V 33). The Aggadist took a historical personage, split him in two, and transfered his locus from Tiberias to Jerusalem. Baer, *Zion* 36 (1971) 169-170 (Heb.), expands on this theme. Baer and Derenbourg at least realized that the Talmudic account is legend, not history. Klein, *Galilee* 41 accepts the story at face value and theorizes that Kompsos and his brother Crispus (= ציצית הכסת) moved from Jerusalem to Tiberias! Both names (Qamẓa and Kompsos) are quite rare—I have been unable to locate a second example of either—and it is not impossible that a very rich man may have played a prominent role both in Tiberias and Jerusalem, but the identification of a historical personage of Tiberias attested in a text of the first century with a legendary figure of Jerusalem attested in a text a few hundred years later is clearly so speculative as to be practically worthless. Derenbourg 268 suggests that the Joezer of the delegation (BJ 2.628//V 197) is the Joezer of M. ʿOrlah 2.12. The only certain attestations of the major figures of V are Simon ben Gamaliel (V 190-192; Rabbinic material in Neusner, *Traditions* 1.377-388) and Jesus ben Gamala (V 193 and 204; Rabbinic passages listed in Klausner 22-23). This Jesus probably is identical with the Jesus of AJ 20.213 and 223; thus Schürer 2.273; G. Hölscher, *Die Hohenpriesterliste bei Josephus* (Heidelberg 1940) 18 nr. 26; Y. Efron in *In Memory of Gedaliahu Alon: Essays in Jewish History*, ed. M. Dorman et al. (Israel 1970) 125 n. 286 (Heb.); Smallwood, *Jews* 313 n. 83. The only reason to distinguish them (as Niese and Feldman do in their indices s.v. Jesus nr. 11 and 14) is the change in the patronymic from Gamalas to Gamaliel but Josephus is very careless in such matters. Schalit (*NWB*) cannot decide. He recognizes two Jesus' (nr. 3 and nr. 17) but only one Gamaliel/Gamalas. In any event, the Rabbinic Simon and Jesus are not revolutionaries.

[37] S. Lieberman, *Greek in Jewish Palestine* (N.Y. 1942, repr. 1965) 179-184. See too Alon, *Studies* 1.266-267 n. 63.

Another interpretation. *'Flee my beloved'* (Song of Songs 8.14), when did it happen? In the time of Menahem and Hillel, when a dissension arose between them, and Menahem left together with eight hundred students who were dressed in golden scale armor; Ḥanin ben Matron came, and Juda the brother of Menahem kicked him to death. Eleazar and the students arose and killed Elḥanan and cut him to pieces. At that time the Romans went and encamped in Jerusalem where they defiled all the women. Eleazar and the students arose and brought the soldiers down from the camp; thereupon dissensions and quarrels broke out in Jerusalem. (It is in reference) to this hour that the verse says: *'Flee my beloved'*.

The passage is very confused. Menahem, the colleague of Hillel, is confused with Menahem the revolutionary. Eleazar ben Simon, the leader of the Zealots who killed Ananus ben Ananus (= Elḥanan, according to Lieberman; see BJ 4.315-316) is identified with Eleazar ben Ananias, the leader of the priestly party who massacred the Roman garrison (BJ 2.453-454). The order of events is reversed (Ananus was killed a year or so after the massacre of the garrison).[38] If anything can be extracted from this text, it is that Menahem's party killed Ananias ben Nedebaeus (identified by Lieberman with Hanin ben Matron; see BJ 2.441) and that Eleazar's party massacred the Roman garrison. Without BJ's assistance this passage would be totally incomprehensible. With BJ's aid we see that it is not reliable.

The second text is from the Fathers according to Rabbi Nathan, version A chapter 4 = version B chapter 6 (pp. 10a and 11b ed. Schechter), one of the versions of the Yohanan ben Zakkai saga. When Vespasian (in version A) or Yohanan (in version B) asked the Jews why they persisted in their insane struggle, they responded:

A	B
Just as we fought the two who were before you and killed them, thus we shall fight you and kill you.	Just as we fought the earlier generals and killed them, thus we shall fight this one and kill him.

The difference between the "two" of version A and the "generals" of version B is slight (שרים/שנים) and which is original is unclear. Before Vespasian the Jews had faced Cestius and another general who may be Florus or Metilius.[39] The Jews killed none of these

---

[38] If we resolutely wanted to save this text, we could emend "Elhanan" to "Menahem" and all would be fine.

[39] See Derenbourg 284-285 and L. Finkelstein, *Introduction to the Treatises Abot and Abot of Rabbi Nathan* (N.Y. 1950) 38 n. 63 (Heb.).

(although cf. Lydus on Cestius and Suetonius on Metilius, both cited above) and the Aggadist (or the Jews!) is guilty of exaggeration. At least this section of the Yohanan saga seems plausible.

Lamentations Rabbah 2.2 p. 53b Buber = Y. Ta'anith 4.8 p. 69a is our next passage.[40]

> The register [41] of three towns used to go to Jerusalem in a wagon: Chabul, Asochis, and Taricheae.[42] All three were destroyed, Chabul because of dissension, Asochis because of magic, and Taricheae because of fornication.

The three towns were once so wealthy that a wagon was needed to carry their *tomos* to Jerusalem, but, for various reasons, they were destroyed. When? Klein suggests the Galilean war of 66-67 CE. He cites BJ 2.503-504, the plunder and burning of Chabul, and BJ 3.462ff, the capture of Taricheae. The destruction of Asochis will be a new piece of data not provided by Josephus.[43] Klein may be correct but another historical context may fit just as well. Galilee was the scene of warfare on a number of later occasions, and notably in the 350's when the Jews revolted against Ursicinus and Gallus. The sources—mostly Christian—speak of the destruction (obviously an exaggeration) of Tiberias, Sepphoris, and (in the south) Lydda. The revolt was centered in Galilee and archaeology shows that Beth Shearim was destroyed at this time.[44]

---

[40] There are some textual disagreements between the Palestinian Talmud (whose text here is identical in MS Leiden Scal. 3 folio 646 [see the photographic edition published by Kedem, Jerusalem 1971], the editio princeps [Venice 1523], and the vulgate edition [Krotoschin 1866]) and Buber's edition of Lamentations Rabbah, but they do not affect our discussion.

[41] Reading הטטמוס, "the τόμος." For the various explanations of this word, see the standard lexica. The text in Lamentations Rabbah is corrupt.

[42] מגדל, with or without צבעייא, is Taricheae. See Klein, *Galilee* 199-201.

[43] Klein 50-51. We cannot be certain that the three cities were destroyed at the same time. For Aggadic compression see Neusner, *Development* 8, and Heinemann, *Darkhe ha Aggadah*, chapter four. Josephus subsequently pitched camp at Chabul (V 213, 227, 234); this is uncertain evidence, perhaps more likely to indicate that the site had remained empty. That Josephus still refers to it as a κώμη could be explained as a reference to the ruins.

[44] The best modern account of this war is by M. Avi-Yonah, *The Jews of Palestine* (Oxford 1976) 176-181. The archaeological evidence from Beth Shearim is conveniently summarized by Avi-Yonah, *Encyclopedia* (n. 1 supra) 1.229 and 234. A synagogue of Caesarea too was destroyed in the middle of the fourth century; see *Encyclopedia* 1.278. S. Lieberman, *JQR* 36 (1945) 329-344, minimizes the extent and importance of this revolt, but, even if the Christian sources exaggerate, we cannot dismiss the archaeological evidence; see Lieberman's clarification, *JQR* 37 (1947) 423-424. See further

Asochis is on the road from Ptolemais, the base of operations for Romans operating in Galilee (as in 67), to Sepphoris. Chabul is nearby. Taricheae borders the other center of the revolt, Tiberias. The pericope thus *may* refer to this Galilean war.[45]

This fighting in the 350's can explain another reference to the destruction of Galilee. The text is Y. Shabbath 16.8 p. 15d.

> R. 'Ullah said, "He (R. Yohanan ben Zakkai) spent [46] eighteen years in that town of Garaba but only these two cases came before him. He said, 'Galilee, Galilee, you hated the Torah. Your end will be to...[47]'."

The Mishnah records only two cases which R. Yohanan ben Zakkai adjudicated while in Galilee, apparently before the war of 66-70. R. 'Ullah noticed this anomaly and deduced the moral placed in R. Yohanan's mouth.[48] R. 'Ullah was a contemprorary of the war of the 350's [49] and so it seems reasonable to understand his statement as a commentary on the troubles of his own day.

We mention last the references in *Megillath Ta'anith*, a calendar

---

S. Baron, *Social and Religious History of the Jews II*[2] (N.Y. 1952) 398 n. 11 and J. Neusner, *History of the Jews in Babylonia* 4.28-29 and 31-32 n. 3. The editing of the Palestinian Talmud is usually ascribed to the late fourth century. The date of Lamentations Rabbah is uncertain. It may be as late as the seventh or eighth century (see n. 30 above) but it is certainly not earlier than 350.

[45] An analogous case of ambiguous identity can be cited from the midrash on *Lamentations* 1.17 which lists five pairs of mutually hostile cities, among them Tiberias and Hippos (Lamentations Rabbah p. 46a ed. Buber). This passage could be taken as a commentary to V 42, but the list seems to refer to conditions of the late third century. See M. Avi-Yonah, *Carta's Atlas of the Period of the Second Temple, the Mishnah, and the Talmud* (Jerusalem 1966, repr. 1970) 89, map 137 (Heb.).

[46] Codex Leiden fol. 377, the editio princeps, and the editio vulgaris agree on עביד הוי יהיב. R. Nissim Gaon on B. Shabbath 47b (to which I am referred by B. Ratner, *Ahabath Zion ve Yerushalayim* on Y. Shabbath [Vilna 1902, repr. 1967] 151) has a doctored reading, י״ח שנין עבד רבן יוחנן בן זכאי, יתיב בהדה ערב. The text seems to be conflated from עביד הוי and הוי יהיב) יהיב is obviously corrupt).

[47] The meaning of לעשות במציקין is obscure. See the repertory of conjectures in Neusner, *Life*[2] 51 n. 1. Some testimonia (including MS Leiden) have מסיקין which does not affect anything; cf. B. Baba Qamma 116b.

[48] Cf. Neusner, *Development* 133-134, "The likelihood is that the saying is pseudepigraphic, and that 'Ulla is responsible for it. He may have taken a famous maxim and put it in Yohanan's mouth."

[49] See the standard biographical dictionaries: Z. Frankel, *Mebo ha Yerushalmi* (Breslau 1870, repr. Jerusalem 1967) 119b; A. Hyman, *Toledoth Tannaim ve Amoraim* (repr. Jerusalem 1964) 974; M. Margalioth ed., *Encyclopedia of Talmudic and Geonic Literature* (Tel Aviv 1960) 716 (Heb.).

of the holidays on which fasting was prohibited. The calendar
itself consists of laconic entries in Aramaic, all obscure. The Hebrew
scholia are late and nearly worthless. The classic edition considers
four dates as references to the events of 66-67 CE but the matter
is so uncertain that a policy of reserve is the best course.[50] The
one identification which seems least uncertain we have accepted
above in chapter one.

D. *Conclusion*

A survey of all non-Josephan sources [51] confirms what was
already known. Our knowledge of the early stages of the war
depends almost entirely on Josephus. External data verify the
following points: the pro-Roman sentiments of Sepphoris, the defeat
of Cestius and the general course of the war. New data is provided on the death of Cestius. But on the situation in Galilee, on
the political parties within the revolutionary movements, and on the
central command of the war before 68 CE, the sources are silent.

---

[50] H. Lichtenstein, "Die Fastenrolle: Eine Untersuchung zur jüdisch-
hellenistische Geschichte," *HUCA* 8-9 (1931-32) 257-351. See his discussion
of 25 Sivan, 4 Elul, 17 Elul, and 22 Elul, on 302-307. On the entry for 17
Elul see chapter one above note 3. Klein, *Galilee* 50-54, cites other alleged
Rabbinic references to the Galilean war, but all are problematic.

[51] I have deliberately avoided discussion of Hegesippus, Josippon, and
the Slavonic Josephus. All three betray that peculiar blend of fact and
fantasy in which medieval historiography delighted. A full collection and
study of all the medieval traditions which supplement Josephus is needed.
Perhaps some of these traditions will be of value.

SYNOPTIC OUTLINE OF V AND BJ

For the convenience of the reader I print here in synoptic form an outline of the entire autobiography and the section of BJ parallel to it. Items which appear in different sequences in the two works are enclosed in parentheses. In this table the order of V is taken as the base and the order of BJ as the variable; on pp. 68-69 is a table which has the order of BJ as the base and the order of V as the variable. These synopses help elucidate the literary structure of each work. For an outline of the chronological contradictions between V and BJ, see pp. 3-7.

	Vita		BJ 2
1-12	Pedigree, youth, education		
13-16	Embassy to Rome		
17-23	Opposition to war		
		449-456	Massacre of the Roman garrison
(25-26	Massacres in Syria)	457-480	Massacres in Caesarea and Syria
(46-61	Conditions in Gamala)	481-483	Noarus attacks Jews
		484-486	Rebels take Cypros and Machaerus
		487-498	Riots in Alexandria
24	Defeat of Cestius	499-555	Defeat of Cestius
		556-558	Distinguished Jews flee to Cestius
25-26	Massacres in Syria	(457-480	Massacres in Caesarea and Syria)
27	Massacre in Damascus	559-561	Massacre in Damascus
		562-568	Appointment of generals
28-29	Appointment of Josephus		
30a	Josephus arrives in Galilee	569a	Josephus arrives in Galilee
30-31	Conditions in Sepphoris		
32-42	Conditions in Tiberias		
43-45	Conditions in Gischala		
46-61	Conditions in Gamala	(481-483	Noarus attacks Jews)
62-69	Destruction of the palace in Tiberias		
(79	Josephus establishes a supreme council)	569b-571	Josephus establishes a supreme council

(77a	Fortification of cities)	}	572-575	Fortification of cities
(186b-189	Fortification of cities)			
(77b-78	Military arrangements)		576-584	Recruitment and training of an army
70-76	Schemes of John of Gischala		585-592	Schemes of John of Gischala
77-78	Fortification of cities and military arrangements		(572-584	Fortification and recruitment)
79	Josephus establishes a supreme council		(570-571	Josephus establishes a supreme council)
80-84	Josephus' integrity and popularity			
85-103	John at Tiberias		(614-623	John at Tiberias)
104-111	Josephus and Jesus at Sepphoris			
112-113	Refugees from Trachonitis			
114	Agrippa attacks Gamala			
115-121	Josephus skirmishes with Romans			
122-125	John tries to remove Josephus		593-594	John tries to remove Josephus
126-148	Dabaritta affair		595-613	Dabaritta affair
(85-103	John at Tiberias)		614-623	John at Tiberias
(369b-372	Dispersal of John's followers)		624-625	Dispersal of John's followers
(190-335	Delegation from Jerusalem)		626-631	Delegation from Jerusalem
(372b	John is restricted to Gischala)		632a	John is restricted to Gischala
149-154	Refugees from Trachonitis			
155-173	Revolt of Tiberias		632b-645a	Revolt of Tiberias
174-178	Josephus and Justus			
179-186a	Philip, Agrippa, and Gamala			
186b-189	Fortifications		(573-575	Fortifications)
190-335	Delegation from Jerusalem		(626-631	Delegation from Jerusalem)
336-367	Digression against Justus			
368-372a	Dispersal of John's followers		(622-625	Dispersal of John's followers)
372b	John is restricted to Gischala		(632a	John is restricted to Gischala)
373-380	Revolt of Sepphoris		645b-646	Revolt of Sepphoris and Tiberias
381-389	Revolt of Tiberias			
390-393	Flight of Justus			
394-397	Revolt of Sepphoris			
398-406	Fighting with Sulla			
			647-651	Situation in Jerusalem
			652-654	Situation in Akrabatene and Idumaea

BIBLIOGRAPHY

A. *Editions and Translations of Josephus*

Feldman, Louis H. See Thackeray below.
Haefeli, Leo. *Flavius Josephus' Lebensbeschreibung.* Münster i.W. 1925.
Marcus, Ralph. See Thackeray below.
Michel, Otto, and Bauernfeind, Otto. *Der jüdische Krieg.* 4 vols. Bad Homburg/Munich 1960-69.
Naber, Samuel A. *Flavii Josephi Opera Omnia.* 6 vols. Leipzig 1888-1896.
Niese, Benedictus. *Flavii Josephi Opera.* 7 vols. Berlin 1885-1895.
Pelletier, André. *Flavius Josèphe: Autobiographie.* Paris 1959.
Reinach, Théodore, ed. *Oeuvres complètes de Flavius Josèphe.* 7 vols. Paris 1900-1932.
Ricciotti, Giuseppe. *Flavio Giuseppe tradotto e commentato.* 3 vols. Torino 1949.
Schalit, Abraham. *Flavii Josephi Antiquitates Judaicae in linguam hebraicam vertit.* 3 vols. Jerusalem 1963. (The introduction to this work is cited as "Schalit, introduction".)
Simḥoni, Y.N. *Yoseph ben Matityahu: Toledot Milḥemet ha Yehudim ʿim ha Roma'im.* Jerusalem 1956.
Stein, Menaḥem (Edmund). *Ḥayye Yoseph.* Tel Aviv 1959.
Thackeray, Henry St. John; Marcus, Ralph; Wikgren, Allen; and Feldman Louis H. *Josephus.* 9 vols. Harvard 1926-1965. Loeb Classical Library.

B. *Editions of Classical Authors*

I have regularly used the Teubner editions with the following exceptions:
Aeneas Tacticus and Onasander:
    Illinois Greek Club. *Aeneas Tacticus, Asclepiodotus, Onasander.* London/New York 1923. Loeb Classical Library.
Aristeas:
    Pelletier, André. *Lettre d'Aristée à Philocrate.* Paris 1962.
Lucian:
    Homeyer, H. *Lukian: Wie man Geschichte schreiben soll: Griechisch und Deutsch.* Munich 1965.
Photius:
    Henry, René. *Photius Bibliothèque.* Paris 1959ff.
Suetonius:
    Ailloud, Henri. *Suétone: Vies des douze Césars.* 3 vols. Paris 1931-1932. (I have retained Ihm's section numbers.)

C. *Books and Articles*

Works cited only once or twice are normally not listed here.

Alon, Gedaliahu. *Studies in Jewish History.* 2 vols. Israel 1967. Heb.
——. *Toledot ha Yehudim be Erez Yisrael bi Tequfat ha Mishnah ve ha Talmud.* 2 vols. Israel 1967.
Applebaum, Shimon. "The Struggle for the Soil and the Revolt of 66-73 C.E." *EI* 12 (1975) 125-128.
Attridge, Harold. *The Interpretation of Biblical History in the Antiquitates Judaicae of Flavius Josephus.* Missoula 1976.

Avenarius, Gert. *Lukians Schrift zur Geschichtsschreibung.* Meisenheim/Glan 1956.
Avi-Yonah, Michael. "The Foundation of Tiberias." *IEJ* 1 (1950/51 160-69).
——. *Geographia Historit shel Erez Yisra'el.* Jerusalem 1951.
——. "The Missing Fortress of Flavius Josephus." *IEJ* 3 (1953) 94-98.
Baer, Yizḥak. "Jerusalem in the Times of the Great Revolt." *Zion* 36 (1971) 127-190. Heb.
Baerwald, Aron. *Flavius Josephus in Galiläa, sein Verhältniss zu den Parteien insbesondere zu Justus von Tiberias und König Agrippa II.* Breslau 1877.
Bar-Kochva, B. "The Fortresses of Josephus in Galilee." *IEJ* 24 (1974) 108-116.
Bardy, G. "Éditions et rééditions d'ouvrages patristiques." *Revue Bénédictine* 47 (1935) 356-380.
Baron, Salo W. *A Social and Religious History of the Jews: Ancient Times I-II.* 2nd ed. N.Y. 1952.
Bardon, Henry. *La littérature latine inconnue II: L'époque imperiale.* Paris 1956.
——. *Les empereurs et les lettres latines d'Auguste à Hadrien.* 2nd ed. Paris 1968.
Bauer, Walter. "Jesus der Galiläer." *Festgabe für Adolf Julicher zum 70. Geburtstag.* Tübingen 1927. 16-34.
Birt, Theodore. "Verlag und Schriftstellereinnahmen im Altertum." *RhM* 72 (1917/18) 311-316.
Bloch, Heinrich. *Die Quellen des Flavius Josephus in seiner Archäologie.* Leipzig 1879.
Blumenthal, Fritz. "Die Autobiographie des Augustus." *Wiener Studien* 35 (1913) 113-130, 267-288; 36 (1914) 84-103.
Brandon, S. G. F. *Jesus and the Zealots.* N.Y. 1967.
Briessmann, Adalbert. *Tacitus und das Flavische Geschichtsbild.* Wiesbaden 1955.
Brunt, Peter A. "Josephus on Social Conflicts in Roman Judaea." *Klio* 59 (1977) 149-153.
Burck, Erich. "Wahl und Anordnung des Stoffes; Führung der Handlung." *Wege zu Livius.* ed. E. Burck. Darmstadt 1967. 331-351.
Cadbury, H. J. *The Making of Luke-Acts.* N.Y. 1927.
Collomp, Paul, "La place de Josèphe dans la technique de l'historiographie hellénistique." *Publications de la Faculté des lettres de l'Université de Strasbourg 106: Études historiques.* Paris 1947. 81-92.
Derenbourg, Josèphe. *Essai sur l'histoire et la géographie de la Palestine d'après les Thalmuds et les autres sources rabbiniques.* Paris 1867.
Destinon, Justus von. *Die Quellen des Flavius Josephus I: Die Quellen der Archäologie Buch XII-XVII = Jüdische Krieg Buch I.* Kiel 1882.
Drexler, Hans. "Untersuchungen zu Josephus und zur Geschichte des jüdischen Aufstandes 66-70." *Klio* 19 n.F. 1 (1925) 277-312.
Drüner, Hans. *Untersuchungen über Josephus.* Marburg 1896.
Eisler, Robert. *Jesous Basileus ou Basileusas.* 2 vols. Heidelberg 1929.
Emonds, Hilarius. *Zweite Auflage im Altertum: Kulturgeschichtliche Studien zur Ueberlieferung der antiken Literatur.* Leipzig 1941.
Everts, P. S. *De Tacitea Historiae Conscribendae Ratione.* Utrecht 1926.
Farmer, William R. *Maccabees, Zealots, and Josephus.* N.Y. 1956.
Feldman, Louis H. "Hellenizations in Josephus' Portrayal of Man's Decline." *Religions in Antiquity: Essays in Memory of E. R. Goodenough.* ed. J. Neusner. Leiden 1968. 336-353.

Frankfort, Th. "La date de l'autobiographie de Flavius Josèphe et des oeuvres de Justus de Tibériade." *RBPh* 39 (1961) 52-58."
——. "Le royaume d'Agrippa II et son annexion par Domitien." *Hommages à Albert Grenier.* ed. M. Renard. Brussels 1962. 659-72.
Gelzer, Matthias. "Die Vita des Josephus." *Kleine Schriften III.* Wiesbaden 1964. 299-325.
Goldstein, Jonathan. *I Maccabees.* N.Y. 1976.
Graetz, H. *Geschichte der Juden III.* 5th ed. ed. M. Brann. Leipzig 1906.
Gutschmid, Alfred von. "Vorlesungen über Josephus' Bücher gegen Apion." *Kleine Schriften IV.* ed. F. Rühl. Leipzig 1893. 336-589.
Hägg, Tomas. *Photios als Vermittler antiker Literatur.* Uppsala 1975.
Har-El, M. "The Zealots' Fortresses in Galilee." *IEJ* 22 (1972), 123-130.
Heinemann, Isaak. "Josephus' Method in the Presentation of Jewish Antiquities." *Zion* 5 (1940) 180-203. Heb.
Helm, Rudolf. Review of Laqueur. *PhW* 41 (1921) 481-493, 505-516.
Hengel, Martin. *Die Zeloten: Untersuchungen zur jüdischen Freiheitsbewegung in der Zeit von Herodes I bis 70 n. Chr.* Leiden 1961.
Hill, George F. *Catalogue of the Greek Coins of Palestine.* London 1914.
Hölscher, Gustav. *Die Quellen des Josephus für die Zeit vom Exil bis zum jüdischen Kriege.* Leipzig 1904.
——. "Josephus nr. 2." *PW* 9, 2 (1916) 1934-2000.
Hornbostel, Wilhelm. *De Flavii Josephi Studiis Rhetoricis Quaestiones Selectae.* Halle 1912.
Jacoby, Felix. "Justus nr. 9, Justus aus Tiberias." *PW* 10,2 (1919) 1341-1346.
——. *Die Fragmente der griechischen Historiker.* 15 vols. repr. Leiden 1964-1969.
Jones, A. H. M. "The Urbanization of Palestine." *JRS* 21 (1931) 78-85.
——. "The Urbanization of the Iturean Principality." *JRS* 21 (1931) 265-275.
——. *The Herods of Judaea.* Oxford 1938.
——. *Cities of the Eastern Roman Provinces.* 2nd ed. Oxford 1971.
Kadman, Leo. *The Coins of the Jewish War of 66-73 C.E.* Jerusalem 1960.
Kindler, Arie. *The Coins of Tiberias.* Tiberias 1961.
Klausner, Joseph. *Historiah shel ha Bayyit ha Sheni V.* 2nd ed. Jerusalem 1951.
Klein, Samuel. *Galilee.* Jerusalem 1967. Heb.
Kreissig, Heinz. *Die sozialen Zusammenhänge des judäischen Krieges.* Berlin 1970.
Laqueur, Richard. *Der jüdische Historiker Flavius Josephus.* Giessen 1920. repr. Darmstadt 1970.
Leo, Friedrich. *Die griechisch-römische Biographie nach ihrer litterarischen Form.* Leipzig 1901.
——. "Die römische Poesie in der sullanischen Zeit." *Ausgewählte Kleine Schriften I.* ed. E. Fraenkel. Rome 1960. 249-282.
Lichtenstein, Hans. "Die Fastenrolle: Eine Untersuchung zur jüdisch-hellenistische Geschichte." *HUCA* 8-9 (1931-32) 257-351.
Lieberman, Saul. *Greek in Jewish Palestine.* 2nd ed. N.Y. 1965.
——. *Hellenism in Jewish Palestine.* 2nd ed. N.Y. 1962.
Lindner, Helgo. *Die Geschichtsauffassung des Flavius Josephus im Bellum Judaicum.* Leiden 1972.
Luther, H. *Josephus und Justus von Tiberias. Ein Beitrag zur Geschichte des jüdischen Aufstandes.* Halle 1910.
Malinowski, Francis X. "Galilean Judaism in the Writings of Flavius Josephus." PhD dissertation, Duke University, 1973.

Marrou, H. I. "La technique de l'édition à l'époque patristique." *Vigiliae Christianae* 3 (1949) 208-224.

Meshorer, Ya'akov. *Jewish Coins of the Second Temple Period.* trans. I. H. Levine. Tel-Aviv 1967.

Misch, Georg. *A History of Autobiography in Antiquity.* 2 vols. London 1950.

Möller, Christa, and Götz Schmitt. *Siedlungen Palästinas nach Flavius Josephus.* Wiesbaden 1976.

Momigliano, Arnaldo. *The Development of Greek Biography.* Harvard 1971.

Motzo, Bacchisio. *Saggi di Storia e Letteratura Giudeo-Ellenistica.* Florence 1924.

Naber, Samuel A. "Observationes Criticae in Flavium Josephum." *Mnemosyne* n.s. 13 (1885) 263-284, 352-399.

Narkiss, M. *Coins of Palestine I: Jewish Coins.* Jerusalem 1936. Heb.

———. "The Sepphorenes and Vespasian." *Bulletin of the Israel Exploration Society* 17 (1953) 108-120. Heb.

Neusner, Jacob. *A History of the Jews in Babylonia I* and *IV.* Leiden 1965 and 1969.

———. *Development of a Legend.* Leiden 1970.

———. *Life of Yohanan ben Zakkai.* 2nd ed. Leiden 1970.

———. *The Rabbinic Traditions about the Pharisees before 70.* 3 vols. Leiden 1970.

———. "Josephus's Pharisees." *Ex Orbe Religionum: Studia Geo Widengren ... oblata I.* Leiden 1972. 224-244.

Niese, Benedictus. "Der jüdische Historiker Josephus." *HZ* 76 (1896) 193-237.

Nissen, H. *Kritische Untersuchungen über die Quellen der vierten und fünften Dekade des Livius.* Berlin 1863.

Otto, Walter. *Herodes: Beiträge zur Geschichte des letzten jüdischen Königshauses.* Stuttgart 1913.

Palm, Jonas. *Ueber Sprache und Stil des Diodoros von Sizilien.* Lund 1955.

Pelletier, André. *Flavius Josèphe adapteur de la lettre d'Aristée: une réaction atticisante contre la Koiné.* Paris 1962.

Peter, Hermann. *Die geschichtliche Litteratur über die Römische Kaiserzeit bis Theodosius I.* 2 vols. Leipzig 1897. repr. Hildesheim 1967.

———. *Historicorum Romanorum Reliquiae.* 2 vols. Leipzig 1906-1914.

———. *Wahrheit und Kunst: Geschichtschreibung und Plagiat im klassischen Altertum.* Leipzig 1911. repr. Hildesheim 1965.

Petersen, Hans. "Real and Alleged Literary Projects of Josephus." *AJP* 79 (1958) 259-274.

Prager, I. *Ueber das Verhältniss des Flavius Josephus zur Zelotenpartei beim Ausbruch des jüdischen Krieges.* Breslau 1873.

Radin, Max. "The Pedigree of Josephus." *CP* 24 (1929) 193-196.

Rajak, Tessa. "Justus of Tiberias." *CQ* n.s. 23 (1973) 345-368.

Rasp, H. "Flavius Josephus und die jüdischen Religionsparteien." *ZNW* 23 (1924) 27-47.

Rhoads, David M. *Israel in Revolution 6-74 C.E.* Philadelphia 1976.

Richards, G. C. "The Composition of Josephus' *Antiquities.*" *CQ* 33 (1939) 36-40.

Roth, Cecil. "The Pharisees in the Jewish Revolution of 66-73." *JSS* 7 (1962) 63-80.

———. "The Constitution of the Jewish Republic of 66-70." *JSS* 9 (1964) 295-319.

Rühl, Franz. "Justus von Tiberias." *RhM* 71 (1916) 289-308.

Russell, D. A. "Plutarch's Life of Coriolanus." *JRS* 53 (1963) 21-28.
Schäublin, C. "*Mēte prostheinai mēt' aphelein.*" *MH* 31 (1974) 144-149.
Schalit, Abraham. "Josephus und Justus: Studien zur Vita des Josephus." *Klio* 26 (1933) 67-95.
——. " 'Ematai katab Yoseph ben Mattityahu 'et Sepher Ḥayyav ?" *Zion* o.s. 5 (1933) 174-186.
——. *Namenwörterbuch zu Flavius Josephus.* Leiden 1968. (cited as Schalit, *NWB*).
Scheller, Paul. *De Hellenistica Historiae Conscribendae Arte.* Leipzig 1911.
Schemann, Friedrich. *Die Quellen des Flavius Josephus in der jüdischen Archaeologie Buch XVIII-XX = Polemos II cap. vii-xiv, 3.* Marburg 1887.
Schlatter, Adolf. *Der Bericht über das Ende Jerusalems: Ein Dialog mit Wilhelm Weber.* Gütersloh 1923. repr. *Kleinere Schriften zu Flavius Josephus.* ed. K. H. Rengstorf. Darmstadt 1970. 1-64.
——. *Wie sprach Josephus von Gott?* Gütersloh 1910. repr. *Kleinere Schriften zu Flavius Josephus.* ed. K. H. Rengstorf. Darmstadt 1970. 65-142.
——. *Die hebräische Namen bei Josephus.* Gütersloh 1913. repr. *Kleinere Schriften zu Flavius Josephus.* ed. K. H. Rengstorf. Darmstadt 1970. 143-272.
Schneider, Rudolf. "Griechische Poliorketiker." *Abhandlungen der königl. Gesellschaft der Wissenschaften zu Göttingen, philol.-hist. Klasse* 10-12 (1908-1910).
Schreckenberg, Heinz. *Bibliographie zu Flavius Josephus.* Leiden 1968.
——. *Die Flavius-Josephus-Tradition in Antike und Mittelalter.* Leiden 1972.
——. *Rezeptionsgeschichtliche und textkritische Untersuchungen zu Flavius Josephus.* Leiden 1977.
Schürer, Emil. *Geschichte des jüdischen Volkes im Zeitalter Jesu Christi.* 3 vols. 3rd and 4th ed. Leipzig 1901-1909.
——. *The History of the Jewish People in the Age of Jesus Christ I.* trans. and ed. G. Vermes and F. Millar. Edinburgh 1973.
Seyrig, Henri. "Irenopolis-Neronias-Sepphoris." *Numismatic Chronicle* 6th ser. 10 (1950) 284-289.
——. "Irenopolis-Neronias-Sepphoris: An Additional Note." *Numismatic Chronicle* 6th ser. 15 (1955) 157-159.
——. "Monnaies Hellénistiques: Les Eres d'Agrippa II." *Revue Numismatique* 6th ser. 6 (1964) 55-65.
Sherwin-White, A. N. *Roman Society and Roman Law in the New Testament.* Oxford 1963. repr. 1969.
Shutt, R. J. H. *Studies in Josephus.* London 1961.
Smallwood, E. Mary. *The Jews under Roman Rule from Pompey to Diocletian.* Leiden 1976.
Smith, Morton. "Zealots and Sicarii: Their Origins and Relation." *HTR* 64 (1971) 1-19.
Stein, Menaḥem (Edmund). *The Relationship between Jewish, Greek and Roman Cultures.* Israel 1970. Heb.
Stern, Menaḥem. *Greek and Latin Authors on Jews and Judaism I.* Jerusalem 1974.
Tcherikover, V. A. "Was Jerusalem a 'Polis'?" *IEJ* 14 (1964) 61-78.
Thackeray, Henry St. J. *Josephus the Man and the Historian.* N.Y. 1929. repr. N.Y. 1967.
——. *A Lexicon to Josephus.* 4 parts. (parts 2-4 with R. Marcus). Paris 1930-1955.

Van Unnik, W. C. "De la regle *mēte prostheinai mēte aphelein* dans l'histoire du canon." *Vigiliae Christianae* 3 (1949) 1-36.
Wacholder, Ben Zion. *Nicolaus of Damascus.* Berkeley 1962.
———. *Eupolemus: A Study of Judaeo-Greek Literature.* Cincinnati 1974.
Weber, Wilhelm. *Josephus und Vespasian: Untersuchungen zu dem jüdischen Krieg des Flavius Josephus.* Berlin 1921.
Westermann, Antonius. *Biographi: Vitarum Scriptores Graeci Minores.* Braunschweig 1845. repr. Amsterdam 1964.
Wolff, Alfredus. *De Flavii Josephi Belli Judaici Scriptoris Studiis Rhetoricis.* Halle 1908.
Yavetz, Zvi. "Reflections on Titus and Josephus." *GRBS* 16 (1975) 411-432.

ADDENDA

32 n. 29

The Qumran Temple Scroll's thematic rearrangement of the legal portions of the Pentateuch is similar to Josephus'; see Y. Yadin, *The Temple Scroll* (Jerusalem 1977) 1.62 n. 73 (Heb.).

36 top:

An exception to my generalization is the book of *Samuel*, several different recensions of which were current in the first century. The nature of the text which Josephus used when paraphrasing *Samuel* has been investigated in a recent book by E. C. Ulrich.

36 n. 46:

But Josephus did manage to tame the barbaric "semitic" character of the Greek of I *Maccabees*; see p. 45 n. 80.

88-89 n. 11:

For other examples of Josephus' newly found concern for purity, see AJ 18.37-38 (discussed on p. 140) and AJ 19.331 (discussed on p. 148).

92-93 n. 26:

Note the striking parallel between the following two thematic transitions: Moses, having successfully completed his legislation (*nomothesia*), turned his attention to matters of war (*polemika*), especially his army (AJ 3.287); Josephus, having established the laws (*nomima*) for the governance of the cities, turned his attention to security matters (BJ 2.572), specifically fortifications (BJ 2.573-575) and an army (576-584). This parallel too, I think, is the result more of Josephan thematic technique than of an attempt to portray Josephus as a second Moses.

106 n. 27:

On a youth's tour of various philosophical schools, see N. Hyldahl, *Philosophie und Christentum* (Copenhagen 1966) 148-152, who discusses V 10-12.

111 n. 45:

The sloppiness of Josephan procedure was unappreciated also by I. Lévy, *La légende de Pythagore de Grèce en Palestine* (Paris 1927) 236 (on the appearance of the Pharisees in AJ 17.41).

111 second paragraph:

"John (70)" probably should be deleted since Josephus claims that he is reporting an observation he made in 66 CE.

167 middle:

Wherever Solyme may have been, V 187 (Josephus fortified Seleucia and Sogane) seems to contradict BJ 4.4 (Sogane and Seleucia were won over by Agrippa at the beginning of the revolt). On the exaggerations of the fortification list see p. 205 n. 45.

171 n. 219:

103 years apiece for the Maccabeans and the Herodians is the calculation also of the *Seder 'Olam Zuta* p. 71 ed. Neubauer. Cf. too Joseph ibn 'Aknin, *Divulgatio Mysteriorum Luminumque Apparentia: Commentarius in Canticum Canticorum*, ed. A. S. Halkin (Jerusalem 1964) 451 (Heb.).

176 n. 236:
   AJ 18.37-38 too seems to have been added after 93/4; see p. 140.

186 n. 10:
   I realize that my exegesis of BJ 2.651 does not follow the natural meaning
of the text which seems to apologize for Ananus' revolutionary actions by
asserting that Ananus was not fully committed to the war even in the fall
of 66. If this interpretation is right, BJ 2.651 is wrong (in addition to the
arguments advanced here see p. 204) and comes as a surprise after BJ
2.647-650.

191 n. 21:
Thackeray mistranslates BJ 2.343; cf. 2.421.

220 top:
   On Josephus' support in Tiberias, see p. 126 n. 96.

232 middle:
   The *de mortibus persecutorum* motif is illustrated not by V 424-425 but
by its parallel BJ 7.437-453. In V Josephus speaks of the benefactions he
received from the Romans and therefore neglects to mention that Catullus,
the governor of Libya, was the moving force behind Jonathan's charges
against him. Contrast BJ 7.

INDEX

This index does not list every passage and subject discussed in this book nor does it repeat the entries of the table of contents.

INDEX OF PASSAGES

A. *Josephus*

II. INDEX OF SUBJECTS

COLUMBIA STUDIES
IN THE
CLASSICAL TRADITION

under the direction of

WILLIAM V. HARRIS (Editor) — W. T. H. JACKSON
PAUL OSKAR KRISTELLER — STEELE COMMAGER
LEONARDO TARÁN

VOLUME VIII

LEIDEN
E. J. BRILL
1979

JOSEPHUS
IN GALILEE AND ROME